THE COMMERCIAL BANKING HANDBOOK

Also by Dimitris N. Chorafas

THE MARKET RISK AMENDMENT
AGENT TECHNOLOGY HANDBOOK
TRANSACTION MANAGEMENT
INTERNET FINANCIAL SERVICES
NETWORK COMPUTERS VERSUS HIGH PERFORMANCE COMPUTERS
VISUAL PROGRAMMING TECHNOLOGY
HIGH PERFORMANCE NETWORKS, MOBILE COMPUTING AND PERSONAL
   COMMUNICATIONS
PROTOCOLS, SERVERS AND PROJECTS FOR MULTIMEDIA REAL-TIME SYSTEMS
THE MONEY MAGNET
MANAGING DERIVATIVES RISK
ROCKET SCIENTISTS IN BANKING
HOW TO UNDERSTAND AND USE MATHEMATICS FOR DERIVATIVES
DERIVATIVE FINANCIAL INSTRUMENTS, MANAGING RISK AND RETURN
FINANCIAL MODELS AND SIMULATION
ADVANCED FINANCIAL ANALYSIS, WITH DERIVATIVES TRADES
CHAOS THEORY IN THE FINANCIAL MARKETS
BEYOND LANs – CLIENT–SERVER COMPUTING
INTELLIGENT MULTIMEDIA DATABASES
MEASURING RETURN ON TECHNOLOGY INVESTMENTS

The Commercial Banking Handbook

Strategic Planning for Growth and Survival in the New Decade

Dimitris N. Chorafas

Foreword by Brandon J. Davies

Treasurer, Global Corporate Banking, Barclays Bank

First published 1999 by
MACMILLAN PRESS LTD
Houndmills, Basingstoke, Hampshire RG21 6XS
and London
Companies and representatives throughout the world

ISBN 0-333-73624-9

A catalogue record for this book is available from the British Library.

This book is printed on paper suitable for recycling and made from
fully managed and sustained forest sources.

10   9   8   7   6   5   4   3   2   1
08   07   06   05   04   03   02   01   00   99

Printed and bound in Great Britain by
Antony Rowe Ltd, Chippenham

Contents

Foreword

How did I come to write this introduction? I suppose these are the words quietly spoken by most people who take on the task and then some months later have to complete it. In this case, however, I have known what I wanted to say all along, and it certainly is not a task but a pleasure. I have known Dimitris for more years than either of us would now like to admit. We met through a shared interest in what computing technology combined with mathematical technique could bring to predictive modelling of interest rate and exchange rate behaviour, at the time I was Head of Financial Engineering at BZW. We shared a wide interest and long standing fascination with banking as business, art and science.

A mathematical economist by training, my original background in banking was in branch banking and marketing and it was this, I think, that created the spark between us. Dimitris' ability to cover the broad scope of the subject, and yet to bring order to what so often appears as chaos, interested me, and this is why I would recommend Dimitris' work to anyone interested in banking. There can surely be few senior bankers who do not have at least one of Dimitris' works to hand; personally, I have several.

The actual course of events that led me to write this foreword began in August 1997 when, in an exchange of correspondence, I mentioned to Dimitris that 'I think the whole area of interest rate risk management in retail banking is not well understood, as evidenced by both the depth of available literature and the often poor understanding shown by bank treasurers.' I should of course have known better because, by 12 August, Dimitris had invited me to contribute a section on my thoughts.

Like Dimitris, I can never confine myself to the role of observer alone but have opinions on the matter that I hope provoke thought and understanding in the reader, even if they do not lead to agreement. That is, I think, the essence of Dimitris' success as a writer and, I would add, a lecturer. He does not just convey facts, he makes you think.

BRANDON J. DAVIES
Treasurer
Global Corporate Banking
Barclays Bank

Preface

Commercial banking is not a market you can attack without a road map. Once you have clearly stated your objectives and completed the plan, you can decide if you want to execute it *as is* or if you prefer to revamp it. The plan itself must be factual and documented – but also complete and detailed. Most importantly, it must be capable of being executed.

Every commercial bank has its unique way of planning for the years ahead, even if it appeals to a general market. Each bank has its own culture, objectives, method of operating, relationship management profile and philosophy of business. With deregulation, globalization, the effects of technology and market push and pull, retail banks develop new products and address new markets. There is no one best strategic planning method for all banks, but there are principles and procedures which developed out of experience in positioning *our* bank against the forces of the future.

The transmission of this experience to a wider public of retail bankers is the goal the present book has thrust upon itself. At top management level, it is addressed to board members who need to decide on the guidelines to be followed by banking strategy, chief executive officers who must set the directives of the strategic planning process for their institution, and the executive vice presidents for marketing, sales, product development, finance and human resources whose input to strategic planning is so crucial.

At upper-middle management level, this book guides the hand of the strategic planner and his immediate assistants in elaborating master plans against competition, and in developing innovative approaches which can revitalize commercial banking; also, in counteracting the moves of non-bank banks, setting the framework which permits improvement of service quality and managing the process of change.

Other contributions of the text the reader has in his hands, at middle management level, include product pricing and the elaboration of a policy for fees. The case of non-banks is brought into perspective and suggestions are made on how retail banks can retain their share in spite of competition by new entrants.

Attention is paid both to loans and to derivative financial instruments. One chapter covers the 1996 Market Risk Amendment and its aftermath in terms of marking-to-market, marking-to-model and the resulting capital requirements. Another chapter warns the reader about security issues, taking as a case study credit cards and smart cards. The text also explains why strategic planning must be collaborating most closely with marketing, all the way from new product planning to the establishment of effective sales plans and the elaboration of relationship banking. For practical examples, attention is paid to direct banking as well as private banking systems and strategies.

The contents of this book can be instrumental in assisting senior management as well as strategic planners, marketing specialists, product planners and financial analysts in the evaluation of the bank's profitability. The emphasis on the pricing mechanism necessary for retail banking products and services is preceded by the fundamentals of research and development, with an explanation of the way leading institutions use simulation and experimentation in connection with their products.

* * *

The 16 chapters comprising this book divide into three parts. Part One explains the need for a banking strategy, starting, in Chapter 1, with a factual presentation of the role retail banking has played over the last 20 years. The reader will also find in the same chapter a discussion on what can be expected in the foreseeable future.

Chapter 2 outlines the goals of a strategy in commercial banking and the decisions to be taken in order to establish a business perspective which promotes the bank's image. Chapter 3 contrasts the business opportunity open to banks and non-banks – from regulation and supervision to globalization of financial services and their profitability.

Because service quality has become a competitive weapon, particularly in connection with income-generating retail banking services, Chapter 4 addresses this subject as well as its importance in the sense of value differentiation. Value added products for investors are already offered by mutual funds, as Chapter 5 explains, and different sorts of funds have proved to be superior to banks in the management of change.

Marketing and competition is the theme of Part Two. Chapter 6 examines the common ground which exists between marketing functions and retail banking strategy. It explores the sense of niche and unique product markets, and brings the reader's attention to the tough requirements which have to be met by a commercial bank to be successful in a mass market.

Chapter 7 elaborates on relationship banking and the role being played by the branch office network. It starts with sales strategies, core competences and banking fees, following up with branch management and the needed re-engineering effort. Using practical examples, Chapter 8 introduces the concept of direct banking and its practical implementation by commercial banks. It also disucsses the ancillary services retail banks increasingly handle.

Chapter 9 focuses on the profitable business of private banking, starting with the notion of wealth planning for a sophisticated clientele. It extends beyond equity investments and bonds to include the ways and means derivatives enter into private banking. Responsibilities taken on by retail banks which may involve some significant risks must be settled through the legal clauses of a customer contract. This is the focal point of Chapter 10, which explains how the customer relationship can be strengthened through a well-studied contract for wealth management.

The subject-matter of Part Three is pricing, profitability, regulatory action and security. Chapter 11 explains how and why setting a pattern of markets, products and bank profitability is a cornerstone of the improvements every bank hopes to make in regard to its bottom line. This chapter also says why, to keep ahead of competition, a commercial bank has to be very sensitive on the issue of cost control. Organizational fat is the enemy of profitability.

A number of practical lessons are brought into banking from the manufacturing industry, since manufacturing has been the first to tackle tough cost control problems. Step by step, Chapter 11 discusses why the commercial bank must look at each of its customers as the ultimate profit center. This goes well beyond being customer-aware, which is the usual line of reference in the banking industry.

Chapter 12 takes a generic look into another activity brought into commercial banking from manufacturing: the research and development (R&D) effort. It gives advice on how R&D can be managed in a retail banking setting, brings to the reader's attention practical examples from the investment banking industry and provides advice on ways in which new product failures could be avoided. Chapter 12 also makes the reader aware that data must be managed in volumes larger than ever, and explains what it takes to gain technological leadership.

Chapter 13 looks more deeply into the problems associated with the pricing of financial products and comes up with suggestions which can have an immediate applicability. Loans policies and economic studies are rather closely related, as Chapter 14 demonstrates. The same chapter provides management with a profit and loss (P&L) pattern for the loans portfolio.

The subject of Chapter 15 is credit risk, market risk and the new regulations introduced by the Basle Committee on Banking Supervision, particularly the 1996 Market Risk Amendment. In a comprehensible manner, this chapter covers value at risk, backtesting and the sense of the green, yellow and red zones. It explains the notional amount and brings the reader's attention to the differences between marking-to-market and marking-to-model.

The theme underpinning Chapter 16 is security. The case studies chosen to dramatize security issues which are wanting hinge upon credit cards and debit cards. Attention is also paid to ways and means to improve the security of customer payment systems. This discussion extends all the way to the Internet. The possible effects of cybermoney on the money supply are also considered.

Let me close by expressing my appreciation to everyone who contributed to the research which led to this management report, and therefore to making it successful. A complete list of companies, senior executives, banking experts and computer specialists is found in the Acknowledgments. Particular mention should be made of the advice provided by Brandon J. Davies and by Dr Heinrich Steinmann. I am indebted to Keith Povey for the editing work and to Eva-Maria Binder for the artwork, the typing of the manuscript and the index.

Valmer and Vitznau DIMITRIS N. CHORAFAS

Part One
The Need for a Commercial Banking Strategy

1 Money, the Banks and the Bankers

1 INTRODUCTION

Banking has an established history of at least 37 centuries, according to some accounts. Historical evidence supports the likelihood of the existence of banking-type organizations for almost two millennia before Christ. One of the earliest evidences of banking operations dates from the Code of Hammurabi, the founder of the Babylonian Empire (1728–1686 BC). It laid down the standards of banking procedures as a uniform public law.

But banking has greatly transformed itself over the centuries. In antiquity, it generally functioned without the aid of a currency. While barter agreements dominated, the standard unit of value was defined in various ways:

- it has often been an established weight, a measure of agricultural produce or of some precious metal,
- but the available financial services were a far cry from what we think of today.

In recent times, in the financial history of Europe, different names were given for generally the same sort of services, while over time some banking products took on distinct forms and functions practically under the same name or frame of reference. There have been merchant, investment, private, deposits, savings, agricultural, popular and discount banks. There have as well been mortgage and savings associations or building societies. In Medieval Italy there were principally three types of operations which provided banking services: pawnbrokers, money-changers and deposit banks.

- Money-changers had a bench, or banca, conducting business largely in exchange of currencies, with no element of credit.

This model however changed and, over time, money-changers evolved into:

- Exchange bankers who remitted funds, and
- deposit bankers who transferred funds locally, and sometimes made loans.

Italian city-states such as Venice and Genova recognized the public-good aspect of the banking business, therefore they required financial institutions to

3

follow certain standards. Reserve banks came later, the first on record being Sweden's Riksbank.[1] The Bank of England was formed in 1694, the Bank of France in 1800. The British fiscal evolution took place in the period 1688–1740, the French only after the Revolution of 1789. The bank note came into widespread use in Britain in the 18th century. Bank deposits spread from around 1826, but the practice accelerated after 1850.

Strategic planning in the financial industry is a development of the late 1960s to early 1970s. In the 1960s, industrial companies hired bankers to run their treasury, and banks returned the compliment by hiring industrial strategic planners. This gave a vigorous impulse to banking activities, as we will see in this and the following four chapters.

2   THE WIDENING ROLE OF BANKING DURING THE LAST 20 YEARS

Since the Industrial Revolution the bank has been *an intermediary* between society in one side and industry and commerce in the other. The bank accumulates capital from depositors. Business companies use this capital to invest in producing goods and services as well as to trade. The role of an intermediary is to correct a mis-match:

- Capital is becoming available in one sector of the economy
- But it is needed in other sectors who are willing to pay a price for money.

This role of an interface between the availability and use of funds underpins the banking industry as we know it. But the bank's role is eroded by *non-banks*: department stores, insurance companies, acceptance corporations, various funds, the postal banks, brokers and other companies dealing in money market instruments.

Asked in 1979 to describe the financial institution of the future, then Citicorp Chairman Walter Wriston replied: 'It's called Merrill Lynch.' The Glass-Steagall Act, which divided investment banking from commercial banking, sees to it that Merrill Lynch is a broker not a retail bank. But because of deregulation brokers have found ways to enter into all sorts of banking.

American law defines a bank as any institution that accepts deposits payable on demand and makes commercial loans. A company, for example, taking only the sort of deposits that require notice of withdrawals, does not fit into this definition and therefore, strictly speaking, it is not a bank. Hence the concept of non-bank banks.

In 1984, in America, the Federal Reserve Board attempted to halt the proliferation of non-bank banks – or at least to regulate them – by amending its Regulation Y. The Fed redefined a bank as any institution that:

- accepts deposits that as a matter of practice are payable on demand, and
- engages in the business of making any loan other than a loan to an individual for personal, family, household or charitable purposes.

This newer definition of a loan by the Federal Reserve Board included the purchase of retail installment loans or commercial paper, certificates of deposit, bankers' acceptances and similar money-market instruments.

But in September 1985, officials in the Reagan administration said that the Fed's redefinition of a bank was an attempt to 'usurp congressional banking policy'. This expanded definition was challenged in court by Dimension Financial Corp. of Kansas, which planned to set up limited-service banks in 25 states. In January 1986, the US Supreme Court (*Board of Governors of the Federal Reserve Systems V. Dimension Financial Corp. et al.*) found that the Federal Reserve Board did not have the statutory authority to redefine what is a bank. According to this ruling, even if an institution makes commercial loans and offers Negotiable Order of Withdrawal (NOW) accounts, it is still a non-bank bank.

- This ruling has been significant inasmuch as in banking it is common practice to obtain NOW deposits without prior notice,
- but the US Supreme Court pointed out that 'the requirement of prior notice of withdrawal withholds from the depositor any legal right to withdraw on demand'.

The 1986 Court ruling also determined that the Federal Reserve Board's redefinition of commercial loans was unreasonable inasmuch as 'the term "commercial loans" is used in the financial community to describe the direct loan from a bank to a business customer for the purpose of providing funds needed by the customer in its business. Money market transactions, which the Board characterizes as "commercial loan substitutes", do not fall within the commonly accepted definition of "commercial loans".'

In my book, the Federal Reserve has been right in its redefinition both of a *bank* and of a *loan*, but because it interprets the law of the land, in a way to create jurisprudence, what the Supreme Court said has a great deal to do with the future of banks and of banking. A European banker who took the time to look at an early draft of this text was to comment that this is an 'American approach which is irrelevant to many bankers'. To pre-empt any similar thinking, let me say that there are a number of reasons why such argument is near-sighted:

- one should not write off the largest banking market in the world because 'what happened there would not happen here';
- with globalization, the law of the land in one country regulating what banking *is* and *is not* tends to expand to other countries – particularly among the G-10;
- from country to country, the banking business has much in common. An IBM study found that in commercial banking 80 percent is the same stuff in a cross-country sense.

The ruling by the US Supreme Court also helps to demonstrate that the correct definition of 'what is a bank' is no academic business. It is both a fundamental functional issue and formidable ammunition in the bitter power struggle under way between banks and non-banks that could well decide the fate of the banking industry worldwide.

The battle about what banking is and is not pits commercial banks against investment houses, brokerages, insurance companies, department store chains, finance corporations, telephone companies and other business entities.

- It engages prestigious names both in the banking and in the non-banking business, and
- it obliges banks to establish strategic plans as well as to search for new financial products.

Chapter 2 will explain that banks not only need to redefine in clear, unambiguous terms the business they are in but also they must differentiate between the different types of a financial institute they want to be. As Figure 1.1 suggests, it is not enough to distinguish between retail and wholesale.

The definition of the line of business must be precise enough to permit focusing the bank's activities in one market. Is *our* retail bank primarily addressing itself to the general public or to private banking? Is the primary goal of our wholesale bank loans to large companies and/or to governments? Or is it treasury activities, trading in currency exchange futures, interest rate swaps and other derivative financial instruments?

Whichever specific business line they choose, in order to survive banks must overcome 50 years of inertia in as many months. They must also use high

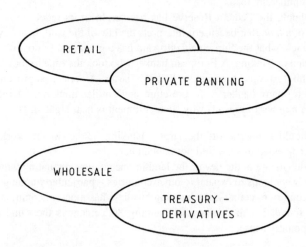

Figure 1.1 Strategic planning should avoid fuzzy answers to the question: 'What sort of bank?'

technology better than their competitors, employing computers, communications and software with return on investment (ROI) in mind. Computers are just another commodity which must become an income earner for the bank.

3　THE NOTION OF MONEY AND ITS FUNCTION IN FINANCIAL TRANSACTIONS

Money is classically used to facilitate arrangements and commitments into which enter two or more parties. There is no precise historical answer to the question 'Who invented money?' It may have been the Chinese, Sumerians, Babylonians, Hittites, Assyrians or Lydians. No matter who invented it, the power of money comes from the fact that it is a generally accepted commodity, but it is limited in its supply.

A banker who looked at this text commented: 'I do not understand why a section on the notion of money and its functions is included.' Let me spell out the reasons for this choice:

- money is the raw material in banking;
- in any industry a good manager will start by studying the raw material;
- if we don't appreciate the raw material, we will never master its transformations – and the end product.

A person unable to understand the raw material his company is using will never be able to understand the products which he handles. If he does not know and appreciate the input, he will never learn much about the output. Therefore he will be unable to sell his company's products and services to the clients. This is as true of banking as it is of any other industry.

In antiquity the first widely used currency was the unit of coinage established by Gyges, King of Lydia in 687 BC. It was an alloy of gold and silver cast in a uniform shape and weight. Money began to acquire its modern character when it assumed the dual function of unit of measurement and instrument for transacting business. Today money plays many roles, the most prevalent being the following:

1 *A unit of measurement.* It makes possible metrics and provides a frame of reference. It also constitutes the basis for double-entry accounting as well as for keeping accounts, P & L statements and balance sheets.
2 *Raw material* for the banking industry. Without it, banks cannot take deposits and give loans, hence they cannot act as financial intermediaries.
3 *A store of value.* Many commodities represent wealth, but the practice is to translate them into a common denominator which is money. Money's value comes from the fact that it is limited in supply.

4   A means for *transacting business*. It permits expressing the value of other commodities in a uniform way, subject to currency risk and to country risk.
5   A means of *exchange*. Money is substituting for barter agreements, but inflation destroys the money's value.
6   The object of *government controls*. Reserve banks regulate money supply and watch after the velocity of circulation of money; they also try to influence interest rates and exchange rates.

Several of these definitions complement one another, but some also overlap: for instance, the notions of unit of measurement, raw material and store of value; Also the sense of transacting business and being a means of exchange. This multiple frame of reference, however, makes money transfers possible.

• Money makes it feasible to move remittances from one place to another through networks.
• Banks do so without transporting bulky commodities or valuable metals over long distances.

Money and technology have a common ground, such as plastic money. Just the same, technology is inseparable from modern banking, and vice versa. As Figure 1.2

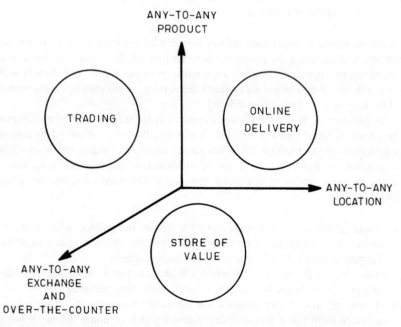

Figure 1.2   Redefining the notion of money as the means for business transactions

suggests, today and tomorrow a bank must be ready to trade any product, from any location, in any exchange and over the counter (OTC). Technology takes the credit for this *globalization.*

Once an accepted unit of value had been established, business can be transacted at an increasing level of sophistication. The evolution in the exchange of assets and liabilities illustrates the change in the character of money from a real, or tangible, entity (such as the coins of King Gyges) into one which is virtual and intangible.

- Money acts as a means of exchange because it is generally acceptable.
- This is true whether or not it is backed by precious metals or other reserves.

What makes money acceptable is the issuing authority standing behind it. The same is true with lending. Though several American municipalities defaulted in the 19th century and brought to bankruptcy British banks, nobody today thinks that the US government will default. This is not impossible, but it is most likely.

Other borrowers and issuers of money are seen as less dependable. Hence the concept of *counterparty risk* (or credit risk) and the need for *collateral.* According to financial history books, acceptance of gold deposits, for exchange purposes and as collateral, was instituted by the Casa di San Giorgio in Italy, as early as 1582. On payment of bank money and presenting the receipt, a claimant could have the exact specie back, less a small fee.

- The receipt could be renewed if the specie was not withdrawn.
- If not renewed, the specie would accrue to the bank.

Money is not only put in circulation by the central bank. It is also created by the banking system – either indirectly or directly. An example of indirect creation of money by the banking system is the issuance of loans based on the bank's deposits or bought money, minus 'x' percent reserve requirements as stipulated by the central bank; 'x' is a percentage which varies by country and with time.

An example of direct money creation by commercial banks is the *negotiable Certificate of Deposit* (CD) devised by Walter Wriston when he was chief executive officer (CEO) of Citibank. At the origin of the CD has been the fact that New York's money center banks were losing corporate business to the US Treasury, which issued bills paying higher interest than banks were allowed by the Federal Reserve.

As a store of value and of wealth, money is a key ingredient of *capital,* and capital is the world's most cowardly commodity. It cuts and runs at the barest jiggle. Money constitutes the raw material of both the capital market and the money market. Yet, as Table 1.1 shows, the two are quite different in a number of ways.

Capital market transactions are typically medium-to-long term. Practically all banks are active in the capital market, though the underwriting of securities is the

Table 1.1   Capital market versus money market

Capital market	Money market
Medium to long-term maturity	Short to very short-term maturity
Can be liquid or illiquid	Is generally liquid
Low credit risk	High credit risk
High market risk	Low to medium market risk

business of investment banks. As far as commercial banks are concerned a major activity is the issue of bonds and promissory notes.

The capital market addresses itself to both private and institutional investors. In the general case, it can divide into two segments: domestic and foreign – for both issuers and borrowers.

The *money market* focuses on short-term debt instruments which are issued and traded. Typical money market transactions are for terms considerably less than one year. In terms of its evolution, the money market became important with the deregulation of the banking industry, which took place in the late 1970s and early 1980s. Money markets flourish when legislation does not penalize short-term transactions.

4   LOOKING AT BANKS AS SERVICE COMPANIES WHICH WORK FOR A PROFIT

Whether a financial institution is more active in the capital market or in the money market, whether it is retail or wholesale, whether it is local, regional, national or international, the first crucial question is: What is a bank's purpose? What has it set out to accomplish?

'I question whether "What is a bank?" is the right first question,' said a reviewer who was supposedly knowledgeable in banking strategy. In other words, a banker should start elaborating a strategic plan without clear definitions and the spelling out of goals and functions.

- Admittedly, it is not easy to define what is a bank, because this involves precision regarding both the objective and the underlying transformation process.
- But this is precisely the reason why, without the slightest doubt, we should begin with this intellectual exercise of definitions. Only eager-beavers will start in the middle.

After this first question has been answered, the next one is: What is the bank's main service: taking money, giving money, paying bills, trading in derivatives? Then, a third question comes up: Who pays for the services, and how much? Figure 1.3 maps these queries in successive layers. Management must start at the top and address each lower layer, having responded in a factual and documented

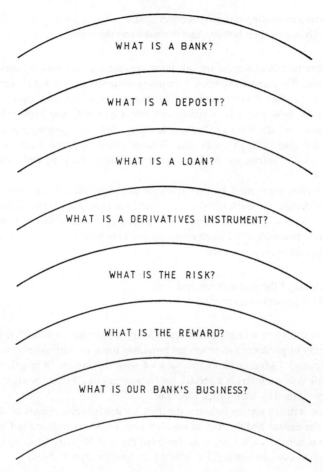

WHAT IS A BANK?

WHAT IS A DEPOSIT?

WHAT IS A LOAN?

WHAT IS A DERIVATIVES INSTRUMENT?

WHAT IS THE RISK?

WHAT IS THE REWARD?

WHAT IS OUR BANK'S BUSINESS?

Figure 1.3 Functional layers change slowly but the characteristics of each layer change rapidly in function of risk and result

manner to the question posed by its metalayer – the one standing above it. Such replies mean commitments which have strategic implications for the bank.

As banks are indeed service companies, bankers are faced with another critical question: How to care for the effectiveness of these services, their evolution, the market appeal, the risks assumed with them, their costs and their profits? As business organizations, banks must

• organize and price their services like industrial products,
• select the right customers to offer them,

- do so in a marketing-intensive manner, and
- carefully watch their bottom line: the risks and the costs.

This means that banks must rethink their mission and the way in which they carry it out. They must establish a *business strategy*, do market research, get involved in product development, pursue strategic planning, and appreciate that new markets, new products, sophisticated client demands and high technology have accentuated the need for lifelong learning. Not only people, products and markets, but also skills die with time. Without *steady training*, banking experience becomes obsolete; the banker loses the ability to face the demands of his customers.

Service companies must be very sensitive to human skill. Some years ago, in the United States, the Bank of Wachovia found out from a study that in five years a banker who is not steadily trained loses 50 percent of his skills. In France, the Banque Internationale des Placements said that new products which did not exist 18 months earlier accounted for

- 35 percent of the transactions, and
- about 50 percent of its profits.

To be competitive as a financial service industry, a bank has to look after a bewildering array of products and processes providing the necessary support to sustain them. Figure 1.4 gives a bird's eye view of what this means in practical terms. On the left side, each box is a service the bank offers its clients. The right column lists a few of the key back-office functions.

Because it runs a service industry, the bank's top management must be very sensitive to the market and the way in which it evolves. As we will see in Chapter 2, it must position the bank against the forces of the next 10 years – raising its sights above day-to-day commitments and facing its broader responsibilities:

- establishing and explaining objectives,
- defining long-term policies,
- developing milestone plans, and
- ensuring that such plans are properly executed.

The plans which are made and the acts of management which follow them must guarantee a products stream, steady cash flow and respectable profitability. Every bank with a substantial interest in growth and survival should not only have strategic plans but also critically re-examine them.

In the present climate of downsizing and shortened planning horizons, it is tempting to retrench from commitment to longer-term development, but this can be counterproductive. A logical solution is to say that there should be a balance

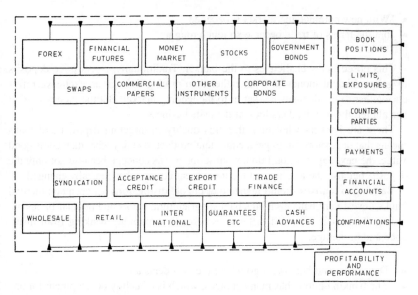

Figure 1.4　Every bank has a network of functions and processes necessary to serve its products and services

between shorter-term and longer-term perspectives, toward beneficial goals. The solution of the clients' problems and survival in the financial industry are inseparable goals. To provide its clients with first-class solutions the bank must understand their business and their opportunities in the shorter and the longer term. Client problems must be approached in a coordinated effort because banking is dealing with both people and money.

Increasingly, the concept of the bank as 'a money shop' is shifting to that of an *agent for development*. Today the biggest assets of a financial institution is *not* its balance sheet, but its customers, its people and its technology.

5　REDEFINING THE PROCESS OF FINANCIAL INTERMEDIATION

Traditionally, *intermediation* means the job of bringing savers and borrowers together. Until recently, the process of intermediation was largely dominated by commercial banks and thrifts (savings and loans (S&L) associations in the US, building societies in the UK), which took in individual and institutional deposits and lent those funds to other individual borrowers and to businesses. Then insurances companies and other non-bank organizations came into the game.

- With new entrants, the market broadened
- but the terms of trade became so much tougher.

This posed many challenges to the banker. Traditionally, banks price deposits to gain sufficient money to lend, rather than pricing through an exclusive reference either to the deposits market or to the lending market. But the money market has altered the way bankers look at deposits business.

There are bankers who think that this duality in targeting deposits and loans means that depositors fail to get a consistent product: one day what they get is good value, the next day it is not. I do not subscribe to this concept, because not only the deposits but also the lending and the investment business has radically changed.

Banking executives should realize that the old distinctions between commercial banks, investment banks, savings banks, agricultural banks and popular banks are fading. The same is true of differences formally separating banking from insurance and brokerage.

- Depositors and borrowers go where the best deals are.
- The banking public has many choices, which is a healthy development for any economy.

Competition has increased because intermediation barriers have come down, and innovation is on the rise. Equally important is the fact that companies and wealthy, sophisticated investors know how to shop around and how to choose the banks they should deal with.

- Companies can borrow or raise equity through a number of financial instruments.
- Savers can shop in the market for an ever-increasing array of products with a good return.

The whole intermediation process has become much more efficient on a worldwide scale. Because of the Internet, private networks and databases, physical proximity has become irrelevant. It is as easy to deal with a bank in New York, London, Paris, Frankfurt, Zurich, Milan, Tel Aviv or Tokyo as with one in your own home town. Finance is today a world-class business.

In manufacturing and merchandizing as well as in the service industries, board members, chief executives and treasurers must be aware of the opportunities as well as alert to the ongoing change. Otherwise their company risks being the victim of events they do not control, therefore losing ground to competitors.

Not only has the profile of loans and of the loans industry as a whole changed, but there is also a merger between the loans and investment domains. Figure 1.5 shows that there is a common ground between loans and investments, making this

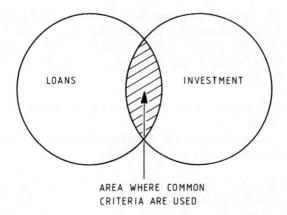

AREA WHERE COMMON
CRITERIA ARE USED

Figure 1.5 There is a common area shared by loans and investments characterized by trust in the future

a reasonable merger. Both loans officers and investment officers look to the future for their decisions:

- the loans officer watches out for the lender's ability to repay;
- the investment officer looks after the company's ability to generate cash flow and turn a profit.

The ultimate borrowers and investors are governments, business firms and households. The latter look for personal loans, mortgages and installments. The ultimate lender is the households, even if books on economics and finance state that the reserve bank is the lender of last resort.

- In a globalized economy which increasingly depends on *virtual resources*, the role of intermediation is redefined by a *new finance* algorithm.
- This algorithm characterizes modern business, and it says that the ultimate lenders buy securities issued by the ultimate borrowers.

So far, the direct finance algorithm has been successfully applied in connection with industrial and commercial companies. At the consumers' level this *direct* type of finance has rarely worked because individuals do not have ready access to the markets – at least not an efficient type of access. This, however, is now changing. Internet and the direct banking policies, which we examine in Chapter 8, alter the aforementioned conditions, making direct finance possible at consumers' level. This will come by stages, the first stage being market information like that made available to subscribers by providers such as Reuters and Blomberg.

Another handicap for direct finance at the consumers' level is reliable credit information, which is a metalayer of general financial news and prices. Until now, individuals have suffered from insufficient credit information, such as the risk of default, but global financial networks are easing this constraint. By so doing, they are altering the market landscape.

- Direct finance contrasts with *indirect finance* which requires the existence of banks as intermediaries.
- It is essentially extending the financing alternatives where competition between banks and non-banks has been tough.

The problem faced by commercial banks and saving and loans in connection with non-banks during the last 15 years is that credit unions, pension funds, insurance companies and others act as intermediaries in an indirect finance sense. They have been channelling funds from depositors to the market, the way the banking industry used to work. The challenge from direct finance is different. Big-name companies no longer pay fees to an intermediary to sell their commercial paper. They market large chunks of it themselves.

IBM has set up the IBM Money Market Account, marketing commercial paper to its shareholders, but it is also open to anyone with $2,500 to invest. British Petroleum created its own in-house investment bank that:

- issues commercial paper,
- does mergers and acquisitions, and
- performs interest rate and currency swaps.

Du Pont has a mergers and acquisitions unit which does an average of 20 deals a year, ranging from $5 million to $500 million. Eastman Kodak conducts foreign exchange trading and hedging, up to $25 billion yearly. General Motors Acceptance Corporation, the financing arm of the auto maker, was one of the first to handle its own commercial paper. Today it has a total portfolio in excess of $26 billion.

Philip Morris bought Jacobs Suchard, a Swiss coffee and candy producer, for $4.1 billion, using its own staff. It only engaged investment bankers for market analysis and fairness opinion. But since 1990, the Securities and Exchange Commission (SEC) has elaborated new rules which tend to make direct placements more difficult.

Companies complained that, with the curbs on commercial paper including short-term, highly liquid, corporate IOUs, they will be forced to pay a lot more for loans. Concerned by several defaults by commercial paper issuers, SEC aimed to protect investors in money market funds from future débâcles. This sounds reasonable because the funds hold one-third of the outstanding commercial paper – but it only restructures; it does not stop direct finance.

6   IS THE SIZE OF BANKS PLAYING A DECISIVE ROLE?

Big does not necessarily mean beautiful, nor is life easier for big banks. For instance, it can be more difficult for larger books to rebalance should liquidity dry up, since they move the market against themselves.

In a way, the bigger the portfolio, and therefore the exposure, the more sensitive a bank or an investor is to how well business opportunity is analyzed, risks are controlled and the balances are put right:

- *if* the trading book and the banking book are not thoroughly managed,
- *if* there is a concentration of maturities of loans due and other events,
- *then* the bank is in trouble; the more the imbalance, the greater the troubles can get.

Risks have to be rigorously managed,[2] but it is not possible to eliminate them entirely. It is very difficult to have well balanced loans and investment profiles across the whole book when *intraday* the market moves so much that every bank can have a big short position at some point.

'Risk is explored but largely for corporates and ... may or may not be appropriate for a retail banker, but is relevant to the investment banker,' said one of the experts who looked at an early draft of this text. Let me answer this contradictory assertion in block letters: RISK IS MOST RELEVANT TO EVERY BANKER, and risk is a very important concept to every living person.

Only the dead might escape this dictum – not all of them, of course, because some may lose, post-mortem, their reputation. Even a bureaucrat who is doing nothing takes the 'nothingness' risk, but an active banker takes risks every day.

- The Savings and Loans, which in the the late 1980S failed in America and left a $800 billion black hole, were *retail bankers*.
- Crédit Lyonnais, which so far has cost the French taxpayer FF230 billion ($38 billion) in silly salvage operations, is a *commercial bank*.
- Barings, which went into bankruptcy because it did not manage its risks, was an *investment bank* – and the only one to qualify for risk management according to a shrinking breed of bankers.

It is not easy to manage risk in a global manner, and the bigger the bank the more complex becomes the control of risk. This gives a distinct advantage to small size which is more easily managed and can be more flexible – even if big financial organizations tend to have more clout. The size of banks and their wealth can be defined in different ways:

- by assets (including loans), deposits, capital, and reserves;
- by capitalization in the stock market; and
- by the network of their operations.

Today a key criterion in judging a network is globality. On a global scale, one of the problems in comparisons is that assets and liabilities are often counted in local money, and currency exchange values, like all commodity prices, change steadily. For example, the rise of oil as a commodity and the fall of the dollar, together with restrictions on banking between different countries, helped to diminish the role of the American banks compared with their rivals in Europe and Japan. 'Ten years ago all the ten largest banks in the world were American,' Walter B. Wriston complained in 1980. 'This year there were only two of them.'

But even at local or national level there may be several problems in making comparisons between banks in terms of size. The usual approach is to consider assets, but this is incomplete without deducting contra accounts which are often kept by a financial institution close to its chest. For instance:

- bank acceptances,
- letters of credit,
- customer securities, and so on.

Still another problem in making meaningful comparisons is that each type of bank (as well as each country's banks) has its (their) own national attitudes and relationships with government(s). While on the one hand the rivalries between the bankers and governments add to the uncertainty of evaluations, on the other the big banks are more or less certain that the reserve bank, the Ministry of Finance or both will pull them out of the crevasse.

This essentially means that smaller banks must be much more careful in the way they manage their assets and the assets of their depositor. Rather than being handicapped by their size, they should use their smaller dimension as a strategic weapon by means of:

- strategic planning
- marketing expertise, and
- product development.

To survive in a highly competitive market without becoming subservient to bigger banks, the top management of smaller institutions must be supported by advanced technology. Sophisticated software should make it feasible to have at management's fingertips at any time quantitative and qualitative information on business opportunity and on exposure in terms of:

- investment in liquid and illiquid assets;
- capital, reserves and current commitments;
- consolidated accounts sorted out by risk class, customer relation, branch office and other criteria.

While the classification of crucial factors can vary from bank to bank and country to country, at the core there exists a common frame of reference. The radar chart in Figure 1.6 provides a practical example. The gradations are from 1 (low risk) to 5 (high risk).

Critics may say that a sophisticated level of bank engineering is not really necessary for small to medium size banks. Many are still bread-and-butter in their operations, yet they make money. There are three answers to this statement. First, big banks have no monopoly in being leaders in financial engineering. You can be a small bank but strategically positioned and geographically focused, therefore requiring the institution to be innovative in products and services. This calls for information technology support which goes way beyond what the classical 'electronic data processing' (EDP) shop can provide.

Second, the size of the exposure may vary, but the nature of credit risk and market risk associated with the on-balance and off-balance sheet activities is not that different between big and small banks. In both cases, risks have to be clearly identified and their list is typically long. The better the internal controls and the sharper the technology the bank uses, the better it is able to confront these risks.

Third, while a minimum size is a criterion, clear-eyed bank management will capitalize on the diseconomies of scale hitting the big institutions. To survive in a financial market which is more competitive than ever, smaller banks have

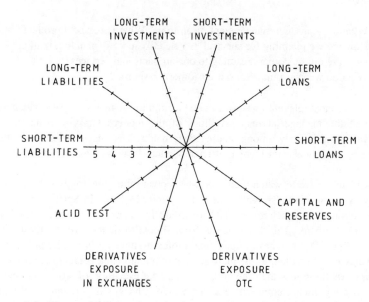

Figure 1.6 The crucial factors in evaluating exposure can be mapped in a radar chart to help in top management decisions

to be more flexible and more responsive to the customer than bigger banks. To compensate for their smaller size, such institutions must always be on the alert. They must also be very careful about their cost structure.

7 LOOKING AT BANKING AS A BUSINESS IN TRANSITION

Thinking of banking as a service industry necessarily brings attention to functions such as marketing, research and development (R&D), production and distribution. Marketing and distribution activities take place at the *front desk* but also through online *networks*. Production is done in the back office.

Marketing concepts in the banking industry have changed over the last 20 years on account of deregulation, globalization and the impact of technology. All three forces see to it that a big chunk of the banking business is in transition – and this process is nowhere near its end. The fact that banking is a service industry is not new. What is new is that the classical banking products are increasingly feeling the pressure of competition, while new products are introduced to the market all the time.

As bankers, do we know what we are producing and what we are going to produce? Are we the leaders or followers in the market to which we appeal? Can we answer in factual and documented manner crucial questions such as the following?

- What does product management mean to us? What is our next product?
- How are we planning for survival in a steadily more demanding market?
- How are our customers reacting to our products and services?
- What do we do to improve our customer's response?

These are most relevent questions in connection to the new functions which have entered the managerial responsibilities of the modern banker during the last 40 years, particularly among leading edge banks. The answer to many of them must be analytical, and involve efficiency controls as well as a golden hoard of critical ratios.

All banks have to watch their credit-to-deposit ratio, a metric which varies not only by country but also within the same country by bank. In Spain, for instance, this ratio is: 0.61 for Barclays, 0.83 for Crédit Lyonnais, 0.96 for Deutsche Bank, 1.18 for Citibank. The difference is from simple to double, yet all these banks have 200 to 300 branches in Spain, and profess to have fairly similar policies.

Many of the challenges the management of a retail bank is facing are *organizational*. Anything less than the adoption and able execution of structural changes means a significant competitive disadvantage. Changes in a commercial bank's functional organization are not weighted in weeks, but still there is an impressive list of them accumulated during the last three decades.

- In the early 1960s, formal planning and control.
- In the mid-1960s, analysis of operations and costing.
- In the late 1960s, profit centers and cost control.
- In the early 1970s, distributed information systems.
- In the mid-1970s, decision support systems.
- In the late 1970s, formal strategic planning.
- In the early 1980s, personal workstations and local area network (LAN).
- In the mid-1980s, the use of expert systems.
- In the late 1980s, with the City's Big Bang, the commercial banks' expansion into investment banking.
- In the early 1990s, the boom in derivative financial instruments.
- In the mid-1990s, the overleveraging of the real economy by the virtual economy.

The off-balance sheet financial instruments have significantly increased the gearing, therefore the risk faced by all banks: hence the 1996 Market Risk Amendment on capital requirements and marking-to-model, published by the Basle Committee on Bank Supervision in January 1996, which became mandatory as of the end of 1997.

Both *risks* and *costs* must be controlled rigorously. Top tier banks have been organizing in this direction since the early 1980s, but the laggards have not yet done their homework in terms of *profit centers* and the way to handle exposure as well as waste. A good example comes from another service industry: computers and software. Softbank, one of Japan's fastest growing companies, is run as a network of 64 profit centers. Its founder came to this concept while the company was still small and an illness prevented him from being in charge over a considerable amount of time.

Masayoshi Son capitalized on his inability to work on the spot and began decentralizing, organizing his workers into groups of 10, each with profit and loss statements that would be updated *daily*. Those who ran out of cash ran out of luck. 'Son likes measuring everything,' explains Softbank Holdings' Reischel (*Business Week*, August 12, 1996).

Well-managed software companies provide a good example for banks also for another reason: the impact of the advances in banking technology. It helped to revamp the delivery mechanism through electronic tellers, automated teller machines (ATM), electronic funds transfer (EFT), point of sale (POS), cash management and home banking – though it had a limited success in terms of paperwork simplification in the back office. Even if some of the goals are not reached management must always watch out. There is no time for complacency, for feeling comfortable with the current solution. Also competitive pressures can bring a downturn,and technology may pass by any bank while competition leaves it behind.

Bankers should never allow themselves to forget that the growing interdependence of economies and of financial markets, as well as the breaking down of barriers between institutions engaged so far in different lines of business, happen against a background characterized by profound changes in financial regulation and legislation. Both legislation and regulation have sometimes encouraged new trends and sometimes adapted to them. Precisely because of the uncertainty characterizing the future course of events, the requirements for survival are a comprehensive strategy for growth, caring for the depth and range of resources, being able to produce innovative financial services, strengthening *our* client base, developing specialized expertise, improving capital adequacy and knowing how to use high technology for profits.

8   BANKING CAN BE FUN

The late Dr Jack Morgan, one of the best-known investment bankers of the 20th century, once said: 'My job is more fun than being king, pope, or prime minister, for no one can turn me out of it, and I do not have to make any compromises with principles.' This nicely expresses what can be the goal of the 21st-century banking professionals.

To succeed, bankers have to be both lean and mean. 'Be nice, feel guilty and play safe. If there was ever a prescription for producing a dismal future, that has to be it,' Walter N. Wriston was to suggest. Taking risks is part and parcel of banking, provided the professionals are able to:

- appreciate the risks which they are taking;
- ensure that the expected return is much higher; and
- steadily control their exposure.

Not all people are fond of banking: 'Banks have done more injury to morality, tranquility, prosperity and even wealth of the nation than they can have done or ever will do good.' It was not Lenin who said this, but US President John Adams (1819).

Another American President, Thomas Jefferson, regarded the expansion of credit, not as a virtue, but as an evil. In his most fanciful vision of the future, he wished the United States 'to practice neither commerce nor navigation but to stand, with respect to Europe, precisely on the footing of China'.[3]

Knowledgeable bankers appreciate that their actions may be beneficial to society, but they also understand that, though the risks can be unlimited, the benefits are subject to constraints. Strategic planning can be instrumental in easing some of these constraints.

As I never tire of repeating, to survive, bankers have to overcome 50 years of management tradition in as many months. This cannot be done without strategic guidelines. Yet, as recently as 1990, over half the banks worldwide had no formal strategic planning functions. Only in the 1990s did senior bankers begin to realize that strategic planning is an urgent need which has to be approached most carefully, as Chapter 2 will explain. Strategic planning is also a good way to gain and hold *market leadership*.

Lee Iacocca wrote, 'If I had to define in one word leadership, I would say it is decisiveness' (*Talking Straight*, 1988). It is primarily because of the decisiveness he had shown in practically all his financial operations that J.P. Morgan considered his job to be more fun than being a king, pope or prime minister.

To be successful, the banker's decisions must be focused. Clausewitz said: 'Keep the forces concentrated in one overpowering mass.' This is why, throughout this chapter, there has been so much insistence that banks and bankers must redefine the business they are in. As for the business philosophy which must underline restructuring:

- all business operations can be reduced to three words: people, products and profits;
- successful financial products are innovative, of a high quality and offered at competitive cost.

Experienced bankers know that service quality and productivity are two sides of the same coin. The *industrialization* of the bank's production activities places increasing emphasis on online distribution of products and services. Both in production and in distribution, emphasis is placed on swamping costs in order not only to become competitive but also to remain so.

In its fundamentals, *financial engineering* has been born out of the need to merge a fast-advancing technology with the more classical aspects of banking business. One of the most valuable lessons financial engineering teaches is that the old pyramid of a hierarchical organization is counterproductive.[4] New, flexible structures are horizontal, as exhibited in Figure 1.7.

Whether we like it or not, organization and structure in the banking industry have changed considerably during the last two decades. Today *bank profitability* greatly depends on how well a merger is performed:

- between bankers and technologists, permitting the creation of new, profitable financial products; and
- between the network of branch offices and electronic banking put at the disposition of consumers, professionals and client firms.

In terms of planning, developing and selling financial products, bankers who are worth their salt think in terms of the client's interest(s) which they try to satisfy through innovation and excellence in service. They do so not only because of profitability but also for reasons of *credibility*.

alignment

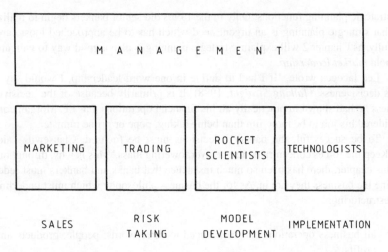

Figure 1.7 A dynamic organization needs only two layers and a synergy between business people and quants

A bank's and a banker's credibility in the financial market is something which can only be earned over time. If one has not earned it, one cannot use it. The banking culture has to change precisely because of these business considerations:

- bankers have to become faster and more entrepreneurial;
- the new culture must be the result of what leading-edge banks have discovered works.

The first successful implementation of the new banking culture within *our* organization must serve as the blueprint when we start to restructure the rest of the institution. It must also make clear to every person that there exists a new set of *do's* and *dont's* in banking, which make the business so much more fun.

Among the *dont's* are the following. Don't sleep on your product and service laurels, because your competitors will swing ahead of you. Don't take your clients for granted, because they will find another banker for doing business. Don't let your costs eat up your profits; use computers, communications and sophisticated software to swamp costs. Don't focus only on production costs, because distribution costs cut deeper into your profit figures. Don't underestimate the role of high technology in banking, because it provides the best assurance for competitiveness and product innovation.

Don't think that the risks your bank is facing in the future will be similar to those it has confronted in the past. Every time we think we have hit a limit we find solutions that take us further – but also bring in new risks.

Notes

1. D.N. Chorafas, *The Money Magnet. Regulating International Finance and Analyzing Money Flows* (London: Euromoney, 1997).
2. See D.N. Chorafas, *Derivative Financial Instruments. Strategies for Managing Risk and Return in Banking* (London and Dublin: Lafferty, 1995).
3. Bray Hammong, *Banks and Politics in America* (Princeton: Princeton University Press, 1957).
4. D.N. Chorafas, *Measuring Returns on Technology Investments* (London and Dublin: Lafferty, 1993).

2 Goals of a Strategy in Retail Banking

1 INTRODUCTION

Chapter 1 made the point that a retail bank which cares for its survival must position and steadily reposition itself against the forces of the 1990s and beyond. To do so, top management must raise its vision above the day-to-day commitments and face a broader range of *responsibilities*. Under no condition can survival be taken for granted.

- About 80 of the top 100 American industrial companies, ranked by assets in 1917, were no longer at the top in 1997; several have disappeared.

Not only companies, but whole industrial sectors change.

- The 50 largest US computer and electronics companies now employ more people than the US automakers who were once considered to be the country's industrial might.

Within a globalized financial market and with a fast advancing information technology, what banks need to position themselves is *recognition* by the market. Recognition comes with the ability to develop and sell products that the rest of the industry does not master.

Chapter 1 has emphasized that strategic planning is instrumental in classifying senior management's thinking. It also helps in making critical choices. No bank can be a leader in all fields, but it must lead at least in some products which will become:

- Its key market thrust and
- Its income earner(s).

Product and market choice are not random. Within a competitive and demanding business environment, *banking strategy* is exercised through skill and forethought. Artifice is necessary in carrying out plans, making moves and engaging in business interactions.

Each action must be based on expectations from own moves and on a prognosis of the moves of other banks, over which we have no control. It follows logically from this proposition that strategy is *a master plan against an opponent*. This definition contains three elements that set strategy apart from other plans:

- It is a *master plan*, not just a list of individual actions.
- It is *against*; hence it involves competition, a basic ingredient in any strategy.
- It has an *opponent*, another person, group or organization, without which the competitive situation could not exist.

A banker who had a chance to look at this text in its early form, suggested that there should be 'reference to the strategic choice between differentiation, low cost and focus in the sense of management planning'. This argument was not accepted because it rests on the wrong premises.

While there are strategic choices between differentiation, low cost and focus (the way these three concepts are used in this chapter and will be much more fully exploited in Chapter 6 – see the omega curve, Figure 6.5), the choice to be made does not alter the foundations of management planning. My credo is: Who fails to plan, plans to fail.

A sound planning methodology should characterize every strategy, and it should be established in a detailed way. There are, however, people who prefer not to plan, because they look on planning as bother.

Let me make a final point. Strategy has been applied to war and its extension, propaganda, but fundamentally it is a much broader concept, having implications in politics, banking, industry and commerce. Strategy is not an objective in itself, but a master plan toward accomplishing objectives.

2 THE FIVE MAJOR COMPONENTS OF A MASTER PLAN

Strategy is not the same thing as a mission, but it incorporates a missionary zeal. True enough, like a vision, a mission contains directions and intent. However, it does not necessarily involve choices. Few people have the skill and the guts to make choices in time, if at all.

A reviewer who looked at this text twisted this concept somewhat by suggesting that 'strategy deals with the available tools and mechanisms and determines how to use and combine customers' defined needs more effectively'. The cognizant reader will appreciate that this is a parody of strategy.

- What this quotation says is basically tactical stuff.
- Nothing is served by shrinking the concept of strategy to the point that it becomes useless.

Strategic concepts and strategic plans are brought forward only by higher-level organizations that have experienced, and can present, thinking ability. True thinking involves intelligence, integrity and ingenuity. Because strategy is a master plan against an opponent, it integrates within itself planning premises addressing the following:

- *human resources* – our clients, our employees, our stockholders;
- *marketing* and sales within our chosen market(s);
- *product* development, product appeal and life cycle(s);
- *financial* resources and financial staying power;
- *technological* competence, moving ahead of competition.

As outlined in Figure 2.1, banking strategy is the kernel of a process which involves all five major plans we have been talking about. These plans have not necessarily been written in order of importance, though many knowledgeable strategists are advising that our clients, and our employees, should be at the top.

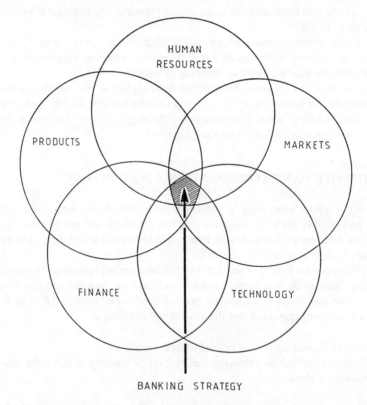

Figure 2.1 Strategy is a master plan which integrates other strategies focused by area of endeavour

A master plan would rest on the able building and execution of these five major component plans. When it does so, it will be in a position to address the challenges facing commercial bankers today. These include, but are not limited to:

- product line choices,
- market segmentation,
- delivery channels,
- marketing and branding,
- pricing strategy,
- risk management strategy,
- scale of operations, and
- operations in the back office.

Some of the issues underpinning these eight bullet points are poorly understood by many bankers, who continue thinking in vanilla icecream terms. Yet all eight points are very important – even if, in many cases, the solutions to be given are tactical rather than strategic.

The human resources strategy is the most fundamental. The careful reader will recall from Chapter 1 that the bank's most important asset is not cash in its vaults, but its employees, its customer base and its customers' confidence. Closely connected to human resources is the fact that during the last decade the basic service philosophy has changed: from *class banking* and *mass banking* to the *customization* of services, including product design, production and distribution.

An important issue concerning strategic planning in connection with human resources is the bank's own personnel – including its management. This involves selecting and hiring; the establishment of individual responsibilities, indicators and objectives; the able handling of management inventory; lifelong learning; promotion and salary; and the careful watch over headcount and overhead factors.

Management should not only be keen to assure that the overall culture and skills of the bank's personnel are in full evolution, but also that there is no great friction between bankers and traders. Tensions arise because these two populations belong to different cultures and are performing different functions.

A *trader* buys and sells securities: bonds, stocks, options, futures, commercial paper, certificates of deposit, Treasury bills. He does so either for clients, for which his company collects a fee, or by investing directly the bank's own money. To win in the game, the trader must make quick and firm decisions during or after hurried phone calls.

Bankers usually have a longer perspective, and they often invest several months or years in cultivating a relationship before it turns into a client. They earn fees for serving as financial consultants; advising on investments and managing portfolios; and putting together new proposals, as in the case of project financing. The management of a client account is no longer the vanilla icecream it used to be.

While most of the aforementioned functions – excluding project financing – are performed by retail bankers, wholesale bankers recast them in a more complex manner for corporations. For their part, investment bankers address themselves to mergers and acquisitions – or to downsizing and divesting companies. All types of bankers need handholding with the customer base.

The third key element in the bank's human resources is its shareholders. Their role has often been played down or they have been taken for granted. Yet, as we will see in section 8, not only are the shareholders the owners of the company but they can also help in promoting the bank's business and image. A similar statement can be made about the bank's bondholders.

While the human resources strategy focuses on how to identify and handhold the customer base, as well as how to recruit key members of the management team, *marketing strategy* is concerned with ways to identify the bank's market and develop a plan to reach it in the most effective way. This is a job whose tools are changing over time. Part Two is devoted to marketing strategy.

Correspondingly, the bank's *product strategy* looks at the range of services offered to the market; the way they are priced; whether or not they respond to market requirements; and how well they are being supported through communications, computers and software. This is a steady, never-ending process requiring market perception and foresight in product design, as explained in Part Three.

- In spite of what many theorists in the financial industry are professing, there can be no valid market plan which is distinct from the product plans – and vice versa.
- Still, while accounting for this synergy, it is necessary to look at product plans and market plans on their own merits – not to use the strengths of the one to cover the weaknesses of the other.

The pyramid in Figure 2.2 expresses this duality in a stratified manner which permits an appreciation of the different issues coming into play in a master plan. Notice that, at the base is 'Understanding the market' and only at the top – provided all functions are performed in an able manner – can we talk about 'Ensuring success'.

Strategic planning for products and markets must coinvolve market research, R&D, product planning, marketing proper, management accounting and the chief economist. The functions of R&D in banking are explained in Chapter 12; those of economic analysis in Chapter 13. Those responsible should make a census of market response to each one of the bank's products and examine each product in terms of:

- business opportunity analysis,
- market appeal versus competition,

Figure 2.2 Strategic planning is a polyvalent enterprise from market perception to sustained profits

- cost of sales, production and distribution,
- the risk factors it involves now and in the future.

In terms of marketing, the bank's specialists must define opportunity in an objective manner in each one of the market(s) to which the bank addresses itself – whether this market is local, national or international. In connection with branch offices, for example, this should be done under the dual perspective of bricks and mortar and an online network. We will return to this subject in Chapter 7.

3 FINANCIAL STRATEGY AND THE IMPORTANCE OF HIGH TECHNOLOGY SUPPORT

The fourth component of any strategy is connected with financial staying power, which constitutes a fundamental ingredient of any master plan. *Financial strategy* looks after the planning of liquid resources and those easily converted into cash without financial loss, in spite of uncertainties and turbulence. It also aims to protect and grow the economic resources available to the bank.

- Financial strategy should see to it that needed controls which are often parochial and standalone integrate into one comprehensive system.
- By focusing on market appeal and return on investment (ROI), as an example, Figure 2.3 suggests a frame of reference which has been implemented in several financial institutions.

The concept behind Figure 2.3 is simple but effective. What should be continually under senior management's watchful eye is the plan/actual comparison of *budgets* – and by extension of, income, cash flow and costs. This is what the best managed banks are doing.

The second dimension is *timetables*, including those of technology deliverables – since information technology, new product development and market

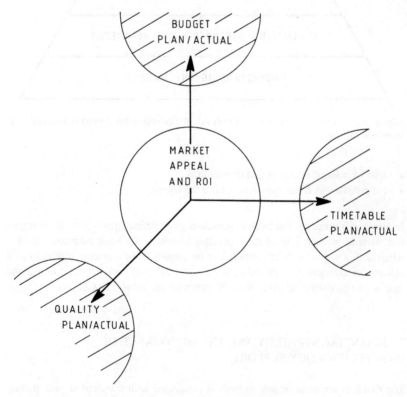

Figure 2.3 The needed controls are often parochial and standalone, which should be integrated into one system

appeal are today indivisible. The third dimension in Figure 2.3 is *quality* of financial products and services. Many boards tend to forget that the quality of banking services is *their* responsibility, it is not something to be relegated down the line.

For each axis along this frame of reference, as well as in terms of strategic planning, we must coinvolve: Treasury, budgeting, management control, as well as general accounting and cost accounting. Emphasis should be placed on current and projected financial needs. This necessarily brings into perspective prognostication in terms of

- cash flow,
- liquidity,
- volatility,
- interest rates, and
- currency exchange rates.

As underlined in section 2, the strategic plan must focus on the bank's financial staying power, a matter which involves both sources of income and expenditures. Both the *interest* budget and the *non-interest* budget must be carefully examined.

- The *interest budget* covers what the bank has to pay as negative interest to the depositors and for bought money. It roughly corresponds to two-thirds of the year's total budget.
- The *non-interest budget* addresses all other expenses, the major one being personnel, but also rental, utilities, software, computers, communications and all other costs.

While all components of the master plan require a great amount of rigorous experimentation by means of modeling, none does so in a more intensive manner than the financial plan.[1] Therefore the master plans of finance and technology correlate. The able use of high technology can be instrumental in better focusing the non-interest budget, decreasing overheads and bettering its punch.

In connection with finance, as well as in regard to any other of the master plan's components on which we have focused, technology is an *enabling tool* making it possible to reach more effectively the goals of the different other plans. Therefore all component parts of strategic planning must involve information technology (IT) sustaining an absolute and relative level of technological advancement and addressing

- technology investments,
- return on each investment,
- solutions by competition,
- modeling and experimentation,

- available functional performance, and
- technology transfer requirements.

Figure 2.4 gives a snapshot of what is involved in strategic planning for information technology. As the reader can appreciate, part and parcel of the strategic IT plan is a whole range of crucial factors. This is a dynamic list, evolving over time, as our own bank and its competitors move forward.

A fast advancing technology is one of the reasons why banking is in transition, experiencing a period of profound, rapid changes. (See Chapter 1.) Networks permit the development of integrated approaches to data, text, graphics, video and voice – in short, multimedia.

The global aspect of online communications, hence of the way of doing business, changes one flavor-type banking into one of many flavors. While computers came into the banking industry for paperwork simplification, today the most important aspect of technology in banking is not cost cutting, though this too is valuable. It is *added value*.

- A prerequsite of business strategy is developing an understanding of where value is added, as opposed to where cost is incurred.

It is crucial to invest in those capabilities necessary to gain and maintain a lead over rivals in key banking activities. Profitability can only be sustained by creating an edge. Often this requires making up a new value chain.

- Profits are far from being an automatic consequence of business. In competitive environments they are hard won and it is just as hard to maintain them.

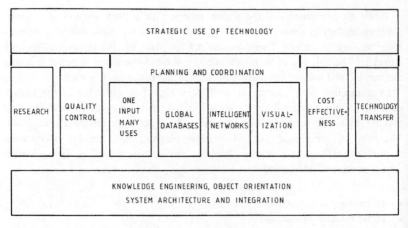

Figure 2.4 Strategic planning for information technology involves a broad range of crucial factors

Financial institutions which do not benefit from the advantage in pivotal activities, particularly those in evolving value chains, only make the modest returns more powerful rivals allow them to make. They find themselves 'dictated to', obliged to follow a certain course by those that exercise leadership.

Economic history teaches that profits accrue to those in a position of power. This position can be created by having the foresight to invest in building those capabilities which are particularly important, as the market undergoes an inevitable, albeit possibly gradual, restructuring. As a general frame of reference, Figure 2.5 presents an index of technology results in terms of return on investment.

- Banks which are able to sustain ROI of 18 percent to 20 percent do so because they are sophisticated users of technology.
- The laggards get no return on investment or, at best, less than 3 percent. This is a pitiful result which does not warrant spending large sums on technology.

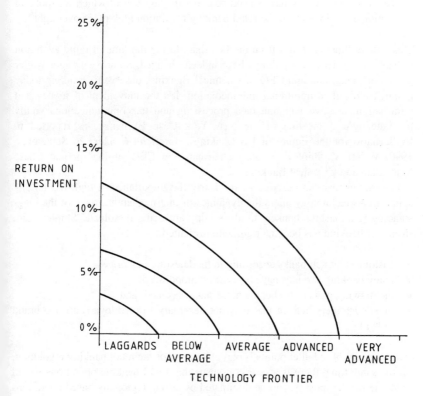

Figure 2.5 Index of technology and return on investment

If we cannot catch up with sophisticated developments in communications, computers and software, employment in our bank will grow faster than the numbers of transactions. If we cannot continue with competitive enhancements, six months from now most other banks will have copied the best of what we have done, cutting into our services and our market. This is something a modern bank can ill afford.

4   WHAT IS MEANT BY THE RETAIL BANKING REVOLUTION?

Leading-edge banks which over the last 20 years established and followed strategic planning premises have brought to the industry what is generally being called the *retail banking revolution*. In reality, this is an evolution which to first-rank financial institutions has come by relatively small steps which took place in rapid succession.

- The pace-setter banks have progressed relentlessly over time, reaching and passing some significant milestones.
- To those banks which have stayed behind – the laggards of which we spoke in section 3 – it looks as if the retail banking revolution took place overnight.

This optical illusion comes from the fact that, during the time of rapid evolution in banking services, many things have indeed changed. Some years ago, Walter V. Shipley, chairman and CEO of Chemical Banking, observed: 'Banking today is much more than traditional intermediation. It's the movement of money and information, a movement that data processing and telecommunications vitally facilitate.' (At a meeting of the New York Cash Exchange, as reported in 'A Scenario for the Future of US Banking', *American Banker*, 26 September, 1990. Walter V. Shipley is today chairman and CEO of the merged Chase Manhattan and Chemical Banking.)

Few statements can describe more clearly the importance of high technology support. 'As technology alters the dynamics of intermediation, many of the long-standing relationships bankers used to enjoy are being dissolved,' Shipley said. 'Much of banking has become transaction-oriented:

- customers switch banks according to the latest money prices;
- many banking services have become commoditized;
- the drawing power of a bank's name has weakened; and
- most customers believe that it is not necessary to owe loyalty to one brand of bank.'

Every one of these bullet points is part and parcel of the retail banking revolution. At the same time, there is a near consensus that retail banking operations would continue for the most part to be dominated by strong regionally based operations even if money center banks are stealing the show.

A European banker who had a chance to look at an early draft of this text had this to say: 'Shipley's view presents a very dated view of retail banking. The four bullets take us in a wholly inappropriate direction – and one the more enlightened banks are trying to reverse. They are trying to build customer loyalty – and are enhancing brand.' It is always wise to listen to contrary voices, even when they seem to be nonsense. The pseudo-enlightened banker who made this comment no longer works with the bank he used to, while Shipley is the chief executive of the largest American bank, and a very successful one at that. As for 'customer loyalty', it is long gone in a globalized economy, and for some banks 'branding' is so misused that it has almost become an unsuccessful gimmick (as will be explained in the appendix).

The same European banker also thinks that technology is breaking down the cartel of money transfers and, therefore, strong regional grouping in the European Union is nonsense. I object to the use of the word technology as if it were penicillin – let alone that this statement is basically wrong. The careful reader will also appreciate that, as far as strong regional grouping is concerned, there will be many developments in the years ahead. To better appreciate this, one needs only to study what has happened in the United States with Nations Bank and the *superregional* drive.

All options are open for the time being. A few pan-European universal banking groups could well emerge, even if the cost of establishing such financial networks is considered by many financial analysts prohibitive in the general case. But a faster pace of consolidation may characterize investment banking.

In the banking industry as in any other, mergers do not happen for the fun of it. The nature of local markets has much to say on which way the chips may fall. Figure 2.6 gives an example of differences among eight countries in terms of banking public and people with credit cards.

According to the prevailing wisdom among banking experts, the major multinational competition will occur on specific products or with well-defined customer groups. This is particularly true of the corporate sector and of high net worth individuals. At the same time, the transformation taking place sees to it that

- banks are becoming more focused, more consumer-oriented and more cost conscious, a fact reflected in their strategic plans.

Because global expansion is not easy and it also requires lots of funds, there is an emerging strategy of alliances:

- About 70 percent of European banks have engaged in collaborative ventures in the last 10 years, both at home and abroad.

Mergers and acquisitions are also taking place. Major Swiss, French and German banks have been particularly active in acquiring stakes and whole firms throughout

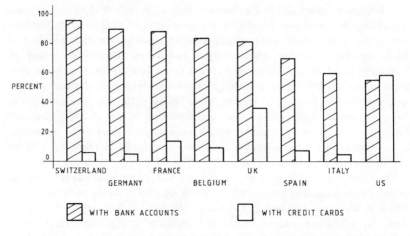

Figure 2.6   Percent of adults with bank accounts and with credit cards

Europe. One of the best examples to this end is the rush of continental European banks in acquiring investment banks in London. Mergers can come either because of strengths or because of weaknesses. In countries like the Netherlands, over-capacity and the prospect of competition from bigger, richer European, American and Japanese rivals have led to spectacular mergers. But Denmark and Norway have another reason for bank mergers: near bankruptcies.

The foray into some foreign markets for retail banking business had pluses and minuses. Citibank is reasonably successful, but quite the contrary can be said of Crédit Lyonnais. Therefore financial analysts believe that the more successful banks in Europe will be those that

- stick to their home markets for high street operations,
- while attacking international markets in specific niches where they are particularly strong.

Few financial analysts expect that universal banks from one country will make on a large scale the costly effort of becoming universal banks in another country. Only in the less efficient banking environment of southern Europe, in particular Spain and Italy, where a simple transaction can require as many as four individu-als to complete, will the more efficient northern banks have a good opportunity to move in.

One strategy short of mergers has been to form networks of banks across Europe through minority shareholdings. These forms of limited partnerships can be the basis for joint ventures, provide access to expertise and marketing net-works, and give the bank the international dimension business customers are increasingly demanding.

The transformation taking place in the retail banking industry, however, is not only geographic. Change is particularly intense in the domain of traditional service delivery going after greater efficiency through *networking*. The transformation in services which is still in process takes place over a number of years because:

- without careful planning not only the volume of transactions but also the costs are rising, and
- competition within the financial services industry is taking on a harsh new reality, which makes mandatory strategic moves. (See also Chapter 3 for the role played by non-banks.)

Much of the change in retail banking is market-induced, because customers make new demands for more sophisticated products and better service, while employees ask for fairer pay and more meaningful jobs. At the same time, shareholders are demanding higher returns on their investments.

5   BASIC CUSTOMER REQUIREMENTS INFLUENCING RETAIL BANKING STRATEGY

There is a majority opinion in the banking industry that the prospects of a retail banking strategy which dates *from the 1950s* – when commercial banks launched extensive campaigns to encroach on the retail market – have definitely faded. But prior to making a big switch, leading banks have studied consumer behavior and the consumers' psychological drives:

- their evolving financial condition,
- their need for information,
- the push to earn and spend, and
- the value attached to time and money.

One of the most important elements of financial services which has been identified by these studies is the wealth position of individual consumers. From my experience from the research connected with one of the major planning projects in which I collaborated, it is evident that consumers have four basic financial requirements.

1   *Save and borrow*, in a way which dissociates flow of income and spending patterns. Some bankers call this 'overcoming timing differences' by having money for spending before realized income. One way to do so is through credit cards; another is by means of a line of credit.

2 *Invest and trade* is a process which requires increasingly sharp expert advice. Confidence is the cornerstone of this issue. The bank must convince the consumer and the businessman that it is able to provide a safe and readily accessible home for superfluous funds – whether at home or globally.
3 Make payment in the *least time-consuming manner*. (Hence the need for networks and back office automation.) This is where a great deal of the technology effort should be focusing, contrary to what some bankers believe: that technology relieves people of the necessity of thinking.
4 *Keep dependable accounts* without being bothered by details – by delegating control activities to the bank.

Each one of these basic needs of the retail banking public goes beyond the old concept dominated by the proximity of branches and associated convenience. Even if *proximity* was the original keyword in retail banking, it is less appealing today because of direct banking solutions; hence we should think twice about the costs involved (see also Chapter 7) and the business opportunities.

Let me add one more thought to this argument. There is conflicting evidence in the banking sector about the importance of branches, because there is no uniform response of the banking public on how useful branches are. In consequence, every retail bank must form its own conclusions before it stands any chance of formulating a realistic strategy regarding networks or bricks and mortar branches.

'Save and borrow' fits well into the bank's role as financial intermediary, but the fact that clients put this issue at the top of the list also means that they will more carefully watch out for higher interest in their deposits and lower cost for their loans. This means stiffer competition.

Perhaps in reflection of this fact, Citibank is increasingly, becoming an institution of global consumer orientation, pulling ahead of other banks which look at the market in strictly local terms. While loans to corporate customers are shrinking, consumer loans have soared. But is *our* bank positioned to take advantage of this trend?

Because the profit margins in the 'save and borrow' product line are falling, banks have to sharply reduce their costs. Economies of scale are not the only answer. Greater efficiency through technology is a better approach. Banks also have to improve their bottom line through able pricing policies.

- *Selling* and *faster sales service* have become a crucial ingredient of successful banking, as Chapter 6 will demonstrate.
- Competitively priced payment accounts are the key to cross-selling other services in *relationship banking*, a term discussed in Chapter 7.

'Invest and trade' requires not only expert advice but also policies, systems and procedures insuring against financial loss. This is particularly relevant to private banking, as we will see in Chapter 9. It is also a new culture retail banks have to acquire, because it is what their customers want.

Whether they like it or not, retail banks are today obliged to satisfy a growing range of consumer demands. Able answers should, therefore, be a pivotal point in their business strategy. At the same time, because they cannot be all things to all people and to all companies, retail banks have to decide which market they are *really* after:

- small business orientation for deposits, loans and ancillary services?
- consumer orientation, with higher net worth individuals in mind?
- the mass market, with its large volume of transactions.

A small business orientation has other prerequisites. Ancillary services can play a key role, such as executing all payments, advancing money for the payroll but also preparing the payroll of the client firm, doing the export trade routines, handling the government guarantees, and providing the analytical accounting infrastructure – for a fee.

A strategy focusing on small business can be lucrative if orchestrated in an instrumental manner. A retail bank's loans portfolio is responsible for 65 percent to 85 percent of its revenue. Hence its potential earnings capacity is strongly related to its lending activities.

Up to a point, the same is true with consumer banking and, most particularly, with credit cards and mortgages. But during the 1980s, depressed economic conditions saw to it that one New York bank alone, in one year (1986), had to write off

- $700 million in outstanding credit card debts;
- $100 million on mobile homes in the Southwest, as owners in that depressed region just walked away from them; and
- $350 million for loans on mortgages, as the real estate market went down.

Among the factors which prove to be critical when it comes to *new retail banking policies* is quality of client service, efficiency of operations and low cost – in that order. These should be *our* bank's goals. For the mass market, automated teller machines (ATM) and point of sale (POS) provide 24-hour service, uniformity of procedures, and direct client involvement. Hence they help to improve the quality of service.

In terms of concentrating on handling the accounts of both lower and higher net worth individuals through a common system, some years ago Gotabanken (of Sweden) experimented with a variety of electronic delivery methods. It found that:

- 75 percent to 86 percent of all staff activities revolved around low value services and transactions;

- to change this ratio Gotabanken studied different service delivery systems, their benefits and their costs.

Amongst the lessons it learned from these experiments were that customers quite rapidly accept self-service terminals if they are actively marketed, and that customers generally approve of the informal *open-space* design for branches.

The Union Bank of Switzerland, also, has found that the core of the branch should be characterized by an open plan, with the traditional security screens removed.[2] Staff must sit behind desks rather than counters, creating an office-oriented *selling environment* which can also serve well in:

- providing investment advice, and
- cross-selling products supported by the bank.

Increasingly, cognizant retail bankers question the wisdom of handling high and low net worth individuals through the same channel. A separation effected by some banks leads to another major difference with old-type retail banking, regarding the number and qualifications of staff.

- Where customer-activated terminals predominate, staff are fewer and are given a role *advising* customers.
- By contrast, in the old approach with tellers for everybody there are more staff and less client satisfaction.

A bank's more lucrative clients are also the most demanding in terms of services. High net worth individuals may use the ATM from time to time, but this is not what they expect from the bank. Neither is videotex-type home banking satisfactory to their needs.

To answer home banking requirements in a more appealing way, Virginia's Crestar Bank has introduced PC banking which its customers can use from their home or office, at their convenience. Through their PC they can transfer funds, pay bills and automatically review and update their account transactions virtually 24 hours a day. The difference is made by the software the bank provides. Crestar PC Banking works with either Quicken or Microsoft Money, in conjunction with a Crestar personal checking account. Over and above this networked electronic teller capability, retail banks offer their best clients flexible working hours for investment advice and other personalized services which we will examine in Chapter 8.

6 GRAND STRATEGY AND KEY DECISIONS IN ESTABLISHING A BUSINESS PERSPECTIVE

'In the past, we tended to run the company to occupy space,' Citibank chairman and CEO John S. Reed told analysts. He then vowed that, henceforth, 'We are going to run the company for performance and not try to be in every market'

(*Business Week*, September 11, 1995). Every chief executive officer should think in these terms.

Performance criteria, however, can be elusive unless they are both quantified and qualified. Quantification will address market share; the targeted cash flow; projected level of deposits and of loans; what the bank expects in terms of profits; as well as return on assets (ROA), return on equity (ROE) and return on investment (ROI). Qualification is more subtle and one of its key ingredients is the *grand strategy*. There exist four main alternatives among which to choose.

1 *Lone Wolf*: this is the strategy followed by Citibank, Bankers Trust, J.P. Morgan and Union Bank of Switzerland, among others.
2 *Europartners*, like the Commerzbank, Banca di Roma, Crédit Lyonnais and Hispano Americana alliance in Europe; or Chase Manhattan, First Chicago and Wells Fargo in America.
3 *Tête de Fil*: this strategy is followed by First National Bank of Boston and Mellon Bank – each acting as the technological backbone of some 100 other, smaller banks.
4 *Coop*: examples are BIK in Germany and Ipacri in Italy. They are both cooperative efforts in technology: BIK of German popular banks, Ipacri of Italian savings banks.

'I think that grand strategy is a misnomer,' said a reviewer. 'It suggests this [choice] lies at the heart of strategy whereas the substance discussed is all about means to an end.' The person who wrote this is the same who confused strategy with tactics. In the beginning of this chapter he suggested that tactics is strategy. Now he thinks that strategy is tactics.

The reader must be very careful not to fall into these traps. Sometimes there are tonalities of grey, rather than black-and-white differences, contrasting strategy with tactics, but the difference is always there. 'Global retail strategy might be impossible to achieve on its own, but feasible with a coop strategy,' one of the reviewers advised. He is right. That is exactly why coop is a grand strategy.

The grand strategy should be clearly chosen because the future belongs to those banks who can create the structures needed for today's and tomorrow's more complex and more uncertain financial markets. By all accounts, the beginning of the 21st century will see banking and financial services as a key battleground – with both the scope and structure of commercial banking radically changing in form and content.

Most likely, the radical changes will be in Europe, if for no other reason than that continental European banks are today well behind their American and British counterparts. Traditionally, competition among European banks was primarily confined to one's own country, but this is no more the case.

- Since the mid-1980s, the big three Swiss banks have moved into Frankfurt in an open bid for domestic German business.
- Also in the 1980s, Deutsche Bank and Crédit Lyonnais moved aggressively into the domestic banking business in Italy.

But while importance of transnational networks has grown, and within the European Union there is no longer a national monopoly of the local retail banking market, organization, structure and, most importantly, technology were left behind. The amount of money spent on technology is huge, but ROI is tiny. There is no doubt this must now change.

Apart from the key decision necessary about focusing and putting emphasis on results, the definition of a grand strategy is necessary because today few banks can do everything all by themselves. The cost and complexity of high technology is a case in point. When it became necessary to develop a new sophisticated global network five competitor investment banks in New York such as Morgan Stanley, Goldman Sachs and Bear Sterns, decided to join forces and develop one network which they share. Grand strategies account for the fact that important chunks of the financial business have become multinational.

- not only is the banking population increasing and its needs expanding,
- but also the ability to tap worldwide business is at a premium.

Tough choices are therefore mandatory all the way from intelligent communications networks[3] to product line decisions which are based on projections and forecasts. This started at the end of the 1980s. In 1989, the Swiss Bank Corporation set down a long-term strategy, dubbed 'Vision 2000', which took the view that the capital markets of the 1990s would be driven by derivatives and risk management products. Thereafter, SBS acquired a chicago broker which specialized in financial instruments in order to gain from the cultural transfer which was necessary to position itself against the market forces of the end of this century.

Positioning requires strategic planning, but without an innovative culture even the best plan will have no effect. A grand strategy is also necessary because the lines dividing banks are no longer as clear-cut as they used to be. There is a distinction between retail banking and wholesale banking and Table 2.1 gives a glimpse of the differences.

- The division is blurred, with private banking fitting between these two classes, as technology erased many differences.
- Another opinion in positioning is that private banking stands on its own. It does not fit between retail and wholesale banking.

Whichever opinion is chosen as being closer to reality the layered architecture in Figure 2.7 explains the overall setting. It maps a business architecture

Table 2.1   Two different banking profiles which tend to merge

Retail	Wholesale
Many smaller accounts	Fewer large accounts
Mass of transactions	Relatively few transactions
Small amounts per transaction	Large amounts per transaction
Real-time implementation	Real-space technology
Rather contained investment in technology	Large investment in technology

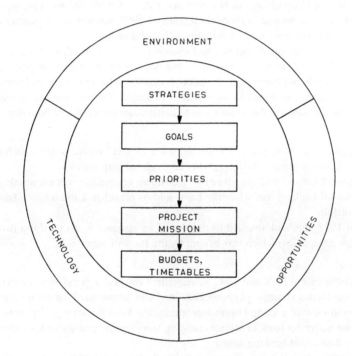

Figure 2.7   A framework for grand strategy decisions on business orientation

adopted by tier-1 retail, wholesale and investment banks in facing the market's evolution.

Entrusted with developing global strategy, senior management must carefully balance the risks and opportunities of market evolution. Both with retail banking and with wholesale banking a sound strategy should involve long-range planning; financial planning and control; budgeting and plan versus actual analysis; the assurance of a steady cash flow; special care in regard to the bank's profitability; and a first-class risk management system.

7   HOW BANKERS TRUST APPROACHED STRATEGIC PLANNING: A CASE STUDY

Today Bankers Trust is known as a merchant bank, but 20 years ago it also had significant retail banking operations, from which it decided to distance itself. This has been one of the first major decisions, or more precisely proposals to the board, made by the financial institution's strategic planning department. That is why it constitutes an important case study.

Historically, the process of strategic planning at Bankers Trust started in 1977 and led to a sharp change in business orientation. Eventually, strategic planning turned the bank around to its original goals of 1903, when it was primarily managing accounts for wealthy individuals and institutions.

Over the years the objectives had changed. By 1977, Bankers Trust was the seventh US bank in terms of assets – but not one of the top 10 in profits. The board also felt that the huge investments necessary in technology would not allow the bank to be all things in all markets. Strategic planning got the mission to study the choices and the answer was to concentrate on wholesale banking.

- Starting in 1979, Bankers Trust unloaded its retail business and transformed itself into a merchant bank serving large global corporations.
- From 1978 to 1982, the (then) new business orientation was wholesale commercial banking, but while the bank sold its branches it did retain a business portfolio.
- In 1982, the bank decided to dispose of its business loans portfolio (to midsize companies) which was bought by the Bank of New York.

In both cases, 1978 and 1982 management reached a grand strategy decision after the bank's strategic planning examined and documented the competitive situation in view of coming business opportunities. With this change, Bankers Trust became a premier bank in services ranging from trading and securities underwriting to investment banking advice.

The three topmost issues characterizing the evolving strategic perspectives at Bankers Trust are shown in Table 2.2. Notice that a distinction has been made between overall strategic guidelines and the most recent thrust. Since most loans originated by the bank are syndicated or sold in the secondary market, by the early 1990s 70 percent of Bankers Trust's balance sheet was made up of liquid securities, with Only 30 percent loans held in portfolio. (*Business Week*, April 22, 1991.) That is a marked contrast with a traditional bank, where the ratio is reversed. To appreciate this evolution and what it meant in terms of return on assets (ROA) and return on equity (ROE) it would be proper to look back briefly at the major strategic moves of the late 1970s and early 1980s which we considered at the beginning of this section.

Table 2.2   Strategic decisions of bankers trust

Overall	Recent thrust
1 Devise a sound strategy to implement returns, and do so successfully	1 Function like a merchant bank
2 Build on expertise in corporate, fiduciary, money/capital and investment banking to develop fully-fledged merchant bank operations	2 Expand revenue from operational products and engage in new product development
3 Significantly improve corporate relationships	3 Improve productivity, service quality and innovation in relationship banking

These have been far-reaching strategic decisions which have influenced the bank's future, fortune and profitability. The fundamental change in business orientation which was decided in 1978 had five major aftermaths. First was *the sale of 57 branch offices* of retail banking business. As a senior Bankers Trust executive commented: 'This was not an easy decision.' These branch offices were bought by National Westminster, Leumi Bank and Royal Bank of Canada. All three banks were strong in retail banking and saw acquisition of the branches as the best way to enter New York's retail banking market.

The second aftermath has been the development of specialization in *targeted industries*. Examples are shipping and aeronautics. This required emphasis on skills that could make Bankers Trust a leader.

The third aftermath has been the structuring of a modern, dynamic and profitable *relationship management* approach to assure customer handholding. This put focus on a technique whereby:

- senior managers are assigned to handle the customer in a global manner,
- while lesser emphasis is being placed on specific channels.

The fourth aftermath has been the institution of a *new personnel policy* to meet the demands of sophisticated customers. Strategic planning documented that leadership in industry marketing and relationship management requires that the bank's own people must be ahead of the customers. The motto has been: 'If you have the right people you get the customers.' This policy led to new approaches regarding compensation, training, the handling of administrative problems and the provision of information system supports. In short, a well-studied package was created able to help Bankers Trust become a premier bank in its chosen domain of activity.

The fifth aftermath has been the redefinition of *advanced information systems*, and the design of sophisticated software – as well as of new and efficient software development practices. A rigorous internal audit found that 80 percent of ongoing

IT projects had little or no usefulness because, as a result of long development timetables,

- competitors had leaped ahead,
- the market needs had changed, and
- delays made certain computer projects practically unnecessary.

This led to a strategic look at IT projects – critically evaluating them against the new policies established by top management. The acid test to which were subjected the bank's business policies documented that market strategy, computers and communications are subjects not independent of each other but closely related into an iterative process. Therefore, objectives must be refined by means of re-educating both sides: the bank's own business executives, and the bank's technology specialist.

It has also been proved that able solutions call for very efficient communications lines. Bankers Trust has given strategic planning the role of 'Devil's advocate' on current business plans. Said a senior executive: 'Even if you are doing well, you risk becoming another big brown industry. That's what we want to avoid.'

Another mission to strategic planning is to use the momentum of banking services going well at the present day, to put in place the next big income earners for the bank. The search for new opportunities is closely tied to the refining of current plans and the development of new products and services. Many banks pay lip service to this principle, but Bankers Trust put it in practical use.

8   BETTING ON SHAREHOLDERS TO PROMOTE THE BANK'S BUSINESS AND IMAGE

Generally speaking, companies do not like to have shareholders with very small odd holdings. While they are usually loyal and vote with management if a proxy battle erupts, shareholder relations are costly. It costs just as much to send annual reports and proxies to a shareholder with 50 shares as it does to send them to one with 50,000 shares – and since many companies look to save money, they offer to buy back odd-lots.

Shareholder relations are, however, a strategic issue, as discussed in section 2. Therefore, other companies take precisely the opposite approach from the one the preceding paragraph stated. They are betting on a widely scattered shareholder base to promote their interests. The Boston Beer Company, for instance, is going out of its way to lure just such small shareholders by:

- placing coupons in its six-packs which eventually lead to share ownership, and
- establishing a toll-free line in the United States to lure customers to buy odd lots of shares.

Boston Beer has set aside 990,000 shares for such small buyers in its planned offering of four million shares. In accord with SEC regulations, the six-pack buyers must first get the formal prospectus for the offering in the mail before buying the stock. To be eligible, they must be at least 21 years old and not work for a brokerage firm or a beer distributor.

Buyers in the consumer offering were able, if they wished, to sell their shares in the public market as soon as the underwritten offering was completed. But as company management expected, few of the new shareholders exercised that right. I see this as a good shareholder strategy for small banks.

There are precedents. The cooperative banks in America follow a similar strategy favoring the small shareholder and the odd lot of shares. There is really no reason why this approach cannot be generalized by the smaller to medium-size retail banks, since it provides benefits to both parties:

- the bank itself gets enriched with new shareholder capital, and
- the public obtains a sense of ownership in the financial institution with which it deals.

Shareholders can serve the bank in more ways than just contributing equity capital. They may become excellent public relations agents, open new avenues for investments and loans, and also oblige management to think more closely of ownership – hence of the longer term.

Big shareholders typically push bank management to improve return on equity (ROE) and to expand the product line. Furthermore, the small shareholders impact counterbalances risk taking because, other things equal, lower net worth individuals tend to be risk-averse. One of the better advantages gained by wider ownership is that, to balance different trends in ownership, the bank's management feels obliged to:

- upgrade the bank's strategic planning process, and
- chart the future course with greater precision.

Cognizant small shareholders will be more prone than big shareholders to ask puzzling questions like: Who are we? What are our products? Who are our customers? Big shareholders would rather focus on queries such as: Where are our markets? What are our *new* products and services? What are our costs?

The very fact of offering equity to small shareholders is for management a way to realize that, in the general case, the days of cheap deposits are gone forever. For the bank, this means narrower interest spreads. Hence management must:

- pay closer attention to analysis of the interest sensitivity of the balance sheet to prevent a large mismatch from developing, and

- work harder at generating floating rate commercial mortgage and installment loans, where small shareholders might help.

Another benefit the bank may derive from small shareholders is that, used as a public relations means, they can attract new accounts by spreading the knowledge that the bank treats its old customers best. It is always better to attract new clients through friends than to spend too much money on advertising.

This in no way replicates the old dictum in banking: 'Don't open a new account for anyone unless you know him personally, or unless proper references have been obtained.' But it extends further out the goodwill circle. If the small shareholders can be turned into asset management clients, the bank will be well positioned to build some extra fee income, including ancillary services like insurance.

Small shareholders may also be a good testing ground for documented answers to queries such as: Are our products priced properly? If we increased the price would we lose the business? Banks should rethink in a factual way all free services they have been providing. Are these still justified? Has *our* institution done its homework in terms of a detailed account analysis on as many customers as possible? (See also, in Chapter 7, the discussion on the customer mirror.)

In conclusion, banking competition has taken a totally new aspect. It is able to attract new accounts not only through advertising but also through direct sales and customer ownership. Contrary to an old banking addage, the modern bank does not *really* know people and organizations for which it opens new accounts. We learn about them as we go. That is why it is so important to:

- cost our services,
- have a customer mirror for profit and loss, and
- maintain an online customer quality history.

In a marketplace which is increasingly demanding and dynamic, banks do compete with one another and with non-banks for business. They do try to attract each other's clients through innovative services and better deals, but also by providing other incentives which attract the customers' attention, excite their interest and make them feel more secure. As cannot be repeated too often, it is no longer vanilla icecream banking.

Notes

1.   See also D.N. Chorafas, *Financial Models and Simulation* (London: Macmillan, 1995).
2.   D.N. Chorafas and H. Steinmann, *High Technology at UBS – for Excellence in Client Service* (Zurich: Union Bank of Switzerland, 1988).
3.   D.N. Chorafas, *Agent Technology Handbook* (New York: McGraw-Hill, 1998).

3 Financial Services Offered by Banks and Non-Banks

1 INTRODUCTION

The term *financial services* is often given a poor definition, and in some cases several definitions which sound as if they were contradictory. In the bottom line, however, such definitions tend to converge towards 'the facilitation of financial flows between two or more agents engaged in market activities'. This simple sentence underpins the concept of financial intermediation as we saw it in Chapters 1 and 2.

Banking strategy, the way we have examined it so far, is applicable in all branches of the financial industry – whether we talk of regulated banks or the so-called 'non-bank banks'. Because all financial institutes engage in a sort of intermediation, they must plan ahead and position themselves against the forces of the competition.

- The process of financial intermediation in all its forms is the justification of the banking system.
- While they perform intermediation activities, banks engage in asset transformation.

But as we have seen in Chapter 2, the line formally dividing different types of banking – for instance wholesale and retail – disappears, as one institution enters the other's turf. The same is true about the line dividing banks from non-banks.

Both banks and non-banks are after deposits of some sort, and they perform maturity mismatching as well as asset transformation by making use of this low-cost funding source. A presumably stable core of deposits helps to change short-term funding activities into longer-term propositions.

One of the interesting aspects of developments in the financial markets during the last 15 years is the trend towards instruments and contractual arrangements that aim to *unbundle risk* and redistribute its components in combination with broader, liquid markets. Examples of risk unbundling and redistribution are derivative instruments like futures, options, forwards and swaps. For instance:

- forward rate agreements (FRA),
- interest rate swaps (IRS),
- underwritten floating rate notes (FRN).

Each vehicle has its own risk transfer characteristics. Aside from intermediation and risk management, a distinct feature of banks and non-banks is to provide a reliable payment system. This, however, is not always cost-effective owing to a number of factors, including the level of technology.

Banks and non-banks do not operate on a level field because of a major difference which needs to be brought into perspective. While the banking system is typically supported through regulation and supervision, the economic forces behind non-banks seem to have a free rein. The fact that banking legislation does not apply to them changes the competitive landscape.

We will start this chapter by taking the proverbial long, hard look at the banking industry as well as at regulation and supervision. While much can be learned by reading the script of the law, it is personal experience and observation that should be used in shaping strategic decisions.

2   THE MANY DIFFERENT TYPES OF BANKS AND THEIR MISSION

Classically, the regulated banking industry has been distinguished into three main classes, *commercial, investment* and *merchant*, as shown in Figure 3.1. Commercial banks are the main intermediaries, as has been discussed in the Introduction. The best definition of a commercial bank in one short sentence is 'A deposit-taking institution, whose primary activity has been that of giving loans.'

Investment banks act as advisors and traders. They are active in the securities business, engage in asset management, act as consultants to other companies, do underwriting, advance bridging loans and focus on brokerage. To a large extent, as descendants of old trading firms, merchant banks invest their own money in business transactions. Classically, they have been the risk-takers.

Figure 3.1 also shows that there are other types of banks with which to reckon. In America the savings and loans associations and in England the building societies are in the mortgage industry. The savings banks in continental Europe are a different proposition, and only partly overlap with the mortgage business orientation.

In America and in Japan, the savings and loans industry is taken as a branch apart from commercial banking. In Germany and in Austria, the savings institutions (Sparkassen) are assimilated to the banking industry, though they preserve some distinct characteristics. In continental Europe, popular banks are numerous, though each one is small or even very small. A reason for the existence of popular banks and credit unions is that of addressing the banking needs of the lower net worth strata in the population, but it does not always work that way. As their name implies, the agricultural banks are supposed to help the farmers, but their role has significantly changed over the years. In some countries, like France, Holland and Austria, the agricultural banks are very strong.

53

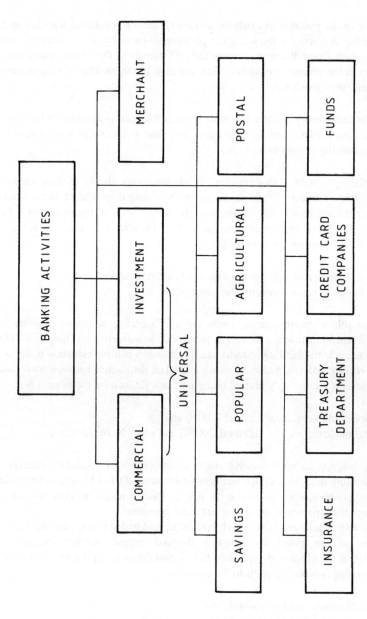

Figure 3.1 There is a multitude of banks in the regulated and non-regulated financial industry

Most of the postal banks (which, incidently, are not regulated) were set up to find cheap deposits for financing the government-owned post and telecommunications authorities. Because they use the PTT offices as their base, postal banks can reach the ultimate consumer. They are also in the middle of a controversy regarding their existence.

- Practically every country has some peculiar financial institutions of its own.
- Because the laws and the privileges vary, there is no unique way to describe the banking system as a whole.

One of the privileges is that banks act as intermediaries. But by so doing they are exposed to a number of risks depending on how long they hold on to the assets. For some instruments, like derivatives, the longer term is the more risky. For others, like loans, the opposite might be true. In terms of *investment horizons* there is a progressive scale which goes:

- from traders and arbitrageurs with a very short horizons,
- to bankers oriented towards the longer term.

In their role as intermediaries, banks serve as a backup source of liquidity for other financial institutions as well as production and distribution companies. This role has made the banking industry the transmission belt for monetary policy – a role recently addressed also by non-banks. The distinction between banks and non-banks is increasingly blurred because of new financial vehicles such as:

- Money market mutual funds (MMMF) and
- negotiable orders of withdrawal (NOW) and super-NOW accounts.

While different among themselves, these examples revolve around the concept of restructuring the classical demand deposit accounts (DDA) by setting new rules like paying significant interest to the holder. This increases the cost of funds to the bank but also makes the instrument more competitive.

The retail banks are those which both benefitted and suffered from the relative demise of the practically cost-free demand deposit account (because of Regulation Q, which was repealed). Retail banking is a major form of commercial banking, addressing itself to the consumer.

- His deposits, and (increasingly so)
- The management of his account(s).

A decisive factor for success in present-day retail banking is an efficient sales organization able to satisfy clients needs by means of products that are designed for greater usefulness and convenience, but are also supported through imagination and skill. The hallmark of accomplishment is when clients begin to make greater use of such services under financial conditions favorable to the user as well as to the bank.

Both product innovation and competitive pricing are cornerstones to improved earnings. All commercial banks currently face the problem of narrow interest margins and they also become increasingly aware that high costs are adversely impacting retail business – but, as it cannot be repeated too often no bank has a lock on the market. Competitive pricing is important.

Table 3.1 shows the results of research I did in August 1997 among four Swiss banks in connection with financing a first mortgage for a private house, on a fixed interest rate over a period of 3, 4 and 5 years.

- Crédit Suisse and UBS are universal banks (see definition in the following paragraphs).
- Migros Bank and Kantonalbank (of Kanton Luzern) are retail banks.

As the reader can see the lowest rates in all three periods were given by a universal bank – and the same is true about the highest rates. Exactly because of these discrepancies, informed customers appreciate there is plenty of scope in shopping around for the best price.

As profitable banks know, they have to capitalize on the fact that the retail sector must be organized to operate efficiently under demanding market conditions. Therefore, while on the cost side they streamline management structures and reorganize their business, at a strategic level they target a clear segmentation of clients by value into:

- retail banking,
- corporate or wholesale, and
- private banking.

In contrast to retail banking, the *wholesale* form of banking is directed to corporate customers who are more demanding – and therefore it needs to be supported by appropriate tools and knowhow. Wholesale banking can be seen as an outgrowth

Table 3.1 Financing of a first mortgage on a 3-, 4- and 5-year timeframe in Switzerland

	Credit Suisse (%)	Migros Bank (%)	Kantonalbank (%)	UBS (%)
3 Years	$3\frac{3}{4}$	$3\frac{7}{8}$	4	$4\frac{1}{8}$
4 Years	4	$4\frac{1}{8}$	$4\frac{1}{4}$	$4\frac{3}{8}$
5 Years	$4\frac{1}{4}$	$4\frac{1}{4}$	$4\frac{1}{2}$	$4\frac{5}{8}$

of merchant and investment banking. Both retail and corporate clients (an example being the company's pension fund) are target populations for *private banking*.

In cases where the law of the land permits, banks combine commercial and investment activities under one roof, into what has become known as *universal banking*. The main issue is culture. Whether commercial or universal, companies in the banking business are often broadly classified into one of three types:

- Money center,
- Regional,
- Local.

Money center banks are so called not only because they do business on a global basis but also, if not primarily, because they buy money rather than depend on deposits. Most money center banks are *wholesale*-oriented, and tend to focus their domestic activity primarily toward the larger companies.

Regional banking organizations tend to be both retail and wholesale, and have some national presence. But typically regionals work on a well-defined territory around their headquarters, serving larger cities and smaller towns – industries as well as individuals.

Local banks do most of their business in the retail banking market. They particularly deal with private individuals and small businesses, featuring a higher proportion of installment and mortgage loans than regional banks. Typically, savings and loans (but not building societies) are local banks.

Because these are fairly different areas of activities and they require different skill as well as different technological solutions, well-managed banks are keen to define the sort of business they are in – and, with this, their culture. As shown in Figure 3.2, the first questions a bank should ask itself is whether it chooses:

- retail or wholesale orientation,
- city banking, agricultural or some other mission.

From factual and documented answers will come a better vision but also more focused questions regarding the products and services we should develop and sell. The strategies which we develop should always keep in perspective *our* competitors.

3   REGULATION, SUPERVISION AND THE DEVELOPING EXPERIENCE IN BANKING STRATEGY

The principles written in Chapter 2 about strategic planning in the banking industry did not exist since the beginning of banking. They developed through patient

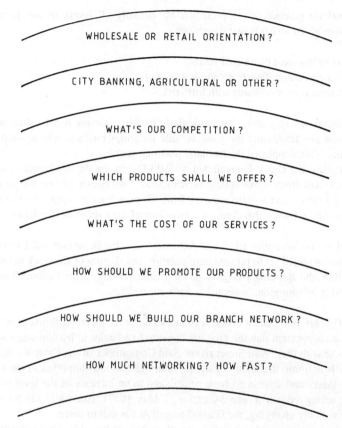

WHOLESALE OR RETAIL ORIENTATION?

CITY BANKING, AGRICULTURAL OR OTHER?

WHAT'S OUR COMPETITION?

WHICH PRODUCTS SHALL WE OFFER?

WHAT'S THE COST OF OUR SERVICES?

HOW SHOULD WE PROMOTE OUR PRODUCTS?

HOW SHOULD WE BUILD OUR BRANCH NETWORK?

HOW MUCH NETWORKING? HOW FAST?

Figure 3.2   An onion skin approach: decision layers in a banking strategy

work, often by means of trial and error, as banks planned ahead and attempted to outwit their opponents in the financial industry.

Not all of the types of banks we have briefly reviewed in section 2 have done strategic planning successfully. Those who did, pulled way ahead of their competitors. This is true of small banks and of big banks; of retail, wholesale, investment and merchant banks. As I have already underlined, strategic planning became necessary because of intensified competition. If we look back more than 60 years, to the early 1930s, we will see that the financial environment was so protected that it hardly required planning ahead.

The history of strategic developments in banking teaches that the nature of competitive advantages in the aftermath of the Great Depression has been quite different from the one prevailing today. The legislation which was put in place made banking pampered and protected by virtually all levels of government. Banks were given an exclusive franchise:

- access to low-cost or no-cost funds,
- little or no competition from non-banks, and
- short-term corporate loans with little risk.

The financial industry and most particularly banking became regulated to avoid speculation and fraud, and the more volatile securities business was weeded out of banking. This simplified the business planning problems.

In America, the Glass–Steagall Act of 1933 forced the deposit banks to separate themselves from banks selling securities. J. P. Morgan could no longer deal with investments, and a quite separate firm, Morgan Stanley, split off to deal in securities. Other banks also divested themselves of their securities affiliates.

- In 1934, the Securities Exchange Act established the Securities and Exchange Commission (SEC) to prevent manipulation and rigging of the stock market.
- In 1935, the Banking Act gave much greater powers to the Federal Reserve Board in Washington, in regard to bank supervision.

Some 50 years later, economists, regulators and other financial thinkers, almost came to an agreement that the time has come to free banks, at least in some ways, to compete with their Wall Street rivals. Said Comptroller of the Currency Robert Clarke: 'It is ironic that many of the prohibitions that are supported in the name of bank safety and soundness have contributed to an increase in the level of risk in the banking system' (*Time Magazine*, 4 May 1987). But while the financial system is slowly changing, the Glass–Steagall Act is still in force.

Both in America and Japan, which are characterized by fairly similar regulatory issues in the banking industry, the debates about reforming the domestic financial systems by updating, respectively, Glass–Steagall and Article 65, have been slowed by political horse-trading. This is making more difficult the management of a situation in which systemic risk gets greater, not less, and the regulatory rules are skewed.

Not only commercial and investment banks but central bankers, too, have to think of strategic planning. The circle that they have to square can be phrased in this way: How to establish a framework of regulation and supervision that accommodates characteristics of the traditional specialized banking system, with the sort of diversified financial services that have evolved?

- The era of strictly focused financial institutions is passing,
- but it leaves behind a regulatory system designed to fit the old requirements.

A single omnipotent regulator for all financial services has so far remained out of reach and things will probably stay that way. Today, regulators everywhere acknowledged the need to preserve assets, while today the need is to cooperate more closely across both business and geographical boundaries. Banks also feel the need for greater harmonization of regulatory standards on everything from risk assessment to reporting requirements. In spite of this, few central bankers foresee anything but the most limited formal merging of existing regulatory agencies, even within single countries. The problems are too complex and the embedded interests too deep rooted too change them in a short span of time. Yet the six decades which followed the early 1930s saw a slow but persistent process of erosion of the old rules which weakened the protective barriers.

- With deregulation, traditional banks lost their access to low cost funds.
- For the bigger banks, however, bought money compensated for such loss, provided they had a strategic plan in place.

Because competitive pressures usually underpin new developments, it is not surprising that strategic planning started with money center banks in the 1970s.

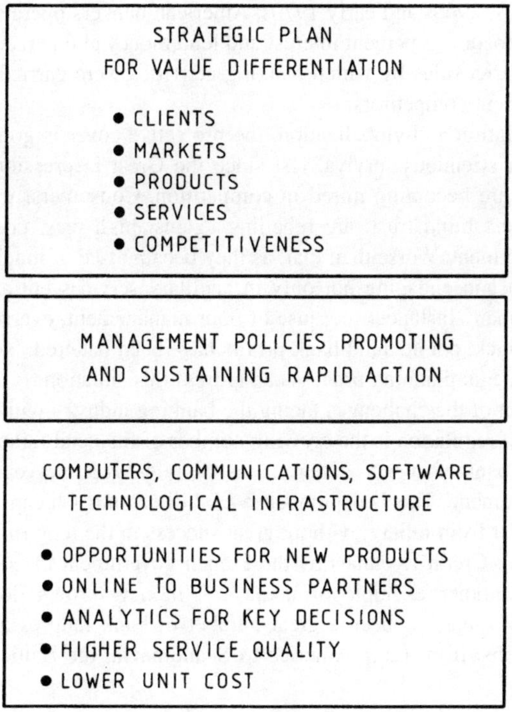

```
        STRATEGIC PLAN
     FOR VALUE DIFFERENTIATION

        • CLIENTS
        • MARKETS
        • PRODUCTS
        • SERVICES
        • COMPETITIVENESS
```

```
     MANAGEMENT POLICIES PROMOTING
      AND SUSTAINING RAPID ACTION
```

```
   COMPUTERS, COMMUNICATIONS, SOFTWARE
       TECHNOLOGICAL INFRASTRUCTURE

    • OPPORTUNITIES FOR NEW PRODUCTS
    • ONLINE TO BUSINESS PARTNERS
    • ANALYTICS FOR KEY DECISIONS
    • HIGHER SERVICE QUALITY
    • LOWER UNIT COST
```

Figure 3.3   Two basic requirements for rapid time-to-market are far-seeing strategic planning and appropriate technological infrastructure

In Chapter 2 we saw an example with Bankers Trust. The need to develop banking strategies spread as smaller, more protected banks felt the pressure of competition.

The statement made about rethinking the regulatory rules and confines has a counterpart in the commercial banking industry. As they got themselves confident with the tools they were using, cutting-edge banks developed far-seeing strategic planning premises. Even if every financial institution takes a different approach in the way it puts together its strategic plan, a common concept underpinning the most successful efforts is a three-layered structure shown in Figure 3.3. At the top is value differentiation regarding clients, markets, products and services. At the bottom is the technological infrastructure. Interfacing between the two are management policies promoting competitiveness.

4   RETAIL BANKING WITHOUT THE
PROTECTIVE UMBRELLLA OF REGULATION

In the post-World War II years which preceded deregulation, which essentially means the 1950s, 1960s and early 1970s, American bankers operated by the '3 to 6 rule': pay depositors 3 percent interest and lend money at 6 percent. Federal and state laws set strict rules by which banking activities were carried out, and protected the different competitors.

With deregulation and globalization, the protective cover is gone and bankers face their most strenuous survival test since the Great Depression. Everywhere they turn they are becoming mired in competition. Consumers, who in the past accorded bankers blind trust, are rebelling against high fees, poor service and impersonal treatment. Worse than that, as they became free of much federal regulation, banks began engaging not only in ancillary services but also in suicidal price wars. In many instances, because of poor management, overzealous lending and some bad luck, commercial bank profits have been battered. Nothing short of a thorough strategic planning process can redress this situation.

An indication of the challenges facing the banking industry without the protective umbrella of regulation is the growing number of financial failures. One of the most dramatic bank rescues to date remains the mid-1983 intervention by the US Federal Government. The Fed pumped $4.5 billion into Chicago's Continental Illinois to save it from failure, without great success in the long run.

The rescue of Crédit Lyonnais by the French government in the 1993 to 1996 timeframe is another example of taxpayers' money thrown down the drain. Elsewhere, too, there has been a great number of bank failures and last-minute rescue operations, from Latin America to Scandinavia, the Baltic countries and Japan.

- In many countries, consumers are increasingly worried by a seemingly endless string of bad-news headlines about their banks.

- Bankruptcies are proof that management does not quite know what it is doing in an environment of fierce competition.

During the years of regulation, bankers could ignore consumers who lost confidence in their institutions as a disgruntled minority. But once banking has gone into the free-enterprise system, and out of a walled environment, competition is bound to shake up a whole lot of things and embedded beliefs. This places emphasis on the need to manage change, as we will see in detail in Chapter 5. The new policy must be established in a realistic way, rather than using vague notions of hope as substitutes for strategic planning.

The optimists believe that the financial industry will fight its way out of today's problems and become stronger than ever, but they fail to notice that many timid, superprudent banks have been pushed to innovation and aggressive marketing without the needed strategies and tools to face the challenges. At the other end of the competitive spectrum are retail bankers who have done their homework in a strategic planning sense. They have rolled out dozens of new services, ranging from discount-catalog shopping to home-equity accounts.

New retail banking products allow consumers to write checks based on the value of their house or condominium. However, in this atmosphere of growing competition many banks are making serious mistakes because they are forced to take on new risks for which they have no contigency plans. A growing number of them are guessing wrongly the aftermaths from their lack of experience with new products.

A history lesson gives muscle to this argument. Periods of turmoil are familiar in the history of banking. The big three banks of 14th-century Florence, the Bardi, Peruzzi and Acciaiuoli, wielded great power until they failed after Edward III of England and King Robert of Naples defaulted on their debts. The fall of Austria's Creditanstalt in 1931 led to financial panic around the world. Throughout most of history, bank failures have occurred with dismal regularity, and neither banks not consumers had protection from them. Even in the booming 1920s, banks closed at the rate of about 500 a year.

- The failure rate rose sharply during the four years following the 1929 stock-market crash when, in America alone, a total of 9,000 banks went under.
- Because many private people got hurt, the Glass–Steagall Act (see also section 3) established the Federal Deposit Insurance Corporation (FDIC) to guarantee the safety of savers' money.

Examining banking failures in retrospect, many people agree that the no. 1 reason for the banking industry's trouble is bad management. Many companies can get away with a fair amount of poor management over a short period of time when the economy is in good shape. But if the economy turns sour, management mistakes are magnified.

The no. 2 reason why many banks face problems is that they are simply unprepared for the rapid change they are facing after regulation and the protection it affords is gone. Typically, banks do not have enough experienced hands to accommodate the industry's changing structure.

- These reasons further magnify the wisdom of engaging in strategic planning, as has been explained in Chapters 1 and 2.
- Another major factor to take into account in banking strategy is *globalization*, of which we talk in section 5.

For banks and bankers, the best way to look at the years ahead is to ascertain that they can use their freedom from regulation to rebuild a strong, stable and confident customer base. This requires skill and imagination, as well as the guts to see that strategic plans are not only developed but also put into action – and that they are fully supported in their execution.

5   THE EFFECTS OF DEREGULATION AND THE GLOBALIZATION OF FINANCIAL OPERATIONS

Globability is needed to underpin financial power, and financial power is necessary to acquire and protect globability in operations. In a world where transborder trade becomes the rule, globalization helps to expand business opportunity and spread risk, but also requires a well-rounded view of the financial organization, as Figure 3.4 demonstrates. The broken arrow shaft tells the reader that this feedback loop is not always present – as should be the case.

Other factors propelling globalization have been advances in transportation and communication which led to a sharp increase in commerce, investment and money management on a worldwide basis.

- As trade expanded, financial institutions began to follow their customers abroad.
- The expanding of the geographic horizons led to creation of new money and securities markets.

The multitude of different financial instruments presented arbitrage possibilities for those institutions capable of taking advantage of opportunities between markets and among instruments within markets. This led to innovations of which the most notable is the development of the derivatives market, offering futures and forwards as contrasted to the spot market.

When we rethink and re-evaluate the effects of deregulation and globalization, it will be proper to include in our strategic plans the fact that protective barriers created in the aftermath of the Great Depression have crumbled. Whatever still

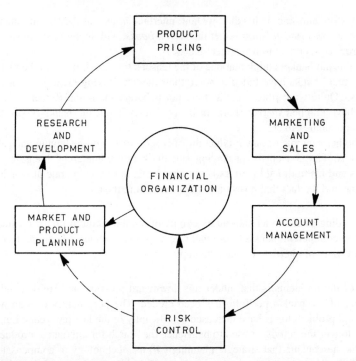

Figure 3.4 Globability requires a thoroughly planned, well-rounded approach to financial operations

remains is under pressure from a combination of social, economic and technical forces. The principle is that, without legislated advantages or arbitrary constraints, the resulting environment is largely regulated by the market.

The reader's attention has also been brought to the fact that technological developments have a major impact in the described direction. The rapid advances in telecommunications, computers and software opened – and continues opening – new horizons with the potential to ignore or bypass many traditional geographic and legislative restrictions. This strengthened the competition by non-bank banks (see sections 7 and 9) and therefore the path to disintermediation.

Strategic planning should pay full attention to technology's role in assisting the emergence of new, cheaper and more efficient market instruments: electronic funds transfers, credit cards, debit cards, commercial paper, Eurobonds, Euronotes, and so on. The most creditworthy customers – typically AAA borrowers – are increasingly bypassing banks, therefore disintermediating them. Banks answer this loss of business through innovation – a steady stream of new products – of which, as already noted, derivatives are the no. 1 example. The problem is not that these new instruments can be handled without intermediaries, but the fact the interme-diaries are *investment banks* rather than *retail banks*, with lucrative business shift-ing from commercial to investment banks.

Cognizant bankers think that one of the reasons for this shift lies in the fact that many retail banks have failed to serve their market, leaving great gaps for other banks. 'Quite what [these] are and are not is barely the point. Rather, it is how they have grabbed market share, in many cases without the banks responding,' said one retail banker.

Another example of new product thrust is *securitization*: the buying and selling of loans. The concept of packaging and marketing commercial loans to other banks and institutional investors is not new. What is new is the rate at which this is done and the fact that investment banks are doing them.

- Lending as the bread-and-butter activity of retail banking is on the decline.
- The commercial bank's traditional role as primary lender is being replaced by a variety of alternative financing approaches.

One of the problems is that, under this downward pressure on loan demand, the quality of the bank's portfolio has been eroded. The percentages of loan write-offs and problem loans have increased significantly in the last few years. Lending is no longer the activity it used to be. Hence the search for alternative products.

It is inescapable that strategic planning will use technology to compensate the loss of business in certain market segments. Technology promotes a new look at financial markets, because it makes it possible to create a de facto 24-hour global reach through interconnected networks. Solutions must blend technological expertise and tradition because there are prerequisites to 24-hour banking which has two different aspects:

- *24-hour retail banking*, based on automated teller machines (ATM), the more sophisticated electronic tellers (ET), point of sales (POS) equipment, and home banking (HB);
- *24-hour wholesale banking* with the axis New York, London/Zurich, Tokyo, addressing large clients, correspondent banks and governments.

Both 24-hour wholesale banking and 24-hour retail banking handle *online*, cus-tomer orders messages, transactions and accounts. In turn, this requires a first-class network increasingly using knowledge-enriched software – as well as real-time analysis and evaluation capabilities as outlined in Figure 3.5. Few retail banks currently provide themselves with solutions which capitalize on technology in an able manner.

Technology can also be used to merge the on-balance sheet capability and service breadth of a commercial bank with the off-balance sheet skills and entrepreneurial

65

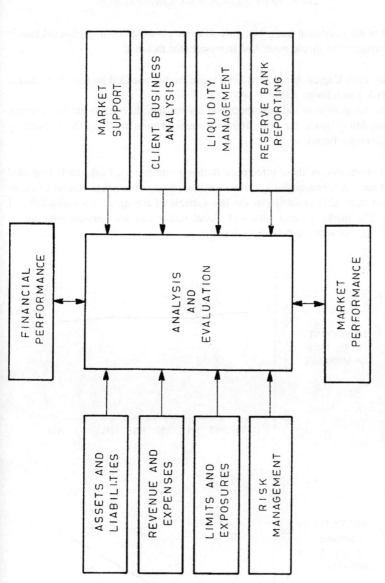

Figure 3.5 Based on a number of inputs and on analytics, senior management's evaluation should target both market performance and financial performance

spirit of an investment bank. Not only strategic planning but also the retail bank's top management should never lose from sight the fact that:

- the 1988 Capital Accord has been significantly amended by the 1996 Market Risk Amendment, and
- the integration of balance sheet and off-balance sheet exposure has become mandatory since the July 1996 recommendations by the UK Accounting Standards Board.

The bottom line of these references is that a commercial bank needs iron-clad real-time risk management systems to assure rapid and accurate control of exposure. A bank able to survive is the one capable of coping with a multiplicity of risks. The market's rapid pace and global nature call for constant attention to positions, exposures and the long list of risks.

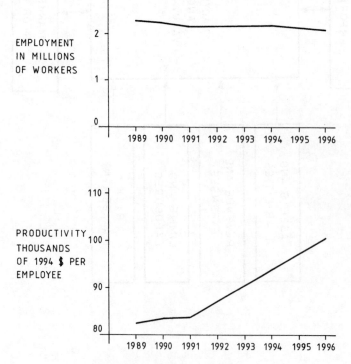

Figure 3.6 Employment and productivity in 1989–96, as the financial business expanded

Dynamic strategies backed up by high technology also necessary to be able to test new products on a trial basis and be ready to transform them into a volume operation to keep up with expanding market demand when they succeed, but also to be prepared to withdraw altogether if the product does not meet with market acceptance.

Cost-effectiveness is an equally important preoccupation. High technology should be used to steadily improve the productivity results. Figure 3.6 shows employment and productivity in the American banking industry in the 1989 to 1996 timeframe. Because of technology, in seven years productivity has increased by 17.6 percent.

6 CAN WE MATCH PROBLEMS AND OPPORTUNITIES PRESENT IN COMMERCIAL BANKING?

Commercial banking and most particularly retail banking as well as the savings and loans business are in decline because they have become less central to the Group of Ten economies. By contrast, non-bank rivals such as securities firms, mutual funds, pension funds and others have been grabbing business.

Adding salt to the wound, bad loans have cramped the commercial banks' room for maneuver, pushing them into derivatives trades. Which are the strategies open to a retail bank when it contemplates remaining a player in the wider financial market?

- A factual and documented response to this query can only be given within the perspectives of a strategic plan.
- Specific measures must be focused according to a bank's position and needs. It does not make sense to advise in a general manner.
- By contrast, general trends can be discussed more broadly and this is what this section is doing.

Stated in a general manner, the advice which I give to client banks is to start by rethinking and re-evaluating the more significant contributions of commercial banking within *their* sphere of influence. This is the job of strategic planning. For instance, in financing productive efforts in the economy, are they addressing primarily business loans or consumer loans? Then they should examine the main kinds of deposits they receive:

- demand deposits,
- time deposits,
- money market funds,
- interbank deposits.

An issue to which strategic planners should pay attention is whether or not *their* bank is taking a fair share of these deposits. If not, what are the reasons? Where are these reasons leading? Where is their bank lagging?

Similar questions should be asked about loans in the chosen domain of activity, and also in connection with reserves in accordance with the 1996 Market Risk Amendment. By total reserves of a bank is meant its total cash assets. Total reserves are composed of:

- required reserves,
- working reserves, and
- surplus reserves.

Adequate reserves are the key to matching problems and opportunities present in commercial banking. *Required reserves* are the minimum total amount of capital a bank needs in function of deposit liabilities in view of reserve requirements. These are also known as legal reserves. Management can optimize the *working reserves* of the bank which are essentially immobilized funds. Working reserves are composed of cash in vault, interbank deposits which are not part of legal reserves, and the legal reserves. Working reserves are essentially a precaution against unforeseen adverse clearing house drains, or unexpected net withdrawals of deposits in currency.

In most cases working reserves appear in the form of deposits in other commercial banks. A wise strategy would see to it that these and other elements in the working reserves class are optimized through simulation and experimentation. Genetic algorithms and fuzzy engineering can be valuable tools in an experimental approach.[1]

Surplus reserves are the portion of total reserves which are neither required nor working by the definition given to each item. Usually, they are not more than 10 percent of the total. A variation in the surplus reserves indicates a difference in the policy of the bank in terms of being more or less liquid.

- An increase in surplus reserves often corresponds to a decrease in activities.
- A decrease in the surplus reserves indicates an increase in the bank's activities.

All this is relevant to strategic planning because the many distractions of the market place see to it that bankers are no more that sharp in the daily management of the institution's funds. Every bank typically experiences a continuous inflow and outflow of money. In normal times the reserves a bank keeps are sufficient to take care of a momentary rush in withdrawals, therefore avoiding illiquidity.

Usually, the models which we build to help in planning the bank's activities are not made for panics. But it would be a good investment to develop a family of models under different hypotheses. This will help to improve total assets optimization at different levels of risk.

Mathematical models and experimentation can also be instrumental in connection with derivative financial instruments, with which many commercial banks are engaged. Experimentation will help promote orderly hedging which abides by pre-established rules.[2] Models on exposure can assist bank management in controlling geared speculation which ends in disastrous results.

Analytical approaches help in clarifying management's thinking even if, in theory, the hedging concept is simple. If a savings and loans or building society wants to protect itself (at a certain cost) for mortgage loans given at low interest rate against interest rate increases, then a forward rate agreement (FRA) may help. But:

- it has to be limited to the level of loans exposure;
- it must be fairly simple, not complex and incomprehensible; and
- management must appreciate that it exchanges market risk with credit risk.

Hedging is the wrong term for such transactions because sometimes a bank doing derivatives trades for its clients takes on a lot of exposure, including legal risk. (See also the cases of Gibsons Greetings and Procter and Gamble against Bankers Trust.) Because some risks are not always appreciated, given that few retail banks and their clients have the derivatives skills they require, exposure can easily get out of hand.

Banks typically enter into these deals because they look for *non-interest* income, therefore for business that generates fees rather than interest. Unhappily for them, the risks which they take with derivatives can wipe out such income and leave a loss. This leads to another argument in strategic planning. Is the bank's role being biased by lust and greed? Are retail and other banks abandoning prudent policies by navigating in uncharted territory? Are they ending by assuming huge risks which they can ill afford?

The following could be stated in conclusion. Over the past years deregulation and innovation have helped banks to do much more than just make loans and hold them on their balance sheets to maturity. Off-balance sheet business can be seen as a new aspect of the banks' share of intermediation; some bankers think of it as a reincarnation of loans.

Because in trying to match problems and opportunities in order to survive, retail banks find themselves in an unfamiliar territory, they must be well aware that sometimes hedging activities tend to run out of control. Therefore the management of retail banks will be well advised to observe to the letter the directives included in the Market Risk Amendment by the Basle Committee and the July 1996 recommendations by the Accounting Standards Board.

7 WHAT IS REALLY MEANT BY A NON-BANK BANK?

Non-banks are of many sorts, and their activities have to do with the circulation of money and with economic forces. Typically, they are not regulated by the reserve institution but thrust upon themselves characteristic functions of intermediation which end in money flows, between borrowers and lenders – as well as different types of investment opportunities.

Non-banks are insurance companies which are giving loans; department stores using credit cards; treasury departments of auto manufacturers and other industries engaging in derivatives; mutual funds with a huge impact on the securities market; pension funds which are becoming the leading institutional investors; and hedge funds going after a fast buck.[3]

What is the difference between a bank and a non-bank bank? If we roughly define a bank as an institution that makes commercial loans to businesses and offers checking accounts and other demand deposits instruments, then theoretically brokers and department stores would not qualify as a bank. But in recent years, many non-bank companies have established quasi-banks that either make commercial loans or take deposits, but not both. General Motors, AT&T, Marks and Spencer, and a golden horde of others issue credit cards which are a sort of consumer loans.

The assumption that, because of non-banks, commercial banks are in decline underpins several aspects of recent financial and economic policy in Group of Ten countries. Banks are being given wider business powers on the grounds that they cannot compete with less regulated entities in the securities, insurance and other industries – including investment funds.

- Bank mergers have been tacitly encouraged as a means of strengthening the industry.
- Banks are even demanding that they should be helped by being paid interest on the reserves they are required to hold with the central bank.

Statistics do not support the thesis that retail banks are generally in decline. They do show, however, that there is a reallocation of financial resources and non-banks are gaining a significant part of the business pie. For instance, from 1960 to 1995, and most particularly since the late 1980s, the share of the market of savings and loans in the US has dropped to practically half of what it used to be.

The situation is by no means hopeless but it is serious. Therefore any strategic plan made by commercial banks should fully account for non-banks and their effect on the market. Many issues concerning competition are very critical to the future of banking as non-banks

- are *not regulated*, hence they have many more degrees of freedom than those of a retail bank;
- *capitalize on other lines of business*, on which they piggy-back their banking activities; and
- can develop *national and international networks*, as easily as banks – or maybe even more easily.

Through their outlets and their networks, non-bank banks can sell any product in their inventory, at any time, anywhere in the market to which they appeal. And they are not limited in their operations through central bank supervision. For instance, in the US, federal law technically forbids banks to branch across state lines.

Many rules which inhibit the expansion of banks have not stopped the inter-state spread of financial institutions that function very much as banks do. Non-banks have been able to circumvent the law because they do not fit the legal definition of a bank: an institution that takes deposits that can be withdrawn on demand and which makes commercial loans.

- Insurance companies, brokers, mail order houses, big retail organizations, card companies and even industrial corporations become a non-bank bank by taking advantage of technology.
- At the same time, while companies which entered the banking field have taken away customers from the traditional banking business, they have also expanded the financial market.

Collaborations between big retailers, mail order companies and non-bank card organizations have been instrumental in promoting both easier credit and the non-bank industry. Many analysts think that this is only the start of what is going to happen as new market opportunities develop.

- Institutional investors, and most particularly mutual funds and pension funds, are becoming the dominant non-bank banks.
- They operate cross-border, which permits them to optimize deals which they do as well as the contents of their portfolio.

What institutional investors need is to position themselves in a way similar to that of large brokerage firms. The brokers' advantage of branch offices can be replaced by networks, the Internet, party-to-party deals and an over-the-counter discount market in which both themselves and the banks are active.

The lesson to retain from these references in terms of increased competition is that the forces of deregulation, globalization and technology are at the heart of a tougher new marketplace facing banks. This involves

- strategic directions and market drives which lead to new departures;
- the enrichment of markets with innovative financial instruments; and
- a dynamic service policy, including rapid product innovation and able marketing.

As we have seen throughout this chapter, high technology is used as a competitive weapon by both banks and non-bank companies who know how best to employ their networks, computers and software. Technology is also the means for swamping the costs of doing business and serves the need for better ways to control risk. To appreciate the growing importance of non-bank banks and the challenge they present to the banking industry, section 8 presents some selected examples.

8 GENERAL ELECTRIC CAPITAL, GENERAL MOTORS AND SEARS ROEBUCK

General Electric Capital Corp. (GECC) is its parent company's largest profit center, accounting for more than a quarter of GE income and, according to some estimates, for half its profits. With about $100 billion in assets under management, GECC is one of America's largest non-bank banks. Other king-size non-banks are diversified financial subsidiaries of Ford and General Motors.

General Electric is generally known as a leader in electrical engineering but, in reality, year in and year out, a large part of its profits comes from financial products. Only a half-dozen holding companies in the United States have more assets than GECC, which is the country's largest leasing firm.

A key component of GECC's success is its top credit rating. Standard & Poor gives the non-bank an AAA grade on its credit quality, and its commercial paper gets a top A1-P1 designation from Moody's, the other major credit rating agency. That pristine rating provides GECC with the abillity to borrow in the short-term money markets at rates that are only a little above what the Treasury pays.

A major reason for GECC's top credit ranking comes from the fact that General Electric itself is a AAA company. The credit agencies assume that, if there was a slip-up at the finance unit, GE would come to its assistance and help it maintain its capital standards. Another reason is that GECC seems to have a lot more liquidity and capital than most banks do, and this is not surprising since many non-banks have stronger reserves than the banks themselves.

No US bank today is left with an AAA rating. GECC lends to many of America's major corporations and has a $12 billion commercial real estate portfolio. It also insures residential mortgages as well as municipal bonds; and it supplies the credit behind millions of retail charge cards from coast to coast. General Electric Capital was one of the first companies to participate in LBO financing in the early part of the 1980s, when some of the most lucrative deals were being crafted. But it seems always to have done its homework and it did not get burned in the process. At present, GECC engages in just about every financial pursuit except ordinary banking: the law prohibits industrial corporations like GE from owning commercial banks.

Unlike a bank, GE Capital does not finance its activities with deposits. Instead, it borrows in the commercial paper market and has some $35 billion in short-term corporate IOUs outstanding, or about 5 percent of all US commercial paper.

If it were a bank, General Motors Acceptance Corporation (GMAC) would be America's fifth biggest – larger than Morgan Guaranty Trust Company. A dozen years ago, in May 1985, GMAC bought the Colonial Group, a mortgage bank. Included in this purchase were *seven* banking and financial servicing companies with a $7. 4 billion mortgage portfolio. GMAC also bought the right to service Northwest Corp.'s $11 billion worth of mortgages. The goal is:

* one-stop financial shopping, and
* complete product offering with credit and debit cards.

Given these examples, a strategic question should be asked: Is *our* bank ready to compete with the GMAC giant, with a high technology GECC, with AT&T and its very successful card offering? These are very practical questions. In banking the value chain is changing because of new market entrants, yet, as is to be expected, not all new entrants into the financial market are that successful.

Among retailers who entered the non-bank business, a success story is that of Marks and Spencer in Britain; also of Rich/Richways in the south-eastern United States. Had this book been written in 1990, it would have been proper to add to the list Sears Roebuck, the American giant department store chain. But today there is a different story.

Sears expanded as a non-bank through several avenues. It bought a broker and an insurance company. Then it launched a credit card. Being a retailer, Sears had many assets on which to capitalize as a non-bank.

* It masters a network of 3,250 stores.
* The Sears Roebuck Acceptance Corporation represents $10 billion.
* The parent company's capital is at the $50 billion level.

When the company *Discover* card was launched, its millions of holders viewed the retailer as a powerful base. Sears' plans were to market brokerage and money market services, while its clients could use Discover to

* get cash from more than 5,000 automated teller machines,
* draw on a savings account paying a money-market rate of interest, and to
* open and manage tax-exempt savings accounts.

Discover also managed to get accepted by the US Customs Service for duty payments, but somewhere the strategic plan of the parent firm went wrong. Too much attention to non-banking activities distracted management from the company's main line: retailing. Other retailers leapfrogged Sears. While Sears tried to function as a non-bank, Sam Walton made Wal-Mart the largest retailing empire in North America.

After several setbacks and loss of status in retailing, Sears decided to retrench. It spun off Dean Witter (the brokerage which it controlled) and along with it went Discover, the credit card operation. Some years down the line, Dean Witter merged with Morgan Stanley. Sears also sold a big chunk of Allstate, its premier insurance company. The non-bank bank experiment was not that successful after all.

9   STRATEGIC ASPECTS OF THE COMPETITION BETWEEN BANKS AND NON-BANKS

The examples we have seen in this chapter help in documenting that, whether their field of operations is commercial or investment banking, established financial institutions face increasing competition from other industries. This does not happen only in one country but, for every practical reason, in every corner of the globe where there is a deregulated market. Such competition has many faces:

- pressure in developing new financial products,
- decreasing time-to-market in order to remain a player,
- the need for improving front-desk and sales support, and
- the urgency of controlling risk and exposure.

Every one of these bullet prints is a strategic issue. It is also a high point of competition between banks and non-banks affecting the priorities of senior managers and of professionals, who need both better training and high-technology support to continue facing the requirements of their job.

Strategic planning is necessary to meet the outlined challenges. Intelligence-enriched software helps in dealing with some of the daily pressures by permitting the design and engineering of financial products that are innovative, appealing to the customer and brought to market faster. But the major ingredient, as we will see in greater detail in Chapter 5, the most crucial element is *cultural change*. To stay competitive, a bank must adapt quite rapidly to market changes.

Quick product definition and speed in the transition to sales have become extremely important aspects of a survival strategy. It is necessary that, when the financial analyst defines specifications, those in charge of trading are preparing the sales approach, while the rocket scientists develop the intelligent software with deliverables produced in record time, and the chief risk management officer looks into exposure.

- This is why, in a technology-oriented sense, all team members should have easily accessible distributed information services, visualize in real time the answer to ad hoc queries, and speak the same technical language.
- The use of concurrent engineering quickly transforms design ideas into realistic models that are interactively evaluated for their features, market appeal, cost and risk.

Over the last 10 years, banking has become a deadline-oriented industry, with *no copyright* in financial products. This is equally true of banks and non-banks, but non-banks are better equipped for the new financial world because of other industrial experience.

In order to survive in a tough market, a financial institution has to come up with new solutions for problems that have surfaced during the last few months, weeks or days. This requires that all of the company's brainpower makes the best possible use of time available.

- Top management must be steadily working on improving its brainpower, enriching it with new skills.
- It must also be keen to integrate different cultures, without killing initiative or adversely affecting skills.

The case to which I am making reference is one of strategic acquisitions in banking. The purchase in 1992 of O'Connor Associates, a Chicago firm specializing in trading equity derivatives, gave the Swiss Bank Corporation (SBC) a chance to push into the Chicago and New York markets and into London in an untraditional way. It did so by importing O'Connor's expertise but also integrating the brokers from Chicago, accustomed to informality and blue jeans, with the bankers from Basle and Zurich with their formal business suits.

Rather than struggling to gain relationships with companies that already had established merchant bank advisory connections, SBC built a trading business based on derivatives. Then it used its edge to devise innovative one-off deals both for industrial companies and for institutional investors.

Other financial organizations followed a different strategy. After it realized that it simply did not have the sort of relationships Warburg and Schroders had in the London market, the management of a couple of other international banks decided to make core profits by trading, and mount ambushes on the better-established investment banks. This was achieved by means of corporate finance deals which increasingly involved off-balance sheet financing as a competitive weapon. Such strategy proved to be successful even if it hardly endears a bank or non-bank to a financial market whose business is raiding.

- Banks which chose this strategy realize that they have little to lose from provoking a conflict;
- their goal is not to be loved but to make up their own comfortable niche.

Non-banks act in a similar way. Some work through derivatives, but others exploit more vanilla icecream financial products – such as factoring and leasing – by capitalizing on better organization and a higher level of competitive advantages deriving from the market they are currently in.

The leading banks and non-banks have come to appreciate the prerequisites which characterize the evolution of a new financial product. They are starting with a strategic plan: address the availability, training or hiring of knowledgeable personnel; pass through the acquisition of the high technology; and develop the ability to manage project evolution in research and sales.

Other prerequisites for a major switch in fortunes relate to financial and administrative management, as well as the ability to continue financing the product brought to the market, save the case of inordinate risk. These issues go beyond the more classical perspective of establishing a client base and of handholding. They also call for paying significant attention to quality service, as we will see in Chapter 4.

Notes

1.   See D.N. Chorafas, *Chaos Theory in the Financial Markets* (Chicago: Probus, 1994).
2.   See D.N. Chorafas, *Financial Models and Simulation* (London: Macmillan, 1995).
3.   See D.N. Chorafas, *Derivative Financial Instruments. Strategies for Managing Risk and Return in Banking* (London and Dublin: Lafferty, 1995).

4 Strategic Planning and the Quality of Services in Retail Banking

1 INTRODUCTION

Transforming a retail bank to operate efficiently in a knowledge society is an imaginative and demanding task. It is demanding because management must shed old-age values, adopt new approaches and establish worthwhile incentives. Among the major contrasts between old and new environments is the fact that *people*, not machines, are central to the productivity of financial services.

Quality is a very complex issue in the service industry because to a significant extent banking is dealing with intangibles. What constitutes a 'quality service' or 'zero defects' is not that easy to describe, as in the manufacturing industry, but it is not impossible either. Since the 1970s, Citibank has had a system with demerits based on customer complaints.

- Quality circles are a proactive way of involving staff in quality issues.
- Merits and demerits provide quantitative yardsticks for management to take action.
- Timely, accurate and focused information permits managers and employees to upgrade their awareness of customer wishes and needs.

Greater power comes to the managers and the professionals who possess up-to-the-minute information and can turn it into knowledge, with emphasis on results. But the transformation of a financial institution will not be done in a vacuum without precise goals – and that is where strategic planning comes in.

Lack of precise goals means deficient market strategies, leading to lack of direction. Quite frequently, management finds it difficult to choose a course of action which permits the attainment of the retail bank's market share and profitability objectives. Lewis Carroll expresses this notion in *Alice in Wonderland*.

"Would you tell me, please, which way I ought to go from here?" said Alice.
"That depends a good deal on where you want to get," said the cat.
"I don't care much where ...," said Alice.
"Then it doesn't matter which way you go," said the cat.

The first place a retail bank should want to get is where it can change its culture. The critical questions are: How can management transform a retail bank accustomed

77

to operate in a protected financial environment into one which can face fierce market forces and succeed? Who should be involved in this transformation? How will it affect the quality of banking services? And how much time has *our* bank to change its culture?

The goal which strategic planning should help *our* bank to attain is a position of strength. But what does 'strength' mean in a market increasingly dominated by online networks? In managing the relations with their customers, retail banks must now take account of competition from Internet Intuit and Microsoft. This competition from independent networks comes over and above the competition from non-banks, of which we spoke in Chapter 3. Networks are becoming another major non-bank bank: one which significantly alters many aspects of *quality of service*.

Networks also impact on organization and structure because they affect both current and projected business aims. Says Hans-Ulrich Doerig, a former Crédit Suisse board member and deputy chairman of Crédit Suisse First Boston (CSFB): 'We are trying to come up with a structure that will hold for the next 10, 15 or 20 years.' A dynamic commercial bank needs to reinvent itself.

2   THE CLOSE RELATION WHICH EXISTS BETWEEN STRATEGY AND PLANNING

Chapters 2 and 3 have given plenty of practical examples showing that strategy and planning are not two separate and independent processes. Strategy is necessary to set priorities and give a sense of direction: from *here* to *there* – the way Lewis Carroll suggests. Planning establishes the detailed road map which we use to get there.

'It is not clear what relevance [a discussion on planning] has to this chapter [on quality],' said a reviewer. 'One might consider it self-evident.' Nothing is less self-evident in business – and the emphasis on planning finds its rationale in the fact that the whole concept of quality in banking has to be included from the very beginning.

- Management's attention to quality will be half-baked if no attention is paid to it at the planning stage.

Only the unable who has been asked by the unwilling to do the unnecessary would leave the quality of banking services out of the picture because 'he has other, more important things to do'.

- Whether we talk of engineering products or of financial services, quality has to be embedded into them, starting at the drafting board.

A planning frame of reference can be established for the short, medium or long term. All three timeframes should be an integral part of the strategic picture which addresses products, markets and back office processes. As far as retail sales operations are concerned, planning should be much more than just a corporate activity directed at marketing: plans must be formulated at every level of the organization outlined in Figure 4.1. Notice that forecasting is a prerequisite to planning and it works within a highly unstructured information environment – where the only constant is change.

Contrary to organizational folklore which considers forecasting an activity to foretell future events, the true sense of prognostication in banking is to help management in evaluating future results of present decisions. What may happen if we increase our fees? How might our customers react? Will our competitors follow? Or will our bank be singled out for higher fees?

Able answers to these questions depend not only on knowing the market but also on knowing ourselves. 'If you know yourself and know your enemies, you don't need to be afraid of the outcome of 100 battles,' said Sun Tzu, the great Chinese statesman and military leader. One of the crucial questions regarding

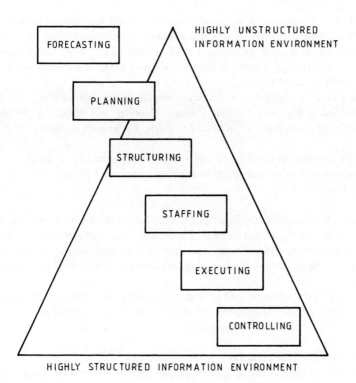

Figure 4.1 The six fundamental functions of management and the information environment to which they belong

strategic planning premises is: 'Do we know where the value in our bank's services is today'; specifically, with which customers and in which channels?

Other forecasting and planning questions concern the strategy our bank decides to follow in terms of products and markets. While these queries are strategic, they should not take a long time to answer. Furthermore, the responses should be focused.

- What may be the aftermath of restructuring our services? What may be the time period for its execution?
- What is the value added being targeted? What is the probability of its being attained?
- How high is the risk our bank can tolerate? For how long?

These are top management queries engaging the responsibility of the bank's chief executive officer (CEO). This statement is true of all basic functions of management presented in Figure 4.1: forecasting, planning, structuring, staffing, executing and controlling.

How many commercial banks are organized along this management-intense line, with what it implies in strategic planning prerequisites? Starting with the major banks, as recently as 1980 over half of them had no formal strategic planning process, though in some of the money center banks strategy became a core function in the late 1970s.

The picture is totally different today. Competition has seen to it that it is difficult to find a big bank without strategic planning, and about 50 percent of medium-size banks have put in place a strategic planning department.

- This, however, is not the case with small banks, particularly in retail.
- For many of them strategic planning is still uncharted territory, and few venture to explore it.

This, too, may be changing. Participants in my London seminars on banking strategy give me the signal that strategic planning is more important to them than it used to be because today the basic product of banks and banking is not money: it is, increasingly, more sophisticated financial products, with emphasis on quality of service.

Smaller banks who now start in strategic planning should learn from the experience of bigger ones. During the last 10 years, the strategy formulated by top-tier banks has had three main components:

- building upon the company's profitable markets (see Chapter 6);
- developing direct banking and/or a private banking business to increase profits from fees (see, respectively, Chapter 8 and 9); and
- controlling costs more tightly all the way to the customer mirror (see Chapter 7).

The approach followed by many retail banks when they establish strategic planning premises is to rethink and possibly revamp decisions connected to profitability versus growth. In banking strategy today the keywords are:

Retain, expand and acquire

while they used to be:

Acquire, acquire and acquire.

Acquiring new clients has become very expensive as the market gets saturated by financial service providers. Therefore many retail banks have come to realize that they better exploit the potential present in their current customer base through cross-selling and the addition of ancillary products.

Something similar can be stated about exploiting the potential of their own personnel, which is often done in an ineffective manner. The same is true of the bank's other assets. A couple of years ago, a study focused on net banking income covering the years 1991 to 1994. A snapshot of the results, given in Figure 4.2,

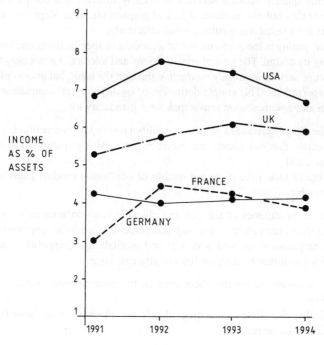

Figure 4.2 The significant difference in net banking income as a percentage of productive assets

presents some interesting statistics. Net banking income as a percentage of productive assets is highest among American banks because the financial industry in the US was the first to engage in strategic planning – followed by British banks. Again followed by banks in the UK, US banks were the first to stress income as a percentage of productive assets. We talk more about this subject in section 3.

3   PAYING ATTENTION TO THE QUALITY OF BANKING SERVICES THROUGH QUALITY CIRCLES

The quality of banking services is both an important and a practical subject, and for good reason. There is sometimes a major gap between what the bank seeks to accomplish and the means it selects to attain its ends. Fundamental issues are the bridges that relate a bank's services philosophy to the way this is executed, linking

- policies to particular commercial programs,
- programs to specific banking practices, and
- practices to the services provided to the client base.

Introducing quality banking services is a fairly difficult and complex process. Because of this, but also because of lack of preparation, some 80 percent of banks who start fail to establish quality control effectively.

Service quality is the conformance of a product to specifications and tolerances set during its design. The goal of specifications and tolerances is not only to make a product or service *uniformly producible* through the bank, but also to meet customer expectations. This simple definition of quality presents considerable challenges in an implementation sense, making it mandatory to:

- be ahead and stay ahead of service quality provided by competition;
- appreciate that our clients are becoming increasingly quality-conscious and choosy, and
- be able to match the projected quality of our bank's product plans with our deliverables.

The change in attitudes of the banking clientele is compelling us to pay more attention than ever before to the way the perceived quality of our products and services impacts on our bank's growth and profitability. Competition and client demand see to it that product quality is a strategic issue.

- The more demanding the client base is, the more attention we must pay to quality.
- Typically, the more demanding clients are those who are also the more profitable to the bank.

Not everybody agrees with this statement. Some bankers say that, to the contrary, the more demanding clients are the *least* profitable to the banks. That is wrong.

With the exception of those clients who are taken to the cleaners by the bank, the way to bet is that the least demanding clients are the low net worth individuals and the companies about to go bankrupt.

- Clients should *not* be taken for a ride, not only for ethical reasons but also because it does not make sense.
- The high net worth individuals and the corporate treasurers know very well what they want, as well as how to play one bank against another for conditions.

Treasurers, institutional investors and high net worth individuals are *very demanding*, but the business they bring carries with it trading profits and fees for investment advice and custody. Let us face it: AAA and AA companies are very demanding and any bank had better pay attention to them so as not to be left with clients nobody else wants.

The awareness of this fact calls for significant organizational effort, which should be appreciated throughout the organizational layers of the bank – top to bottom – as shown in Figure 4.3. Service quality cannot be guaranteed only through top management decree; nor only by initiatives taken at first-line supervision. The overall corporate objective should focus on service quality and the same is true of all intermediate layers in the bank's organization, all the way to the lower layer of supervision. Specifications and tolerances regarding the quality of services our bank delivers should be carefully studied because they underpin the

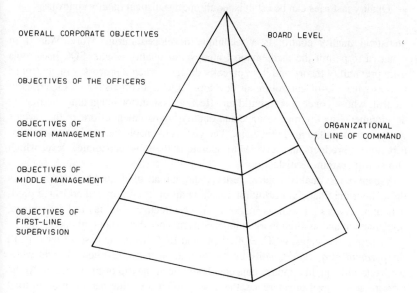

Figure 4.3   Service quality should be addressed at all levels of the organization

concept of quality assurance. In practice, four basic issues converge towards quality in financial services:

1. Bank-wide Quality Control (BQC),
2. Total Quality Control (TQC),
3. Statistical Quality Control (SQC), and
4. Quality Control Circles (QCC).

Quality control circles, or simply *quality circles*, are typically small group activities. They consist of employees from the same work area using problem-solving techniques to address workshop problems and do something about them. We will talk much more about quality circles in section 6.

In a meeting in Tokyo, the Fuji Bank gave a good example on the application of quality circles in the financial industry. The executives I was talking to mentioned a new product their bank had launched in the market. Then they said this product sold well in some branches but poorly in others. An investigation by marketing did not reveal the cause of the problem. Therefore the Fuji Bank instituted quality circles in which branch employees and first-line supervisors participated. The problem, it was found, had to do with lack of understanding of the product by those expected to sell it – and it was quickly remedied.

*   Quality circles can be assisted through quality histories.
*   Quality histories can be established through statistical quality control.

Statistical quality control is a technique developed during World War II in America to permit the mathematical analysis of quality results. SQC uses tools from probability theory and it graphically displays when a process is in control as well as when out-of-control trends develop. [1]SQC is a cornerstone of total quality control, whose concept is to build an effective system for integrating the quality development, quality maintenance and quality improvement efforts of the various groups and departments in the bank. The goal is to enable the production and distribution of products and services to operate at the most economical level which allows full customer satisfaction.

A bank-wide quality control reflects the spread of a quality consciousness throughout the financial institution, reaching all of its current and projected products and services as well as markets. To be effective, this has to be designed, implemented and assured in a homogeneous manner throughout all operations.

These four concepts, QCC, SQC, TQC and BQC, form the basis of what I call *the pyramid of quality*. Quality circles operate at the infrastructural level while the bank-wide quality control concept should be at the top of the pyramid. At the infrastructural level of reference, the goal is to ensure wide participation in total quality control activities by managers, professionals and clerks. This facilitates

the production of financial goods and services of high quality in the most economical manner – as well as guaranteeing customer satisfaction with the services being
rendered, since QCC, SQC and TQC provide the feedback for corrective action.

Time and again, in the meeting I held with senior bankers in the course of this
research, it was underlined that, as long as financial institutions rendered services
for which they did not charge, it was possible to take the liberty of being a little
lax, here and there, in terms of service quality.

- But today fees from services are a major income earner for a bank, and will be
  even more so in the future.
- When we charge for our services, we must be very prudent about the quality
  which we deliver.

As practical experience helps document, it is not enough to talk of service quality:
it has to be implemented and closely supervised. One lesson the Japanese banks
mentioned during our meetings is that they cannot simply transfer their quality
management knowhow wholesale to the branches. Quality transfer requires a
well-organized, concerted effort which is fully backed by top management.

4 NEW RETAIL PRODUCTS, ADDED VALUE AND QUALITY CHARACTERISTICS

Hard to define, impossible to legislate, *quality* starts as an attitude of mind. It is
also the manifestation of a *valid culture* in the financial industry. Therefore product quality should have a prominent position in the strategic plan. Some people
say that automation blurs the focus on quality. This is not true – provided that we
use knowledge-enriched software rather than brute force.

Competitive forces and the advancement of technology have pushed banking
management toward paying greater attention to the services offered to the client
base. In a way similar to that which industry has known over the last three
decades, such services are altering the way most people think about

- institutionalized research and development (R&D) (see Chapter 12)
- assembly line production methods, developed to swamp costs, and
- online approaches to marketing and for product delivery to customers.

All first-rank banks have projects aiming to significantly enhance the profile of
their retail operations. At the Union Bank of Switzerland, for example, the 1994
Liberty package of retail services showed the commitment to a new, broader customer relationship with increased transparency:

- The focus of the new concept has not been a single product offered by the
  bank, but a comprehensive range of services.

- These were designed to allow each customer to shape his or her banking relationship individually – as well as to enhance customer ties.

UBS saw to it that Liberty marked the first time a package of banking services has been protected by a trademark. Its increased transparency, provided through its enhanced information content, opened the way for customers to obtain round-the-clock account information by accessing the bank's computers via the telephone.

To develop and promote this direct banking product line (see also the discussion on direct banking in Chapter 8), UBS undertook an intensive program of customer surveys which provided a better knowledge of customers' needs. It also enabled the elimination of some weaknesses that might have entered product design. For instance, attention was paid not only to service quality but also to ways and means to obtain significant cost savings.

Another retail banking product successfully promoted by UBS has been Fiscaplan-Plus. This provides a variety of insurance options for death and disability and a new pension scheme based on a single premium, completing the bank's former range of private pension plans. Fiscaplan-Plus marked the bank's entry into the individual life insurance market with an extension of its retail product spectrum.

A third example of value-added banking services which required significant attention to be paid to service quality has been the bank's credit card business. Within four years, 1991 to 1994, with a market share of around one-fifth of all Eurocard credit cards currently issued in Switzerland, UBS became the leader in this field, as shown in Figure 4.4. But gaining leadership required a significant effort in terms of service quality and value-added efforts.

To gain leadership in retail products and to improve the saleability of their services, banks must have a finely tuned strategic plan. They must also gain and hold technological leadership. Chapter 2 has underlined the importance of technological support in shaping banking strategy.

One of the fundamental reasons behind the wave of interest in supporting intelligent networks, deductive databases and knowledge-enriched software is the expected improvement in banking services. As the preceding sections demonstrated, quality has become today the terrain where *competitive advantages* most visibly demonstrate themselves with a dual objective: quality must be higher and cost must be lower.

A *service orientation* sees to it that, at the bottom line, computers are just another commodity like oil, potatoes or cabbages. It requires money but no extraordinary skill to buy the machines, though it is somewhat more difficult to develop their software. The challenge is

- to tune computer-based services to the market, and
- to make technology an income earner for the bank.

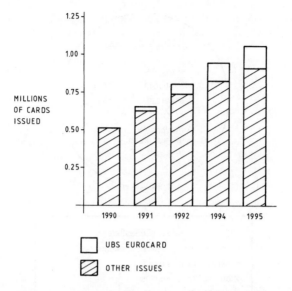

Figure 4.4   UBS share in Swiss Eurocards/Mastercards

Some financial institutions are better able to exploit technological opportunities. In the late 1980s, American Express was among the first to deploy a large scale expert system, the Authorizer's Assistant, which is still in production. Since then, it has deployed and experimented with genetic algorithms, neural networks, speech recognition, scientific visualization and virtual reality.

This new generation of tools has been applied to diverse domains such as automating service bureaus, matching the efforts of sales representatives to customers drives and detecting fraud. The implementation which has taken place has shown a good return on investment, as well as a favorable impact on the ability of American Express to face market challenges by improving the quality which it delivers.

Not only should automated processes be characterized by emphasis on quality control, but they should also be designed with embedded quality control tools. When this is done, software helps to improve the quality of financial products and to enhance the service rendered to the customers. The prerequisite is that we know how to go after high quality goals.

The point made in Figure 4.5 is that computers and communications (C+C) technology is subservient to the strategic plan. Markets, products, services and client handling are all part of the strategic plan – and they condition the C+C infrastructure. But, as will be appreciated, higher service quality is an integral and indivisible part of this infrastructure.

Figure 4.5   A bank's strategic plan can be so much more successful when supported through advanced computers and communication (C&C) technology

In conclusion, quality control should be a strategic objective for every financial institution which cares about its survival, and it should concern all of the services the retail bank provides to its customers. In the long term, we stay competitive and remain in business by

- taking the customer seriously, giving him what he needs, and doing so *now*, not at some future date; and
- assuring the best there is in terms of service – a process which is ongoing, not one-tantum.

The quality of the financial product comes before the money we ask for in fees, but quality is maintained only if *everyone* believes in it. Quality comes before money, because short-term profits made at the expense of quality lead to short-term lives – of products, of services and sometimes of banks.

5   ORGANIZATIONAL PRACTICES FOR CLOSING THE QUALITY GAP IN BANKING SERVICES

Japanese financial institutions and manufacturing companies associate the policy of establishing as well as maintaining high quality in products and services to strategic planning. They look at strategic planning as a process for identifying and implementing solutions to existing and anticipated organizational challenges, quality assurance being at the top of their list.

While different organizations have different approaches to strategic planning, they all try to clarify and simplify objectives, means and tools, in order to arrive at the best practices. At the top level, objectives can be classified into three generic issues:

1. *Goals*: Bottom-line goal(s), product goal(s), market goal(s); other goal(s).
2. *Options*: the so-called 'Six Ms': manpower, markets, money, machines, materials, methods.
3. *Action plans*, which at Japanese banks are typically enacted and coordinated by means of quality circles.

At each of these levels of reference, clear-eyed management is taking steps to integrate quality control activities into their strategic plans and their regular organizational practice. This they see as fundamental in closing the *quality gap*. They prefer an embedded quality procedure to the alternative of making quality control an offline activity – for instance, sole responsibility of a technical staff.

As senior executives of Japanese city banks were to comment during my research, not only is it necessary to incorporate *quality thinking* into basic organizational practices – starting with strategic planning – but there is also need to provide

- measurement systems (see SQC and TQC, p. 84),
- performance evaluation criteria and
- corrective action procedures.

Such references are valid in terms of reaching both policy objectives and technical goals. Besides that, Japanese financial institutions tend to balance the technical and operational issues with people-building goals, because organizations are made of people. People-building goals mean those personnel policies that improve the health, education and skills of employees, from clerks to professionals and senior managers, leading to an increase in their productive capacity. Several banking executives stated that, if institutional policies are rich in people-building goals, broader organizational support for corporate economic goals is obtained.

But, at the same time, Japanese bankers underlined that it often takes about 10 to 15 years to build the pyramid of quality. During the same meetings, it was also

underlined that quality circles can help in strategic planning, precisely because
the latter involves a further-out timeframe than operational business plans.

- It is not easy to make long-term business forecasts, but
- the problem is eased as a quality circles practice coinvolves people of different skills, interests and orientations.

An important reference made in the course of this meeting was that some of
the results reached through quality circles have been instrumental in long-term
planning. This is particularly true in regard to multinational operations which by
necessity involve different cultures.

It was also stated during the same banking meeting that parent firms allowing
their overseas subsidiaries temporal flexibility in matching company goals with
local realities are more likely to demonstrate visible progress in business performance. Such progress correlates to quality practices and it is enhanced by means
of quality circles.

Once an overseas Japanese banking subsidiary elaborates on its business plan,
it typically incorporates the language of quality throughout its strategic goals.
This places quality control activities within the mainstream of business perspectives and organizational practices.

Such a statement is just as true in manufacturing as it is in banking. An example was taken of the Matsushita Electric plant in Taiwan, which is 50 percent less
automated than its parent company's plants in Japan. However, through employee
involvement schemes (hence, quality circles), the quality gap with the parent
company's plants was closed.

The lesson is that, as business firms move towards automated production, giving technology the edge, quality circles facilitate employee acceptance of organizational and technical change. Local management involvement in identifying
options through quality circles adds to both strategic plans and daily business
practices, thus improving overall performance.

The process of coinvolvement of all levels of management and of the clerks in
quality concepts and procedures pays dividends because quality means consistency around a central value. This is characterized by the specifications of the
financial product, of which we have often spoken.

- Unwanted variety may occur if there is no established and normalized method
for controlling the outgoing product quality.
- Low quality is the rule when the services which we offer are not kept within
tolerances – provided such tolerances have been established in the first place.

The investment advice we give to our customers, the financial transactions which
we make and the customer-oriented applications we develop are fertile areas for

the implementation of quality control measures. However, fair judgment not only demands objectivity and impartiality but also a *merit* system. Merit rating is

- a tool for measuring the performance of bankers at the front desk and the back office, and
- a means of appraising the relative qualities of their personality with respect to the jobs they fulfill.

Emphasis on merit rating for people and products grows out of an attempt on the part of bankers to seek means of control over the quality of their financial services. The job is feasible, provided we *really* want to do it, we know how to go about it and we have the skill to build a quality system – not just some scattered applications.

6   USING QUALITY CIRCLES TO EASE THE PROBLEMS PRESENTED BY DOWNSIZING

By linking product and service quality options to the goals of our bank, as well as by involving managers, professionals and clerks in decision-making processes addressing products and services, a retail bank can benefit in a double sense.

- It positions itself in a way which permits the screening and evaluation of the business options which exist.
- It can see to it that its personnel is compelled to become involved in quality-enhancing activities.

This is the best way to establish quality as a norm, and a very efficient one, for that matter. In Japanese financial institutions, for example, managers and supervisors suggest action plans for each option relevant to the daily work of their people. This involves outlining organizational resources and includes steps taken in their employment along four axes of reference: time, funds, staff and space. Each of these four axes of reference is characterized by a quality assurance program, with procedures integrating into one global view of product quality. In Tokyo, the Dai-Ichi Bank described the quality assurance phase of its product cycle in the way presented in Figure 4.6. This constitutes a valid reference for the quality assurance program of every commercial bank.

I have used this approach to quality assurance with a European bank in connection with *downsizing*, and found it to be instrumental in terms of results obtained. The reader may ask what quality circles and downsizing have in common. Let me pre-empt this query.

- Downsizing is a painful experience to any company, because it involves slimming down the labor force.

- Most banks are overstaffed, and therefore they can appreciate the sense of this reference.

But how is downsizing going to be done? I would like to start with the premise that most people do not equate being made redundant with quality. Yet automation or no automation, the quality of banking services greatly depends on people. Redimensioning might be counterproductive if it does not target quality. By contrast, the synergy of these two issues can give good results.

Quite often management hires outside consultants with the mission to cut down the head count. Often the result of this practice is butchery, sometimes cutting muscle rather than fat. Quality circles are a far better alternative because they focus on the need to

- reduce costs,
- increase productivity, and
- redimension the bank.

There are many human aspects in redimensioning which can best be studied internally through quality circles. This is particularly true as, quite often, downsizing

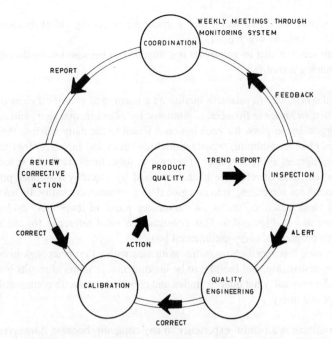

Figure 4.6   A comprehensive view of a quality assurance cycle

is done because banks are facing relentless investor pressure to rethink their services, downsize their branches and cut down their personnel. High-handed approaches lead to significant personnel problems.

- Redimensioning is the means for management to comply by ensuring that its shareholders receive the maximum value for assets that no longer fit longer-term plans.
- That concept includes branches and channels not meeting expectations, as well as services which do not fit within the latest strategic plan.

On the technical side, whether we talk of banking or of the manufacturing industry, downsizing is done to focus on core strengths. That is what Tenneco has done in spinning off its Case Corporation construction equipment unit; Bally Entertainment by transferring to shareholders its health-and-fitness business; and W.R. Grace by divesting its kidney dialysis division, National Medical Care, to shareholders.

Slimming down is also a way of capitalizing on tax advantages. In the typical spin-off, at least 80 percent of the shares of the subsidiary are distributed to holders. When structured this way, the spin-off is tax-free for both the investors and the company. The financial industry, too, can spin off units bought at different times but which it no longer makes sense to keep around because the nature of the business has changed.

In banking a more common form of downsizing is the reduction in branches, which are simply closed. This is a process which should be done with great care, and where quality circles may offer advantages. In July 1996, Crédit Suisse announced a massive worldwide restructuring, with plans to close down a number of branches of its own and its subsidiaries lopping off 3,500 staff from its workforce in Switzerland. This downsizing is more complex than others because it involves not one bank but four banks. (See also the case study on Wells Fargo and First Interstate in Chapter 5.) These are:

- Crédit Suisse itself,
- Volksbanken, which was bought by Crédit Suisse some years earlier
- Bank Leu, a commercial bank in Zurich, and
- Neu Argau Bank, a smaller retail bank.

Technically, the concept of the restructuring was in line with what most commercial banks currently do or aim to do. It has been projected as a strategic move for the future. The merger would result in two new entities:

- *Crédit Suisse*, a bank targeting high net worth individuals, institutional investors, corporations and investment banking;
- *CS Volksbanken*, a low cost operation directed towards retail banking in Switzerland.

The idea was sound, but the strategic plan on how it should be implemented in the most effective manner does not seem to have been worked out in detail. Therefore even the official announcement of the reorganization led to lots of problems. At one point, it was feared that even Moody's might downgrade Crédit Suisse.

A month after these plans were made public, the downsizing entered troubled waters. Management seems to have failed in mobilizing employees and in developing alternative lines of action. This is the people's side of downsizing, which is much more difficult than the technical part.

While not directly related to downsizing one of the approaches used by Japanese banks to mobilize managers, professionals and other employees can provide some valuable insights. The reference is in connection with *service quality*, emphasizing zero defect programs. City banks in Tokyo have been able to close the quality and productivity gap through small group activities which focus on *zero defects*. Through quality circles, managers, professionals and employees can understand in practical language how their work fits into the bigger organizational picture which quite often is invisible to them. Most importantly, managers use quality circles in discussions aimed at fine-tuning the bank's goals and making almost real-time adjustments in the choice of options.

Japanese financial institutions and industrial firms look at quality and performance as an iterative process rippling throughout the company to mobilize its human capital towards mutual goals. Special attention is paid to a number of subjects such as the following:

- discarding unnecessary items (Seiri),
- arranging things in good order (Seiton),
- checking the condition and quality of a service (Seiso),
- disciplining oneself to keep the workplace orderly (Shitsuke).

An example of the way the Organization Department can benefit from quality circles procedures is by reducing the use of unnecessary space. Toshiba mentioned that (in one of its overseas subsidiaries) it was able to increase production volumes by 2.3 times using the same amount of space. This saved the cost of building factory floor space which would have been otherwise necessary in order to add production capacity.

Through quality circles, other companies managed to involve clerks and line workers in gathering production information to standardize processes and identify emerging quality control problems. Clerks and middle managers systematically collected data on yields, defects, outputs, setup and throughput times, as well as physical inventory levels by using quality circles problem-solving techniques and statistical quality control methods.

All this has an evident impact in terms of profitability – whether we talk of manufacturing or banking. The background provided by quality circles permits managers, professionals and clerks to receive feedback on their jobs and to have access to information in order to address quality problems more effectively.

7   COMBINING QUALITY CONSCIOUSNESS AMONG EMPLOYEES THROUGH RIGOROUS ACCOUNTING METHODS

One Japanese bank stated that quality circles activities plus the indispensable technology transfer contributed to a 300 percent improvement in productivity in its back office over a three-year period. Such evidence is overwhelming and it should be exploited to the fullest possible extent by all retail banks.

In other cases, the emphasis placed on the quality of banking services has provided the ground for the development of innovative policies. In some banks, the internal data collecting process has been narrowed down to focus on those measures needed to maintain and support quality characteristics. This permitted the development of products and services that meet the expectations of consumers in a more efficient manner.

A specific example, given during the meeting with one of the Japanese city banks, concerned a quality circle which identified crucial points in the production and distribution of its financial services. This flashed out issues which needed to be more closely monitored in order to assure quality of service.

Another city bank mentioned how quality circles helped in improving the internal reporting structure. Prior to this, the bank featured a uniform reporting scheme. Now, depending on the severity of the problem, the information in question is routed

- to the bank's president,
- to the senior vice president who is directly concerned, or
- down the line to the person who should take action.

In every case when a trouble spot is identified, reporting-by-exception should not only be in real time but also routed to the executive who is responsible for taking timely corrective action. This approach allows the voice of the customer to be reflected in the production and distribution of financial services, leading to a quality deployment function.

The Japanese banks are not alone in this effort of identifying and rapidly correcting trouble spots. Citibank in New York has for several years instituted a merits/demerits process which rewards or penalizes the appropriate section of currency exchange operations:

- rewards (merits) are given for the correct execution of customer orders;
- penalties (demerits) are applied for errors made in processing Forex orders.

Citibank's foreign exchange quality database is accessible online by senior management. Since the late 1970s, when this process started, a minicomputer has been dedicated to Merits/Demerits, linked to an accounting system to integrate the associated credits and debits.

Linkage to the accounting system is also one of the rules in the Japanese implementation of quality control of banking services. Evidently this process impacts on accounting practices. Two general dimensions relate to quality-centered activities. The first is a variant of the cost accounting method, to reflect outgoing quality. In its broadest sense, cost accounting is based on assigning direct labor, direct materials and overhead by production unit in order to determine the allocation of costs. The quality-oriented variant works on the assumption that there is no more expensive process than low quality; hence the allocation of accounting merits/demerits in terms of quality performance, in a way fairly similar to that used by Citibank.

The second is a cost management method, with emphasis on both cost reduction and quality assurance. Cost reduction results from improvements in product design as well as production and distribution technologies. Cost control is achieved by maintaining target prices, eliminating causes of budget variances. Low quality adds to costs and therefore it violates the principle of cost control. Hence it is correct to add quality-induced charges.

Figure 4.7 reflects this approach by introducing merits/demerits due to quality as a separate line from other costs. This concept can be carried all the way to the *customer mirror*, a subject which is covered in Chapter 7.

Both the above methods have been successfully used by tier-1 financial institutions to capture and reflect realized savings. For example, lower error and lower defect rates help in reducing lead times and in promoting flexible back office work as well as product delivery to the customer:

- Through knowledge engineering approaches, the Japanese are masters in producing personalized services, where quality plays an important role.
- They excel in implementing flexible programming and scheduling processes, and have effectively achieved just-in-time (JIT) delivery systems.

It is no less true that benefits such as increased productivity and control of labor cost would not come on their own. Strategic choices in internal banking operations must account for the fact that 60 percent to 75 percent of all non-interest costs are human costs, while 66 percent of all human costs are managerial and professional – subject to *mental productivity*.

The benefits outlined in the preceding paragraphs accrue to those banks which not only are proactive but also care for *computer literacy* among their employees – all the way from president to janitor. After the personal computer became the able assistant of senior management, Larry McGregor, chairman, Premier Banks, Illinois, was to say:

> I believe that, within the next five years, any bank officer who does not use a computer directly in his work will be functionally illiterate. We cannot afford to have functional illiterates as senior bank officials.

In my judgment, computer literacy today is the new minimum educational standard and it strongly correlates to what has been said about quality of banking

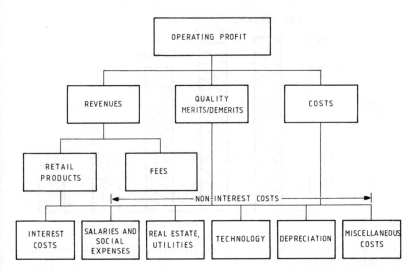

Figure 4.7 Main elements of revenues, costs, quality merits/demerits and profits

services. At the same time, intense and relentless quality control constitutes part of *the new ethics*.

Not only is cost accounting essential for financial reporting purposes, but it must also reflect quality management in order to provide the bank's managers with the necessary information to monitor the operations under their control. The ingenuity lies in blending the cost accounting dimension with quality goals – avoiding cost savings having adverse effects on quality control objectives.

This duality in emphasis placed on banking services can be achieved by integrating into the accounting system cost savings realized through improvements in quality performance, with metrics (*noun, singular*) such as the following:

- percentage of transactions produced with no errors, and no reworking;
- percentage of delivery commitments met;
- shorter product introduction times;
- cross-sales statistics at the branches; and
- cross-sales statistics over the network.

Failure rates in connection with the execution of customer orders and transactions is good metrics in terms of the quality of a financial institution. Figure 4.8 gives a snapshot of average failure rates for cross-border deals involving five of the best-known trading countries.

As for cross-sales, Japanese statistics show that through this approach white-collar productivity can increase by 20–120 percent, sales per person can be 10 to 50 times higher, and return on assets improves by between 30 and 130 percent.

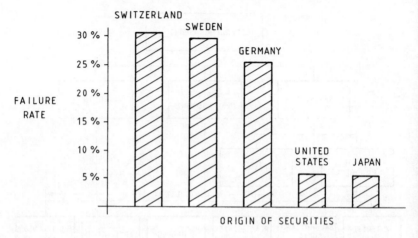

Figure 4.8 Average failure rate for cross-border deals resulting from lack of appropriate infrastructure

However, the adoption of quality as a crucial criterion requires a cultural change in the bank. When this is done, it leads to more effective performance and its timely evaluation, as shown in section 8.

8   THE VIRTUAL INFRASTRUCTURE, QUALITY MILESTONES AND PERFORMANCE EVALUATION

Operational controls used by retail banks subscribing to quality circles focus on decreasing errors and increasing the value of financial products, as well as tracking production and distribution volumes in an effective manner. At the same time, the accounting system draws on data that is

- disaggregate enough to be useful for transaction reasons, yet
- can be easily aggregated for financial reporting purposes.

This multidimensional approach to the exploitation of accounting databases[2] reflects concern, not only about the marketability of financial products and services, but also regarding quality and costs. It also leads to imaginative design specifications and exploitation market niches. The able use of opportunities presented by niches is a good means to produce value-added goods which help the bank to survive and prosper. Yet, as suggested on a number of occasions during my research, this solution seems counter intuitive to local managers accustomed to the classical handling of services, and their pricing on a cost-plus basis.

The fact that top-tier banks have adopted the quality strategies we are discussing, and that they are able to achieve strong return-on-sales figures, should warrant a careful consideration of the points being made. Where factors of production and distribution are relatively equal among banks, as is the case in the financial industry today,

- the able modifications of past organizational practices is one way to gain competitive edge (see also Chapter 5 on the management of change); and
- we should always be keen to adopt solutions which are better than our own, particularly when our competitors are able to turn on a dime.

The previous section explained why quality milestones are an instrumental way to evaluate performance, linking managers to organizational rewards: pay, job advancement, career results. As the Japanese city banks have found, managers and professionals are more likely to participate in quality assurance activities when they are part of their reward structure.

Two aspects of a career development program in Japanese finance (as well as in the manufacturing industry) are typically meant to ensure that managers and professionals receive adequate training in quality-oriented methods – and that they put into practice what they learn.

1. A corporate training program that includes quality circles, statistical quality control, total quality analysis, industrial engineering and value analysis.
2. A series of proficiency examinations connected to job rotation, which in the longer term help to improve position and function.

This gives the bank's employees knowledge of all aspects characterizing a modern bank. Even courses and examinations which may not directly relate to quality assurance activities indirectly do so if they help develop analytical and problem-solving skills.

- The overall purpose is continually to improve the quality skills of an individual over the duration of his/her career at the bank.
- The specific goal is to give managers and professionals the knowledge and working tools necessary to carry out quality improvement activities.

Proficiency examinations are well established among Japanese banks in their operations at home and abroad. The same is true of the link between organizational rewards and quality assurance. Such linkage has been found to be stronger when managers give a high priority to quality results.

Japanese financial institutions, as well as industrial and merchanidizing firms, tend to consider their quality control organization as part not only of the corporate but also of the country's virtual or logical infrastructure (often called 'soft infrastructure', but the term can be misleading), which includes health and education.

A *virtual infrastructure* is judged to be fundamental in transorganizational activities, which means:

• activities that benefit all business partners, from clients to suppliers; but
• activities that any one firm would find it difficult to organize and underwrite all by itself.

As underlined on a number of occasions during the research project in Japan, transorganizational activities are strategic. The common set of functions identified by most virtual infrastructure endeavours includes:

• offering training workshops and seminars,
• providing a stream of up-to-date material,
• dispatching experts and consultants as trouble-shooters,
• organizing conferences and national awards/recognitions, and
• providing technical support such as a rich library and media center.

Financial organizations which operate cross-border invariably find that the virtual infrastructure of some countries is wanting. Therefore they supplement it through their own initiative, as briefly outlined in the above five bullet points.

As far as operations abroad are concerned, the large banks have the in-house resources to set up their own training centers, dispatch experts and sponsor corporate conferences. But the smaller greatly depend on the host country's logical infrastructure.

The importance of the virtual infrastructure and its impact on the service industry has not yet been fully realized by host countries. In the course of my meetings with money center banks, several managers were to note that the lack of the appropriate logical infrastructure in a host country separates the home office from some of the operations abroad.

In conclusion, the attention to product quality in the banking industry, and in the service industry at large, is justified by fundamental reasons which have to do with product quality. The quality of financial services is no subject to be treated once and then put in the time closet. To the contrary, it is flexible, evolutionary procedure which relates to the management of change (of which we talk in Chapter 5) and strategic planning – as well as to daily operations, including the key issue of performance evaluation.

Notes

1.   See also D.N. Chorafas, *Statistical Processes and Reliability Engineering* (Princeton and New York: Van Nostrand, 1960).
2.   D.N. Chorafas and H. Steinmann, *Database Mining* (London and Dublin: Lafferty, 1994).

5 Facing the Invasion of the Banks' Business by Mutual Funds and Managing the Process of Change

1 INTRODUCTION

The railroads were the first means of transportation in history which did not depend on muscular power. After a difficult start in the 1830s, railroad companies became rich and powerful – so powerful and bigheaded that they did not bother to watch out for the new means of transportation based on internal combustion engines which eventually took away from them their most lucrative customers, the passengers, and a good deal of the freight.

Automobile companies, which in their turn became rich and powerful, were not an outgrowth of railroad firms. Not even seed money was put into autos by railroads. Motor vehicle companies were originally made by young and enthusiastic entrepreneurs, who eventually lost out to professional managers – as exemplified by the legendary career of Alfred Sloan at General Motors.

Auto companies, however, failed to see the future of air transport. Aircraft manufacturers started humble. Their origin was quite distinct from that of railroads and automobile manufacturers, with whom they competed. Eventually air transport became a successful industry which, with time, siphoned a huge chunk of traffic – and therefore of customers – out of the hands of auto firms.

A similar story can be found with computers. IBM and Univac, to take just two examples, were uninterested in anything other than mainframes. They missed the bus with minis, and by 1970 this gave Digital Equipment and Data General their chance. Some 10 years later, Digital Equipment looked at personal computers with disdain. A small but imaginative company, Apple is credited with having made the personal computer concept work.

Something similar is now happening in banking with mutual funds. A failure which the transportation, computers and finance industries have in common is that they have paid scant attention to *market positioning* which, as we have seen since Chapter 1, is a basic strategic move. Figure 5.1 demonstrates how skills, management culture and other factors work together in shaping the approach we take in regard to the market – and the resulting aftermaths.

- This is a never-ending evolutionary cycle.
- When even one of its cycles is malfunctioning, market leadership is lost.

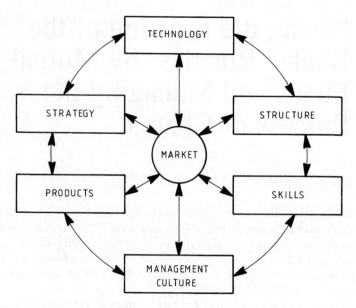

Figure 5.1   Market positioning works both ways, impacting many critical elements

Therefore the history of the mutual funds industry is indivisible from the blunders retail banks made in regard to their product line, as well as from the ups and downs of the regulatory system since the 1930s. Over the years, mutual funds have grown so large and secretive that America's archaic securities laws are no longer adequately protecting investors.

There is basically nothing wrong with mutual funds, pension funds and hedge funds[1] – until proof is provided to the contrary. Critics suggest that part of the proof is the fact that they are not regulated. The aim of this chapter is not to criticize the mutual funds industry but, rather, to demonstrate that this is a business which has for some time been slipping out of the hands of commercial banks that failed in the management of change.

2   A CASE STUDY ON FIDELITY INVESTMENTS

There is today all over the First World an incredible concentration of financial power in the hands of mutual funds. In the US, the top 10 funds control about half of the industry's $3 trillion in assets. Another way to sort out the statistics is to say that almost 50 percent of that $3 trillion is in equity mutual funds, up from $250 billion in 1990. This trend is accelerating. In the first three months of 1996, $71.3 billion of the $79.4 billion flowing into the mutual fund industry went into equity funds. Critics say that so much power in the hands of mutual fund managers could destabilize the stock market – even more so than did the 1987 crash. Other analysts point at Fidelity as an example of business which might have been handled by retail banking, *if…*

As a mutual fund, Fidelity is the largest independent investment management organization in the world. It has a network of fund management operations in America and in Europe, and claims to manage over $300 billion for more than eight million customers. If Fidelity was a bank, it would be one of the largest.

The company traces its origins to 1930, when Anderson & Cromwell, a Boston money manager, established the Fidelity Fund as a vehicle to run clients' investment accounts. In 1943, the fund was acquired by Edward Johnson, who three years later established Fidelity Management & Research to provide investment advice to the Fidelity Fund and other mutual funds launched under the Fidelity name.

Fidelity prospered in the rolling stock markets of the 1950s and 1960s, capitalizing on the skills of its investment managers. A quarter-century ago, in 1972, when Edward Johnson III assumed the reins of management, assets had grown from $3 million in 1943 to over $3 billion – a thousand times up in less than 30 years.

A decline was experienced by the mutual fund market at large during the 1970s, but a combination of new products, innovative marketing, able trouble-shooters and knowledgeable fund managers enabled Fidelity to continue to prosper. The mutual fund offered what, at the time, retail banks were not ready to promote: investment advice to clients, together with knowhow on how to manage equity funds.

- The long bull market of the 1980s was particularly advantageous for Fidelity in growth terms.
- In 1990, it became the first investment company to manage assets in excess of $100 billion, which was a landmark.
- In 1996, the assets managed by Fidelity Investments reached $400 billion – a growth of 13,300 percent in less than 25 years.

Growth continued to be rapid during the 1990s, especially in America, where Fidelity has been strong in market knowhow. Another factor in its success has been the public acceptance of technological innovation, which in America is generally higher than in Europe. For example, in the early 1990s Fidelity and Charles Schwab, a discount broker, introduced brokerage by personal computer. This made it feasible for computer-literate customers to buy and sell equities online. And since most likely computer-literate customers are professionals, hence having higher net worth, this meant good business.

Fidelity and Charles Schwab are highly relevant lessons for retail banks. The careful reader will not fail to appreciate some key issues which go well beyond specific banking laws and deregulation. For instance, in America, by cancelling

Regulation Q (which forbid banks to pay interest on current accounts) the government launched a wave of deregulation which increased the public's acceptance of risk, and brought into the market non-bank players, as the banks took time to wake up. Furthermore, the government helped in this transition by means of tax advantages. With implicit promotions like 401-k accounts, which shield income from taxes, the public continues pumping billions into mutual funds.

In commercial banking, while some of the depositors' money goes to loans, another chunk goes to derivatives (supposedly for hedging) or even to junk bonds, as the Savings and Loans experience demonstrates. In the general case, however, the majority of banks are managed by people who take their responsibilities seriously.

It can be be said that the strategic planning approach taken by well managed funds is no different from that characterizing top-tier retail banks. This is explained in the block diagram in Figure 5.2. What this block diagram does not say, however, is that mutual funds and discount brokers are typically first to hit the market with innovative products. This gives them an edge over retail banks, but it also requires sharp risk management tools.

There are several lessons a retail bank can learn by carefully studying the message in Figure 5.2. One of them centers on the five functions underpinning strategic planning premises:

- two are products and services-oriented,
- two have to do with marketing,
- one concentrates on the back office.

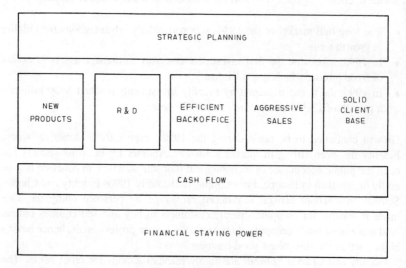

Figure 5.2 Many critical factors can be distinguished between the two main pillars of strategic planning and financial staying power

The second lesson from mutual funds is the emphasis they place on cash flow, which guarantees financial staying power. This is helped by the fact that, as far as mutual funds are concerned, the pace of business expansion has been significant.

Like any industry, mutual funds have ups and downs. In the 1987 to 1992 time-frame, Fidelity both increased the value of funds under management (from $68 billion to $168.37 billion) and improved its share of the US market (from 8.8 percent to 10.5 percent). Only two other groups, Vanguard and Capital Research & Management, experienced similar growth rates.

However, adversity struck in December 1994. Aggressive position-taking by some Fidelity Investments managers, combined with rising interest rates, produced poor results and, according to some Wall Street observers, major losses. Most embarrassing was the fact that the firm's conservative short-term funds were hit. These are the vehicles investors count on never to lose money.

Let us retain two basic issues from this reference in what concerns strategic planning. First, the strategic plans mutual funds are following tend to be more secretive than those of commercial banks, because the clients come flocking as a matter of faith – and there is no regulation. Second, each individual client should also think in terms of strategic planning when he makes investments. He should not be a mere bystander.

3   ARE MUTUAL FUNDS AND OTHER VEHICLES MORE SECURE FOR THE INVESTOR?

Philip Dormer Stanhope, Earl of Chesterfield, was known to have given some good advice to his son and godson. Dispensing wisdom as to the art of worldly success, in one letter dated 27 May 1753, Chesterfield wrote: 'A man who has great knowledge, from experience and observation, of the characters, customs and manners of mankind, is a being as different from a man of mere book knowledge as a well-managed horse is to an ass.'

The dictum fits investment strategies like a glove. Do we really know where our money is being invested if we do not learn how the market works, or if we do not make steady observations and reach crucial decisions? There is a very significant difference between

- active management of an investment account, which requires strategic planning, and
- relegating one's wealth to professionals who, statistics show, are only on rare occasions able to beat the index.

A metaphor related to the train and the autos which we saw in the Introduction can help to visualize a prevailing difference between the mammoth investment vehicle driven by the train conductor and the small motor vehicle where the risks are taken by the man behind the wheel. Even trains running on long-laid tracks have failures, but big investment vehicles have many more surprises. In late January 1995, as shareholders pulled out hundreds of millions of dollars, Fidelity acted to prevent more bad news.

The Boston fund group responded to a concern expressed by the silent majority of its investors by sending out an educational pamphlet explaining the kinds of derivatives used by its portfolio managers. Fidelity's swift action helped reassure most of its clients, but the pamphlet surprised the more knowledgeable investors.

- They thought that their bond fund invested in US Treasuries, Deutsche mark bonds or British gilts.
- They discovered that it also used structured notes, interest-rate futures, currency forwards and other exotic products.

This kind of *position risk* is not so different from that of a commercial bank. After all, mutual funds and banks have fairly similar needs in terms of capitalizing on market movements and hedging in order to protect their investors' and their own wealth. Like a money center bank, Fidelity was also active in the stockmarkets of lesser developed countries.

- In 1994, Fidelity had $8 billion invested in emerging markets.
- It was therefore exposed to the Mexican meltdown, but its reaction to the crisis has been swift. (See also section 4 regarding new measures for emerging markets.)

One of the particularities of the so-called 'emerging markets' is the associated currency risk, as Mexico demonstrated so well in 1995. Because the foreign players dominate, there is little investors can do to hedge their currency exposures. In today's capital markets, when investments can be switched at the touch of a button, institutional and other investors can quickly desert any government with suspect economic policies. This has disastrous consequences on exchange rates, which go into free fall.

Another particularity of emerging market is their very small base of capitalization. The stockmarkets of Poland, Hungary and the Czech Republic have a capitalization about 50 percent that of Microsoft. Still another characteristic of the emerging markets is their high volatility and sensitivity to political events. After the 1996 re-election of Boris Yeltsin, a number of equities on the Moscow stock exchange jumped 300 percent in a few days. They had lost just as much some months earlier when opinion polls showed that Yeltsin could not possibly win the election.

- Emerging markets are not the only iceberg endangering the cruise of mutual funds.
- Depending on the instrument being used, another way of gearing is derivatives.

Let me immediately underline that, among mutual funds, Fidelity is not alone in using derivative financial instruments. Most fund managers employ derivatives as tools to reduce risk. Some use them aggressively to increase returns if their view of interest rates or equity market movements is right.

American mutual funds are more comfortable with these instruments than European portfolio managers. But some mutual funds watch more carefully than others that aggressive hedging does not get out of control. At Fidelity, for instance, the market interpreted the resignation of Thomas J. Steffanci as an attempt to curb the company's conservative funds, which under him had tried to increase yields by taking some risky bets in emerging-market debt. This was one of the moves designed to soothe investors, who pulled $800 million out of Fidelity's bond funds in December 1994 and $100 million more in January 1995. Yet the company also confronted issues facing many funds in the wake of the 1994 historic bond-market débâcle:

- How can one balance performance with conservatism?
- How can one instill some caution into the bond group's investment culture when the market asks for greater returns?

The irony is that, if Fidelity and other mutual funds pulled back too hard, shareholders could suffer. If management was too conservative, shareholders would be less likely to recover past losses or to experience high returns in the years to come.

Another major part of the problems facing mutual funds management these days, as the industry has reached maturity, is that the prevailing compensation system generates handsome annual performance bonuses without accounting for risk. This pushes the traders towards more risk taking for higher profits – hence the need for risk management systems of which we talk in section 4.

Even if some of the premier mutual funds, like Fidelity, have made their message clear after losing a good chunk of their bond fund assets, risk has its place and its price. The challenge is how to integrate it with conservative investment portfolios. This is an issue which also faces the retail banking industry 100 percent. The choices to be made are strategic.

4   A STRATEGIC ANSWER TO PROBLEMS OF RISK MANAGEMENT AND OF GLOBALIZATION

The no. 1 rule in financial strategy is that noble intentions should be checked periodically against results. On 6 December 1994, came the announcement by Fidelity Investments that its Magellan Fund would probably have no year-end distribution, rather than the $4.32 per share previously estimated. The mutual fund said the change 'occurred as part of the normal review and verification process, and does not reflect any recent portfolio activity'.

Though cognizant markets observers agreed that Fidelity's disclosure had much to do with accounting problems, many financial analysts suggested that it underscored the notion that top-caliber investment funds may also report disappointing results.

- Well-informed Wall Street analysts generally attribute those losses to rising interest rates.
- Many suggested, however, that, in a highly illiquid, end-of-the-year market, the fate of any leveraged portfolio is uncertain.

Ironically, the troubles at Fidelity Investment came at about the same time the Orange County bankruptcy hit the market. The Magellan Fund news reverberated worldwide, causing anxiety in New York and London about the stability of mutual funds, respectively in the US and Britain. Such news was also viewed as problematic for European stock markets because it added to the jitters about interest rate increases, and therefore the future of bond holdings.

When the 6 December 1994 event took place, the Magellan Fund was valued at $36 billion. On Wall Street, some wondered if Magellan got stung by derivatives. Morningstar Mutual Funds editor John Rekenthaler said Magellan had realized $900 million in losses through 30 September 1994, according to filings, making it unlikely that the fund could have paid $4.32 a share in income and capital gains, as originally estimated – a forecast which Fidelity said had been a combination of computer and human error.

Quite important is the action the mutual fund's management took subsequent to these events, to ensure that the situation was once more under control. A new risk control system was instituted and management saw to it that investments in emerging markets, which have been frequently used by the mutual fund's managers to beef up performance, became subject to a *liquidity framework* designed to ensure that funds can sell the holdings quickly if that becomes necessary, while risk management was given the task of developing ways to measure the safety of fund investments, including liquidity. This strategy is consistent with the fact that to take advantage of globalization investors have to get out of a market that is about to go down and into another somewhere else in the world that is likely to go up. The general thinking is that a private investor cannot spot these trends and move fast enough. This, however, is to forget that a private investor would be silly to put money into 'emerging' markets.

Theoretically, a fund should be able to know when to get out of a market – whether emerging or mature. It is supposed to have the information and to be capable of picking the right time to switch between markets, enabling investors to take advantage of globalization. That however is theory. The facts do not seem to support the argument.

When to come into and out of a market is the billion dollar question. Evidence suggests that investing through global funds has been more or less a disappointment. At the average fund level there seems to be little, if any, added value from the heralded asset allocation strategy. No doubt there exist outstanding global managers who sometimes buck the trend, but the average emerging markets fund tends to perform worse than funds in the main markets.

This is what Magellan and other mutual funds want to correct in terms of restructuring their current strategy. Management is also trying to cut down on the pack mentality that led so many managers into the same stocks. For instance, it halted the internal distribution of *daily night sheets* listing the prior day's trading records of all portfolio managers. The night sheets had enabled them to piggy-back on one another's trading.

Paying much greater attention to formal risk management procedures is neces-sary, among other reasons, because of the sprawling company size. This is a prob-lem mutual funds did not have in earlier times, but now Fidelity is taking in nearly $5 billion a month. Altogether,

- it has 10 million individual fund shareholders,
- it controls 13 percent of all the money in mutual funds, and
- it expands into virtually all aspects of financial services, including under-writing, brokerage, insurance and credit cards.

This strategy emulates very closely the product lines retail banks are supposed to offer, at least in the national or local market – if not globally. A good example comes from Japan. Because of Article 65 of the Constitution (similar to the Glass–Steagall Act in the United States), securities houses are not allowed to take deposits. But they bypassed this restriction through low-risk investment accounts for lower net worth individuals.

Worldwide, investment houses and mutual funds have another significant advan-tage over retail banks: they are global, while retail banks are local. In global terms, Fidelity is aggressively pursuing offshore versions of its funds in Europe and East Asia. There are constraints as well. Critics say that *size* is beginning to hinder the Fidelity funds. Managers are finding it increasingly difficult to maneuver their huge holdings in and out of the stock market. And the company's prominence has led to an extraordinary level of scrutiny by the Securities and Exchanges Commission.

However, SEC has no charter to tell the funds to stay at home. Had that happened, it would have been against current trend, as financial advisers and the financial press in the US and Britain have been urging the placement of investments overseas. As far as the strategy followed by American financial advisors is concerned, the reason-ing goes like this: since about half the world's stocks are outside the United States, investors should be more diversified, in order to benefit and to hedge.

It comes as no surprise that most US investors chose to invest overseas via a fund, given the difficulties of judging the prospects of investments abroad compounded by unfamiliar economies and currencies. American funds abroad fall into one of two categories:

- international funds, which invest only outside the United States, and
- global funds, which buy a mix of US and foreign stocks.

A growing number of money managers offer global approaches, but recently most investment professionals have favored international funds. They prefer to separate moneys into domestic and international components but often forget that the stockmarkets of the Group of Ten countries tend to move in unison.

On the bottom line, there is probably no single correct answer to making a choice between global and international fund investing. While some decisions are based on rationality, most have to do with trend and fashion. Expert advisors tend to suggest that it is also a function of analysis and hope within the realm of a global trading system which changes rather fast.

5 RETHINKING THE STRATEGIC CONTENT OF MANY DECISIONS BANKS HAVE TO MAKE

Quite often, because appropriate planning procedures are not in place, management finds out the hard way that attempting to provide a wide variety of services to all customers does not yield the most profitable results. Having lost time and money in ill-fated efforts, a financial institution often decides to reconcentrate in sectors where:

- the promise of growth seem to be higher, and
- returns on investment have the greatest appeal to its client base.

The case study we have seen in sections 2 to 4 with Fidelity Investment is instructive for two reasons. First, fund management is the field of activity many banks are now entering with *private banking* (see also Chapter 9) – and it might have been theirs for a long time if they had not left it to mutual funds and to pension funds. Second, the problems which we have studied can well face many retail banks in the coming years.

In my book, the first strategic choice to be made is not the investment per se – hence the product – but the market to which it will be sold. Retail banks with strategic planning experience pick out the consumer segment that they can serve well.

- They avoid the mirage of serving the market by being everything to everybody.
- They do not enter service domains where their expertise is thin.

Conditions of course can change. As we have seen from Chapter 1 on, strategic planning is not something to be done once and then to be left in the time closet.

Table 5.1 Twelve key variables in the banking industry with impact on strategic planning

Financial products	With regulated banking	With deregulated, globalized, banking
Basic characteristics		
1 Number of products	Few	Unlimited, with brand differentiation
2 Content	Traditional, common agreement	Open to innovation
3 Pricing	Uncompetitive, assured income	The market sets the prices
4 Level of innovation	Very limited	Rapid and dynamic
5 Cross-product selling	Limited	Unlimited, but knowledge-based
6 Product life cycle	Long to very long	Short to very short
Mechanics of implementation		
1 Financial analysis	Traditional, with linear approaches	Non-traditional, real-time modeling, non-linear
2 Introduction of new services	Regulated, by the government	Open to fierce competition
3 Means of delivery	Mainly paper	Mainly online
4 Distribution channel	Classical branch office	ATMs, POS, PCs – in full evolution
5 Delivery point(s)	Proprietary	Proprietary and non-proprietary
6 Information technology	Low or average, largely batch	High technology, real-time only

The market changes and the same is true of the strengths and weaknesses of the institution. Neither are strategic plans and associated choices which are made for one market good for all others in which the bank operates.

A great deal of the difference between strategic premises is due to specific market characteristics. Also highly important is the nature of the prevailing regulations characterizing the banking environment. To document this statement, Table 5.1 presents 12 key variables with impact on strategic planning. They divide into two sets:

- six represent basic planning characteristics,
- six concern mechanics of implementation.

Another major factor influencing the degree of novelty retail banks can bring to their product line – and therefore their planning premises – is the affluence of the population to which they appeal. In the United States, for example,

- in the early 1970s, only 4 percent of the population was considered affluent;
- in the early 1980s, that percentage had grown to 12 percent;
- in the early 1990s it reached 22 percent and still kept growing.

Such increase in affluence has brought a change in investment preferences and new demands for the packaging of banking products, chiefly among the so-called 'baby boom' generation. Those banks which profited the most from this affluence were the most proactive. Those who profited the least were characterized by the misguided notion that their prestigious name or elegant image would bring in customers.

Retail customers today no longer connect snobbery with where they shop, but they do watch out for the items they purchase. It is very easy for them to lock onto the item that is considered upscale at the moment and then buy it anywhere, including a non-bank institution. Therefore, to plan correctly, the retail bank needs to know how its market will change in the near future, altering its business strategy accordingly. This is the raw material on which to build a dynamic strategic planning orientation which revolves around

- markets,
- customers,
- products, and
- the use of technology.

How far should the bank plan? As is shown in Figure 5.3 there is a theoretical and a practical answer to this query. The theoretical will be top-down, starting with far-out planning which looks ahead 15 to 20 years. While far-out planning is a good exercise in management, I do not talk of that range in connection with strategic plans for retail banking.

The bottom-up way in planning starts at the rolling year, which is the budgetary horizon, and goes towards long-range planning. For retail banking services I would suggest mid-range as a good target, particularly at the start. But the retail bank should have a concept which can answer vital questions such as the following.

- What will we be doing in 10 years? From where will the business and the profits come?
- Which are our product strategies? Where do we want to be a product leader?
- Is there enough management skill to handle new products and new markets? What can we learn from sophisticated client requirements?

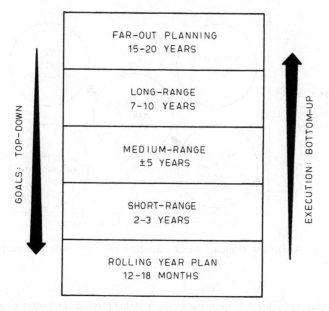

Figure 5.3 Strategic premises must be examined both bottom-up and top-down, under different planning horizons

Another strategic issue to which top management of a retail bank should address itself is that of capital productivity: that is, the amount produced for every unit of capital. A 1996 study by McKinsey found that capital productivity was significantly greater in the US than elsewhere, which helps explain the significant difference in profits between American and continental European banks as well as mutual funds.

* Higher capital productivity generates bigger financial incentives.
* It sees to it that investors both accumulate more wealth and spend more seed money.

McKinsey suggests that European and Japanese managers could do much better in their current business environments by paying more attention not only to capital productivity but also to other strategic issues including improved quality of services and time-to-market. Even if this study has primarily focused on manu-facturing, a good deal of its results apply to banking. Many German companies, McKinsey suggests, waste money by overengineering products. American man-agers cannot afford such luxury because the capital market gives them a primary objective which they have to meet or else. This overriding objective is financial performance.

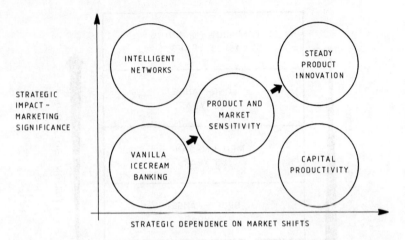

Figure 5.4   A frame of reference which can help retail banks with strategic planning decisions

As shown in Figure 5.4, some banks see to it that products and services are plotted against axes of *strategic impact* and *strategic dependence*. The former gives a measure of marketing significance, the latter shows the level of dependence of the business on market shifts. This analysis enables prioritizing where to allocate capital, people, and time to obtain the best return.

On the bottom line, the winner will be determined by two factors: the capabilities of which he disposes and the degree of planning, skill, judgment and energy applied to doing the job. Just as the choice of customers is very important, so is the choice of products within specific markets which – even if complex – must be fully understood and correctly interpreted.

6   STRATEGIC PLANS, THE CHIEF EXECUTIVE OFFICER, AND THE ACCOUNTABILITY OF THE BOARD

Having considered the competition to retail banking in the form of mutual funds and the resulting loss of market share, particularly in regard to the more wealthy investors, let us now look at the issue of how commercial banks can recover some of their lost turf. A good way is through leadership and superior organization.

- Leadership should be exercised at every level, but most particularly at the top of the pyramid.
- Also at the top, says an old proverb, is the bottleneck – as is the case with every bottle.

The chief executive officer (CEO), the man who commands the enterprise, is not a mere technician. He is the animator, the promoter, the planner, the organizer, the person who should value above all character qualities of hard work, creative imagination, internal drive, independence of opinion and unbiased judgment.

This list of personality traits is fundamental, though to the unaware it might seem to be simplistic. *Expecting the unexpected* and challenging the obvious are two other basic abilities of good executives. The same is true of their ability to sell their ideas and their services to their boss and to their customers. Not all bankers are able to do so.

Depending on the bank and on personalities, the CEO may be the chairman of the board or the president of the bank. In some companies, like General Motors and Dupont, the Finance Committee depends directly on the chairman. In most cases, however, both the chief financial officer (CFO) and the strategic planner report to the president, as shown in Figure 5.5. So does the executive vice president (marketing).

These organizational dependencies are not always clear-cut, with the result that there are overlaps in responsibilities. Sometimes a conflict in authority happens in the business promotion area between marketing and strategic planning. This is a misinterpretation of functions because the promotion of banking activities per se is part of marketing – not of strategic planning.

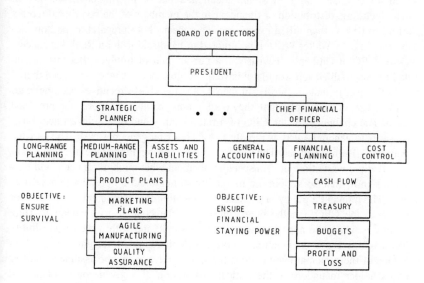

Figure 5.5 Strategy and structure must be tuned to corporate goals in order to ensure survival

In other cases, the conflict of authority is between the strategic planner and the chief financial officer. For this reason in Figure 5.5 I have paid particular attention to separating the two functions. Such conflict, too, rests on misinterpretation of duties because, as we saw as early as Chapter 1, the financial plan is shorter-range and it integrates into the strategic plan.

What kind of personality traits should the chief executive officer and his immediate assistants have? The ideal answer is perfection in preparation, daring in the execution, submission to the facts and impartiality in regard to their own interests. These traits will be found in varying degrees in all great industrial leaders.

- There exist CEOs in the retail banking industry who do things well and accomplish far-out objectives.
- There exist CEOs who focus on the short run but who bring, wherever they go, order, clarity and success.
- There exist other CEOs who have not sorted out their priorities – and therefore bring confusion and unhappiness.

The *gifted* chief executive prepares himself over long, tedious periods of time, to become the man at the center of financial destinies. Destiny cannot be left to chance. More failures, more alibis, less contructive accomplishments are often the results of applying the fallacious idea that not men but the nasty notion of 'chance' or of supranatural forces run the affairs of this world.

In no company, large or small, local, national or international, whether in manufacturing, distribution or finance, can the members of the board of directors afford to be less than gifted executives. This means both preparation and on-the-job training. As Walter Wriston is rumored to have said to John Reid, his successor as CEO at Citibank: 'I wish you a fair amount of troubles. Because if you don't have troubles you would not have the troubleshooters when you need them.'

In finance, in manufacturing, in merchandizing, chief executives become leaders because, other things equal, they obtain more results than those who preceded them. The challenge for the CEO of a retail bank – and of any investment business – is to generate ideas as rapidly as his company generates cash. This is what Warren E. Buffett advises. The chief executive and his immediate assistants cannot afford to waste time in vain speculation about what might have been, and they should know that no system, no marketing strategy and no product is good forever. The moment a policy or a means of executing it is inefficient, inadequate or obsolete, the CEO and the board must have the courage to abandon it. Here exactly is where the need for moral courage starts; and with it the responsibility for insight, creative imagination, intuition, calculation and foresight.

One of the principal justifications for an executive job is the assumed capacity of its holder to undertake the critical exploration of a given course of action, before he makes a decision. It is precisely at this point that incompetence most frequently reveals itself. The executive fails in his job because he did not *expect the unexpected* – not because he did not do his best to avoid the rocks as soon as he saw them, but because he should have been aware of their existence without the need to actually see them.

As far as I am concerned, the loss of market by retail banks to mutual funds is precisely due to this oversight. As the Introduction has demonstrated, there are precedents in the railroad, automobile and aerospace industries. Every chief executive should also be aware of the fact that new policies and new strategies both lead to and require *new structures*. As shown in Figure 5.6, in a dynamic banking environment these new structures have to be endowed with new managerial tools. This concept comes from the late Dr Herrhausen, chief executive of Deutsche Bank, and it leads to the need for *a new culture*.

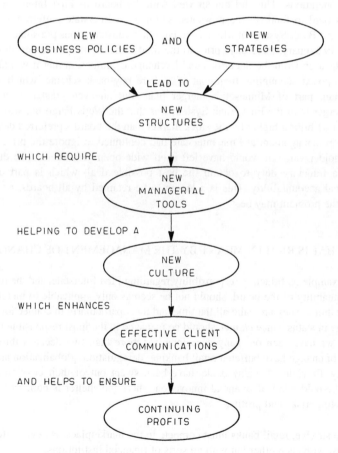

Figure 5.6 Dynamic change in a banking environment

There are also some CEO duties which over the years remain unaltered because they rest on basic principles like *personal accountability* by the chief executive and the members of the board. A good example is the fiduciary responsibilities of board members, both individually and collectively. On 22 January 1995, First Interstate, California's fourth-largest bank, announced that it was in merger talks with Wells Fargo, the state's second-largest. On 24 January, a deal was done at $11.6 billion. This merger meant further consolidation of California's retail banking. It also resulted in downsizing, as Wells Fargo's plan had been to close more than 80 percent of First Interstate's branches and to reduce its staff by 75 percent. (See also in Chapter 4 a similar challenge faced by Crédit Suisse because of its acquisitions.)

Wells Fargo's goal had been to cut $1 billion of annual costs from the consolidated operations. This did not sit well with the board of First Interstate which fought hard to fend off the unwanted suitor. First Interstate preferred a merger with First Bank System of Minnesota, but other considerations prevailed.

On 19 January, three days prior to the final decision on the merger, there was an indication from the Securities and Exchange Commission that it would reject the proposed accounting treatment of a share buy-back scheme, which was an important part of Minnesota's merger plan. But an even greater deterrent to the merger with the First Bank System was that the Wells Fargo bid was valued around $1 billion higher by the stock market than the board's preferred deal.

If top management at First Interstate had continued to ignore the price gap in shareholder value, it would have left itself wide open to lawsuits. The directors have a fiduciary duty to obtain the best possible deal, which is part of their personal accountability. This is a lesson to be retained by all boards, no matter what the problem may be.

7   WHAT IS REALLY MEANT BY THE MANAGEMENT OF CHANGE?

The example on fiduciary responsibility regarding First Interstate, and the resulting accountability of the board, should not be seen as only applicable to mergers and acquisitions. They are valid all the time and most particularly in connection to any change in status, since *change* should be managed in the most responsible manner.

As we have seen on many occasions, for more than two decades three great gales of change have buffeted retail banking: deregulation, globalization and technology. Bewildered, many banks have been swept out of their cosy world and into the cold wind of financial innovation where the shelter is built from R&D, marketing, risks and profits.

- To survive, retail banks must compete in the marketplace as never before, not just with each other but with all sorts of financial institutions.

As we saw in the case study with mutual funds, the ability to face up to a toughening competition is an integral part of top management's accountability.

- In pursuit of new sources of income, many retail banks have strayed far from the business of taking and safeguarding the public's deposits and running the payments system.

While there are, in banking, cases of improprieties – as in all other industries – the no. 1 reason for failure in duties is the inability to *manage change*.

- Competition has forced some banks to range so far, in so many directions and at such a pace, that top management has had no time to take the proverbial long hard look.

'I would question that the [inadequate] management of change is the no. 1 reason for failure,' said a reviewer. 'I would rather identify the failure to recognize and embrace the need for change as even more important.' It seems to me that here we are playing with words – unless the message is that, after the need for change has been identified, the status quo can prevail. There is an American saying about avoiding change by the gimmick of embracing it and falling back: 'The unable is being asked by the unwilling to do the unnecessary.' But I would agree with the reviewer that

- complacency is the real problem, and with it inertia;
- complacency sees to it that the bank is falling behind in the competitiveness battle.

Besides this, getting people to respond positively to change is the most difficult challenge facing management today. It is not just a positive response to short-term tactical change that is needed. What is most important is the willingness to *continue to change* as new circumstances occur.

In practice, the management of change is complex because organizations are made of people. Ideally, the chief executive seeks to induce his subordinates to work in a coordinated fashion toward common objectives, and to do so with enthusiasm and imagination. The trouble is that:

- enthusiasm and imagination conflict with tradition, and many banks are run by tradition;
- individualism is the negation of conformity – and it is difficult to strike the right balance between them.

The need for managing change is a direct reflection of these facts. On the one side we have companies which are so embedded in the status quo that they stay immobile and are hammered. Examples are IBM, Apple Computer, General Motors, Philip Morris, Philips and Westinghouse. On the other side are companies on the move – able to reinvent themselves – like General Electric and Microsoft.

At Microsoft, Bill Gates grew up watching IBM falter and Digital Equipment nearly crash and burn. He understood this could happen to his company and created a culture that spends little time celebrating successes. In late 1995, after a near-miss with Internet, realizing that Web momentum was too great to ignore, Microsoft was able to turn on a dime. Gates saw to it that Microsoft became *Web-centric* – dumping what did not fit and reshaping everything else.

This is the best paradigm for retail banking. In a world where change is the only constant, by standing still banks condemn themselves to a slow death. There are all sorts of theories and techniques for managing change, but in the wrong hands or used the wrong way, they can be lethal. Change is likely to be implemented most successfully when:

- people improve their knowledge of what is new and what is different, before modifying their performance, and when
- they understand their own strengths and limitations, as well as the impact they have on the people around them.

Whether smooth or catastrophic, predictable or unpredictable, change is an appropriate metaphor for our time. Changes can be salutary and, as Voltaire's Dr Pangloss had it, the best of all possible worlds. The management of change could decide whether a banks succeeds or fails in assuring its future.

Change has come at a rapid pace to the retail bank business perspectives. With regulation, banks have been allowed a privileged position, not just among financial companies but among all other commercial activity, in return for performing twin functions:

- turning savers' deposits into investment funds, which is the job of the intermediary, and
- providing the mechanism through which payments can flow to sustain economic growth and prosperity – the job of the clearer.

As we saw in Chapter 3, in exchange for this protective cover commercial bankers were told by the government and by regulators what businesses they could or could not conduct, and how they should conduct what was permitted.

- In regulated markets, competitors were kept at bay virtually irrespective of how good or bad their management happened to be.
- But in deregulated markets such complacency is no longer the case. Retail banks which do not change as the market does go under.

In the environment of the 1990s, bankers feel constrained by their rules as much as protected by them. They want them rewritten. The problem is that rewriting the rules infringes the territory of non-banks, which in return want to be allowed to enter more deeply into the banking business.

American and Japanese commercial banks are pushing their merchant banking arm into the securities business as far as they feel the regulators will let them get away with. For their part, investment banks and securities houses have become direct suppliers of credit to a wide range of financial and non-financial customers, offering investment products that are virtual substitutes for interest-earning demand deposits.

One of the best examples of the need for managing change is the fast-evolving reporting requirements. For instance, the Market Risk Amendment by the Basle Committee on Banking Supervision, published in January 1996, became effective immediately, and mandatory as of the end of 1997.

For many years, banks have been accustomed to mark-to-market their trading book. Some followed a conservative policy of marking-to-market or at original cost – whichever is lower. But many of the items they carry in their trading book and their banking book, particularly those off-balance sheet, have no ready market. Hence the Basle Committee advises that they should be marked-to-model. This will take a great deal of effort to do because it amounts to a cultural change.

8 REASONS FOR FALLING BEHIND IN STRATEGIC PLANNING

Upturn and downturn are twin sisters. My research findings are that,while on the bottom line the aftermaths of a business downturn are most frequently expressed in financial terms, the reasons may be varied: non-appealing products, uncompetitive pricing, low quality of service, inadequate marketing, or a combination of these. Such reasons share a common background characterized by:

- *parochialism*, where many executives do not understand the success of their company's rivals, and
- *contemptuous paternalism*, which shields employees from accountability and therefore from the need to deliver.

Most obstacles to growth and survival inhibit clear vision of the years ahead, and make strategic planning difficult if not outright impossible. Table 5.2 presents a list of the more important obstacles to effective strategic planning, as seen by the banks which participated in this research.

Retail bankers able to view market evolution from the right perspective were to comment that strategic planning and the management of change are so important because every institution's deposit base is at risk. Every day of the week, every other competing bank is there to come after it and get it.

Table 5.2   Obstacles to effective strategic planning in the
banking industry

	Percentage of times this was chosen as no. 1
Unanticipated economic cycles	70
Government regulation	65
Lack of trained personnel	53
Insufficient planning timeframe	49
Lack of interest by top management	21
Lack of reliable data	18
Improper organization of planning function	12

There is a great deal of cannibalization in banking, making mandatory the ability steadily to reposition ourselves against the forces of the competition. One of the reasons for the erosion of the deposits base is that retail banks think of themselves too much as executors of transactions, and too little as sales agents and cross-product marketing experts. This is a direct result of failure in strategic planning. It also constitutes a cultural gap which can have very severe consequences. Let us never forget that every bank and every other company always lives on the edge of its survival opportunities. During the 1980s, 230 companies disappeared from the Fortune 500, the list of top-tier financial and industrial organizations.

• Without strategic planning we cannot position ourselves against the market forces.
• Without the management of change, we cannot adapt fast enough to retain effective positioning.

The way to bet is that, while retail banks fall for many reasons, at the top of the list is lack of understanding of the changes taking place in the market. This leads to a shrinkage in resources, which makes it more difficult to maintain financial staying power.

Inadequate strategic plans have much to do with failing determination by top management to take action, when there is still time to reverse a bad situation. Many retail banks are missing their chances because they simply cannot position themselves in the triangle shown in Figure 5.7.

The 13 reasons presented in Table 5.3 were identified by banks and other companies participating in this research as topmost in their mind in answer to the question why they get into trouble. The irony is that each one of them can be corrected, but do so requires concerted action and co-involvement by top management. Notice that, as a reason for troubles,

• limited financial resources are not at the top of the list, but mid-range,
• forecasting and planning top the list (see Chapter 4), with inadequate internal controls in third position.

In second place in Table 5.3 is 'changes in the marketplace'. Unmanaged, such changes often lead to *business failures* because the company alienates itself from its customers. An example from the computer industry can be instructive, because it says volumes about what strategic planning might have done.

In the mid-1980s, Symbolics was a top-flier. Then it crashed. Financial analysts say that Symbolics management failed to address the market's growing preference for powerful, general-purpose, relatively inexpensive workstations, such as those supplied by Sun Microsystems, Digital Equipment and others.

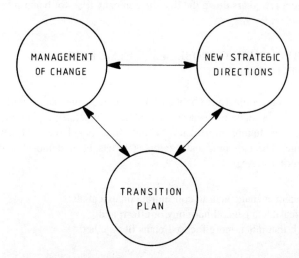

Figure 5.7 Strategic plans can be instrumental in expanding the marketing horizon and in providing continuity in action

Table 5.3 Thirteen reasons why retail banks get into trouble

1.	Lack of forecasting and planning
2.	Change in the marketplace
3.	Inadequate internal controls
4.	Changes in technology
5.	Product obsolescence
6.	Changes in business beyond skills of management
7.	Uncontrolled increases in costs
8.	Limited financial resources
9.	Decreased efficiency of the branches
10.	Inability to chop off dead wood
11.	Internal political conflicts
12.	Obsolescence in knowhow
13.	Tarnished image in the marketplace

- Symbolics kept pouring money into developing its own, more costly hardware.
- While still strong, it failed to move its Lisp software to those other computers.

Within a few years, a shrinking market and associated lack of business opportunity caught up with Symbolics. Its management did not heed the advice of financial analysts who expected sales to plummet. Therefore the company produced another loss. Instead of managing change, it stuck to its old policies, which no longer corresponded to market trends. As adversity struck, it did not learn its lesson – and a few years down the line the company filed for bankruptcy.

9   WHY BY 'AVOIDING PROBLEMS', RETAIL BANKS ARE GETTING INTO TROUBLE

This and the preceding four chapters have provided the reader with plenty of evidence that in a modern business environment the strategic plan and all of its components – including information systems strategy – have to be kept flexible and dynamic. Through practical examples it has been demonstrated that the formulation of a strategy

- helps senior management to concentrate on essentials;
- makes feasible a general harmony of effort; and
- sees to it that other, more focused plans fit together.

One of the top organizational issues assured through strategic planning is that every contributor is playing his full part. This is very important because the growth and survival of every bank rests on human capital, correct market perspectives, competitive products and modern equipment to support them.

Evidence has also been provided that, when we talk of strategic planning we should be sure it allows us to migrate into a larger (or smaller) structure, without having to risk restarting from scratch. But few retail banks really master this process because it is alien to their old culture. Because of this inability to change bad old habits, some financial analysts paint a gloomy picture of American banking. They provide an account of what happened to the financial markets during the 1980s and single out some 2,500 of the nation's 12,372 federally insured banks as being dead, dying or crippled.

What keeps those institutions going, these analysts say, is the reluctance of Congress and the executive branch to face up to the extent to which the banks' assets have lost value. The first step to improving the health of the banking industry, they argue, is to admit the problem and begin revamping the banking industry. A growing chorus of financial analysts, as well as bank executives, suggest that the weakest financial institutions should be sold off or merged. Some studies use a non-traditional approach to identify the weakest banks as those which fall behind because

- they lack market strategy,
- they fail in innovating their products, and
- they are not able to crown promises with results.

Other analysts add to this short list the banks' inability to lead in high technology. This is said with a view to the future, not to the past. Some financial institutions which were technological pioneers in the 1970s are still stuck with systems which are now 20 to 25 years old. Because they are scared about replacing them, they continue to sink more money into them, with diminishing results and a loss of market competitiveness.

While in many financial institutions the current information systems are growing obsolete, there is fear of unknown technologies, as well as hostility on the part of conventional data processing departments toward new methods and techniques. This sees to it that the gap between computers and management continues and is even enlarged.

Obsolescence in information technology is a good example on the price paid by banks for *avoiding problems*. Plenty of cases exist to document that the concept of avoiding problems by avoiding change leads to an even more absurd conclusion: Avoiding to solve problems for not to touch other peoples' turf.

Precisely the same spirit of avoiding to look at the core of problems, let alone to do something about them, is responsible for the huge losses some banks have recently incurred. Mid-June 1996 I was talking to a member of the board of a major European commercial bank, who was exclaiming how great was his institution.

Such a statement was only half true, because it so happened that during the last couple of years this bank was hit by some fairly major losses. Nothing secret about them. They had made the headlines. The executive vice president indeed acknowledged his bank had faced rough weather, but then he added: 'Well, these cases don't concern *me*. They did not happen in *my* department.'(!!!)

If each member of the board looks only after his turf and avoids studying and solving the problems hitting the other divisions, the bank sails straight into trouble. It is therefore not surprising that financial losses snowball. Just look at the red ink which surrounded Japanese banks in 1995.

- Sumitomo Bank, no. 2 in the top 500 Asian banks, lost a staggering $3.36 billion.
- Nippon Trust Bank, no. 118, lost $1.64 billion, and it had to be taken over by Mitsubishi Bank.

Some other Japanese banks went under and rescue came by way of taxpayers' money in order to avoid systemic risk. A short list includes Cosmo Bank, Hyogo Bank and Kizu Credit.

Another casuality has been Yamaichi, Japan's oldest broker and one of its "big four." Cosmo is an interesting case because, when it crashed, it had 73 percent of its loan book not performing. Surely enough Cosmo management should have tried to redress the situation before the loans portfolio went that far beyond repair. But it is easier to avoid looking at problems than to do something about them – until the bank caves in.

Let me close this chapter on a positive note. In the years ahead surviving retail banks will be those which show innovative capabilities, learn to live with increased volatility and uncertainty in the market, are able to control risk and know how to manage change. Other crucial strategies are to assure high technology-based systems, a strict control over costs and the offering of high-quality service to the clients. 'How we do it? We watch costs like a hawk,' says Microsoft president and chief operating officer Robert J. Herold.

Note

1. See D.N. Chorafas, *Derivative Financial Instruments. Strategies for Managing Risk and Return in Banking* (London and Dublin: Lafferty, 1995).

Part Two
Focusing on Marketing and Competition

6 Retail Banking Strategies and the Marketing Functions

1 INTRODUCTION

Retail banks which wish to survive in a market more competitive than ever are obliged to act according to the new patterns of customer behavior which have developed over the last 20 years. Particularly in the countries of the Group of Ten (the United States, United Kingdom, Germany, France, Italy, Japan, Canada, Switzerland, Sweden, Holland, Belgium, and Luxembourg, as an observer) banking has become more sophisticated, more demanding, and more critical of services and products.

This was the conclusion of the 1st International Retail Financial Services Conference for Scandinavia, organized by the Lafferty Group and held in Oslo, 17–18 June 1996. Many Norwegian retail banks participated in this conference, as well as executives from Chase Manhattan, First National Bank of Boston, First Union National Bank, Huntington Bankshares, NatWest, Deutsche Bank, Wasa Banken, Lan & Spar Banken and Fellesdata, the information technology unit of the Norwegian Savings Banks.

If one was asked to write in a nutshell the sense of these two days of meetings on retail banking and the associated marketing functions, the emphasis would be on the way first-rank retail banks answer the complexity of customer demands. The solutions which they provide are both a response to and a motor behind the increasing competition between banks and non-banks. (See also Chapter 3.)

Lecturer after lecturer emphasized that increasing competition no longer permits retail banks to sit quietly and wait for customers to pass by their branch office and knock on the door of their own free will. Bankers have to be aggressive salesmen of their services, which means they have to activate all the whistles and levers of effective marketing.

A similar situation prevails in wholesale banking, where the rules of the game have changed. This change came because today many corporate treasurers are former bankers and in consequence they know first-hand

- what sort of opportunity exists in the market,
- how the fee structure works, and
- what banks should be offering.

Many retail bankers have pointed out that both sophisticated investors and corporate appointed treasurers are tough partners. Their demands can only be answered *if* and *when* the bank has an effective strategic plan – as Part One has demonstrated.

Part One also made the point that the marketing plan is an integral part of the strategic plan, and the same is true of product plans, a subject which is treated in Part Three. A different way of looking at a marketing plan is as the means of reflecting the *bank's identity*, which speaks volumes for the care with which it should be constructed.

2   WHAT IS MEANT BY MARKETING IN RETAIL BANKING?

As the Introduction has explained, in the banking industry the importance of marketing has grown steadily. The coming years will test quite severely retail banks which have not yet found their way in expressing their identity to the banking public and in convincing their clients that they can offer the best advice at an affordable cost.

An expanding market provides opportunities to enlarge business volume and better the market share, but this is associated with the fulfillment of some key requirements. One of them is to provide customers with the right information in a format that makes its exchange or presentation

- easy to assimilate,
- comprehensive in its content, and
- personalized to the customer's needs.

This is not the case today of the information with which banks provide their clients. What they feed them with is often in mixed media format; it is out of date when it reaches them; and usually it is stored in awkward computer systems which are heterogeneous and not readily accessible to the enduser.

Why so much emphasis on information in a discussion on marketing? Because the two are not quite the same, but almost. Theoretically, an advanced communication technology provides powerful support to the marketing function by facilitating access to distributed multimedia databases as well as to technical, sales and financial expertise. Practically, as we will see on a number of occasions, solutions are not that simple.

Attention should be paid both to client information and to market information, or knowledge of the financial services available in the market to which *our* bank appeals – including data elements covering all aspects of market response. This duality of client information and market information makes it feasible to satisfy in rapid succession client requests. In the past, when clients did not really know and therefore appreciate the retail banking products offered to them, the banker told the client what to buy. This is like Henry Ford's famous dictum: 'They can have any color [for their autos] as long as it is black.'

But as the clients became more educated, affluent and sophisticated, it was they who told the banker what to offer. The roles have changed and, at the same time, advanced communications facilitate the forming of *telemarkets* in all areas of business activity, assisted through access to distributed multimedia databases. No banker should underrate the Internet.[1]

On the technical side, advanced communications provide a real-time linkage among workposts, and they provide support for message facilities. They also assist in the consolidation of accounts amongst a number of geographically dispersed points of reference which may interest the same client.

- As customers' requirements become more demanding, the need for quicker and just-in-time deliveries increases.
- Therefore both marketing and operations require substantial technological support to enable more effective sales of banking services.

Said a banker who saw an early draft of this text 'Certainly, customers are becoming more demanding, but speed is not the issue, and even if it were I am not sure this proves that technological support is needed.' This statement is incoherent, but bringing absurdity to its logical conclusion let us turn the clock back 400 years.

- The high tech in transport at that time was horse and carriage.
- Banking was only being done over the 'banca' and at fairs.
- Illiteracy of the population was well over 80 percent.

Under these conditions, the world did not go bust – but it was moving at a different pace. The high gear of business today is broadband telecommunications and intelligent software.[2] To doubt the impact of technology on banking is like living 400 years in the past.

If backward concepts carry the day (at a time when Internet connects in real time the antipodes of the Earth) the only way to reach North America or Australia will be by sail. It is good to be contrarian, but if one does not want to be taken for a fool then one should not make a fool of oneself.

Clear-eyed bankers know there is no time to waste beating around the bush because of so many serious problems which have to be addressed. There is plenty that needs to be done in a focused research and development (R&D) effort, while on the social and political side of the spectrum lies the fact that in banking, as elsewhere, marketing is a creator of images which proceed in a parallel channel to the development of new products.

3 THE CONTRIBUTION OF A MARKETING PLAN

Not only does the making of a marketing plan oblige us to think about our sales goals, but also, once we have developed such a plan, we will have a much better idea of what it takes to launch our product(s). 'Build a better mousetrap, and the world will beat a path to your door,' says a proverb. But many banks are finding that choosing the wrong marketing strategy and sales tactics can kill the competitive advantages of the 'better mousetrap'.

- Time and again bankers find out that the insight which they gain when they develop a marketing plan can be invaluable.
- Precisely because of this insight, and the foresight that goes with it, section 2 characterizes marketing as a generator of images.

Figure 6.1 brings home this message by addressing what is expected by the different functions contributing to the creation of customer-oriented basic images and their impact on marketing. This figure does not follow the beaten path. At least one banker considered it a 'very strange and controversial flow chart', while others liked it and still others said that 'at least it is [an] honest chart'.

Another field where marketing must lead is product planning. This used to be true mainly among the leading banks of the First World, where today the most important tradition is *innovation*. But today little by little such a principle is becoming valid for the whole banking industry: any valid marketing approach depends on constantly pioneering new products.

The bank's laboratories need both new ideas and interactive database mining (see Chapter 12). Marketing contributes to the stream of new products by taking upon itself the task of evaluating the drives, location and extent of the market, the wants or needs of customers and the strategies of competition. In terms of business opportunity analysis, as well as competitive intelligence, marketing must provide the bank's management with a clear picture of what competitors (and our

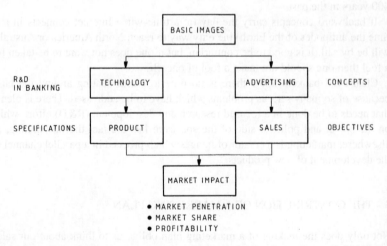

Figure 6.1 Marketing is the creation and exploitation of customer-oriented basic images

own bank) have available to fill the market's needs. Part and parcel of this evaluation is strengths and weaknesses both of ourselves and of our competitors.
Furthermore, new banking products require:

- consistent R&D programs and
- a steady training of the sales force.

One of the important sales planning functions in retail banking is *brand marketing*
(see the Appendix). 'As electronic banking becomes more prevalent, consumer
choices will be dictated by brand marketing,' says Peter Kim, vice-chairman and
strategist of McCann-Erickson. 'Being a bank or even being big is no longer
enough,' adds Michael Wilder of Arnold Fortuna Lawner & Cabot (*USA Today*,
September 11, 1995).

Another important function marketing must fulfill is client segmentation and
targeting. This is critical to new product development as well as to successful marketing campaigns. Both, incidently, require the use of analytical tools.[3] Cluster
analysis, for instance, has proved a valuable method for market segmentation purposes, helping to develop customer groups that are meaningful and actionable.
Customer targeting is used both in direct marketing campaigns and in private
banking – and it has been proved that it achieves a good return on investment.

In terms of mathematical tools in marketing banking services, fuzzy logic and
neuro-fuzzy allow pattern analysis and configuration for the individual needs of
customer and market segments. But, once market focusing has been done,

- the results must be effectively visualized, and
- interactive 3-D color graphics is the best way to proceed.

Because many retail banks feel obliged to enlarge their horizon of saleable products, they thrust upon marketing the responsibility for *ancillary services*. In earlier years, banks offered ancillary services almost by chance, because some senior
executives decreed that such services can turn banks into *financial supermarkets*.
This is no longer the case. Ancillary products must be planned.

Asked in 1979 to describe the financial institution of the future, then Citicorp
chairman Walter Wriston replied: 'It's called Merrill Lynch.' But then he added
that, to survive as financial supermarkets, banks

- must use high technology better than their competitors, and
- they must employ computers and communications as income-earning services.

Technological expertise is a legitimate ancillary service, but it is not so commonly offered because few retail banks have high grade IT expertise. It is indeed

surprising how many banks fail to exploit their technological resources. The more common ancillary services include:

- real estate,
- travel agency chores,
- stockbrokerage,
- insurance policy sales,
- mutual funds, and
- safe custody.

In all these functions marketing plays a vital role, but not everything is in marketing. As Part One has so often underlined, the key to success is low-cost production, easy delivery and good quality – backed by the bank's seal of approval and by the confidence of its customers.

4 MARKETING MORE EFFECTIVELY TO OUR OWN CLIENTS

A person or a company depositing money in a bank essentially faces the credit risk associated with the trust given to the counterparty. The same is true about buying the bank's stocks and bonds. Deposits and other types of investments have a resemblance to the process of giving out loans, except for the fact that in the latter case it is the bank which takes on the credit risk. In these transactions, the degree of risk varies according to:

- the character and strength of the counterparty, and
- the quality and quantity of collateral.

A bank does not give collateral to its depositors. All it gives is trust. Therefore marketing must convince the bank's own clients that they can trust the bank with which they deal. Confidence must be built and sustained both with the current client base and with the new account acquisitions.

Quite often, retail banks fail to appreciate that the most promising marketing avenue lies in their own backyard. Because of this, most banks divert up to 90 percent of their marketing investments and attention to total strangers, while marketing could be more effectively done in cross-sales to the retail bank's existing client base. (We will talk more of cross-sales in section 8.)

When I say 'cross-sales,' I mean capitalizing on the synergy of the range of products we have seen in section 2. Cross-sales lessons can be learned from the manufacturing industry. Some 70 percent of IBM's yearly business comes from its existing customer base. To sustain this business, the company

- develops a line of complementary products,
- trains its salesforce in handholding, and
- uses technology to sustain and enlarge the customer contact.

Database mining[4] can offer marketing management, as well as the relationship banking executives (see Chapter 7), a wealth of information. Interactive access to the bank's database permits marketing to tell the client, 'We appreciate you buy products "A" and "B" from us, but we would like to talk with you about our products "C" and "D". Our offer of "D" services can fill the following needs in your business and your financial transactions…'

This focus on customer needs and requirements is very important today because banks are faced with a *selective client base* which tends to reduce its financial correspondents. In 1980, AAA American companies had on average 36 banks to deal with. By 1996, this number had been reduced to 9, and is still shrinking. Banks which convince the client of the quality of their services and their innovative features continue to be retained and they become the client firm's assistant treasurer. They can remain in this position only as long as they

- are inventive in the type of products which they offer to their clients.
- market these products in a way which is appealing to their clients, and
- keep ahead in technological knowhow, so that their clients continue to need their services.

Not only is this concept the raison d'être of customer-oriented databases, like the example we have seen with the Dai-Ichi Bank, but it is also a core issue in relationship management, as discussed in Chapter 7. Furthermore it is the kernel of a drive towards developing a *sales culture* in the bank.

When in 1987 Royal Bank of Canada posed itself the question of what it had available for the management of the client relationship, it came up with 39 different incompatible bits and pieces which could *not* make up a marketing system. Thereafter a new marketing strategy addressed four distinct but interrelated areas which were retained as the pillars of a valid solution. The marketing effort focused on the ability to manage in the most effective way:

1. the client information,
2. the client relationship,
3. the client profitability, and
4. the sales and marketing effort.

The next target was that of managing the cost of delivery by market segment. Figure 6.2 shows the four market segments the Royal Bank of Canada established as its strategic perspective. Notice that these are not the same as those outlined in Figure 6.4; the latter are based on my own research with a different financial institution.

The retail bank's 8.2 million clients were stratified on the basis of the size of the account the bank was handling, another criterion being income from transactions and fees. Many financial institutions follow this frame of reference, but not

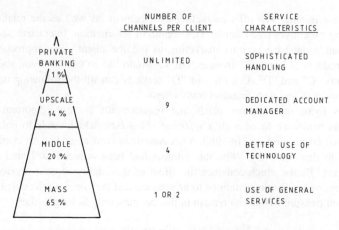

Figure 6.2   Market segments and product policy of the Royal Bank of Canada

all. One of the major banks I have been working with has chosen for the classification of the top 1 percent the level of more than $1 million per account. The
upscale is classified between $200,000 and $1 million; and the middle level
between $30,000 and $200,000.

No two banks establish the same limits. This type of study must be done within
a bank's own operating environment taking into account its market, its products
and its policies. While it is very helpful to know the experience of other banks
based on the marketing strategies they have chosen, there is no substitute for
making one's own strategic studies. This is what the winners in retail banking
do – and that is why they remain the winners.

5   GIVE ME A MARKET AND I WILL MAKE A BANK

Dr Vittorio Vaccari, the president of the Italian Unione Christiana Impreditori
Dirigenti, once said: 'Give me a market, and I will do a company.' Vaccari's apho-
rism is perfectly applicable to finance: 'Give me a market and I will make a
bank.' Not any bank, but one which is full of innovation, has high quality products and is characterized by low cost in production and distribution. This is the
stuff of which successful marketing plans are made, and this is the background
against which a bank will be proud to make information publicly available.

The successful marketing plan for banking products will be characterized by
flexibility. Management will be ready to change strategic plans as the market conditions evolve and technology advances – and the bank will be ready to invest
ample resources, both human and financial, to face market challenges and grasp
the opportunities. Marketing plans must be dynamic and able to capitalize on
business as it develops. There are many products in banking which are still latent

or imperfectly exploited. The same reference is applicable to other industries, until a promoter catches the market's eye and takes hold of the market.

Lipstick, eyeshadow and make-up are terms that were waiting to be invented. The business opportunity was not exploited. Then they were popularized by Max Factor. Factor's power lay in the fact that he composed simple words, which were easily understood by the public. 'Make-up in seconds, look lovely for hours' was the headline in a typical Max Factor advertisement. For millions of ordinary women, Factor simplified the complicated task of looking, or at least feeling, good – and in the process he helped to create the first major international cosmetics business. The message Figure 6.3 gives is applicable to all industries:

- the marketing job is polyvalent, and
- it is an integral part of strategic planning.

Not only cosmetics products but also financial services and whole sectors of the banking industry wait for a Max Factor to exploit latent potential. Those banks which flourish in some countries show others where market opportunities may be. This is dramatized in Table 6.1 through a reference to two sectors: savings banks and mutual and co-op banks. Savings banks have the minimum market share in France: 6 percent, and the maximum in neighboring Italy and Spain with 32

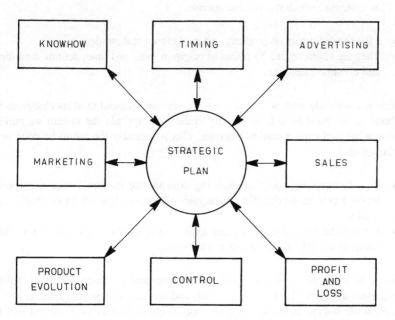

Figure 6.3 The marketing job is polyvalent and it integrates into strategic planning

Table 6.1   Market share of savings banks and cooperative banks

	Savings banks		Mutual and/or cooperative banks	
	Market share (%)	*Number*	*Market share (%)*	*Number*
France	6	35	22	150
Germany	24	704	14	2,778
Italy	32	75	—	—
Spain	32	52	3	100
UK	29	84	—	—
USA	18	1,500	2	368

percent in each country. Mutual and/or cooperative banks have the maximum market share in France and in Germany while they are non-existent in the UK.

To a large extent, the reason for this discrepancy is historical, though in some cases there exist also some legal grounds. 'Historical' essentially means that nobody exploited the latent opportunities, even if many people realize that more often than not we talk of *living markets*. Like living systems, markets have embedded into them aspects of birth, growth, development, mutations, crossovers, ageing and death – hence history. There are changes resulting from *shocks* and other changes induced by *learning*. Both can alter the functions and the structure of the system in which we live and operate.

- Like species, financial products and markets are real entities.
- They are characterized by points of origin in space and time, definite duration and eventual extinction.

This is essentially what we mean when we say that financial markets change and therefore we must be able to steadily update and upgrade the system we build to emulate and exploit market behavior. This is precisely the job to be done by marketing.

- In a fast-growing and fast-changing domain like modern banking, market leadership is not a prize that can be gained once and then left on the shelf as a trophy.
- It has to be won again, again and again – or it will be lost for *our* bank and competition will take away our market share.

Some lessons can be learned from the manufacturing industry. In 1980, IBM expanded a variety of marketing channels and services to improve customer contact, while hoping to reduce its own support costs. This process created *retail product centers* for office machines and small computers, which proved to be a rather cost-effective way to attract new business – until the market changed and the centers were overtaken by low overhead byte shops.

Another of IBM's marketing solutions of the 1980s was the *business computer centers* . There customers could see demonstrations of small systems and make purchases. Such centers operated in 50 cities in the US and 30 cities in other countries, but their life cycle was short, precisely because the market had changed. With reference to these two IBM initiatives, a reviewer said: 'This was exactly where they were making their strategic mistakes which led to their major subsequent problems.' This statement has evident implications for banking and therefore I would like to comment on what it says.

The strategic mistake IBM made in the 1980s was *not* with the retail product centers and the business computer centers – which were the right concepts – but with the fact that it allowed the mainframe culture to persist. In a quite similar way, financial institutions

- which stick to vanilla icecream products and target low net worth clients because 'the high net worth clients are demanding' prepare themselves for lots of trouble;
- the 'mainframes' of any business are not just big irons but a way of thinking which is retrograde. This statement has its counterpart in the banking industry.

Let me continue with the IBM example. Still another Big Blue channel launched in the 1980s was *direct mail and telephone selling* of typewriters, dictation units, computer terminals, small computers and office products; also of data processing supplies. This service which was a forerunner of what has become the immensely popular *help center* was expanded worldwide – and remained valid until the products themselves disappeared from the company's list.

Like telephone banking, which was popularized at about the same time, telephonic selling of hardware has been a marketing strategy which enhanced contact with the customer while it also improved the sales productivity of IBM. Customers were given

- the convenience of toll-free telephone ordering, and
- the ability to use major credit cards.

A further IBM innovation of the 1980s was *customer support centers* that provided users and prospects of the mainframer's intermediate-size computers with sales, education and installation support. These spread to more than 100 of the mainframer's branch offices worldwide and remained valid until the mainframes themselves were no longer wanted by the market.

Whether we talk of computer software/hardware or of banking, the essence of these references is of a new marketing program able to give sales and service teams a comprehensive, structured approach for helping customers manage what we sell them more effectively. The similarity between computers and banking is important because

- the new way to think of banking is as *information in motion*;
- the shift from paper money to electronics is as critical as the change 2,500 years ago from barter to money.

Promoted by able marketing, this shift is profound and it will have long-lasting aftermaths. The problem is that our thinking, our attitudes, our skills and consequently our decisions have not yet caught up with the new realities. The same is true of the marketing culture and associated professional obligations in retail banking.

6   THE COMMON FEATURES CHARACTERIZING PLANNING AND MARKETING

To appreciate the role of marketing in retail banking and its evolution, we should start with the fundamentals of planning processes in a marketing-oriented sense. Planning, as we know it, grew out of the Gantt chart designed in 1917 to plan war production. It was enhanced during World War II through the use of analytical tools and statistics. Similarly,

- market statistics use quantification to convert experience and intuition into definitions, information and diagnosis,
- quantification blends well with marketing which evolved as a result of applying management concepts to distribution and selling.

As prosperity grew in the inter-war years, by the late 1920s marketing pioneers like Thomas Roebuck began to question the way manufacturing and merchandizing was organized. They anticipated how the market behaves, and what can be expected in the next 2, 3 or 5 years, and concluded that the assembly line in manufacturing was a short-term compromise. They thought that, despite its tremendous productivity, Henry Ford's method was poor economics because of its

- planning and scheduling inflexibility,
- poor use of human resources, and
- difficulties in engineering changes.

In the 1920s and early 1930s, marketing too was inflexible. But while Thomas Watson, Sr and other sales wizards revolutionized marketing, it was left to the Japanese to restructure manufacturing and marketing processes along flexible lines. They promoted teamwork through quality circles (for quality circles in banking, see Chapter 4) and promoted the information-based organization (see section 2) as the way to manage human resources.

From marketing to flexible planning, every one of these managerial innovations represented the application of knowledge to work, substitution of information for guesswork and emphasis on solutions rather than throwing money at the problem. They also replaced 'working harder' with 'working smarter'. Working smarter, at least in terms of letter scheduling has not been a 20th century invention. The earliest reference I could find dates back to 1869 when George Westinghouse, an American inventor, turned the pneumatic concept which was used in drilling the Mont Cenis Tunnel into a brake for use on trains. In pipes running under the train, compressed air held back pistons. In the event of a release of air pressure, the pistons slammed forward. The effect was to drive brake pistons against wheels, slowing down the kinetic energy of a train.

With pneumatic brakes, a 34-meter train going at 50 kilometers per hour could be stopped in 170 meters. The result encouraged the idea of *scheduling* more trains, more closely spaced than had previously been wise, which in turn required better *signaling*.

Something similar is happening with marketing in banking. Market research in the financial industry has proved that in selecting his bank the customer not only pays attention to the pricing, the image and where the bank is located, but also – and perhaps most importantly – to *the person* who in his eyes represents the individual financial institution: its motor and its brakes.

- The customers who count most to a bank's profitability are tough evaluators of the bankers they deal with.
- For them, the most important criterion impacting on customer choice is the quality of investment advisors.

As shown in Table 6.2, 12 percent of the clients characterized the quality and knowhow of the bankers they deal with as being 'very important'. Another 45 percent considered the same criterion as being 'important'. To solve the financial

Table 6.2 Criteria for client choice

	Very important (%)	Important (%)	Not too important (%)	Of little importance (%)	Unimportant (%)
Very well known	3	27	35	24	11
Old established house	5	24	45	18	8
Proximity of branch office	7	31	40	16	6
Quality of advisors	12	45	33	10	—

problems of these sophisticated and demanding clients we must approach them
with abundant energy purpose, leaving nothing to chance.

From my personal research, I have a lot of documentation to back up these statistics. I also have the evidence that in the financial industry there is a de facto
market stratification with about 2 percent of clients bringing to the bank nearly
half its profits.

- This stratification follows Pareto's law, as Figure 6.4 suggests.
- The statistics are based on my own research, and therefore differ from those
  we saw in Figure 6.2 concerning the Royal Bank of Canada.

Another 18 percent of the clients, at the top of the pyramid, are quite demanding
in terms of the nature of products and quality of services they want from the
bank. These bring to the institution which knows how to handle them another 30
percent of its profits.

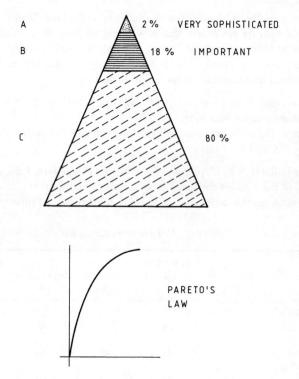

Figure 6.4 Stratification of the client population in terms of requirements for
services

'The point is,' said a reviewer, 'that the private banking market is a different market, it is not the top 20 percent of the retail market.' In other terms, according to this funny logic, the retail market is one flat surface where the peaks of the marketing pyramid have been leveled out by a steamroller. Even a blind man with sunglasses can see the absurdity of this argument.

'Private banking customers are sophisticated and may be demanding, but can be highly profitable,' another reviewer advises. That is right. Where the first reviewer missed the point is that private banking customers did not land on earth last night from planet Mars.

- The majority have been retail banking customers, whom the financial institution cultivated and upgraded to investors.
- It did so by being innovative and steadily improving its quality of service, rather than by treating unequals as equals, feeding them with the banking equivalent of mainframes.

Most evidently, it is the top of the clients' pyramid which should attract the most marketing attention. To do that, Dai-Ichi Kangyo Bank in Tokyo has set up a special database of 1 percent of its business clients. This represents 20,000 out of 2 million accounts, and they receive great attention and care on the management's behalf.

The message these paragraphs intend to convey is that, unless banks fully redefine what business they are in and who are their most important clients, they will go out of business – or, at least, out of lucrative business. In the next few years, we will witness many bank mergers and bank failures, with the price paid by those banks who do not understand how Pareto's law works.

- Fifty years ago, bank failures almost meant the end of the world.
- Today, they are the means to purify the system.

What is essential is that *our* bank does not fail. For this, it needs focus by management and a mighty marketing function. There is nothing as distressing as losing market share at the top of the pyramid shown in Figure 6.4. But marketing involves decision making under uncertainty.

- If all uncertainty is eliminated, we have no opportunity.
- But if none is eliminated, we have only risk.

Therefore we must anticipate the impact of market changes on our institution and respond to them before suffering the negative effects. That means we must conceptualize what business would be good for our bank to be in, and re-establish in a documented manner what business we are *really* in. These two references are not necessarily the same, as we saw through practical examples in Part One.

To handle market uncertainty, we must evaluate the difference between the projected goal and our current position. We should also prepare a plan which makes
it possible to *renew and reinvent our bank* in a steady manner without upsetting
the balances. Skill in longer-range market planning will answer the following
questions:

- What is the role of *our* bank in the next 10 years?
- Do we have the ability to make factual evaluations and develop a transition
  plan?

Chances are that this transition plan will rest on three pillars: market perspective,
human capital and modern equipment, of which we have spoken on several occasions in Part One while discussing strategic planning. There are banks that wait
for the good old times to come back. But the old times will not come back –
while the ground continues shifting beneath us.

7   EXPLOITING NICHE MARKETS AND MASS MARKETS

A retail bank can differentiate itself *geographically*. It can also do so *by product*.
A product-based differentiation addresses the kinds of specialized services it
offers to clients: personal loans, credit cards, business loans, investment advice,
foreign trade assistance, money market instruments, derivatives and so on.

A bank can also differentiate itself through *a market niche*: providing an edge
in doing business that other banks have not yet explored, and that would stand
analysis by the chief executive officer of a client firm. The latter will be probably
asking a lot of questions in terms of service–product relationships his company
needs to remain competitive. The exploitation of niches is also known as *customized marketing*. It is an approach which can be seen as both customer-oriented
and product-centered. Typically, it is a solution which exploits the client–product
synergy by means of customization.

Market strategies in the banking industry can be classified into four main
groups: *niche*, *unique product*, *mass market* and *me too*. A niche product strategy
makes no attempt to change the industry structure. It provides no global view of
doing business but:

- resegments the market, and
- exploits low competition.

Under certain conditions a niche strategy can be rewarding. Table 6.3 presents the
results of a six-month campaign by a retail bank to better its position by exploiting both niches in marketing and the mass marketing channel. The niche results

Table 6.3   Results of a six-month marketing campaign by a retail bank

	Niche marketing (%)	*Mass marketing (%)*
New clients as % of current base	8	12
Business volume growth	26	11
Profitability growth	31	6
Increase in average balance	24	9

proved to be much more interesting in terms of business volume, deposits and profitability. This bank:

- carved out for itself two specific niches,
- followed them in terms of quality services, and
- took a fresh look at its delivery mechanism, to increase customer satisfaction.

Another retail bank which decided on undertaking a mass marketing drive found out that the best way to do so was to take a long hard look at the cost of its delivery system. Management discovered that certain traditional services which used to be advisable had ceased being so. Non-competitive services oblige the bank to get out of some sectors where profits are questionable.

   The strategy followed by the second bank which chose the mass market road was to redesign its network for online order taking and delivery. This was done not only to radically reduce labor costs but also in the belief that, contrary to the niche strategy which is very selective, a mass market strategy is global. In terms of strategic decisions, the second bank:

- addressed the total market in which it was active,
- capitalized on long-term advantages, tuning management thinking accordingly, and
- made compulsory mass-marketing objectives which, as it turned out, needed to be steadily redefined.

Figure 6.5 brings both the niche market and the mass market into perspective. The criteria are: return on investment (ROI) and market size. Notice that, contrary to the other alternatives, a *unique product* strategy involves moderate risk but calls for long, sustained commitment to *innovation*. It uses value-differentiation and aims to

- gain product leadership,
- create a new customer base, and
- capitalize on relationship management.

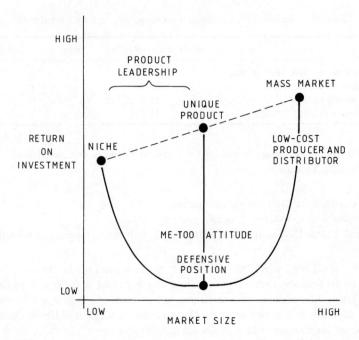

Figure 6.5 The omega curve for niche market, unique products and the mass market

From my experience I can assert that the worst possible strategy is 'Me too': 'If the other retail bank does it, so do I.' With this, the best result which could be expected is a very low return on investment, but the more likely outcome is loss of time and money. Yet it is surprising how many banks rush into this mimicking procedure which has no future and no rewards.

A well-chosen marketing strategy eventually leads to rethinking and redefining the banking environment, which in turn calls for retail bank re-engineering. Any successful attempt at re-engineering should consider the connection which exists between type of market and the channels. This is shown in Table 6.4.

Finally, it is proper to keep in mind that any marketing strategy, no matter how well studied, may fail. The main reasons for failure are lack of clear understanding of what is a niche, a unique product or a mass market; defective product/market orientation; inadequate client relationship management; and substandard preparation of products and people.

Other major mistakes made by retail banks include efforts to disconnect management decisions from customer requirements and market trends, insensitivity to shifts in the niche or the unique product environment and inability to live with vagueness and uncertainty – which every niche implies, this being just as true of the mass market.

Table 6.4   Type of market, type of production and type of distribution

Type of market	Type of production (back office)	Type of distribution
Mass market	Mass production	Online network
Unique product	Series production	Network and cross-selling
Niche	Job lot	Network, cross-selling and personalized offering

As the preceding examples help document, strategic marketing is no abstract idea, but a practical experience. Therefore, to avoid pitfalls, bankers will be well advised to answer Lee Iacocca's questions for management: what are our objectives

- for the next 5 years?
- for the next year?
- for the next 90 days?

In business, we always need the ability to look into the future. 'If you deal with day-to-day crises, you focus on the next month instead of the next year,' says Iacocca. Hence the queries: what are our plans, our priorities, our expectations; how do *we* intend to go about achieving them? Answers like: 'The way our grand-father did it' are not acceptable.

Chapter 7 will demonstrate that the ABC of convenience banking has changed. Proximity of branch and 'old chap' attitudes used to be quoted as the principal reason for selecting a bank. Now, for top-tier clients, the ABC of the principal reasons is the innovative products a bank brings to the market; the knowhow of its people in providing client consultation; and the sophistication of the communications and computers network the bank puts at its customers' disposal.

8   THE DIFFICULT JOB OF PRODUCTIZING AND CROSS-SALES

Section 4 made the statement that, while one retail bank can learn from another, particularly from one with a leading position, it is not good policy to copy the other bank's marketing plans, because each plan should be tuned to the prevailing market conditions and the characteristics of the client base. Procedure-wise, how-ever, there tends to be a convergence which should be brought to the reader's attention:

- The rule for the upper two strata in the schema in both Figures 6.2 and 6.4 is: *know the client.*

These two strata principally require niche and unique product strategies, which have been discussed above. Notice, as well, that much of the productizing effort discussed in section 6 also appeals to the two aforementioned populations.

To 'know the client' means that the banker must have at his fingertips the client history, cross-sales experience, transaction profiles, costs of service, risks taken with the different services and the resulting client profitability.

- The rule for the lower two strata in Figures 6.2 and for the bottom stratum in Figure 6.4 is: *know the market.*

The challenges of 'knowing the market' are quite different from those of 'knowing the client'. We no longer talk about the treasurer of a corporation or about a high net worth individual, but about a whole market segment. First and foremost therefore is the task of market segmentation.

Any market segment will be composed of individual units: physical or logical entities. While the business *our* bank does with them does not have the margins which will permit us to know them in detail one-by-one, we would still want to sort out and prioritize their characteristics – to help ourselves in productization and cross-sales. My experience is that

- database mining helps both in profiling and in cross-referencing;
- it makes it possible to manage not only the client relationship but also the channel.

But to succeed in this strategy we must convert our database from accounting-oriented to client-oriented. When this is done, chances are that we will end up with many surprises in terms of the penetration of our products into the client base.

Banca Provinciale Lombarda, one of the retail banks I have been working with as a consultant to the president, had 425,000 customers and these featured some 675,000 accounts. This means 1.6 per customer. In the average each customer bought 1.6 products, yet

- the bank featured 18 product channels of which nine were considered by top management to be basic;
- a thorough analysis, however, has shown that of these less than 10 percent were truly marketed.

In other cases statistics can be even worse. The UK's TSB (formerly Trustee Savings Bank, now part of the Lloyds TSB Group) handled 7.5 million customers. These customers used an average of only 1.2 of the bank's total offering of around 100 products. I was told in my London seminars that this low figure tends to be in line with the experience of other British banks.

This is not written in the sense of a criticism because it is indeed difficult to organize a client-oriented database and engage in cross-sales. Even the bank's own employees may not be trained to understand this concept and its importance to the survival of retail banking. But proper organization and high technology can ease the job.

In fact, a growing number of retail banks, like Abbey National, which took the initiative to revamp their database, changing it into a client-oriented structure, have had a similar experience to that of Banca Provinciale Lombarda. They found that to intensify product marketing they had to alter the organization and make customer information available interactively to management and the account-handling officers – all the way to the tellers. They also reached the conclusion that the bank's database structure should not be accounting-oriented, but client-oriented.

As the name implies, an *accounting-oriented* database is primarily concerned with accounting data. This is the old model in data processing, from the punched card era, which still today dominates 90 percent of the banking industry and the vast majority of computer programs.

By contrast, the kernel of the *client-oriented* database is customer identification made in a way to facilitate the exploitation of the customer relationship. This goes well beyond demographics, into customer history, *customer mirror* (profit and loss by account and by transaction) and service-accounting links. Accounting databases can be converted, and are being converted, to client-oriented databases. This has been accomplished by several banks which found out through practice that it is very rewarding to market to their own clients. As a result,

- they set appropriate marketing strategies, and
- get organized to capitalize on their customers' trust.

It is fairly difficult to extract meaningful service relationships from accounting-based structures. But it is easy to exploit customer-oriented databases, if for no other reason than that they have been specifically designed for that purpose.

Once a customer-oriented database is in place, we can exploit its contents for customizing and productizing reasons. *Productizing* is a fairly recent term, coined to differentiate between a product which is still at the research and development (R&D) stage and one which is ready to be launched in the market.

There are many reasons why a product may stay for a long time in R&D, or even may never come out of the laboratory, as with, for instance, precompetitive research or bank engineering weaknesses. But the most fundamental reason is management inertia and lack of knowhow. This is highly counterproductive:

- not only does the bank not earn income on the R&D money it has spent,
- but also it loses some of its best clients who are attracted by new products in other banks.

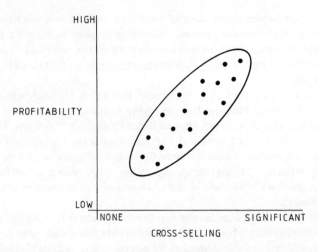

Figure 6.6 Cross-selling intensity and profitability correlate between themselves and with client loyalty

For the top 2 percent of the retail bank's clients who, as cannot be repeated too often, are the more demanding and more lucrative, new products are key to *cross-sales*. Based on a recent research project, Figure 6.6 suggests that cross-selling intensity and profitability correlate between themselves and with customer loyalty.

9   IN THE YEARS TO COME, THE BANK IS THE NETWORK

To overcome our opponents in the retail banking market, exploit business oppor-tunities as they develop and control risk, we must launch a fighting machine perfectly adapted to these tasks. Never should we consider our adversary to be petrified in his habits, thoughts and decisions – even if evidence says this might be so.

Because we know, or at least we should know, that our competitors will be attacking our customer base, targeting our most lucrative clients, we should orga-nize our defenses around high technology, aggressive marketing and relationship banking.

- Through networks we should be able to reach our clients at any time, in any place and for any product.
- Our clients should be in a position to access online our bank, for any place, at any time, for any product.

Part of the client relationship information which can be effectively mined is what some banks call *entitlement information*, identifying the kind of service this client is entitled to. Other interactive database mining activities track each one of the products, aiming to answer questions such as:

- Which products move, which do not move?
- Which client class, demographics or other criteria relate to the best product's performance, and to the worst?
- Which client characteristics best promote cross-selling, and which are the least attractive?
- Which client requirements call for what type of productizing?

These questions make a great deal of sense because the more sophisticated of our clients appreciate that the bank they are dealing with has to espouse the new marketing philosophy of managing the *market space*, rather than the *market place*. Real-time networks see to it that the market space is what constitutes banking in the future. Marketing management will be responsible for the development and marketing of the emerging channels of service. Among the better known are:

- multimedia kiosks,
- automated teller machines,
- point of sales,
- telephone banking,
- home banking,
- PC banking and
- the use of the Internet.

Every one of the items in this frame of reference is networked, with Internet being the most recent development. Whether we want it or not, competing means looking at the future, and in competing for the future we must develop new concepts in terms of: products, channels and brand.

A retail bank can sell more services by becoming a source of advice and counsel to its clients, as well as a reference in regard to product innovation. People and companies buy products because of the *value* they perceive from the product and its provider. This value may not be immediately apparent. Hence the need to personalize the product for the important customer. A financial product is valuable to its customers if it can

- save them time,
- save them money, and
- save them trouble.

Quality is remembered long after the memory of price is gone. Quality is what makes relationship banking. Greater service is what generates cross-sales. We will return to these issues in Chapter 7.

Retail banks should never allow themselves to forget that in terms of marketing they compete with non-banks who have skills in many areas influencing the market of the future. We have already spoken of different examples like Microsoft, Intuit, GE Capital, AT&T and Charles Schwab. Another example is Virgin.

Few retail bankers have heard or, if they did hear really appreciated, the wisdom of H.J. Stern who, on his retirement from the helm, advised the investment bankers he called inhouse to sell his firm: 'A company isn't like an oil well where all you have to do is hold a pan out and collect the oil. It's like a violin. And I'm not sure my sons have what it takes to play the violin.' No other expression than 'It is like playing the violin' can better apply to what has been recently called 'brand banking', of which we spoke in Part One. The brand manager is in charge of developing new products to meet the demand of consumers such as:

- foreign exchange products,
- investment funds,
- travel-related products,
- credit cards and debit cards,
- business lending,
- home ownership,
- house improvement,
- children's education and other loans.

Because he must research methods to improve the service, the brand manager must work interactively with local and remote databases. Since they are essentially marketing managers, brand managers are also given the responsibility of coordinating efforts within the bank's branch network and at headquarters.

It is also part of the branch manager's mission to monitor the bank's corporate image portrayed in its branch office network. Much of this work has to be done online and in a way it resembles the mission of the trader who must *access* and *analyze* databased information as well as

- dealing in each one of the major money markets,
- executing buy/sell orders, and
- moving funds from market to market and currency to currency.

This is the *one bank, one network* approach which has proved to be an effective business strategy. In a similar manner, also online, the brand manager will develop and market products and services to different customer strata or populations. For instance, for the younger generations these include Kids' Account, On Campus Loans and PC Loans.

The concept of 'The Bank is the Network' permits the development of valid strategies which channel the retail bank's activities where it counts in the market. In the years to come, relationship managers and brand managers will be the agents responsible for tailoring products specifically for a given market, and following up relationships to ensure a high customer retention rate. But, because neither brand managers nor marketing managers are supermen, they have to be assisted to a very significant extent by technology. This is one more confirmation of the fact that, in the years to come, the bank is the network – and the network is the bank.

10   IS IT REALLY TRUE THAT IN THE FUTURE INTERNET TAKES ALL?

What I mean when saying that 'the bank is the network' is that, through networking, those retail banks which know how to manage technology are well positioned to face the future in distribution. As we will see in Chapter 8, when we talk about direct banking, the convergence of computers and telephone changes the banking industry and revamps its products. Currently existing telecommunications networks are dominated by the delivery of either narrowband voice and data, or analog broadcast of entertainment. But in the coming years broadband services will be delivered digitally, and they will be characterized by interactive multimedia. This will have a tremendous impact on a number of banking products.

Chapter 8 will make the point that direct banking for all sorts of financial services can be done through open or closed networks, the latter being the banks' own – or proprietary. The most classical example of an open network is the plain old telephone service. A much more sophisticated reference is *Internet*.

In October 1995 Huntington's Bankshares and the Bank of Wachovia made a joint venture on Internet – the first of its type – which, in terms of investment, represented a tiny $2 million. This US Internet set-up is the only one which currently processes transactions on the Web. The two banks' investment boomed to $40 million in just six months.

Internet may not provide the best current technology in banking, and for sure it is not going to be the ultimate, but as an online delivery channel it is a communications solution some banks would not want to miss. Table 6.5 classifies different technology-influenced products into mature, maturing and emerging. Internet falls into the emerging class; because developments happen at a rapid pace we will be able to judge the results by the year 2000.

As far as financial services are concerned, the greatest enemy of Internet is security; and security may prove to be its undoing. Never believe the software vendor who tells you that it has solved the security problem through encryption, firewalls and other goodies. A 100 percent security does not exist – and, under current technology, it is not even approximated. (Security is discussed in Chapter 16

Table 6.5   Financial tools and products influenced by technology

Mature	Maturing	Emerging
ATM	Direct banking	Internet
POS	Private banking	Intranets
Kiosks	Branding	Agents
Direct deposits	Financial supermarket	Interactive online banking services

in connection with smart cards.) Still, in spite of widespread concerns about security, some banks have gone ahead with using Internet for retail banking, as shown by the Huntington's Security First Network Bank example. Let me add that:

- some analysts considered the Security First venture to be a bold bet;
- others looked at it as seed money with a very uncertain outcome.

While Huntington's Bankshares says that this Internet investment has paid off handsomely, it should be kept in mind that, originally, the no. 1 purpose was not return on investment but rather the test of an open network market. Also it was a test to see what it can provide in terms of competitiveness. The huge popularity of the Worldwide Web, its millions of subscribers and the fact that it features a global implementation capability brought a windfall. In the years to come, these same factors may see to it that there is a major redefinition of the customer interface in the financial industry. This will in all likelihood include not only the electronic channels, But also a direct, online salesforce.

Cognizant people in the industry think that open networks like Internet will not only reduce the number of bricks-and-mortar branches but also lead those remaining towards specialization and streamlining, with more flexible opening hours and more focus on quality of services and on low costs.

One of the senior retail bankers with whom I was talking about Internet's influence on his business mentioned during the meeting that in the late 1980s his institution tried to get in PC-banking but failed. It was as if nobody wanted the service. The same happened a couple of years later with the smart card. Smart cards are still not wanted by the market, but open networks have taken on considerable weight.

There are, however, a number of questions in connection with electronic banking, and most particularly the open networks. One of the most crucial is: *Who is going to own the network* ? This is no academic query but one which will permit the bank to be at the center of customer relationships.

In conclusion, the bank has traditionally been the bricks-and-mortar network. Computers, communications and sophisticated software change that old paradigm. But who is going to take command of the customer relationship? This is the billion dollar question which no banker yet feels able to answer in a factual and documented manner.

Notes

1. See H. Steinmann and D.N. Chorafas, *An Introduction to the New Wave of Communications and Networks* (London: Cassell, 1996).
2. D.N. Chorafas, *Agent Technology Handbook* (New York: McGraw-Hill, 1998).
3. See D.N. Chorafas, *Chaos Theory in the Financial Markets* (Chicago: Probus/ Irwin, 1994).
4. D.N. Chorafas and H. Steinmann, *Database Mining* (London and Dublin: Lafferty, 1994).

7 Relationship Banking, Customer Mirror and the Branch Office Network

1 INTRODUCTION

A 19th-century merchant from Frankfurt is credited with having said that to buy a gem from a man who wants to sell it and resell it to one who wants to buy it, is very easy. But to buy a diamond from one who does not want to sell it and sell to one who does not care to buy it, that is business. This is also, in a nutshell, the function of relationship banking.

Traditionally, a branch office network was put in place for proximity banking purposes, but branch office managers and their people did not feel compelled – or even required – to produce concrete sales results. Yet the reason for the existence of a branch is sales: from the acquisition of new customers to cross-sales of the retail bank's products.

Not only have sales not been given a priority in traditional branches but also customer relationships are handled in an accounting way, without any great concern for business performance. Things are changing, however, and top-tier banks consider a number of functions as fundamental in justifying the existence of a branch office network. For instance:

- fee producing services,
- effective customer handling,
- retaining the most valuable existing clients,
- attracting new high net-worth customers,
- motivating the staff to sell, and
- managing the cost of delivery of services.

The new mission given to the retail bank's branches must reflect the fact that matter-of-course client loyalty to a single institution is in decline. Whether the retail bank's services are marketed through networks or bricks-and-mortar, customers increasingly compare and evaluate product quality and the cost of services. Month-by-month, products and services wanted by the most profitable clients become more complex, as the top 20 percent of the client base looks for an integrated range of sophisticated services. The maintenance of account relationships becomes important both to the client and to the bank.

As the banking population becomes more affluent, for customer retention purposes knowledgeable bank counsellors are likely to become the financial institution's most critical resources. Investment advisors must be mobile, visiting the customer at his place rather than waiting for him to step into the branch. Here is how Thierry Lombard, of Geneva's Lombard, Odier, sees the bank's business developing: 'Our clients still come to us, but more and more we have to go to them.' Christopher Reeves, chief executive officer of Morgan Grenfell, was to state: 'Clients want to deal with people with original ideas. So new rules have to be created. We must not believe that rules are written on tablets of stone.' This is the credo of the modern bank.

Also, as we will see in this chapter, the challenge of greater sales productivity is on the table. Because retail banking is an industry, we have to carefully account the results the bank's employees deliver. This means our people have to be able to fill their *quotas* – a notion which is standard in industry but is new in banking.

Finally, a word of caution. Some people might say that the three components of the chapter's title – relationship banking, customer mirror and branch office network – are barely related. This is not the case. Relationship banking and customer mirror highly correlate; the same is true of the branch network and relationship banking, with the latter acting as the pivot of the other two references.

2   SALES STRATEGIES, CORE COMPETENCES AND BANKING FEES

Chapter 6 has documented that one of the most popular strategies followed by retail banks in the 1990s is cross-sales to the existing customer base. Another is the offering of innovative products to the top of the customer pyramid: from cross-sales to the bank's own customers, to the acquisition of new customers from carefully targeted market segments.

There is no general agreement on the effectiveness of cross-sales. While more and more banks today feature ancillary services, insurance being one of the favored, some bankers say that is not effective. In fact

- many banks are finding that adding an extra channel adds costs overall, despite expectations of the inverse;
- this is written in the sense of a warning, as well as a call for careful exploration of 'pluses' and 'minuses'.

We have spoken as well of other strategies such as cost reduction within the branch network over the short, medium and longer term. As we will see in Chapter 8, this is associated with the usage of new approaches like direct banking. Still another strategy is the achievement of higher levels of customer satisfaction. Customer retention can be improved through more sophisticated financial services.

One of the reasons retail banks are so keen to increase the appeal of their products, as well as to better their quality while reducing their costs, is that many services which used to be offered free have now become part of the fee structure. No two price lists are alike, but all have in their background a certain sense of value differentiation: among different banks, and between one customer population and another.

The segmentation and differentiation criteria are not necessarily demographic. Rather, they divide the overall customer population along one or more dichotomies which permit focusing on products and services offered or to be offered to each market segment. Market segments may be fundamentally different. Figure 7.1 uses wealth and time as criteria.

- Some customers are *money rich* but *time poor.* These constitute the best population for innovative fee-earning services.
- Other customers (the majority) are *time rich* but *money poor*. These should be served with tough cost-control in mind.

Many retail banks understand what is implied by this dichotomy, but only a very few have a strategy able to capitalize on its existence. For instance, while most banks get the bulk of their revenues from loans and investments, State Street Boston concentrates on businesses that generate fees.

- Fee income at State Street provides about 60 percent of revenues.
- This is almost twice the 33 percent at most big banks of the Group of Seven nations.
- It is practically at par with what Swiss banks target for their revenues.

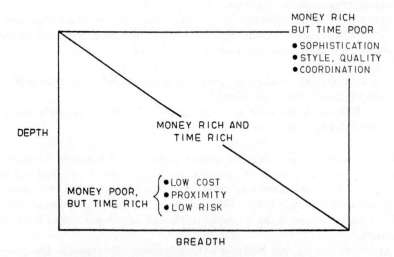

Figure 7.1   Wealth and time constraints in the client base

But there are prerequisites to a strategy on fees. If we charge the customers for our services, we must ensure that what we offer is not only up-to-date but also of the highest quality and very efficient.

Without wanting to downplay interest earnings, emphasis on fee income is not something which characterizes only the big banks. I had in my banking seminars in Vienna senior managers of one of the smaller Austrian agricultural banks. From them I learned that their institution had just 11,000 clients and 72 percent of them featured 100 to 100,000 schillings ($4,800) in deposits. This was a skew distribution, with this lower level of the pyramid representing 82 percent of transaction, but only 6 percent of income. But in a way which surpassed the statistics from big banks, this small Raiffeisenkasse had 80 percent of its income from only 12 percent of its clients. (In a money center bank, as we have seen in Part One, about 20 percent of the clients represent 80 percent of profits.)

It is only to be expected that, when faced with such statistics, banks target fees to make up the missing profits in the P&L. Is there no other alternative? What about innovation? In the early- to mid-1980s the place to be for retail banks would have been credit cards, but because non-bank banks have swept through this domain, banks lost a good chunk of their share. In six years in America the credit card market share controlled by banks has dropped from 95 percent to 75 percent of the total credit card business.

Credit cards used to be innovation in retail banking, but in most Group of Ten countries this market is by now mature. Other classical product lines of the financial intermediary which are shrinking are business financing and revolving credit. 'The credit card market is not mature,' said a banker, indirectly implying that, where the old magnetic stripe plastic money ends, the 'new' smart card is beginning to make itself felt. I will dispute both statements.

- Even though credit card profits continue to grow in North America, Britain and some countries of continental Europe, the credit card is mature.
- As far as the smart card (in its present form) is concerned, it is a non-starter. Any product which languishes for more than 20 years – as the chip-in-card did – is a dead duck.

Over and above this, as we will see in detail in Chapter 16, a major hindrance with electronic money, and smart cards, is security. It would be schizophrenic to criticize Internet banking because it is not secure while promoting smart cards which are even more unstable and untested as a system – no matter what Mondex and other similar projects may say.

Contrary to these as yet untested banking products, asset management is a well-established business in commercial banking, and this is where fee income is going up – at least among those institutions having the appropriate infrastructure. Other product lines which depart from the beaten path can be found at the common frontier of fee income-generating services such as forex, securities and assets management. Below, in a simplified form, is an example of advice given by many portfolio managers in a major commercial bank.

1. *Taxation*, which in all likelihood in the coming years will be high for companies and high net worth individuals.
2. *Inflation*, expected to be relatively low over the next few years but to pick up by the end of the decade.
3. *Interest rate changes*, which will most likely be characterized by significant volatility in some of the main countries and currencies.

The common frontier in fee services also involves the need for focusing on a few key currencies, on a well-balanced portfolio of securities and on a selected number of commodities which interest the client firm. These references help demonstrate, the kind of advice to be given to the client, for which a fee will be asked.

For fee income purposes, the most important requirement today is that a bank concentrate on developing *core competences*. These must be supported by flexible skills and high technology, to allow the production of a stream of distinctive services that cannot be easily imitated by a rival. Outside plain vanilla icecream banking, core competences have no universal definitions. A bank may have 17 or 20 channels for doing business, but only a third of them will be strategic and even fewer will constitute core competences. Because in terms of core competences every bank is on its own, it will be appropriate that its management studies:

• what constitutes a core competence in its particular environment;
• how a core competence should be chosen among alternatives;
• what it takes to achieve a core competence or acquire it;
• how to use a core competence to create a cash flow and profits stream.

Deposits of all sorts, as well as securities and payments, tend to be core competence subjects for commercial banks. But with deregulation commercial banks have branched into other fields which they now consider the core of their business. Sometimes the core subjects do not necessarily correlate, though they do have in common a need for high-grade skills.

• Cultivating such skills means putting effort into recruiting, leading and training star employees.
• The true core competences reside in human capital and in less obvious things such as critical mission statements and goals.

The question of core competences should not be taken lightly. The decisions a retail bank is making today commits management to personnel qualifications, delivery channels and information systems the institution will have in the 21st century.

As Part One advised, to be able to position ourselves against the forces of the coming years we have to understand the evolution in customer needs – and prepare to meet the *future* requirements. This is the personal side of financial relationship, over and above the technological aspects.

Chapter 6 also made the point that a major force in repositioning is the bank's network, and the real-time interactivity which it provides. In the past, banking was restricted to banking hours and the branch office. Today it is 24-hour banking, anywhere for any product. This is promoted by:

- rapidly decreasing costs in the technology, and
- a growing customer acceptance of the benefits flexibility provides.

But while it is necessary to increase steadily the efficiency ratio (see sections 6 to 8) to keep in the race – as low-cost producer and deliverer of banking services – it is just as vital to understand the profitability of customer segments, all the way to the individual customer. We will talk of the customer mirror in section 4.

3   PRODUCT MARKETING AND RELATIONSHIP MANAGEMENT

Some people say that this or that country is overbanked. This may be true of vanilla icecream retail banking, if we examine the number of retail banks, their branch offices and the number of personnel they employ. But it is not necessarily true of investment banking. Top-tier investment advisors are rare birds.

The strategy and the means for handling the customer makes the difference. For long years, customer management services had not changed and the technology was somehow kept out of the roots of the relationship banking system. Now, however, a great deal has changed and we will be well advised to take note of it. Chapter 6 has already introduced the concept that, to a very substantial extent, *marketing* means *relationship management* and vice versa. The broader answer to the query of what is done by a bank which specializes in relationship management is that it helps the clients shape a long-term relationship, as opposed to simply doing some deals. This notion is exemplified in Figure 7.2, which shows both forward action and feedback in a solution for relationship banking which focuses on the longer term. Not all approaches, however, follow longer-term horizons, and this is pity.

Some bankers say: 'Relationship banking is only a branch of marketing,' but then they add, 'Relationship management is the art of managing the relationship with customers, of which marketing is but one part of a complex management matrix.' All this is playing with words. The best way to look at this linguistic controversy is to forget the legalistics and go back to the fundamentals. A fundamental issue in business (as well as in technology) is that nearly every time we think

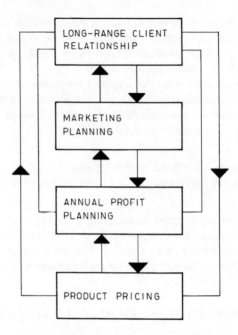

Figure 7.2 Forward action and feedback mechanism for a policy in relationship banking

we have a limit we find a new concept or a new tool that takes us even further. That is the best definition of what relationship banking is.

- Relationship banking helps to overcome short-term pressures by bringing the longer term into perspective.
- While building longer-term relationships is not inconsistent with producing short-term results, both aspects of business are important.

When in Chapter 9 we talk about private banking, which is one of the best examples of relationship management, we will emphasize the fact that the short term is meaningless in building a high net worth clientele. Not only is the longer-term perspective important, but there are as well organizational prerequisites for relationship management. They include:

- the existence of a system able to mirror all business activity products,
- able approaches to cross-sales in the existing customer base,
- customer mirror services to evaluate what a relationship costs and what the bank gains, and
- databases which are accurate and up-to-date by profit center, product and client relationship.

We have spoken of the importance of database mining in Chapter 6. An able execution of database mining operations makes mandatory: speed of access for ad hoc queries; clear and easy understanding of the displayed message; simplicity of manipulation by end users; and ability to obtain as much information as possible from different sources.

But while it is important that the retail bank puts at the disposal of its people the best that technology can offer, it is just as crucial to remember the importance of the well-trained relationship manager, and so do something about it. Relationship bankers must learn a great deal about product selection, packaging, selling and delivering of services in:

- money management,
- financial planning,
- income sheltering,
- tax advising,
- brokerage of securities,
- project financing, and
- different insurance schemes.

Most of these products show up time and again, but their form and their content change. This is the result of market research and product development which, in a dynamic financial industry, is a never-ending process. Figure 7.3 hints at the feedbacks this process involves.

A crucial question is how to deliver a customer-oriented approach at reasonable cost while observing high-quality service policies. The use of high technology can help, but this does not deliver all the necessary price advantages, because the crucial skill on the banker's side may be difficult to find – or too expensive.

The advice which is often given, 'Make your customers feel that you appreciate their loyalty – but also reflect to them *your* readiness to help in recognition of the uniqueness of their situation,' is good, but incomplete. Retail bankers should never forget that a good customer relationship is essentially marketing, and should involve a fair amount of cross-sales.

With any action involving personal account management, there exist essential factors in developing and strengthening banking relationships: the creation of personal contact, the able maintenance of handholding, person-to-person marketing and timely response to personal preferences.

In its way, banking has become quite similar to the consultancy business. The relationship banker is the consultant assigned to a specific project, and the way he acts can make or break the customer contact. Retail bankers will therefore be well advised to learn from consultancies. A consultant's views on products and markets will come under the heading *customers*. The consultant will look at R&D and product description, but also at *competition*. He will examine production facilities and production costs. He will also evaluate marketing skills and distribution services.

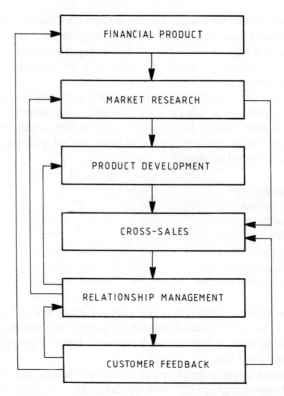

Figure 7.3 Research and development on banking services is a steady, creative process

Another paradigm describing the action of relationship bankers is that of *trust bankers*. In a number of cases, the trust bankers' thinking is that the best approach to customer handling is not to sell specific services but to attract, maintain and augment client confidence.

A further paradigm which can help in strengthening relationship banking comes from product planning and the way it is practiced in the manufacturing industry. Working in close collaboration with marketing, the product planner sees his mission as one of selecting, designing, combining, packaging and tailoring products for *client satisfaction*. In a similar manner, in the financial industry, the relationship banker aims to maintain and extend the collaboration which exists between the bank and its customers. This targets not only new products but also other banking services already existing, but which a customer has not been using in a way which might be profitable both to him and to the bank.

In conclusion, while relationship banking has much to do with the bank's profitability, it does not need to work strictly on short-term profit-oriented goals. Rather, it should take the path of an intensified longer-term trust relationship.

The winners in relationship management are those banks able to understand *their customers* better than others.

4 CUSTOMER MIRROR: THE MEANS FOR EVALUATING ACCOUNT PROFITABILITY

A short time ago I was talking with the executive vice-president, marketing, of a well-known European commercial bank about his bank's priorities for the next 12 months. His answer was: 'Our first priority is ways and means to gauge customer profitability. This is critically important in terms of our ability to retain the high-value customers.' As this and similar references help document, relationship management has underlined the need for a *customer mirror* able to reflect all aspects of a partnership. Classical marketing models focus exclusively on customer acquisition and, then, on customer stratification. By contrast, experts in marketing now accept that

- it costs between four and 10 times as much to acquire a profitable customer as it does to retain one; and
- a narrow segment of the customer base typically accounts for 80 percent or more of a bank's profits – as we saw in Chapter 6.

But without the assistance of a customer mirror and its quantitative indicators, the relationship banker (and therefore the bank) cannot really know to which customers he should pay most attention; which customers really generate a profit to the banker and which tend to create losses; or from what kind of transactions these profits really come.

The need for such awareness has resulted in placing emphasis on the customer mirror. In turn, an accurate customer mirror can become a driving force behind relationship marketing.

- One reason for the need of quantitative indicators is that, in modern retail banking, customer filtering is not that simple.
- We need the customer mirror to tell us, among other things, what kind of discounting our bank is doing, and whether this is justified by the business the customer brings in.

Mapping all aspects of the customer relationships is a 'must' in an industry in product line expansion like banking. The tools we make available to ourselves for customer relationship management must permit business actions in response to, and in anticipation of, actual customer behavior:

- determining the most profitable customers,
- understanding how to retain them, and
- identifying the most vital elements for sustained earnings.

The customer mirror was invented by banks which are sophisticated technology users to identify ways making it possible to bring up the value line. The mechanics are simple, starting with online transactions executed by tellers and with customer information elements in the database:

- cross-referencing accounts and clients,
- managing the total client relationship across all delivery channels, and
- doing a financial tracking of individual P&L based on transactional profiles.

The object is to provide the senior management of the bank, and most evidently the relationship banker, with a single view of the business done with each important customer. This should properly identify:

- products being used by the customer,
- the transactions he is making,
- the cost of each of these transactions,
- the risk involved in each of these transactions,
- the fees the bank charges for each transaction, and
- other profits the bank is making relative to the customer relation.

Both statistics and accounting data are important. The customer mirror is a good example of what in Chapter 6 we called a *customer-based* database system. We also spoke of the transition taking place from accounting-based to customer-based solutions.

Transactions should be recorded as they happen in real time and database mining should be used to reveal *patterns*. Such patterns are instrumental in making the financial organization and its managers increasingly *customer-oriented*. They can also assist in ensuring an integrative approach which brings into perspective:

- client-related risks, and
- the prevailing trend in risk-taking.

Another advantage provided by the customer mirror is that it is essentially leveraging existing information at the bank's point of sales. This both permits better relationship management and increases the sales prospects with every customer contact.

Some of the benefits provided by the customer mirror come from the fact that, as has been explained on plenty of occasions, relatively few relationships account for the big chunk of the retail bank's profits. It is therefore important to:

- learn the most about key profit drivers, and
- find more clients with similar characteristics.

The customer mirror is essentially a means of visualizing client data. It makes feasible monitoring whether critical relationships are getting stronger or weaker. It also provides effective means of targeting profitable customers. What the customer mirror does is to display *periodically* and *ad hoc*:

1. all transactions done with the customer, by channel;
2. the cost of these transactions to the bank;
3. the monetization of the risk the bank has taken with these transactions;
4. the customer collateral, formal and informal;
5. the fees the bank charged for these transactions;
6. other fees pro rata, like portfolio management and safekeeping;
7. the cross-sales in relationship banking;
8. the milestones in the historical customer relationship (strengths and weaknesses); and
9. P&L with this customer profit center.

Many banks have data on their customers that cannot be described as information because they are buried in accounting files rather than being readily accessible, yet only readily accessible information can help the bankers in the front line who:

- meet the customer,
- sell banking services, or
- plan marketing campaigns.

By interactively visualizing customer data we create information which underpins relationship management as well as helping in cross-sales and in effective retention of those customers that are profitable. Figure 7.4 explains the benefits this strategy can provide.

Through the complex relationship of its component parts, the customer mirror assists in selectivity, permits better market planning, enhances sales thrust and introduces a totally new game: the real-time exploitation of customer information. The modern banker must have this information online, interactively at his fingertips.

The first customer mirror application which I helped to develop for a commercial bank was in 1972 for Commerzbank in Germany. A few years later I did improved versions for Banca Provinciale Lombarda, Credito Commerciale and Istituto Bancario Italiano, in Italy. In all these applications in retail banking,

- the customer mirror proved to be a necessary foundation for the able management of customer relations;
- its use provided extensive information about a customer, combined with decision support systems and marketing databases.

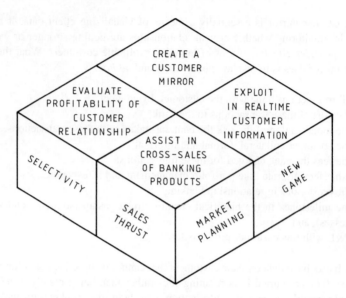

Figure 7.4   A realtime customer mirror can give polyvalent assistance to the banker

In practically all banks which have developed customer mirror applications, the information being provided is perceived to be relevant and to add value to the customer relationship. It has also helped to make delivery channels more flexible, enabling new products to be incorporated and new services to be brought to market quickly.

5 MARKETING SAVVY AND TECHNOLOGY FOR IMPLEMENTING THE CUSTOMER MIRROR

In the financial services industry the focus on customer profitability is driven by real business issues such as the declining effectiveness of traditional marketing, rising customer expectations for sophisticated financial services and an increasingly competitive banking environment. The motor power of competition pushes towards

- customized products,
- relationship management,
- new distribution and communications channels,
- multiple pricing options, which are client-oriented, and
- a customer mirror to learn more about individual P&L.

Each one of these issues and all five together drive banks towards focusing on sharper policies and better ways to conduct business. At the same time that relationship management poses significant challenges to the retail bank in terms of qualified personnel requirements, the customer mirror makes urgent the need for financial metrics and models to help understand customer profitability and customer lifetime value. A sophisticated technology is needed with systems and procedures, including applications able to store and manipulate massive amounts of detailed data which reflect not only transactions, but also interactions during the entire course of the customer relationship.

One of the challenges is integrating the disparate information from multiple operational systems and tying these data to individual customers in order to understand the entire context of the relationship. An even greater challenge is to take the proverbial long, hard look through strategic planning.

- From a strategic perspective, this is a process allocating organizational resources to those activities that have the greatest return and impact on profitable customer relationships.

The careful reader will recall the discussion in Chapter 5 about the management of change and its importance to the survival of the bank. Figure 7.5 presents in a nutshell the sense of that discussion in terms of customer profitability, using this occasion to give a reminder that, before having a customer mirror, we must carefully define products and services, and study the market and the customer and develop models, as well as software for computation.

- From a technological viewpoint, relationship management requires capturing, analyzing and sharing all the facts about the customers' transactions and other activities with the bank.

Strategic and technological perspectives converge in requiring activity-based costing, detailed transaction data on customers, database mining operations, dynamic

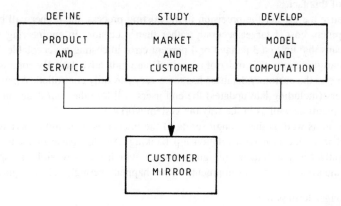

Figure 7.5 For evaluation of customer profitability the customer mirror should be online, fully interactive, with 3-D visualization

algorithms able to reflect actual customer behavior, and real-time point of contact. An effective customer relationship management calls for a significantly different infrastructure than what is available with legacy systems.

As we saw in section 4, the presentation of information must be made more attractive by transmitting multimedia messages through networks and computers whose functions are becoming integrated. Enabling technologies are the new communications vehicles essential to support the rate of information transmission and to mine large amounts of data and extract meaningful information. One of the enablers is the shrinking cost of technology. The prices of both hardware and software continue to fall, making available affordable analytical solutions. This changing world is increasingly supported by the convergence of several formerly distinct management information systems (MIS).

- Sophisticated tools make feasible an increasingly fine customer profile program.
- Interactive database mining procedures see to it that critical information becomes available instantaneously.

A prerequisite to this type of implementation is the thorough revamping of legacy systems. I often hear in my practice: 'How do you build up the customer mirror?' The answer is that a bank has to start with a customer-oriented database, as explained in Chapter 6. The next step is the costing of transactions. Transactions are associated with channels (product lines). To built up the infrastructure, in my practice I start by costing one product line while ensuring flexible interfacing to permit adding on other channels. As each new channel is taken onboard in a costing sense, it is important to provide for consolidation to make feasible a comprehensive view of client relationships, with ad hoc cross-referencing. Attention must evidently be paid to the *quality of the cost database*. Not all retail banks are aware of this fact.[1]

Because the greater the precision in the costing process, the higher will be the development cost, I target accuracy rather than precision. In engineering terms this means that up to a 3 percent or 4 percent error in costing is acceptable. What particularly interests us is order of magnitude and indicative data. By contrast, the error rate in the customer database has to be very carefully controlled. When there are errors (including late updates) the end users will lose the confidence in database contents as well as in the way the system works.

Crucial, as well, is the re-engineering of the interfaces to permit expert system support in connection with relationship banking. Another basic element is the development and sustenance of agile software, which makes feasible transparent use of the system. Such developments do not happen overnight. They require:

- a longer-term policy,
- the establishment of criteria which permit value judgment, and
- value differentiation towards other banks.

I insist on these technical aspects because the able implementation of a customer mirror is not something that can happen in the old EDP way. Mapping the customer relation can only be done through knowledge engineering. Expert systems can be of help

- in visualizing whether critical client relationships are getting stronger or weaker, and
- in detecting changes in behavior through the identification of patterns.

Massaging the contents of the customer database can show whether there is an increase in customer attrition at a particular branch, or negative events happening in connection to a given product. Integrating the customer mirror and market mapping activities can highlight shifts in demand.

Another way of looking at the mirror is in terms of *customer research* which can reveal why people and companies select banks: is it on the basis of physical proximity or other criteria? This is fundamental in revealing whether *our* distribution network measures up to the needs of important customers. The major cultural change is to appreciate that

- the customer is the ultimate profit center, and
- the products and the branches or any other business unit are there to help the customer.

Legacy methodologies for measuring and understanding internal profitability bear little relevance to the practice of the customer mirror, the way it has been described in the preceding paragraphs, in driving for

- client visibility,
- operational efficiency, and
- marketing differentiation.

Every function within the enterprise – finance, treasury, accounting, forex and securities – must take account of customers in its decision-making processes. Traditional product-oriented management is not able to scale up to handle this more complex information environment. The modern retail bank must be measuring activities across multiple product categories and diverse channels, and constantly changing decision points.

6   CAN WE MEASURE THE CONTRIBUTION OF THE BRANCH OFFICE NETWORK?

Section 5 has explained that the customer is the ultimate profit center. But there are other profit centers as well for which we should be accounting. An important one is the *branch office* (BO) network, which has been traditionally taken as synonymous with retail banking. There are two classical ways for banks to offer services:

1. operate from one central location, or
2. establish a network of branches.

Nederlandse Credietbank, BHF Bank and Bankers Trust are examples of financial institutions which formerly had middle-sized BO networks, but have phased them out. Other commercial banks have engaged in a very significant downsizing of the number of their branches. In the mid-to-late 1980s, this took place on a grand scale in America; today it is happening in Europe. A good example is Crédit Suisse.

Over the last few years, research focusing on the service industry at large has been pointing out that the most profitable service industries, hotels and banking, have branch networks, which are either *very small* or *very large*. It is not so much a matter of a general notion of economies (or diseconomies) of scale, as of the overheads required for

- *brand marketing* approaches and name recognition,
- *creative offering* of new customer-tailored products, and
- *increasing competitiveness* by swamping costs which tend to rise rapidly in a service industry.

In earlier times, the management of branch office network was a relatively easy operation, but competition and market demand have changed this aspect. To survive, each profit center must be able to turn itself into a marketing powerhouse, evaluating its exposure in real time, to offer client consulting services and to be able to do simulation and experimentation – all beyond what an old-concept BO stood for. Among first-rank retail banks the visible part of the new branch divides into:

- *sales activities* oriented towards the current client base and new prospects;
- *client consulting* for investments, loans and ancillary services;
- *transaction-type* operations, classified into higher risk (forex, securities, derivatives) and more traditional;
- *client self-service* supporting 24-hour banking through electronics; and
- *back office* work which should become highly automated, reducing the human costs.

Retail bankers advance a number of reasons for the ongoing rationalization in branch office operations. The most important can be described in three

words: *risks, costs* and *competition.* These are the three generic references, but
there are as well others varying by market and by bank.

Competition, for instance, pushes the idea of a *data center* at the branch office
for business clients. This is equipped with PCs and telecommunications, permitting all types of data services, including access to databases and messaging. Also
supported through networked PCs are *electronic tellers* which offer marketing
support, such as

- list and description of products and services,
- assistance in marketing different products, and
- the possibility to execute transactions beyond classical self-service banking.

Those banks which are more advanced technologically put at the disposal of their
clients means for financial simulation, regarding loans, cash flows, analysis of
annual reports and investment analysis. This, however, does not need to be provided at the BO. It can also be exercised from the client's premises with the retail
bank providing the software – as does the Crestar Bank in the United States.

All these competitive weapons are a far cry from what the client used to get at
branch level. But it is no less true that today, in America, Europe and Japan, many
companies as well as investors are far more knowledgeable about technology and
even financially more sophisticated than the banks they deal with – and banks are
trying to catch up.

In terms of supporting its own operations through technology, the new branch
office needs a range of services, a number of which are outlined in Table 7.1.
Real-time support based on networked personal computers is intended to serve
both the front desk and the back office. Online work at the back office includes

Table 7.1   The new branch office

Client-oriented services:
  Online teller/cashier
  Electronic teller, ATM, self-service
  Marketing, cross-sales
  Investment consulting
  Corporate banking/home banking
  Integrated customer services

Support for front desk and back office based on networked personal computers:
  Management decision making
  Corporate memory facility
  Interactive client mirror
  Electronic mail, faster communicating
  Time management (calendaring), personnel scheduling
  Greater clerical productivity
  Local, specialized applications

---

general accounting; payments of all sorts (bills, and so on); orders of payment (giro); certified checks (bankers' checks); check handling; letters of credit; commercial and financial paper; squaring out cashier operations; registration of transactions; processing of standing instructions; and generally the administration of customer orders as well as of internal activities. Very significant, in a functional sense, are

- *market planning and sales*, with control of obtained results through the fulfillment of quotas;
- *management planning and control*, from budgeting to costs, service proper and quality of service;
- *risk management* to ensure that both government regulations and the bank's own rules regarding exposure are rigorously observed.

Figure 7.6 presents an integrative view of functions typically executed at branch office level and supported through information technology. These include managerial activities, cross-sales functions, the online execution of client-oriented banking services, relationship banking and control entities to ensure compliance.

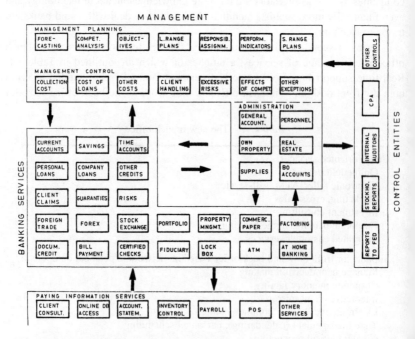

Figure 7.6 Every box in the figure must be supported through software, which by becoming increasingly sophisticated offers the bank a competitive advantage

The ability to use *agents*[2] for tracking transactions pertaining to each one of the boxes in this block diagram will go a long way to answering questions often posed by top management and marketing management in regard to the cost-effectiveness of the branch office network (and of each of the branches).

- Where should client handling services be enhanced, or downsized?
- Which product(s) are particularly appropriate at each BO? How much innovation do the clients demand?
- Where should *our* distribution capability be strengthened?
- Which customer relationships underpin current profitability? How well are they managed?
- Is there client attrition in the branches? In which branch does it hurt?

Other questions to be explored through database mining by BO and at the level of the whole branch network include the following: How to maximize the potential of each branch and of the system? Are current tools enough for relationship banking? Are they adequate for the evaluation of profitability? Which new tools and methods are needed?

In the background of these queries is the ultimate concern whether the retail bank's distribution capability is fitting well with the characteristics of the customer base. Or, are banking services being offered because of historical reasons which are no longer valid – with the result that the bank is losing contact with its market?

7 BRANCH OFFICE MANAGEMENT AND THE NECESSARY RE-ENGINEERING EFFORT

As public and private financial networks spread and the number of services which they support increases, there is not much of a compelling business reason for customers to come into the branch any more. They can conduct their banking online. This is the concept underpinning the use of networks for 24-hour electronic banking. Yet there is still room for person-to-person finance. The reason underpinning person-to-person relationship banking is that, as old services get automated, we should be keen to develop new ones which require expert assistance.

John B. McCoy, the CEO of Bank One, was among the first bankers in America to radically revamp the branch. The first trial with the new approach came to life in the late 1980s. It was a branch in Sawhill, Ohio, that featured blue neon signs and a huge skylight. Tellers stood way in the rear, like cashiers in a retail store, and customers were enticed by various loans and investments departments on their way to the teller and back.

In two years, this Sawhill branch office grew to hold $35 million in deposits. McCoy has since opened other similar branches. The idea that tellers should be located at the back of the branch office rather than in the front was first suggested to Bank of America, in the early 1980s, by a consultant the bank hired from the merchandizing industry. The Bank of America consultant was a former executive vice president, marketing of Safeway, the supermarket chain. His suggestion was that money being the commodity most wanted by BO clients, it should be handled the way Safeway handles milk.

- The refrigerators with milk and butter are located at the back of the shop, not at the front.
- To reach them, mamas must walk all the way through alleys full of goodies, so that themselves and their kids fill the cart.

Radically restructuring the branch office is no easy decision, and it should be made with strategic objectives in mind. Before the bank decides on re-engineering, it should study what branch design and merchandizing techniques are being used by competitors, and learn how to turn its branches into an effective and profitable *sales environment*.

It is wise to analyze carefully and discover how to engineer a successful bank branch for the 21st century. This means finding out how to create a bank branch to serve the evolving customers' needs, understanding the new concepts underpinning in-store banking, and providing instant services.

Part of the re-engineering job regarding the branch should be flexible work hours, permitting customers to see their investment advisor, loan officer and other staff, at a time convenient to *them*, rather than to the bank. Another vital part of re-engineering is to study how the branch manager spends his time. Is he devoting

- one third to direct customer handling,
- one third to marketing operations, and
- one third to management work and leading?

Or is he swamped by paperwork so that he cannot attend to his more important relationship banking functions. If the branch does not give the example on relationship management, the way to bet is that this job will be done by subordinates without inspiration and leadership. The principles we have seen in sections 3 and 4 will be violated all the way.

Figure 7.7 presents in a nutshell some of the critical decisions to be made by the BO manager in leading his clients and his people. While planning and control of the customer base is strategic, and should be done by top management, many local decisions are tactical:

- the branch manager should have the freedom to reach them, and
- he should be controlled at the end of the year on profit and loss.

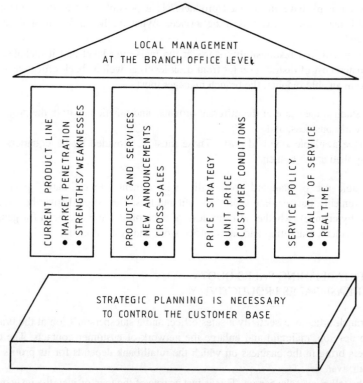

Figure 7.7 Decisions to be made by the management of the branch office

A good way of re-engineering the branch office is to give to its sales efforts a *market orientation* by industry: hotels, restaurants, entertainment, auto merchants and their clients, pharmaceuticals, electronic shops, hospitals, city government. Before the choice is made, we should calculate the potential of each sector for *our* business.

A critical question in deciding on market orientation is to define whether the target is the mass market or a niche market, as discussed in Chapter 6. The next question is the potential for *market penetration*, and with it the identification of the means to gain control of the chosen segment.

- Can we attack the chosen market in an able manner?
- What are our strengths and weaknesses?
- Can we base our strategy on our strengths?
- How fast can we build up our potential, particularly the human resources?

Some of the tactical decisions the branch manager should be concerned with is the *share of the market* he is after. What is the goal in terms of market penetration?

Does the bank have the needed products? Is it possible to provide continuity? What is the cost-effectiveness of the services? What are the marketing skills at the branch?

Profit and loss responsibility starts at the marketing level and it includes the estimated cost of distribution (at front desk level) as well as back office costs. To do so in an able manner, the branch manager must

- establish the share of the different products and functions within the projected yearly business, and
- have available standard costs. These must be provided by headquarters and applied at the branch.[3]

The able use of standard costs will be instrumental in estimating personnel requirements, but also in evaluating profit and loss. They should cover both direct labor by channel (whether at front desk or back office) and overhead for general management, marketing and sales, office work and systems cost.

8   ESTABLISHING SALES QUOTAS TO INCREASE SALES PRODUCTIVITY

A branch office is essentially a sales office, and a salesperson's job at the branch is to develop, maintain and enlarge the network of customer contacts. The customers bring in the business on which the retail bank depends for its profits and its survival.

The teller is a salesperson. This is just as true of the loan officer, the investment advisor, other professionals employed at the branch and the BO manager himself (see also section 7). Sales office productivity depends on all major functions performed by management and the salesmen who are responsible for:

- relationship banking,
- investment advice,
- investment transactions,
- current account transactions,
- currency exchange operations, and
- derivatives trades, and so on.

Winston Churchill once said that, in order to move, the human donkey must see a carrot in front and feel a stick at the back. Applying this dictum to banking, the retail bank will be well advised to use incentives as the carrot and a quota system as the stick.

- *Quotas* are quantitatively expressed commercial objectives applicable down to the level of the single salesperson.

- *Market forces* indicate how to structure a quota system; the other parameter is product availability.

Quotas in banking should be given a triple role: to promote individual initiative at the front desk, to help in better relationship management through financial incentives, and to provide a means of gauging sales results. Quantitative sales objectives should be established yearly for salesmen, traders and account managers. They should reflect number of new clients, wealth brought in by new accounts and through cross-selling fees provided to the bank, and other business opportunities. Every one of these issues has already been discussed to a certain extent in Chapter 6 and in the present chapter.

The setting of sales goals is best done at sales meetings held at the branch and by speciality departments. Sales quotas are that much more effective when the salesmen themselves are brought into the picture. Typically, sales meetings fine-tune guidelines given by product managers and product planners (brand managers), reflecting the bank's strategic decisions.

Let me repeat. Front desk operators, account managers and other relationship banking representatives should be an integral part of the quota-setting system. This procedure is more effective (and better documented) when based on analysis and modeling taking into account

- economic and financial forecasting,
- competitive intelligence,
- business opportunity analyses, and
- strengths and weaknesses evaluations.

What sort of guidelines should be followed in establishing quotas? In the course of a project centering on this subject, the team of which I was a member came to the conclusion that five basic considerations should be taken into account in elaborating individual sales quotas.

1. The nature and extent of the sales effort and of available supporting functions.
2. The penetration of the bank into a certain market and the fertility of that market.
3. The product mix of banking services the salesperson will be required to market.
4. The orientation of the sales effort, particularly in what concerns cross-sales and industry marketing.
5. The quality history of a salesperson, including his or her business experience and personal characteristics.

In banking, in manufacturing, in merchandizing, even in the law enforcement industry, experience with quotas shows that the productivity of the individual worker depends – in a very significant manner – on the person himself. This is particularly true when quotas are sweetened by incentives. Table 7.2 summarizes the factors on which sales productivity depends at management level, in communicating information to clients and in sales.

A good deal can be learned by studying how manufacturing companies have handled the challenges posed by quotas, given that they have had in this domain much more experience than banks. Originally, IBM calculated the salesman commission on the basis of the *point system*. In the mid-1950s, when computer marketing started and data processors were rented,

- for new accounts the salesman got a commission equal to one point per dollar of monthly rental;
- for cross-selling to existing accounts the commission was only half as high.

When rented equipment was being taken back, its rental value was flatly subtracted from the rental value of the newly installed equipment, and commissions were only paid on the difference. But quotas and commissions became more complex as

- the products multiplied,
- the unit price dropped,
- the market expanded, and
- sales territories varied substantially as to their potential.

In a quota system, *market potential* is based not only on market size but also on how rich it is, the nature of competition, the force of competitors and the availability of products to fill the existing and developing customer needs. All these factors are important.

- As the market changes, quota systems must be reset.
- The algorithm must be shaped so as to propel *sales productivity*.

Table 7.2   Factors on which sales productivity depends

In management	*In communicating with clients*	*In sales*
Forecasting	Contacting the client	Product characteristics
Planning	Taking orders	Market segmentation
Organizing	Answering order status queries	Market penetration
Directing	Giving valid responses	Customer profiling
Controlling	But also pricing:	Account Planning
	product information	Profiling each
	transactions, and	relationship
	other bank services	Resource scheduling

In many companies, IBM being an example, the sales engineer tends to have half of his salary fixed and the other half on commissions gained by reaching and exceeding the quota. In the case of equipment sales, for instance, half the commission is received on signing the contract, the other half after the customer accepts in writing the new installation.

Sales productivity can be immensely improved through commissions and quotas. Yearly established quantitative goals are, as well, an excellent means of gauging what a salesman contributes to the firm. It is improper to pay equal salaries for unequal effort.

Table 7.3 gives a real-life example from the computer industry – a sales office with 10 salespersons. This is a German business equipment company which was not very well managed (since then it has gone bankrupt). Therefore there were no quotas and no clear sales guidelines. Each salesman had to handle the whole line of products, but was free to choose the product that he could push best. From top to bottom, the productivity among salespeople varies widely – as it can be attested both in dollar terms and in number of units.

This sort of silly business also happens in retail banking. In every branch office there are people who are working hard, and others who are loafing. A well-tuned

Table 7.3 Sales statistics by salesman in information technology (DM amount converted into dollars)

Salesman	Dollars	In units	Price
'A'	1,800,000	38	47,300
'B'	504,000	63	8,000
'C'	248,000	12	20,700
'D'	847,000	93	9,100
'E'	24,000	8	3,000
'F'	300,000	27	11,100
'G'	97,000	6	16,200
'H'	255,000	20	12,750
'I'	687,000	35	19,650
'J'	258,000	19	13,570
	5,020,000	321	

Averages
Price per unit — 16,137
Units per salesman — 32
Dollars per salesman, per year — 502,000
Ranges
Price per unit — 3,000 – 47,368
Units per salesman — 6 – 93
Dollars per salesman, per year — 24,000 – 1,800,000

quota system helps to weed out the unable, the unwilling and the unnecessary. It is immoral to pay people equally for grossly unequal work.

9   WHEN BANKS JOIN FORCES WITH SUPERMARKETS: THE TESCO–NATWEST EXPERIENCE

One way to increase sales productivity in retail banking is to spin off operations relating to small loans and deposits – that is activities oriented to the lower part of the customer pyramid. This business can best be conducted by means of a specialized subsidiary with very low overheads, which can still make profits when dealing with very thin margins. The Union Bank of Switzerland did so with Afina.

Another way, which can be seen as complementary rather than as an alternative, is to join forces with people who know best how to deal with polyvalent retail operations. Non-banks, like department stores and supermarkets, capitalize precisely on this knowhow. Both may be a good partner for banks. NatWest joined forces with Tesco – the good retailer.

To my knowledge, the first partnership between a bank and supermarkets took place in New England in the late 1970s, with Money One. This was a network of check verification devices operating online to the bank's databases. It involved a number of supermarkets, department stores, other merchants and some 100 local banks. The First National Bank of Boston was tête-de-fil.

Check verification devices were installed prior to the cashier's position and, as the name implies, permitted the customer to certify the amount on his check – which was in real time withheld from his account. He could then not only pay for the merchandise with the check but also receive cash, using the cashier of the supermarket as a bank teller. The bank guaranteed to the supermarket the amount of the verified check.

By the end of the 1970s, another experience in retail bank–supermarket collaboration took place in New Jersey. It involved the opening of a small kiosk in the floor of the supermarket manned (full-time or part-time) by a banker who could open customer accounts, sell other services and answer queries. This application was localized. It did not spread far.

In my book, joint ventures in retail banking make sense. When we go through a supermarket or department store we see thousands of items the store's company does not make. To people accustomed to challenge the obvious, this poses questions:

- Why should we not add money to the items on sale?
- Why should we sell our bank's products only in a branch office?

The banking and merchandising worlds are moving so fast that we have to leverage the skills: both those of ourselves and those of others. We cannot do everything by ourselves. Hence the cooperation between NatWest and Tesco makes sense. It is an experiment to be watched carefully for its results – but it may also have pitfalls.

A British banker suggested that one of the pitfalls is the superiority complex of successful supermarkets. For instance, this reviewer said: 'Tesco thinks its customer relationship is better than NatWest's (or the banks' generally). Hence it intends to harness the customer contact, leaving banks to provide the processing'.

- The underlying suggestion is that this hardly makes a promising basis for a joint venture for a bank.
- A joint effort is tacitly accepting that the bank cannot build customer relationships as effectively as a supermarket does.

These are not my concepts but those of the reviewer. The same banker also brings attention to the fact that selling financial products elsewhere than through branches is not a new idea, but it begs the key question of whether banks are retailers or manufacturers. 'Joining forces with UK supermarkets,' says this expert, 'is like going into the lion's den – after all, they are very good retailers.'

From this comes the hypothesis that joining supermakets may be the first step a bank takes towards a concentration on manufacturing. To my mind, this may be all right if it is done as a conscious decision. But it can become truly dangerous otherwise – that is, if the market decides for the bank. The market is a tough judge:

- Tesco can brand financial products in a way that NatWest and other commercial banks cannot do.
- The food retailer was anyway moving into banking, having confirmed that it will turn its loyalty card into a payment card (*Retail Banking International*, Issue 350, 5 June 1996).

Tesco is an aggressive supermarket in the UK, which in five years it has moved from fifth to first position measured in terms of purchasing trips to their store. Its most recent thrust started with a loyalty scheme, turned into a bank account and followed this with rewards such as paying higher interest rates than are available in a bank's current account. From June 1996, customers have been able to pay a standing order into their Tesco Clubcard Plus account which is managed by and cobranded with NatWest. They can use their balance to pay for grocery shopping, as well as utilities such as gas bills, at Tesco stores.

- Money held on deposit on Clubcard Plus will attract an interest rate of 5 percent.
- Customers will be able to get cash back at tills or at any of NatWest's 2,500 ATMs throughout the UK.

NatWest is being paid a fee to operate the accounts, process cards transactions and manage the credit risk. It also gains a brand name, as its logo appears on the card. Interest rate risk is taken by Tesco. Credit is available on application, at 9 percent per year up to the level of the customer's monthly standing order.

- This presents a reasonable improvement in financial services at retail outlets over Money One.
- A further contribution by British Telecom may lead to Interactive TV in personal finance.

'This is no more than a glorified videotex,' said one of the cognizant people I was talking to in London. Personally, I do not think much of set-top boxes and other trivialities, but as long as other people are ready to spend money on new experiments even those not expected to provide great results are worth consideration. We should always learn from other people's mistakes.

Notes

1. See D.N. Chorafas and H. Steinmann, *Do IT or Die* (London and Dublin: Lafferty, 1992).
2. D.N. Chorafas, *Agent Technology Handbook* (New York: McGraw-Hill, 1997).
3. See D.N. Chorafas, *Bank Profitability* (London: Butterworth, 1989).

8 A Popular Marketing Policy: Direct Banking

1 INTRODUCTION

The drive towards direct banking has many origins, one of them the growing sophistication of customers who are not seeking service gimmicks but better value for their money as well as ways and means to save time. Relationship banking means more competition among banks who need to be conscious of their reputation for:

- openness,
- responsiveness, and
- fairness.

Not surprisingly, banks want to differentiate themselves and their services from those of competitors by providing better ways of delivering financial services than vanilla icecream banking. Next to this *strategic* perspective, a salient issue in direct banking is to *contain* costs (as we will see in Part Three). A similar principle applies, incidentally, with discount brokerage, because fees are much lower than in traditional banking since no investment advice is provided.

The concept of direct banking is not new, but it is only rather recently that it has become popular. Since the late 1970s, the Japanese have offered a service called ANSER. It is a voice response system operated by Nippon Telegraph and Telephone in collaboration with the city banks. For the price of 10 yen (5 pennies, or 8 cents) the consumer can ask for the balance of his account and last deposit. In France, the Banque Régional d'Escomptes et Dépôts (BRED) has operated a voice response system also since the late 1970s, and in America several retail banks have done the same. While 20 years ago technology did not permit doing fancy things, the concept was there and the solution was available to those clients who liked to work online.

On the technical side, direct banking is done today through a number of devices. The simplest is the plain old telephone through a touch-tone set. A more modern approach is the smart phone consisting of a screen and a processor – essentially a network appliance. In the early 1980s, videotex was used (not that successfully) for direct banking. A French version is the Minitel. Since the late 1980s, direct banking has also been done by fax, though some banks have a policy not to accept customer orders by fax for security reasons. A more flexible approach is using the personal computer with appropriate software, whether for office banking or for home banking, for current accounts or for investments.

Some banks have installed and operate multimedia kiosks, which they also classify as direct banking (which is not quite correct). Others consider the electronic teller as a direct banking instrument and practically everybody looks on the Internet as the ultimate solution.

2 THE BUSINESS OPPORTUNITY ASSOCIATED WITH DIRECT BANKING

Some people say that direct banking can be done through a telephone, TV, PC or the Internet, and they add: 'The choice is not that important.' I disagree with this statement. The choice *is* important because it conditions how the bank handles its customers and their banking needs.

Twenty years ago I had in one of my seminars the newly elected president of a small American bank who introduced telephone banking, as the direct banking process was then called. He did that in order to attract young urban professionals as new customers, having found out that the average age of his existing clientele was over 60 and this population was being steadily depleted. The strategy worked out well. This retail bank nearly doubled the number of its customers and tripled its deposits. But bare-bone telephone banking will be of practically no appeal today. We no longer live in the late 1970s.

- Young urban professionals are very demanding.
- They will go for nothing less than Intuit software.

I can also appreciate the argument advanced by some banks that the reason they are interested in direct banking is that it provides a way to avoid the huge costs associated with acquiring new customers. It does not really make sense to advertise indiscriminately. But I would add that the same argument about costs is true when a bank overrelies on the direct banking strategy.

The successful case studies we will see in this chapter are not random but carefully chosen. For each of these positive references there is more than one failure. Failures happen when the necessary preparatory work has been skipped over. What should precede a direct banking decision is a basic study able to establish

- where exactly the customers are,
- what precisely they want,
- what is the most likely market potential, and
- what is the most probable return on investment.

When a retail bank makes plans for direct banking, its management should never forget that the services to be offered to customers are limited by the constraints of the solution to be used as well as by *security* considerations. For instance, lack of visual display on the classical telephone limits the type of transactions possible. At the same time, no solutions so far have been able to demonstrate truly rigorous security – in spite of claims and counterclaims. (See also Chapter 16.)

Because direct banking is considered to be the 'in' thing, many banks go for it on the basis of vague beliefs that 'it will be for the best'; or that 'the potential market for direct banking' is bound to be millions of people, mostly among the young and technologically-minded; or that 'a good security solution will eventually be found'. This euphoria prevails even if the entry costs are relatively high, or the technology being chosen is unexciting. For instance, in Germany, Comdirect, which began operating in February 1995, provides personal service between 8am and 10pm, with standard queries answered by recorded voice. This is so a banal as to be unworthy of spending time reviewing it.

Twenty years ago, or even ten years ago, offering instant access interest-bearing deposits would have been a novel service, particularly through value differentiation: for instance offering low-cost brokerage, sales of mutual funds and loans. Today sophisticated customers demand much more. With 'more' comes up the question of costs. Some financial institutions have chosen to discount their services. Others do not. Rather than going down the discount banking road, they have adopted a strategy which permits customers to choose between

- higher-quality services where advice is included – but also fees – and
- cheaper telephone-based services needing no counseling.

Some banks which offer direct banking services have chosen to look into core accounts first and see where cross-selling and new business can be generated, and also what might be gained in terms of relationship banking by making the client's bank account a seven days a week, 24-hours a day *electronic address*,

- automatically linking account to account so that they become system-centered, and
- seeing to it that the handling of transactions becomes transparent to the user.

Return on investment is an issue which should be quite definitely associated with these and other direct banking solutions. Costs will be significant. Are expected benefits over a two-to-three-year timeframe covering expenses and producing profits? Cost-minded banks look at the P&L at different levels of transaction expectancy.

- Will fees and cost savings be able to cover new costs?
- Will new business justify a big chunk of the investment?

Let me repeat where the fees and the cost savings may be coming from. To attract technology-minded customers, some banks promote access by telephone, fax and personal computer on a full range of current, savings and investment accounts along with discount brokerage and credit services. But only a very few retail banks look in a rigorous way at direct banking in conjunction with their branch network (see Chapter 7) and at their transaction streams:

- Can *we* restructure products to increase transaction levels and amortize direct banking costs?
- Can we convince customers to switch to electronic channels to generate savings from economies of mass and from reducing the labor content of transactions?

As for the prospects of eliminating branch offices because of direct banking, projections made by many banks may be rosy, but actual results do not look so good. The pie chart on the left side of Figure 8.1 comes from research done in Germany. The message it conveys is that the large majority of customers would rather stick to the branch office. Even among those who said they like the novelty, only 5 percent would go only for direct banking. The other 10 percent also wants the branch office.

The reader will notice that this response is not uniform. The right side of Figure 8.1 shows results from a US survey: 55 percent of small businesses prefer to deal by PC and phone rather than through the branch. The other 45 percent was fragmented between those who were neutral, those who thought that the delivery medium was not that important and those who did not have a clear opinion.

- These American statistics are not that bad for direct banking, but they are not particularly good either.
- Other things equal, it seems to be that small businesses want direct banking much more than the consumers.

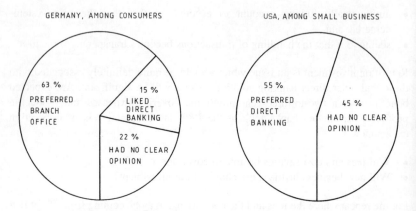

Figure 8.1 Response to the attraction of direct banking from studies done in Germany and the United States

The real problem is not that the customers, particularly the consumers, are not interested at all in direct banking, but rather that most retail banks offering this service do not know exactly what they sell – what they are after. It is always very important to map the battlefield, choose the proper strategy, concentrate, refine and be patient. Or to keep out of direct banking altogether.

3 CAREFUL SELECTION OF DIRECT BANKING GOALS AND SUPPORTING PROCESSES

Even if direct banking is today a popular marketing policy, it does not mean that a bank should go overboard in adopting it. After learning what direct banking is and is not, top management should ask itself: What are my alternatives? For whom will I be developing the new service? What can *we* really expect in terms of P&L, in cash flow, in new clients, in cross-sales?

Factual and documented answers are necessary because no two banks so far have had the same experience with direct banking. The market is in the pocket of no retail bank, no matter what its management may be thinking about this issue. Different retail banks have tackled the establishment of electronic banking in different ways.

- Some opted to emphasize direct bank services to their existing client base, hoping to cut costs and increase cross-sales.
- Other retail banks, as well as several non-banks, chose to target market share and a new client base, rather than selling to their own customers.

Both strategies have much to do with *home banking*, a field which so far has had many more failures than success stories.[1] Starting in 1979 with videotex, home banking targeted the consumer population via TV and simple keyboards, as a reincarnation of distance banking done via the phone. In these early experiences, home banking offered the attraction of operating from the customer's living room by means of visualization, but the consumers did not quite bite.

- In the US, the UK and continental Europe, consumers proved difficult to move and banks learned that they had to be patient.
- Banks and non-banks which went into home banking for a fast buck got out of it in tears, licking their wounds, which amounted to millions of dollars.

In the US, the list of wounded retail banks includes First National Bank of Minneapolis, Bank of America, Chemical Banking (with Pronto) and many others. Among non-banks are the AT&T/Knight Ridder Enterprises joint venture. In the UK there is among others, the Nottingham Building Society. Only in France has a retail bank hung on to its home banking offer on Minitel and made some minor profits.

It has taken nearly 20 years for consumer behavior to start changing and even now this is not sure. It has also taken some painful lessons for the banks' marketing organization to appreciate that home banking (and today's direct banking) require enlarging the time horizon. Patience is crucial in offering a hope of success, but also:

- there is no substitute for good management;
- there is no escape from an interactive verification of results along the lines which Figure 8.2 suggests.

How long the time horizon should be is dramatized by *First Direct*, a Midland Bank subsidiary, which a couple of years ago boasted a new customer rate of 10,000 every month. First Direct started as a standalone telephone account service, in 1989. By 1994, when it began to take off, other high street banks and building societies were already offering similar telephone access.

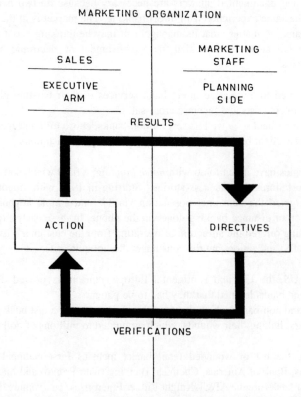

Figure 8.2 To function properly, a marketing organization must steadily verify obtained results versus those planned, in the light of standing directives

- The generation of a mass effect is one of the important issues among direct banking goals.
- While the entry by several retail banks (and non-banks) into direct banking increases the competition, it also has salutory effects.

Competition creates a market. The British Bankers Association suggests that, after the market took off, telephone banking grew by nearly 60 percent in the 1995–6 timeframe, to three million accounts. By the end of the century, high street banks predict that one in three accounts will be telephone-based.

These statistics, however, do not tell a great deal about competitiveness and the sophistication of the service, although sophistication is necessary both to attract professionals and to sell ancillary products. Recent research in the UK is suggesting that one in every two people would now be willing to buy life assurance, pensions and other products over the telephone.

- Consumers are starting to be attracted by products and services accessible online, or at least so it seems.
- They are also responding to the fact that increased competition is now providing better value for money.

Slowly, direct delivery of banking services is emerging as a bank's effective response to its customers' changing lifestyles. For their part, banks today are more sensitive to the fact that – as we saw in Chapter 6 – a few people, particularly higher-income customers, account for the bulk of retail banking profits.

- Typically, upscale customers have neither the time nor the inclination to queue for service when they visit a branch office.
- Direct delivery provides them with the possibility of banking whenever they want from wherever they are.

As we saw in section 2, automated voice-response units which have been utilized for 20 years, can handle routine queries and transactions for a fraction of the cost of operator-assisted telephone banking. But are there possibilities for cross-selling with low-tech telephones? What improvements can be expected, for instance, with the screen phone?

There are a lot of queries in connection with new forms of retail banking, waiting for factual answers. In principle, what can keep direct banking as an ongoing commercial proposition is the steady increase in the sophistication of services without a corresponding increase in costs. But are cost savings in personnel wiped out by the higher costs in technology? These questions must be answered in an able manner for direct banking to continue providing a convenient and cost-effective way of dealing with a multiplicity and diversity of customers' transactions. As we will see in Chapter 11, the future of any product is in its evolution. Can direct banking be transformed into a selling tool?

It is too early yet to provide a definite answer. Much will depend on what strategies are adopted by the direct banking leaders – and on the aftermaths. How far are direct banking experiences rewarding in financial terms? To what extent are they providing a better level of service? Are they able to attract higher net worth individuals? Equally important are the answers to negative questions:

- What are the drawbacks of direct banking?
- What pitfalls have the innovators encountered?
- How successfully have they tackled the problems which came their way?

Enthusiasm is good, but not enough to carry the day. The fact that very few banks in the direct banking business know their costs and have precise goals is, to my mind, a big negative. All banks want to be profitable, but few take care in doing so.

For better or worse, there are no universal answers to the queries this section has posed, even if the general opinion is that direct banking seems to be generally attractive to the market, and may become even more so over the next years. Therefore the case studies which we will see in this chapter should be seen as references, not as proofs. Those banks who take nothing for granted and do their homework in a meticulous way will probably be the winners. The others will contribute the red ink.

4   PROVIDING DIRECT ACCESS FOR BANKING SERVICES AND FOR INSURANCE

Section 3 made reference to First Direct, of Midland Bank. This is one of the better known stories and therefore an often quoted example of success in direct banking. As the experience progresses, Midland appears to be on target to achieve one million direct banking customers by the year 2000. The 500,000 customers which it has already attracted represent about 1.5 percent of the British banking market. So far, so good.

But what does this *really* mean in terms of banking through bricks and mortar branches? A successful branch office handles about 3,000 new customers a week. Midland is evidently aware of this. Its management considers that the expansion of direct banking is equivalent to opening four or five new branches each month. I consider this an overstatement. Another statistic caught my eye, however. Midland seems satisfied with its direct banking efforts because, management says, *over 80 percent* of applicants are not the bank's own customers. Other British banks which do not offer the service are paying the price in terms of client base attrition.

Midland also counts the costs as being rather reasonable. In terms of real estate, all that is required for First Direct is to take up a few extra square feet of office space at its relatively low-cost Leeds complex – or so it is stated. But other financial institutions have a dilemma.

- Direct banking has a high entry price.
- It requires considerable marketing skill.
- It costs a lot to run at the technological end of the service.

Yet, because direct banking has become a catchword, costs and relative lack of skill do not discourage new entries. Even not so sophisticated banks join the telephone banking bandwagon, and they do so by offering goodies. In June 1996 in the UK, the Co-operative Bank decided to give away 100,000 mobile telephones. Selected customers were offered an Orbital 905 mobile phone enabling them to bring up their account balance or a mini-statement on the phone's display screen.

The strategy which was chosen by the Co-operative Bank and some others is that followed by Gillette. It calls for giving away the razor but charging for the blades. In the case of direct banking, there is no charge for the mobile phones, but customers would have to pay:

- an initial connection fee,
- monthly line charges, and
- individual call costs.

For a personal user, the initial fee is £30 ($45), line rental is £17 ($26) a month and calls are charged at 30p (45 cents) a minute at peak rate, 10p off-peak. A business user will be charged a £30 initial fee, and a rental fee of £27.50 ($42) a month. Calls will cost 20p a minute during peak times and 10p a minute off-peak.

- A couple of years down the line we will see if people are ready to pay that silly money, or whether the product went under.
- My best estimate is that the second option is more likely than the first, but I may as well be wrong.

This and similar initiatives in costly services rest on the hypothesis that busy people prefer buying direct from the bank's database than having to visit bank branches. Theoretically, clients who shop by telephone can compare prices faster than by walking around a shopping center. Practically, with closed systems like the one offered by the Co-operative Bank, shopping around is not feasible.

Another closed system in the United Kingdom is offered by Abbey National Bank. It has operated as a national 24-hour telephone banking service since May 1995 and seems to get a fair response. Still another is *DirectLine*, the Royal Bank of Scotland subsidiary. This system saw its 1996 half-year pre-tax profit fall to £5 million ($7.6 million) from £45 million, as a result of competition. The shortfall came in spite of the fact it increased market share.

DirectLine value-differentiates itself from other examples by the fact that it has entered into the bank's ancillary services by targeting *insurance* – both motor policies and household policies. In the first half-year of 1996 it had

- 2.2 million motor policies, up from 2.1 million in the same period in 1995, and
- 773,000 household policies as against 633,000 in 1995.

In the UK there are several competitors in the online insurance sales business. *Virgin Direct*, for instance, is offering life insurance and health cover. Virgin charges no commission, no investment element or cash-in value, and the monthly premium is guaranteed for the duration of the policy. We will talk more of Virgin's direct access products in section 7, when equity investments are discussed.

While there is nothing wrong with selling insurance online, and indeed this may be a profitable business, banks must be aware that this is a double-edged knife. Insurance companies, too, are entering the direct banking business, while there is a beginning of megamergers: in August 1997, Winterthur (Switzerland's largest) merged with Crédit Suisse. Nor should we forget that the Dutch ING, which bought Barings after its bankruptcy, is the result of a merger between a major insurance company and a bank. There is a search for synergy in the financial industry, and bankers will be well advised to keep it in perspective.

In England, Prudential, the country's largest life insurer, took on banks and building societies when it opened for business as a bank in October 1996. The insurer officially launched its branchless mortgage lending and deposit taking following an emerging trend in the British life insurance sector: Scottish Widows and Friends Provident, the mutual life insurers, have already got into banking services. Prudential's strategy is an attempt to

- expand its customer base, and
- capitalize on existing clients.

The underlying reasons are clear. About 250,000 life insurance policyholders receive £1 billion in maturity money each year, but the company's research has shown that about 70 percent of that money remains in a building society account for a year after it matures.

With the new scheme, customers will be able to buy financial products through Prudential's 6,000-strong direct sales force, who visit them in their homes – or over the telephone. Customers will also be able to make deposits or withdraw funds from the Pru's savings accounts through branches of Midland Bank or any bank where they hold current accounts.

Brokers, too, are on the same track and banks try to get a step ahead of them. In February 1996, DirectLine test marketed its *Tracker* Personal Equity Plan (PEP) which the Royal Bank of Scotland also offers to non-DirectLine customers. The minimum investment is £30 ($42) per month or a £500 ($720) lump sum.

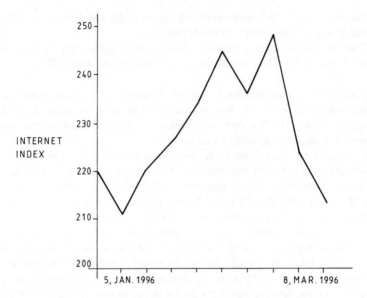

Figure 8.3 The ups and downs of the Internet index

Its plan tracks the FT-SE 100, while trying to keep administrative and management charges down. Direct debit charges for the PEP are low: 30 pence (20 cents) per transaction. But while the transaction cost may be low, the value at risk for the investor may be high. Like any index, the FT-SE 100 is volatile. Stock exchanges whose prices go one way, UP, have not yet been invented. Figure 8.3 shows, as an example, the volatility of the Internet index during the first couple of months of 1996.

By contrast to these examples, open universal direct banking systems present a much greater interest to the cognizant user. People who know exactly what they want to buy in terms of banking services can simply order by phone – after doing their homework online. That is true for simple products. At the same time, for complex financial instruments,

- clients could find it harder to say what they want without a face-to-face meeting;
- at the same time, the range of new services available over the telephone may be limited.

What all cases of open and closed online banking systems have in common is the battle for the control of the distribution channel. The (presumed) low cost of direct distribution is changing the face of retail financial services industry and sees to it that banks and non-banks are taking the direct route.

- The winners in this environment will be cost-effective, focused companies which are in close contact with their customers.
- Some predictions suggest that direct insurers will capture 50 percent or more of the market for motor and property insurance before the year 2000.

I doubt that this will be the case, in spite of the success of Centraal Beheer in the Netherlands, Topdanmark in Scandinavia and Churchill Insurance as well as DirectLine in the UK. But there is a market for direct distribution channels in connection with a number of financial services.

A similar statement can be made about branchless banking. The truth of the matter, however, is that to maintain and build market share banks must harness the potential networks. This proposition is fairly well understood therefore, not only Midland and the Royal Bank of Scotland but also Barclays, Lloyds-TSB and NatWest in the UK have introduced direct banking facilities.

The most severe problem with direct banking and direct insurance sales is that they are characterized by 'me too' strategies which, as we saw in Chapter 6, is the way the loser takes. Most banks follow this road just to be there, irrespective of whether or not it is wise to do so, or even whether and when they might break even. One of the lures of direct access for banking and insurance is that it is unhampered by regulatory restrictions. But at the same time it cannot use the obsolete technological infrastructure featured by most banks. It also requires new pricing policies designed to serve unorthodox players whose goal is to exploit direct distribution channels.

The pricing problem of which I speak is not connected only with direct access. It also enters into the retail bank's classical business lines, requiring them to rethink all other pricing issues – and most particularly that of the tellers. Section 5 addresses this subject, while Chapter 13 concentrates on the pricing policies to be followed with financial services.

5   WHAT WILL HAPPEN IF WE CHARGE THE COST OF TELLER SERVICES?

In the US a teller handles about 200 transactions per day. This corresponds to 50,000 transactions per year. These transactions are typically of a simple nature – deposit/withdrawal type – but are increasingly involving online access to the bank's database.

Therefore, when we talk of the cost to the bank of a simple transaction, we should count not only the teller's time but also overheads, utilities, materials – and of course technology. Some years ago, in a seminar I gave to Rabo Bank in Holland I was told they had costed the simple transaction and found that it eats up six guilders. Today, this would correspond to about seven guilders or four dollars. Other, more complex transactions evidently cost more money. Table 8.1 gives an

Table 8.1   Cost of doing business for investment
banks in London

	£
Money market or forex transaction	13–17
Cancellation	35
Contract for exchanges	25
Complex swap, per event	125

Note: Average ratio, front end to back office (including IT): 1:3. But the Range is 1:0.6 to 1:7, depending
on organization and technology. The better the organization and higher the technology, the lower is this ratio.

idea of costs based on the input I have received from investment banks in London.
No doubt in costing their services banks must account not only for front desk and
technology expenses, but also for back office costs. Table 8.1 gives some ratios
which could be used as benchmarks.

Starting with the premise that, with current technology, direct banking
addresses mainly simple transactions, the figure which interests us per event at
the teller is $4 (£2.60). Direct banking also costs money, but if we are using
sophisticated software then – because of reducing the labor content – the main
costs will be technology and utilities.

- Banks do not charge a fee for direct banking, otherwise they will not sell the
  service. They absorb the costs.
- But with few exceptions, mainly in Sweden, they do not charge a fee for teller
  transactions either – even if they cost $4 each.

Assuming direct banking transactions are less costly, which will not be the case
until the system dedicated to them is properly utilized, banks have an interest
in pushing clients towards operating online. They should also offer incentives for
a limited time on a promotional basis.

One of the best policies to induce the customer to use an online service is to
charge for teller services, while offering direct banking free. This should be done
in full understanding of the fact that such a strategy might be risky because the
competition can turn the tables. To succeed, it requires industry-wide understanding and collaboration.

In April 1995, First Chicago introduced a new pricing menu of current
accounts. With it came the announcement that it would charge a $3 fee on all
routine teller transactions over a maximum of four free visits, or six for direct
deposit customers. This move made P&L sense, but the public relations campaign
was wanting and it brought a firestorm of negative publicity, despite the bank's
insistence that 80 percent of its retail customers would now enjoy reduced fees
and minimum balances. It also opened up the market to competitors.

In May 1995, Citibank, a First Chicago competitor in Illinois, announced that it would eliminate all remote banking fees with the exception of transactions at non-proprietary ATMs. This was done regardless of customer balances, which has evidently been a public relations coup, suggesting that it was reducing fees while First Chicago was levying new ones.

In June 1995, Chase Manhattan announced ChaseDirect, a package of remote banking services supported by dedicated telephone bankers. With this program Chase decided to eliminate most remote banking fees for customers with balances over $6,000.

- Analysts saw Chase's announcement as a relationship banking package.
- It has been designed to cross-sell to affluent customers who prefer the convenience of remote delivery.

If we look into the issue of pricing banking products, the moves of First Chicago and Citi addressed a fundamental subject: the need to rationalize delivery costs by moving customers away from costly teller visits. Electronic banking transactions can be the answer if we make them much less expensive to process than teller transactions.

Let me take this opportunity to underline that asking customers to pay fees for teller transactions is no silly business. Such a move began in the US as early as 1987, when Wells Fargo introduced a low-cost current account for customers who agreed to pay fees for routine teller transactions. Wells says that 20 percent of its retail customers now use this account.

Neither is it sure that banks really know how to price their products and how to promote those which have a lower cost. In England, high street banks charge for ATM transactions while taking up the time of the teller is free. In France, Crédit Agricole charges fees for telephone banking, particularly account inquiries, but gives the teller's time free of charge.

The more rational pricing scheme Wells Fargo invented has found a good echo. In 1992, Bank of America introduced a similar account, and in 1995 Huntington Bankshares brought to the market DirectAccess (See also section 8), a low-cost package of remote services supported by a new generation of technology. Huntington hopes eventually to move 65 percent of its customers to DirectAccess. (The original projection, 'within three years', has not yet been fulfilled.)

As these examples help document, the 'best solution' is not necessarily evident. It cannot be a matter of general definition and it is not the current 'in' thing either. Though the way to bet is that the best solution for our bank will be heavy in technology, computers, communications and software are not the only parts of it. Marketing savvy is necessary as a long, hard look suggests that:

- deposits still account for *60 percent* of all teller transactions;
- account inquiries comprise *90 percent* of all telephone transactions; and
- cash withdrawals make up *70 percent* of all ATM transactions.

Customers who use ATMs for withdrawals continue to make deposits inside the branch. And while many analysts believe that – if they are properly motivated – consumers are ripe for mass migration to remote banking, this is a question which still remains wide open.

The lesson to be retained from all these references is that if direct banking is an innovation, which it is, we should be studying in a rigorous manner how this innovation affects the whole system. This should be done for each channel of the bank and for all channels taken together. It should be precise, not general; and it should be based on facts and figures.

As Figure 8.4 suggests, we should be keen to study the market potential of any innovation as well as its implementation details. But we also should be examining the existing service(s) which it replaces and what this means for the years to come in terms of:

- incurred costs,
- projected profits, and
- replacement of current products or processes.

Direct delivery of banking services both complements and competes with tellers and ATMs. It takes away part of the business of each while it brings, hopefully, new clients. Even if the potential seems to be great, the entry price can be stiff and old cultures risk killing the projected profits. The same is true of old tariffs and irrational pricing schemes regarding new and established banking products.

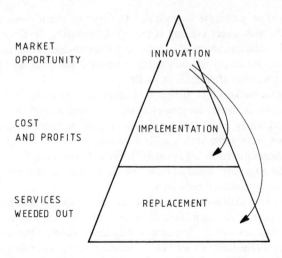

Figure 8.4 A new banking service must be studied from different viewpoints and levels of reference

6   PUBLIC REACTION TO DIRECT BANKING SERVICES OFFERED BY GERMAN BANKS

In Germany, Deutsche Bank, Dresdner Bank and Commerzbank offer direct banking services of sorts. To understand how this channel is positioned and what may be its chances, it is wise to review briefly the characteristics of the German banking market. This should be done under what section 5 indirectly suggested:

- that innovative products should pass quickly into implementation,
- but prior to designing them the concept should be subjected to market research.

Starting at the manufacturing sector as frame of reference, one of the basic characteristics of the German market is the close links existing between industrial companies and banks. Bankers provide short- and long-term funds, but also, at least until now, German banks have a major financial stake in the companies to which they extend loans.

While this 140-year-old policy may now be changing as the big German banks convert to the Anglo-American investment banking model, it still dominates current practice. Because one bank acts as *tête-de-fil*, this leads to dependence on a single institution with which the majority of business is done.

- The effect is that a German bank typically knows much more of the company it finances than does a US or UK bank.
- At the same time, relationship banking is at the board level, with a senior banking executive sitting on the manufacturing company's board of directors.

It should be of no particular surprise that this type of much closer relationship impacts on the way direct banking is projected. Similarly, the German banking community is uncertain about advantages and disadvantages concerning the promotion of direct banking – which is rather impersonal and could lead to increased competition which has aftermaths on profits.

Some German bankers look at increased competition as a vicious circle leading all the way from industrial companies to the consumer market. Not long ago, a Deutsche Bank study found that more than 80 percent of traditional retail customers do not want more than vanilla icecream banking. (As reported at the Lafferty 1st International Retail Financial Services Conference, Oslo, 17–18 June 1996.) But the 20 percent upscale, including small business, requires better banking services and specialized personnel.

Like retail banks in other countries, German banks estimate that between a fifth and a quarter of their clients make a negative contribution to their bottom line. In other terms, they are a drain. But as well they are of opinion that in many cases this is the fault of the bank: either bankers promise too much, or they do not know their costs and their risks, or they treat all of their customers the same way. Like everywhere else in the world, German banks seem to be overshooting some of their clients and undershooting others in terms of services. As Burkhardt Pauluhn, the executive vice-president of Deutsche Bank in charge of retail banking who lectured at the 1996 Oslo event was to say: 'It is possible to make losses with a customer holding more than DM1 million in securities by splitting responsibility and failing to vertically integrate.'

German banks do not have the profits American and British banks have from credit cards, because Germany is typically a non-credit card country. To compensate, Deutsche Bank, and other commercial banks, got into ancillary services. For general insurance, for example, Deutsche Bank employs 300 sales agents.

Though the three major German financial institutions now invest in direct banking, nothing is sure about the success of this project. If used as a precedent, Videotext (Bildschirmtext) started in 1983 and took 10 years to reach half a million users. Now it grows by about 10 percent annually. Internet is just starting. Deutsche Bank launched a direct banking service known as *Bank 24*, which expects to have up to 500,000 customers in four years. In a way reflecting what was said in section 5 on fees, at Bank 24 the cost of some services will be half the fees which are charged by the parent bank, with marketing emphasis that of providing 24-hour online service.

Deutsche Bank has invested heavily in Bank 24 to create a strong brand image. Still, Bank 24 assets are tiny. It only has a very small base of deposit and savings accounts, and loses money. Management predicts break-even will happen by the the year 2000. Current customer contacts are

- by telephone (62 percent),
- by fax (30 percent) and
- by electronic mail (8 percent).

It is being said that an estimated 80 percent of Bank 24 customers have PCs, compared with a German national average of 18 percent. This seems to me too far-fetched. If it were so, much more than 8 percent of Bank 24 customers would have been using electronic mail.

Other estimates, too, sound awfully optimistic. Deutsche Bank management hopes that over half of Bank 24 customers will come from the savings banks. However, not to be left behind, the savings banks are reacting with direct banking operations of their own.

There is as well T-Online, a Deutsche Telekom PC-based network which has entered the remote banking business on the coat tails of the telephone company's strength. This is an open network used by an estimated 1,200 credit institutions to service 2 million accounts.

- The savings banks have 400,000 accounts on T-Online.
- Deutsche Bank has the biggest presence of the universal banks with 140,000 accounts on this system.
- About 400,000 Postbank customers also use T-Online.

Another competitor is the Direct Anlage Bank, a subsidiary of Bavaria's Hypo Bank, which focuses on brokerage. But because the discount brokerage concept is new in Germany, a lot of advertising is necessary as well as an educational effort directed at clients and prospects.

Also in Germany, Citibank is active with a direct banking scheme. It launched a limited service CitiPhone Banking in 1989 and a full service CitiPhone Banking in October 1995. The phone banking service has 500,000 calls a month. The direct banking option, which sells all of the bank's products, has 45,000 calls a month from about 18,000 customers. Tiny numbers.

7   MAKING INVESTMENTS ONLINE, THE DIRECT WAY

Some cognizant retail bankers say that their institution's entry into direct banking is rather defensive; it has not been born out of their customers requirements but as a response to competition. Other retail bankers suggest that they found out the hard way that many of their customers somehow got the impression they were no longer wanted because of the bank's emphasis on:

- high net worth individuals
- high potential customers, and
- high profitability goals.

According to this point of view, direct banking is supposed to give a sense of belonging to those customers who might have felt left out of their bank's new business goals. Not everybody, however, subscribes to this argument. A number of people think that even if the current thrust to direct banking is indeed a defensive move, it is so for a different reason: the aggressive stand taken by non-banks. (See also Chapter 3.)

Richard Branson started in the music business with the Megastore and the Virgin Record label. Then he moved quite successfully into air travel. Now he is trying his hand in finance. Branson recently created *unit trusts* (mutual funds) investments vehicles taking advantage of what he knows best:

- being a low-cost producer,
- being a master of advertising, and
- capitalizing on selling over the phone.

Like a similar product by Marks & Spencer, the department store chain, Virgin Direct provides a convenient service for experienced investors. However, novices should think twice before rushing to buy an equity-based product simply because it comes from a household name.

Like the Royal Bank of Scotland, Virgin established a tracker fund which follows the FT 100 index. Marketing and feedback can be done most effectively by using models and realtime computers which weight the fund and help in making management decisions much more effectively than using lots of people. (See also section 8 on database mining.) Branson is said to have come to this vehicle after observing that many professional managers do not beat FT 100. So he set the course of following the FT 100 while keeping management costs low. The other side of his success story in selling financial investments is his gift for publicity.

Virgin's aim is both to widen the PEP market and to take business from traditional investment services providers. The message is simple: why pay a broker commission? In insurance, too, Virgin offers underwritten quotes over the phone, taking as little as 10 minutes to arrange life insurance and filling in the forms which the customer has only to check and sign. The company said these are:

- the first life policies to be sold exclusively over the phone, and
- the first personalized policies, which tailor premiums very closely to each individual's preferred risk level.

A staff of 90 at Virgin Direct's call center is on hand for direct customer contact seven days a week, between 8 am and 10 pm. Among non-banks, Virgin is not alone in direct access deals. Marks & Spencer also has had a low-key execution-only PEP operation going since 1989. In 1995, the retailer joined the tracker bandwagon with an offer of a PEP invested in its FT-SE 100 Index Tracker unit trust. Designed specifically for customers among its five million charge card account holders, wary of the risks of stock market investments, this offer guarantees to return investors' original capital on the fifth anniversary if the value has fallen.

M&S also has a customer investment vehicle in its long-running Tax Free Savings Plan. This offers a choice of two actively managed unit trusts. All these schemes, however, face problems when the market turns down and investments lose value. Their promoters must use derivatives to hedge themselves.

How are the banks reacting to the non-banks appeal to investors? Citibank has launched three asset allocation mutual funds, or *CitiSelect funds*. They have been studied so that they can adjust shareholders' assets among stocks, bonds and cash. This is done according to market conditions, and it features three different risk tolerances. Known as CitiSelect Portfolio 200, 300 and 400, these three different risk tolerances are sold by brokers at Citibank's branches. They use the bank's existing asset allocation software to recommend the funds to conservative, moderate and aggressive investors. The lowest investment is $1,000 and the funds charge a front load, or sales commission, of 4.5 percent.

CitiSelect marks the first time that Citi had put its own name on proprietary mutual funds, allowing itself to sell house funds and earn management fees.

By creating a fairly complex multi-manager, international asset allocation product, the bank has made a major move into a popular offering in the capital markets.

In mid-1996, NationsBank also announced it would sell at its branches its proprietary funds with loads. But it also stated that it would sell the same products without loads by phone and mail. Its subsidiary *KeyCorp* is offering different fund groups for different investment channels. This difference in strategy front-load/no-load can be seen as the counterpart of fees to be applied for teller transactions, of which we have spoken in section 5. The fact that sales commissions are waived with direct banking has introduced a great deal of uncertainty among retail banks on how to price their services. Innovation does not make things easier for bankers, though it does present many opportunities if the right technology and pricing systems are in place.

8   USING THE DATABASE AS A STRATEGIC TOOL IN DIRECT BANKING

Practically all of the examples on direct banking we have seen so far rest on two pillars: networks and databases. Retailers were the first to use their customer base as a strategic tool to hammer out more business. Marks & Spencer has been employing its customer-oriented database to sell financial products such as

- life insurance,
- market funds, and
- pension funds.

Marks & Spencer has great experience in the able use of its customer base. With American Express in the US and Diamond Credit (a Mitsubishi credit card company) in Japan, in the mid-1980s M&S was one of the three best examples worldwide of using expert systems for database mining. The first significant application was the automatic evaluation of lines of credit – and it brought major advantages to the three market leaders.[2]

The knowledge engineering models developed and used for the evaluation of lines of credit through database mining can be nicely extended to other applications domains like a direct banking implementation known as *Instant Loan Answer*. At Marks & Spencer, in a matter of minutes the customer can obtain a yes/no on his loan application, then he can drive to a branch to sign up the loan. How best to handle this loans application is still in evolution. Many banks and non-banks use expert systems. And they keep on adding functionality like signing the document in the screen and automatically crediting the current account, which can do away with going to the branch.

As another example focusing on *direct loans*, in the United States in June 1996 Huntington's Bankshares sent out 65,000 preapproved loans to prospective customers for their next auto. The paperwork was done through expert systems and the bank issued a plastic card (not credit card) as an activation device.

- Investigated through knowledge engineering, the credit was good for six months.
- Over the life cycle there is no need to go back to the bank for approval.
- The instrument is novel and it seems to have obtained good market response.

What knowledge engineering and database mining do in connection with direct banking is the routine administrative work of clearance and control, the calculation of values and credit line, and providing automatic link to current account and general ledger. Documentation remains in the database, rather than on hard copy, but information is enriched by computer.

Proactive knowledge engineering constructs like *agents*[3], and database mining through expert systems, permit much greater flexibility at the front desk and significant efficiency in the back office. This dual improvement is most welcome because today practically every company invades another company's turf.

- Insurance companies, for example, also come into banking, opening up deposits facilities.
- There is a proliferation of products and plenty of competition for insurance from retail banks.

Insurance companies say they have to invade other financial industries' domains because in recent years banks have emerged as the most important new channel for insurance sales – at least in America. But at the same time they have gravitated toward branch office-based sales, leaving the door open for innovative direct marketers.

One of them is discount broker Charles Schwab, of San Francisco. Schwab began direct marketing of low-cost insurance products which, like life insurance, can be an integral part of a diversified financial portfolio. Schwab (and several banks) capitalized on the fact that, as industry studies show, half of the American population has no insurance agent even if people want to buy insurance. Competitive advantage is provided through database mining.

- With over $200 billion in assets under administration, Schwab serves 3.6 million investment accounts.
- Its OneSource no-transaction-fee mutual fund program has gathered over $20 billion in assets since its inception in 1992.

Schwab will initially sell three types of insurance: 10-year term life which only provides death benefits; universal life, which also offers an interest-earning policy

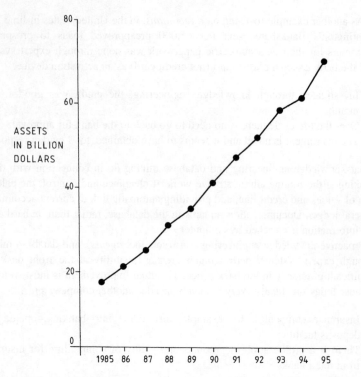

Figure 8.5 Allstate Insurance: assets have increased by 400 percent in 10 years

value account; and survivorship universal life which covers two lives and pays a benefit on the death of the second insured – typically to cover the estate settlement costs.

In different terms, direct access does not just take clients away from banks and insurance companies but also helps to innovate both professions. One of the reasons why banks and brokers are so keen to enter the insurance market is the wealth they find there. As Figure 8.5 documents, the assets of Allstate Insurance have increased by 400 percent in just 10 years.

9   SMALL BANKS TOO HAVE A FUTURE IF THEY KNOW HOW TO MANAGE TECHNOLOGY: THE CASE OF LAN & SPAR

The references in this chapter to successes and failures with medium to larger banks might convey the wrong message that only big banks have a future – if and when they are able to exercise control over technology. This would be the wrong conclusion, as the case study in this section helps document.

Peter Schou is the chief executive of Lan & Spar Bank, a small Danish savings and loan bank. He is not only computer-literate but also a very imaginative person who used high technology in his bank to leapfrog ahead of competitors, including the larger Danish banks. Starting with more recent developments:

- Lan & Spar has a homepage on Internet: WWW.laan-spar.dk, which began operating in late 1995;
- customers can download programs as well as finding interactive conferences
- customers can also access through Internet Lan & Spar's PC Bank.

As a real-time project, the PC Bank went alive in August 1994 and, two years down the line, in September 1996, it featured 165,000 transactions. This reference concerns the direct connection to Lan and Spar software, not through Internet.

Schou's concept correctly started with product design. A bank lives off the products it sells to its customers. At his lecture at Lafferty's 1st International Retail Financial Services Conference for Scandinavia (Oslo, 17–18 June 1996), he said, 'We cannot afford to exclude a section of the market by designing products in which they are not interested.' This is not Citibank talking. It is Denmark's Lan and Spar, based in Copenhagen with headquarters in the Parliament Square (Hojbro Plads). It has 90,000 customers, 270 employees, and a return on equity (ROE) of 12 percent per year – which many big banks would give their soul to get. Lan and Spar features

- 11 branches through the country, and
- one direct banking outlet in Copenhagen.

Product design in this small bank is both a lesson and a prototype for big institutions to follow. (See also Part Three.) The first rule Peter Schou made is *pursue content*, by properly establishing what customers truly need. Under an able executive, a small bank has the salt of the earth to appreciate this issue – contrary to many big banks whose management lives in an ivory tower.

The second rule of Peter Schou, which should be written in block letters and which every executive can see in his office is *navigation*. This means providing agile electronic support to permit customers to find what they need without being computer wizards.

If the first two rules are market-oriented, the third basic rule focuses on internal administration. This, too, is an important issue which helps to separate *well-managed* from *badly-managed* retail banks. Figure 8.6 shows in a nutshell what Lan & Spar has obtained *since* it sorted out its technology problems and managed to gain IT leadership. The statistics reflect a *21-month* trend.

- The number of transactions increased by 50 percent.
- The number of new customers has grown by 22.6 percent.
- The number of employees increased by *zero* percent.

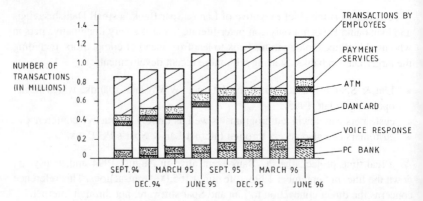

Figure 8.6 Self-service in Lan and Spar Bank statistics

Self-service by banking customers has been instrumental in obtaining this result. While the number of transactions grew from 870,000 to 1,280,000, and in spite of a significant increase in the customer population, over the same period the increase in the number of transactions made by the bank's employees has only been 2.5 percent. These numbers show the trend among well-managed financial institutions. Peter Schou is proud to say: 'We have been able to increase our business volume with only a minor increase in costs.' So have other banks which are ahead of the curve – big or small.

The emphasis on customer-actuated transactions should not go unnoticed. Lan & Spar looks after productivity improvements by dividing all transactions into

- those generated by employees in branch offices, and
- those generated by its customers through direct service banking.

As Figure 8.6 demonstrates, the latter consist of PC Bank, voice response, Dancard (the Danish debit card), payment services and credit cards.

Market segmentation played an important role in strategic planning. While not excluding corporate customers from its clientele, Lan & Spar particularly focused on the consumer market. Its chief executive had the vision necessary to implement market segmentation the way any sophisticated bank would do, dividing its private customers into three groups:

- blue-collar workers,
- white collar workers, and
- academics.

Having focused on the customer strata he would like to consider for his bank, and studied their requirements in terms of banking services, Schou squeezed his product range into

- five leading *lending* products, and
- five leading *sales* products.

Lan & Spar had the wisdom to see the synergy which exists between *thinking technology* and *thinking profit* – the way strategic planners should do. As Peter Schou said in his lecture, unless you have the rocket scientist[4] and the advanced information technology,

- you cannot design sophisticated products, and
- you should not take risks.

Short of human and technology resources, a bank must keep a low profile, characterized by risk aversion. Even with plenty of financial resources, it should concentrate on what it knows best – establishing its niche and sticking to it. (See Chapter 6.) This policy is in principle the best for a small bank, even if it has qualified personnel and high technology.

Working along this strategy, Peter Schou was able to launch a successful *direct banking* activity. While Lan & Spar established branches in the major Danish cities, it also covered the country from its Copenhagen-based direct banking service. We spoke about it in connection with Figure 8.6. The chief executive officer also positioned his bank in terms of price/quality in a way which made sense versus the competition. Most significantly, after gaining technology leadership, Lan & Spar has added *new income-making services*. These include:

- a pension program,
- energy-saving programs,
- a new wine program, and
- a program about the government's grants policy toward students.

At the same time, the bank incorporated several improvements into existing services. But remember: *all this became possible only after this small retail bank became a technology leader*, because high technology supports and low technology inhibits the way in which the bank addresses itself to its client base.

- What is shown in Figure 8.7 is the transition Lan & Spar experienced from 1990 to 1996 – just six years.
- This very significant trajectory in cost and quality is a model all banks will be well advised to understand and follow.

What I particularly appreciated with Peter Schou is that he created new ideas – he did not imitate others. This was a refreshing presentation after that of the executive vice-president of a major European financial institution who had said: 'If the

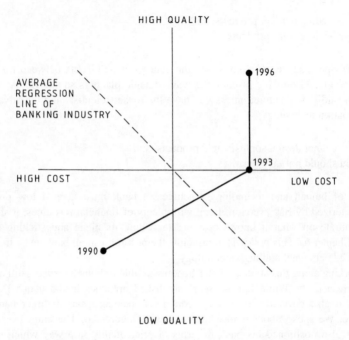

Figure 8.7   Positioning price/quality versus competition by Lan & Spar of Denmark

competitor offers something new, we have to copy it. We cannot afford not to do it.' That is absolute nonsense. We have seen in detail in Chapter 6 that 'me too' is the worst possible strategy. Also a bad strategy is the use of mainframes which some other lecturer at the same conference had promoted. Mainframes would have ruined Lan & Spar. But its chief executive

- wisely put all customer services offered to the market under DOS and Windows;
- while the sophisticated software he provided made this small, dynamic outfit a *multimedia bank.*

Let me offer some more food for thought. Most people say that technology 'reduces barriers to entry'. This is patently false. Properly used, technology increases barriers to entry, because most banks lack the technology to compete with those which know how to move ahead.

Lan & Spar offers one of the best examples of what should be done in terms of using affordable technology in an ingenious way to raise barriers. In a nutshell, the strategy is: build the infrastructure, package the product, choose the content, provide for navigation, and

- sell,
- transport,
- deliver.

Every one of the employees at Lan & Spar is computer-literate. Information technology is fully distributed. Every branch has its IT advisor. The bank builds only the software which it considers to be competitively crucial. A small central IT group leads in standards and architecture, as well as keeping control over the bank's IT strategy. There is no fat and there are no delays: two qualities which eat up for breakfast big and rich banks.

Notes

1. See D.N. Chorafas, *Interactive Videotex. The Domesticated Computer* (Princeton: Petrocelli Books, 1981; D.N. Chorafas, *Interactive Message Services* (New York: McGraw-Hill, 1984).
2. See D.N. Chorafas and H. Steinmann, *Expert Systems in Banking* (London: Macmillan, 1991).
3. D.N. Chorafas, *Agent Technology Handbook* (New York: McGraw-Hill, 1998).
4. See D.N. Chorafas, *Rocket Scientists in Banking* (London and Dublin: Lafferty, 1995).

9 The Profitable Business of Private Banking

1 INTRODUCTION

The five chapters on strategic planning in Part One provided the evidence that, in the banking industry, a few large customers account for the largest percentage of income and of profits. The same is true in other industries, an example being the telephone companies, where

- the top 1 percent of clients of the Bell system accounts for 25 percent to 35 percent of toll revenues,
- while, for AT&T, the top 4 percent of business customers make 62 percent of all long distance calls.

Given these statistics, a critical issue for the service industry is retention of existing customers and expansion of the products which they use. The question management asks itself and its people is *how to capitalize* on the convergence of marketplace and technology in creating the melting pot from which new business opportunities are emerging.

Chapter 8 said that one way to do this is *direct banking*. This is correct but not necessarily complete, and this for two reasons. First, it addresses most particularly the middle and lower strata in the client base which want convenience banking, ancillary services and sound investment advice. Second, while it constitutes a competitive proposition, the process of direct banking is not generating a fee income. Rather, it is swapping costs. While theoretically direct banking is addressing both costs and revenues, the top issue on which it focuses is: 'Can we cut costs without deteriorating the relationship?'

While cost cutting is important, we need more than that for our top 20 percent of customers, taking account of the non-bank competition. A question in the mind of many retail bankers in Britain is: 'How can our bank differentiate itself from Ford UK, "The Drive-in bank" with over 1,000 branches nationwide?' The answer is

- personal finance, and
- care through private banking.

Private banking is a strategic move. Several banks today identify personal banking as *their* business opportunity. An example is Britain's Lloyds Bank, which

212

made the strategic decision to downplay corporate banking. By contrast, NatWest and Barclays have chosen corporate banking as their top strategic product. (See Chapter 11 on the definition of strategic products.) There is a difference in terms of chosen strategies because the market is polyvalent and every institution perceives business opportunity in a slightly different manner. Both corporations and wealthy individuals are demanding in their relationship. Those banks going into private banking should appreciate that high net worth clients

- are sophisticated, and
- they want instant gratification.

If a bank does not have highly qualified investment advisors, account managers and salesmen – as well as advanced, knowledge-enriched software – it cannot offer private banking successfully, because it is not possible to sustain quality of service. Private banking requires a great deal of preparatory work:

- analyzing the customer preferences,
- meeting needs for specific products, and
- value-differentiating *our* bank from the competition.

Therefore, prior to entering personal banking, the management of a retail bank will do well to study where the banking market is growing, what the professional people are demanding, what do younger people need as they start creating wealth? Is the investment banking market too far away from *our* bank's culture. Can we offer our clients the value they want for their money?

2 THE GROWING BREED OF PRIVATE BANKERS AND THE FEES OF THE INDUSTRY

Because that is the way the trend is going, most financial institutions want to be private bankers. The winners are those who remember that this is not a faddish business. Private bankers have to look after the private fortunes of rich people – and they must do so in an environment of globalized, computer-based banking. Figure 9.1 shows the pillars on which a successful private banking effort rests.

The processes underpinning private banking are characterized by an all-round personal service that includes current account, investments, loans, mortgage(s), foreign currency, insurance and pension needs. A number of issues such as investment preferences and profiles, fund management, overdraft charges, loan rates and interest paid on deposits are practically negotiated individually.

Some confuse private banking with *relationship banking*, of which we spoke in Chapter 7, because most often the bank manager gets to know each investor socially. He may even become executor of his or her will. The difference is that

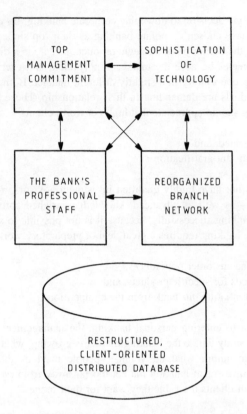

Figure 9.1 Critical success factors in private banking

the process of relationship banking is much broader – both private banking and corporate banking are part of it – and it concerns a policy rather than a procedure. By contrast, private banking is a matter of specialization.

- Relationship banking is a marketing concept.
- Private banking is investments and assets management-oriented, using relationship banking methods and tools.

As the rich get richer, the market for private banking is growing. Both inherited wealth and newly created wealth are factors driving demand. Forecasts say that, up to the year 2000 and beyond, we are going to see very significant increases in private wealth – and this wealth has to be managed.

Not everything is positive in private banking. 'The private sector,' suggests a study by the Union Bank of Switzerland, 'might even suffer some setbacks in the longer run as bank secrecy and the treatment of tax evasion come under attack by the European Union' (UBS Economic Research, 'EMU and European Finance',

Union Bank of Switzerland, July 1997). To overcome the difficulties, the same study advises:

- the need to focus on expertise in international investment management, and
- the need to ascertain political support for the operation of financial centers.

The UBS study further suggests that the European Monetary Union will foster a restructuring of the banking industry. Mergers will increase, but margins will remain very low because of high research costs, while banking instruments will tend to grow rapidly as a more sophisicated investment culture develops in Europe, and private banking plays a role in it.

Private bankers screen customers on the basis of their *investible assets*. The term means excess cash beyond the cost of home and living expenses. And since the other side of private banking is fee income for the bank, given the charges, soon would-be lower net worth clients become aware that private banking is not for them.

Private banks levy fees for consulting, asset management, keeping the mail, using a numbered account and other services. They also tend to impose charges on current accounts when the deposit falls below an agreed minimum. In terms of fees for account management, policies differ and the same is true of minimum amounts.

- Most Swiss banks set SF500,000 ($420,000) as a minimum.
- The minimum in England tends to be £75,000 ($115,000).

Fees vary widely. They are typically standard at the bottom of the scale (as in the foregoing examples), but tend to be negotiated when the wealth of the private account exceeds a certain amount, for instance $5 million. Standard fees are at 1.5 to 2.0 per thousand per year. Negotiated reductions can chop off up to 50 per-cent of this amount.

Even with discounts granted to the more important clients, a 1.0 to 2.0 per thousand fee rate can mean a significant income for the bank. This is further attested by the fact that a growing number of banks manage their investment advisors as profit centers.

The income being generated is so much more important when the bank obtains from the client discretionary powers, which practically every institution tries to do. Neither is the 1.5 to 2.5 per thousand the only charge.

- Many banks are charging the client hidden fees like services for coupon collection in a bond portfolio.
- They also profit from the private clients' orders to buy and sell assets – which means a hefty commission.

As we will see later on, some private banking institutions also charge for the time of their investment advisor. This is done through a flat fee, for instance $3,000 per account per year, rather than per hour. Some banks and brokers send to their clients copies of their financial studies; others do not.

Institutional investors, treasurers and high net worth individuals particularly appreciate the results of economics studies and of fundamental and technical research which they receive from the bank they deal with. This often amounts to a stream of information. The deeper meaning of this is that financial research and new product development capabilities are quite crucial to success in the relationship banking business. But the best managed banks do so in an able manner.

In order to provide the most valuable input, the bank's research focus has to rapidly adjust to the new requirements of investors. The most appreciated input is that which has a lead time on the economic and financial developments taking placed in the national and global economy – and in the markets. Therefore

- the specialization of the financial analysts and researchers tends to increase, and
- research focuses not only on companies and instruments but also on the market potential of certain instruments, such as mid-caps or small-caps.

From sales to handholding, investment advice as well as a steady stream of economic and financial analyses, private banking can involve significant costs. Therefore, as we have seen, several experts advise against the danger of overestimating the profitability of this business.

Private banking can be a rewarding business, but it is as well to remember that even financial institutions which have prestigious private banking activitites find that this is not a super-profitable part of their organization, as competition trims the margins.

- The trouble with very rich people, some bankers suggest, is that they are too savvy to hand over excessive fees to the bank.
- At the same time, research and marketing studies cost money – and this is also true of the globalization efforts made by a bank to better serve its most important clients.

Not everybody agrees with the statement that private banking – for the treasuries of multinational corporations and high net worth individuals – is one of the financial industry's moving gears. However, this is my experience, based on the strategy of the banks I have been associated with. Beyond doubt, other people and other banks can have a different experience.

3   INVESTMENTS NEEDED TO CONFRONT THE CHALLENGES OF PRIVATE BANKING

Because private banking requires investments on behalf of the financial institution – from human capital to technology – management should not enter into it light-heartedly, even if the projected fees sound great. A basic question is: do local conditions warrant these investments? In the case of *our* bank, is emphasis on private banking justified?

As the marketplace becomes more competitive, 'me too' can mean death. We have spoken of this in Chapter 6. Private banking is the opposite of vanilla ice-cream banking. Therefore the bank should develop a strategy to deal with the new challenges. For instance:

- Should we reorient branch offices to private banking? All of them? Some of them?
- How can we provide service differentiation in *our* services, to obtain price differentiation?
- Which are the marketing and distribution options we should adopt in relationship banking?
- What kind of technology do we need to back up our client contacts *our* advisors' judgment?

The first question is that of market potential, but even growth statistics may lie. For instance, even if the private banking business of a branch office grew by 10 percent, we actually lost share when the private banking market grew last year by 20 percent.

Demographics, income statistics and geographic information systems (GIS) can provide some insight into the population of customers and potential customers. GIS should not only be used for new branches but also for re-evaluating performance of existing branches. The business perspectives change and we have to steadily rethink our marketing strategy and investments. The wisdom of offering private banking services hangs on able answers to these issues.

As a matter of principle the customer relationship in private banking will tend to be polyvalent, as Figure 9.2 explains. Precisely because of the change in culture which it requires, despite the fees it may not be profitable to *our* bank. Hence we need to perform cost–benefit analysis by

- client,
- client group,
- channel and
- branch.

It is indeed regrettable that quite often such analytical studies take a back seat and operational decisions are done with a lot of hype. This should not be the case with private banking where, as I have found in many cases, particularly inaccurate is the estimate of competition.

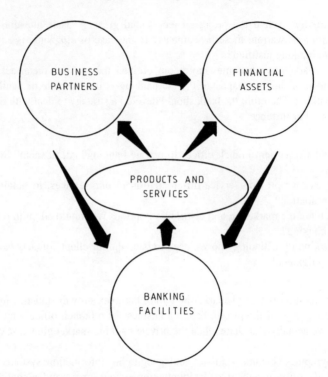

Figure 9.2 A customer relationship definition can be polyvalent, with financial products a focal point

Some people say that private banking can benefit from economies of scale, when it is spread through the branch network. This is a false supposition because with private banking the old type of banking skills, which are still rather widely available, are counterproductive. As we saw in Chapter 8 with Lan & Spar, advice orientation needs:

- content,
- navigation and
- personalization.

These are neither old-style banking nor mass market issues, but characterize niches and unique products. Neither is private banking served through mainframes on the side of technology, the sort of solution prevalent among low IT banks.

Few institutions truly appreciate that the ability to develop and use high technology is the key in gaining leadership in the private banking market. Yet, in all domains, including the able use of new technology, banks have to face competition not only from other banks but also from discount brokerage houses and the Internet.[1] Current studies tend to indicate that

- the increase in competitive pressures will be greatest at the retail level, and
- in the European Union, a unified currency and advanced transaction technology will undermine the currently existing national franchising.

Both a unique currency and any-to-any networks present rich opportunities to high-tech banks and non-banks to capture lucrative market share, particularly among young urban professionals. At the same time, new debt and equity instruments, particularly derivatives, serve as the spearhead of competition in the integrated markets.

Over the coming years, the Euro will also have an interesting effect on banks and the technology they are using. It will significantly increase the speed of consolidation that has lagged behind in most European retail banking markets, and oblige senior management to reconsider and revamp the computers, communications and software solutions the bank is using.

Shielded by a very protective nationalistic legislation, the umbrella of the local reserve bank and the parochial currency of the country, retail banks in Germany, France, Italy, Sweden, Spain, Austria and other continental countries have not yet faced the earthquake of the technological revolution.

- Technology-wise banks in these countries remained laggards and now they face painful (and costly) restructuring to match the American and British banks.
- Not only can this experience be traumatic, but the situation is exacerbated by the fact that it becomes increasingly difficult to find the needed technologists.

To better appreciate the sense of the second point, take notice that in America today some 190,000 jobs for information technologists remain vacant because people with requisite skills are not available to fill them (*Strategy Weekly*, 2 July 1997). This gap is bound to grow, because US universities produce a mere 30,000 information scientists per year.

The statement has been made in a recent publication by Prudential Securities that: 'America's financial services expertise is among our most important export.' This was followed by the remark that 'Through its actions and inactions [Washington] has created a wonderful fostering environment for the transformation of healthy and diversified banks.'

- The lion's share in this transformation is leadership in information technology.
- Such leadership is a rare quality in continental Europe.

When the executive vice-president, IT of one of the well-known banks in Europe said in the course of a meeting, 'The electronic channels supported by our main-frames have limitation of capacity,' I thought he knew what he was talking about. Then he added: 'As for software packages, they are all pretty similar.' With this, I lost all respect.

Banks which think that way are not fit to provide private banking services to their clients, because private banking flourishes on innovation and expert advice. Therefore, it is a culture alien to static forms of thinking – and to mainframes. The private banking market may be significant, but so are the requirements it imposes on the retail bank.

4   WEALTH PLANNING FOR A SOPHISTICATED CLIENTELE AND TAX ADVISORY SERVICES

Major changes have occurred in private banking and the market's expansion has led to a large increase in competition. As a result, banks are searching for ways to differentiate themselves in order to compete more effectively, establishing an identity by introducing distinct elements which can influence the client's perception.

While a visual identity may seem to be skin-deep, the concept behind it is that people always make conscious and subconscious judgments about what they see. It is in this sense that private banks seek to create competitive differentiation in the marketplace, developing and implementing value-added strategy across a wide range of services. This strategy of value differentiation is in full evolution. Having concentrated primarily on high net worth individuals, there is now a trend to capture the growing market of customers with mid-range disposable assets or income. The target of private banking services is no longer exclusively the very rich client, but a wider market segment with money to invest. However,

- in the 1990s, mid-range net worth customers have also become more informed and sophisticated;
- they are demanding clear and precise information on the services offered, and on tangible benefits to be gained.

The real driving force behind the current changes in private banking marketing perspectives has been the need to gain a larger base on which to depreciate costs of the expanding demands of sophisticated customers who are seeking more and better services. This brings into perspective a key subject touched on by section 3: the impact of high technology on private banking.

Correctly used, technology underscores the human element, and this is very positive because in private banking human capital is most critical. Technology also breaks down barriers. Former Citicorp chairman Walter Wriston once stated: 'As far as banking is concerned, technology is making the old legal barriers irrelevant.' But technology can work both ways: it can be a friend to those banks who know how to use it, and a foe to those who do not.

Technology is very important in wealth planning for a sophisticated clientele, because more and more of investment and asset management decisions are done today through *modeling*. An example is compliance with taxation, which can be greatly assisted through an experimental approach permitting its optimization.

Tax advisory services are in demand because quite often rich families fail to transfer their wealth to their children in a planned way. In the United States, 90 percent of the money made by 'Dad' is frittered away. The greatest share of it goes to lawyers as the children fight for shares of the estate. Another part disappears because the family business is mismanaged by the second and third generations – and a big chunk is taken in tax. Equipped with

- simulators which permit experimentation,
- optimizers responding to client preference criteria, and
- expert systems focusing on compliance,

the more technologically oriented private banks move ahead of the pack, offering their clients factual and documented advice on wealth planning and inheritance.

Tax advisory services are a means of value-differentiation because many other products provided by private banks are quite similar – and unique services are what matter. It is important to identify the needs of individual customers and design the wealth management service according to what is important in a fully personalized sense.

While specialized tax lawyers may have a greater competence on inheritance and other tax issues than the legal department of private banks, the latter have the customer handholding experience. Banks promote the offering of legal services to their customer base because

- it provides them an income service, and
- it spreads the cost of the legal department the banks themselves need for other reasons.

Sometimes, the law restricts how the bank presents itself to its clients. For instance, out of many big and small banks in Switzerland only 22 are allowed to call themselves private bankers under Swiss law and, for this elite, Geneva is the heartland. We will talk more about this in sections 5 and 9. This legal restriction has its reason. Private bankers are totally responsible for their clients' money and legislation must give confidence to the banking public. To appreciate the aftermaths of private banking regulation, it must be remembered that, at the end of the 19th century, there were 266 private banking companies listed in Geneva alone – and 25 years ago there were 49.

A number of factors have thinned the ranks. Not the least have been succession problems: because Swiss private bankers are organized as partnerships, at least one partner must carry the name of the bank or it has to be changed. For many families, keeping one of their members as 'banker on tap' through the generations became an impossible feat. In other terms,

- wealth planning and inheritance problems do not interest only the private bank's clients but also the private bank itself;
- it is indeed curious that many private banks do not apply to their own business the advice which they give to their clients.

While some private banks were taken over by large commercial banks, an occasional scandal also took its toll. The most recent among Swiss private bankers has been the collapse of Geneva's Bank Leclerc when partners evidenced less caution than is customary. But that happened back in 1977, a statistic pointing to the fact that such an event is not common.

Another reason why the ranks of Swiss private bankers have been dwindling is that some have been the victims of their own success. Bank Julius Baer and Bank J. Vontobel in Zurich, as well as Bank Sarasin in Basle, changed from partnerships to shareholdings largely because their growth called for a more widely-based capital structure. But other private bankers have taken a different approach. In Geneva's Lombard, Odier, founded in 1798, and Hentsch which began in 1796, members of the founding families are still partners. These banks are still emphasizing the continuity of private institutions. Although much of the wealth they manage comes from families who have banked with them through generations, there has been a substantial increase in new client activity, particularly from institutional investors.

In other countries, too, the bank's name and its tradition in private banking are vitally important. Classically, private banks such as Coutts and Hoare, in the UK, have relied on their names to convey the image of long-established and trustworthy private banks. But name alone will not tip the scales.

- wealthy individuals not only require efficient service and high performance,
- they also want their bank to have a message for them in a way which is comprehensive and comprehensible.

Private banking flourishes when certain preconditions are met. The outer layer is the bank's culture, the whole structure being based on the pillars shown in Figure 9.3. Not all institutions which have entered the private banking market are able to fulfill the prerequisites this figure shows.

In conclusion, next to business confidence and continuity, the success of private bankers comes from ingenuity, value differentiation and flexibility, and also from concentration on niches. A further factor is that private bankers today are being forced to think internationally. This is an area in which Swiss banks excel.

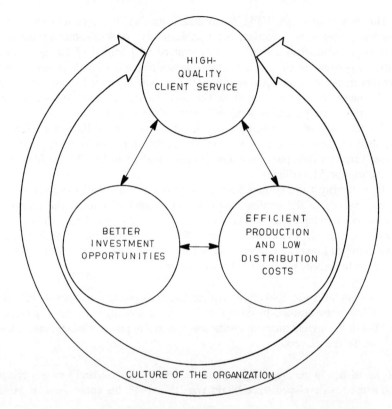

Figure 9.3   Private banking flourishes when it is based on good foundations

5   INTERNATIONALLY INVESTED PERSONAL WEALTH AND THE PRIVATE BANKING BUSINESS MADE IN SWITZERLAND

Since the early to mid-19th century, lacking a significant industrial base in Geneva, local bankers have built up their contacts abroad. During the Industrial Revolution, they helped finance industrialization throughout Europe and travelled to America to seek out further investment opportunities.

At the turn of the century, turning adversity into opportunity – because they were way behind in resources compared to large public banks – the private bankers of Geneva concentrated on managing assets for wealthy individuals. This might be seen as the beginning of private banking. European and international clients sought the security of neutral Switzerland as wars and political upheaval ravaged their countries, while frail currencies and heavy taxation represented other major risks for them.

However, it was after World War II that Switzerland became the world's pre-eminent private banking marketplace. Cognizant analysts believe that it is the destination of more than a third of the estimated $4.3 trillion of *internationally invested personal wealth* – which means money placed outside its owner's home country by people with liquid assets over $1 million. Figure 9.4 shows the origin of this money in order of magnitude. The internationally invested personal wealth originating in the US makes about 40 percent of the total.

But internationally invested personal wealth is only part of the picture. If total numbers are considered, current estimates put the amount of assets managed by Swiss banks for their portfolio clients at between SF1.8 trillion ($1.3 trillion) and SF2.2 trillion ($1.5 trillion).

From the Big Three (Union Bank of Switzerland, Swiss Bank Corporation and Crédit Suisse) to the smaller banks, the investment of foreign and domestic wealth is a thriving business. The country's Big Three banks stand well ahead of their nearest rivals. Even relatively small Swiss private institutions, such as family-controlled Lombard, Odier; Pictet and Julius Baer rank as considerable participants in the private banking market worldwide.

- A study of Swiss banking by Arthur Andersen predicts that private bankers will increase business by more than 10 percent annually in the coming years.
- But of the myriad financial institutions engaged in private banking, only a few are the real players.

As mentioned in the preceding paragraphs, much of Switzerland's money center attraction has developed since World War II. In 1945, the entire Swiss banking

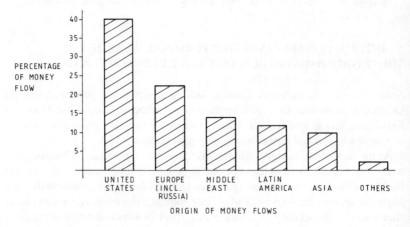

Figure 9.4 Estimated origin of about $4.3 trillion in internationally invested personal wealth

system had deposits and other liabilities of only SF15.5 billion ($11 billion). This is small fry compared to today's figures, even accounting for inflation.

As far as internationally invested personal wealth is concerned, not only Swiss bankers but practically everyone is chasing the trillions in assets that high net worth individuals have around the world, and that are available for investments. By some estimates, this wealth is expanding at a double-digit rate every year. New wealth zones are found everywhere as

- entrepreneurial activity spreads across the developing world, and
- a growing number of people reach their prime income and savings years.

However, the point has been made in sections 2 to 4 that, while all banks are dearly interested in this wealth, very few have the knowhow to proceed with *private banking*. Swiss banks are a case in point. Commission income, which is an important measure of private banking activity, now amounts to an estimated $8 billion (*Business Week*, June 24, 1996) – with most of the growth having occurred in the last 20 years. This is an approximate figure based on the fact that asset management fees, trading fees and other expenses approximate less than 1 percent of the $1.3 trillion to $1.5 billion attracted by Swiss banks. Therefore the true figure in fee income may stand much higher.

Felix W. Zulauf, a money manager and former private bank strategist in Zug, Switzerland, estimates that wealthy clients pay fees equivalent to 1 percent or more of their assets. This is 10 times as much as what banks can charge pension funds or other big institutions, therefore high net worth individuals are the clientele of choice. There are, as well, other reasons which make wealthy private investors a better client target than institutional investors. By and large, institutional investors by now know how to manage their money. Not only do they negotiate the fees they pay but also they often specify who should be the broker(s) and the custodian(s). This ties the hands of private banks. By contrast, consumers usually do not have that knowhow. They do not know how to do their shopping for low costs and they ignore credit risk and settlement risk. This makes their handling so much easier and more profitable. But increasingly private investors insist on the quality of service which they get from their private banker. That is why in Part One, on strategic planning, the whole of Chapter 4 was devoted to the quality of banking services.

There are other differences between consumers and institutional investors. Money center banks look on private investors as a widely distributed population, much more so than institutional investors can ever be. Therefore they address them not only from headquarters but also – if not mainly – from local private banking operations they have bought in America, the UK, Germany, Japan and elsewhere.

Among private banks, there are variations in private style. While the smaller institutions focus on handholding, the Swiss Big Three and their private banking activities are turning toward high-technology fund management, as well as towards derivatives. This is becoming the case with all major banks addressing the private banking market.

How and why derivatives enter into private banking is discussed in sections 8 to 10 of this chapter, while Chapter 15 is dedicated to the 1996 Market Risk Amendment by the Basle Committee on Banking Supervision, and the way in which it impacts commercial banking. No self-respecting book on commercial banking can leave out the derivatives subject – and its risks. Let me, however, quickly state at this point that not all bankers are convinced that derivative financial instruments and private banking match. The reason given is that there seems to be no special link to the very wealthy.

I do not agree with this argument, and this for a number of reasons. First, that more bread-and-butter derivatives have by now entered into the banking infrastructure. Second, major financial institutions repackage derivative instruments in a way which bypasses restrictive laws, and offer them to both wealthy clients and institutional investors. A third and just as important reason is that some wealthy clients *want* to include derivative instruments in their private banking portfolio. There is as well the case of proprietors, treasurers or traders of companies who use derivatives in their daily business – or who simply are after above-average returns.

Over and above these reasons, all of the larger financial institutions targeting private banking are keen to develop their asset management subsidiaries that they acquired in recent years to pump up their global investment returns. Practically all are offering more sophisticated products than those available some years ago, and this necessarily means derivatives.

As far as Swiss private banking institutions are concerned, the fact that Switzerland did not join the European Union enhances their standing because it attracts German, British, French, Italian and other EU capital. By contrast, capitalizing on its position as a banking center for high net worth individuals, Luxembourg has bet on stricter bank secrecy laws and other advantages, as will be shown in section 6.

6   WHERE ARE LUXEMBOURG AND THE OFFSHORE FINANCIAL CENTERS IN THE RACE TO PRIVATE BANKING?

Luxembourg's strength in private banking is that it has no withholding tax. This unsettles its neighbors, France, Germany and Belgium, which are demanding an EU-wide withholding tax to stem the flow of untaxed money from each of these three countries (and many others) to Luxembourg.

As is to be expected, Luxembourg's response is to suggest that withholding tax should be imposed throughout the OECD. This means that, if the country cannot have an advantage over its neighbors, nobody else can, as an OECD-wide withholding tax would also include the Channel Islands.

Luxembourg's argument focuses attention on the offshores. Wherever they may be, offshore centers are chosen mostly for being a tax haven, but geography also plays a role. Luxembourg's proximity to Germany made it the recipient of one of the biggest movements of flight capital ever seen.

- Luxembourg has been the main destination for an estimated DM360 billion ($200 billion) in capital that took flight when Germany imposed a 30 percent tax on interest payments in 1993.
- Not to be outdone, in 1996, Switzerland was the beneficiary of the next wave of German flight capital, because Germans distrust the Euro while they like the Swiss franc.

Not all internationally invested personal wealth follows the same criteria. With about 40 percent of the total amount in personal banking coffers, Americans search for better investment performance. By contrast, for Europeans the key words are confidentiality, security and tax efficiency – in that order.

How big is the market for the offshores? This is synonymous with asking how big the internationally invested personal wealth is now – and will be in the future. Recent estimates indicate that about 2.6 million to 3.0 million people worldwide have liquid assets of $1 million or more. These statistics include global wealth, whether invested onshore or in the client's home country (onshore).

Among the onshore, the largest share is held by the US private banking sector, while most money invested offshore is heading for the traditional European private banking centers. However, the growth of Asian wealth has brought other financial centers, such as Singapore, into prominence.

Among American financial institutions in the private banking market, Citibank is the best known player, with an estimated $90 billion in private banking assets in 35 countries. Yet, huge as this sum may be, it is small game compared to the money mastered by the three big Swiss banks worldwide, as we saw in section 5. For value-differentiation reasons, some private banking projects are specializing. Citibank and rivals JP Morgan, Republic Bank of New York and Chase Manhattan are addressing the fastest growing affluent group: entrepreneurs. On Wall Street, Merrill Lynch, Goldman Sachs, Morgan Stanley and Lehman Brothers are mounting their wave of competition.

In the UK, the top private banker is the National Westminster subsidiary Coutts & Co. NatWest is also rapidly expanding its global product line with big acquisitions on Wall Street. And HSBC Holdings accounts for some $40 billion in assets in Asia alone.

Because of the institutionalization of private wealth, chances are that many of the currently diverse asset management criteria will converge. Increasingly, high net worth individuals are using investment techniques ranging from optimum asset allocation to securities lending, which until recently were the speciality of institutional investors and large banks.

Furthermore, as we have seen, high net worth individuals are not the only players in the international personal investments market. Some banks have identified a group of potential clients who occupy the middle ground:

- high-salaried persons with needs well in excess of basic banking, and
- professionals who do not yet have permanent assets which require high-level personal relationships, but who might, eventually.

In these terms, the essential difference between the middle and top tier of private banking is in today versus tomorrow. This influences the way of personalizing, packaging and present financial services – as well as the future of the offshores. A similar statement can be made about product planning. Full customization is done for the upper tier, while to the mid-tier the bank offers for sale packaged products and the client chooses from this selection. This, however, will most likely be changing towards full customization as competition intensifies.

Also changing is the answer to the query: 'What does it take to make the ideal private banker?' The classical requirements include a smooth manner with clients, relationship banking skills, continuity in handholding and exacting service standards – but also straight fund management abilities. Newer requirements focus on skills such as dependable knowledge of taxation and inheritance laws (see also section 4), as well as ability to advise on exotic-type investments (see sections 8 to 10). As a result, without support through database mining and sophisticated software, very few people have the range of experience often considered necessary.

Because personal banking takes time, high technology is needed to face in an able manner the time requirements necessary for personal attention. Time allocation has changed dramatically over the last dozen years, from 1985 to 1997, as Figure 9.5 suggests. This change in time allocation to meet the market's demand is feasible only if we use high technology to assist the personal advisor and account manager in his duties. But, as cannot be repeated too often, though they spend an inordinate amount of money on technology, most personal banks do not have the skill and the means to proceed effectively with IT restructuring.

Another 'must' is personnel development and career planning to minimize staff turnover. Some personal banking institutions, like Switzerland's Pictet, pride themselves on having a staff turnover of no more than 3 percent a year. Bigger banks probably lose 10 to 15 percent of their private banking staff each year and some international banks even reach 30 percent. That is bad. Not only do high net worth clients hate to see their interface at the bank frequently changed, but also bankers with high-grade investment skills can often take some of the best clients with them when they move. This leads to an instant loss of deposits and of fee revenue – and, in the longer run, it reflects negatively on the bank's name.

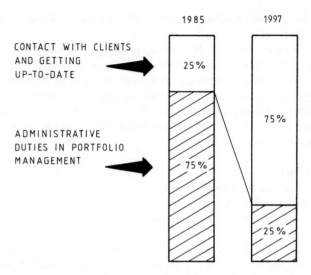

Figure 9.5 The dramatic change which has taken place in the use of the personal banker's time

7 THE PRIVATE BANKING BUSINESS IN BRITAIN AND IN GERMANY

In England Child, Coutts and C. Hoare have been the traditional names in the private banking world. Traditionally, the British private banker is a man of estimable courtsey and charm. At Coutts he used to wear a long frock-coat; at Child's, a tailored pin-stripe.

According to English tradition, the private banker is trained to deal with different clients. One of his skills is dissuasion: he will gently dissuade anyone with less than, say, £500,000 in *investible assets* from taking significant market risks – or with less than £75,000 in investible assets from even opening an account.

England's oldest private bank, Child & Co, was founded in 1584. It was banker to the royal family until William and Mary closed the royal account, which is now held by Coutts. Among other prizes, Child's boasts an IOU for £800 from Nell Gwyn, the mistress of Charles II.

Founded in 1672, C. Hoare & Co. is the last remaining wholly independent private bank in Britain. Heavily invested in South Sea stock in 1720, the bank's early partners were among the few to sell out before the bubble burst, saving their institution from certain collapse. Scotland's Adam & Co opened in 1983, and since then it has served the wealthy of Scotland. It claims to be the only private bank offering a fully itemized account service.

Apart from NatWest (which owns Coutts) and Royal Bank of Scotland (which owns Child and Adam) the big clearers are latecomers to private banking. Lloyds

Private Banking was established in 1985. Midland Private Banking opened for business only in January 1995.

A similar reference is valid about money center German banks which, after the Big Bang of the deregulation of banking industry in the mid-1980s, in Britain, acquired investment banks in the City and slowly moved to their investment banking and private banking operations. Deutsche Bank even restructured itself to compete better in the big league of global finance. On 9 July 1996, the then chairman Hilmar Kopper announced that the board had decided to divide Europe's largest lender into four divisions:

- private banking,
- commercial and institutional banking,
- investment banking, and
- a unit handling information technology.

The model for the make-over of the three operating divisions is Deutsche Morgan Grenfell, the parent company's London-based investment banking unit, where managers already have global responsibilities. But Deutsche Bank's centralization of information technology, rather than its distribution to the operating divisions, goes counterclockwise to the more prevalent current trend and, in my judgment, it will hamper operations.

There are as well some cultural differences regarding what is and what is not private banking. As defined by Deutsche Bank, a private bank is private capital market banking. Deutsche Bank prizes the total value of its securities accounts which exceeds DM125 billion, features some 73 mutual funds and has an estimated 200 independent salesman with whom it holds exclusive contracts.

Deutsche Bank is also active in ancillary services, particularly in insurance. In terms of strategy, management seems to have concluded correctly that *retail investment banking* is a world of difference as compared with vanilla icecream banking. Furthermore, its characteristics change rapidly and therefore it requires a complex approach in regard to

- managerial functions,
- building up of the customer base,
- developing and marketing products, and
- retraining the bank's own personnel.

Other German banks whom I met in my research emphasized the importance of innovation in customer handholding, and the need to develop customer profiles – beyond knowing how many retirees or how many professionals one had as private banking clients.

American banks have made a similar point, adding that the able execution of such strategy has permitted a tremendous improvement of the marketing of private banking services. As always, the change in culture led to significant market impact, which is vital as customer contact points multiply, and so does the number of products.

8   IS IT ADVISABLE TO USE DERIVATIVES IN RETAIL BANKING AND IN PRIVATE BANKING?

There exists a great number of derivative financial instruments, each with its own characteristics and level of risk. The way popular opinion has it, derivatives are for hedging. This is not true, but many people go for this hype, either because they do not know the facts or because they do not care to learn about them.

For instance, while the constituent parts of an Index are more volatile than the Index itself, Index trading is a risky business, as the bankruptcy of Barings documents. Derivatives have a place in retail banking if, and only if, the following policies are set by top management:

1.   Hedging must be done under strict rules to be observed at all times.
2.   Clients must be advised about the risks, and the transactions done for them must be conservative.
3.   The development of new products for clients gives priority to risk control over higher profits.
4.   Speculation – that is, hedging in a vague and ill-defined sense – is strictly avoided.

About 77 percent of derivative financial instruments are treated over the counter (OTC), not in exchanges. The OTC market is huge and to manage this exposure bankers need effective measurement procedures – as well as a deep understanding of the risks. It is the unfamiliar and the misunderstood that generally cause lasting problems for the financial markets.

The contractual commitments with the OTC deal specify a *notional principal amount*. With rare exceptions, notional principal is neither paid nor received by the counterparties – but it is the basis for the calculation of what is due, usually a fraction of the notional amount. For risk control reasons, it is therefore appropriate to redimension the notional principal using a divisor, or *demodulator*, for instance 25 or 30 (for a practical implementation example, see Chapter 15):

•   Say, for instance, that the notional principal of an interest rate swap (IRS) is $200 million.
•   But, given the state of the market and our past experience, we estimate the risk we take at 4 percent.
•   We can then demodulate the notional amount of the contract by 25, which will bring our exposure on this contract to $8 million.

For risk management reasons, the use of a decompiler of contractual notional principal amounts helps to convert off-balance sheet exposure to loans equivalence. Such conversion makes sense because many more bankers understand loans than understand derivatives. Furthermore, in July 1996, a discussion paper by the UK's Accounting Standards Board advised that on-balance sheet and off-balance sheet exposure should be integrated.[2]

The fact that derivative financial instruments are inherently risky does not mean they should not be traded. During the mid-to-late 1980s and the 1990s, derivatives provided the means for new business as well as for confronting financial risk.

- Initially, off-balance sheet instruments were almost exclusively oriented to large players.
- But, by 1992, they had been offered at the retail level, while the number of large players put on the block skyrocketed.

Since 1994, the private banking operation of Chase Manhattan Private Bank has been promoting among its wealthy clients the more settled type of derivatives. Generally, these are considered to be mainly structured products which are thought to be able to preserve capital while offering the potential for enhanced returns. Derivatives have been promoted to private banking clients as the way to eliminate capital risk and reduce the volatility of yields. But Chase has added another twist to this argument by suggesting that they enable clients to benefit from the movements of an underlying market or currency, without being directly exposed to that market or currency.

This is of course less than half-true. In their Asian offering, for instance, the customized products – which are chiefly based on two of the so-called 'exotic currencies,' the Thai baht and the Indonesian rupiah – allow the customer to name his view of a market and invest accordingly. But such deals also carry a very high amount of risk.

While there are major concerns about the suitability of derivatives for low net worth clients, it is increasingly considered that for high net worth individuals derivative instruments might be appropriate, because they help in risk mitigation in a dynamic financial environment. I see this argument as being more evident for medium-sized businesses than for individuals. In a globalized economy many businesses need to hedge:

- Interest rate risk
- Foreign exchange risk, and
- Commodities which they buy abroad or at home.

There are, however, prerequisites to a wise use of derivatives. These start with the ability of users to identify different types of risk and deal with them, and have as a common denominator the force to restrict to *hedging only* rather than run the company's treasury for profits, and end up with huge losses.

Medium net worth individuals, too, might use some packaged bread-and-butter derivative products for house financing and property indexation. In the first case, a home buyer seeking a mortgage could mitigate his risk by entering into two transactions: a mortgage loan, and a hedge against changes in interest rates. But only a sophisticated investor should aim at the use of derivatives as a means to increase his flexibility in changing either the loan or the hedge as new circumstances develop. A similar statement can be made of property indexation.

For instance, a futures contract which is based on an index of house prices can enable the homeowner to protect himself against unwelcome house price movements – as distinct from changes in interest rates, though the two are related. A similar scenario can give the lender a way of sharing in the appreciation of house values in return for offering a lower interest rate on the original mortgage.

Another suggestion made by retail bankers concerns private investment instruments. There is now a derivative focusing on home income streams. This might enable homeowners to borrow against virtual incomes from their houses, in a way similar to that whereby Swiss authorities tax homeowners, on the basis of hypothetical income.

In a paper, 'Derivatives for the Retail Client' (CSFI, London, 1994), Andrew Dobson suggests some form of House Price Indexation (HPI) which might allow reduction of the principal risk in home ownership, as well as of cash flow risk. This might take the form of

- a house price-indexed futures contract, subject to availability of a suitable index, or
- a funding instrument with principal indexed to movements in the HPI, paying interest on the original invested sum at a given rate.

The borrower would still be left with a risk to the extent that movements in the value of his property deviated from movements in the index. If he knows how to handle it, this risk would be rather different from the one he faces today.

Hedging property values, moreover, is not altogether an alien concept to homeowners, but the different schemes existing so far have not functioned so well. An example is the *home income* variety, involving borrowing on the security of a home, often at floating interest rates, to reinvest in a fixed annuity.

- The annual debt service usually came to exceed the value of the income purchased with the proceeds.
- A more painful experience still has been that property prices fell, rolling up the deficit.

The core problem is that nobody can say in advance what will be the outcome with an untried vehicle like property index linking. Theoretically, a fixed interest rate would allow the principal proceeds to be used either to purchase an annuity or to invest in a form of fixed rate instrument. But the more complex the financial instrument becomes, the more difficult it is, for the typical homeowner, to understand what the derivative is all about and how it can be managed.

9 MAJOR SWISS BANKS: THEIR GLOBALIZATION AND DERIVATIVES INSTRUMENTS

As transpires from the examples in section 8, there has been a growing interest in the retail market for derivatives. Though this is still a small percentage of overall business, a number of banks comment that they can see it exploding in the future to the point of representing a third of their derivatives business.

Swiss banks and insurance companies provide a reference. However, prior to examining specific cases on the use of derivative financial instruments in the private banking market, it will be wise to take a look at how the banking industry works in globalized off-balance sheet trades.

I have taken the major Swiss banks as an example because Swiss commercial banks were among the first to introduce derivatives to the consumer market. In a way, the reader may wish to regard this section as a continuation of the text in section 5 on Swiss private banking.

Swiss Bank Corporation (SBC) and Union Bank of Switzerland (UBS) – which have merged since this text was originally written – bought London broking firms in the 1980s with the Big Bang. In the beginning, UBS made the most substantial purchase in Phillips & Drew. SBC's acquisition of Savory Milne turned rather sour, but then it bought Warburg as well as three American investment banks. Crédit Suisse merged its international investment bank with the US firm of First Boston in 1988. Generally, however, none of these efforts worked wholly as planned.

- UBS had difficulty integrating Phillips & Drew with its own operations, though it finally managed to do so.
- SBC found it had not gained true access to London markets through Savory Milne or for that matter through Warburg.
- CS First Boston was plagued by internal divisions until the early 1990s, because it was run as a collection of regional operations rather than a single unit.

These results called for stern measures and, since the early 1990s, SBC and UBS have restructured international operations and tried to make them more coherent. CS Holding adopted a dual strategy of expanding Crédit Suisse operations and making CSFB more effective. It also linked the two with a joint venture, Crédit Suisse Financial Products, to engineer and sell derivatives.

These efforts seem to have borne fruit as, in the 1990 to 1994 timeframe, the trading income of all three major Swiss banks increased significantly, as shown in Figure 9.6, because the Big Three Swiss banks had positioned themselves to take advantage of the strength of bond and equity markets. They also benefitted from the European currency turmoil which started in September/October 1992.

Financial results permitted UBS to raise pre-tax profits by 69 percent in 1993, with a third of earnings coming from abroad. Trading income, much of it generated abroad, formed 37 percent of CS Holding's profits. In the opinion of financial analysts in London, one of the main reasons for the rapid progress made in the 1990s by the three Swiss money center banks has been their strength in derivative financial instruments.

- They are by now used to trading in currency derivatives in the Swiss bond market.
- They know how to use derivatives to push into markets where they are weak in underlying cash products.

On 7 November 1995, less than six months after he persuaded top management to buy S.G. Warburg – as head of investment banking operations of Swiss Bank Corporation – Marcel Ospel replaced George Blum as group chief executive. Six other SBC Warburg board members were promoted to the group executive board.

Financial analysts say that Marcel Ospel's promotion demonstrates the importance SBC attaches to its global financial business, as well as its interest on

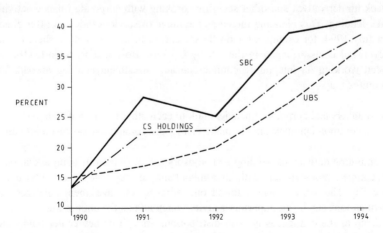

Figure 9.6 Trading income as a percentage of revenue in the 1990 to 1994 timeframe

building up expertise in derivative financial instruments in a global sense:

- In December 1992, SBC bought O'Connor, a Chicago-based options-trading firm.
- Within a couple of years, O'Connor partners were put into top management jobs at SBS.

Two of the latest appointments to SBC's executive board, David Solo and Andy Siciliano, come from O'Connor. A third, John Dugan, is at top management level. The strategy behind infusing Chicago blood into Basle is to transform SBC's international operations.

Still, while the O'Connor partners were good at derivatives, they seem to have lacked fund management experience, which Warburg possessed. The takeover of Warburg was risky, scale being one of the problems. A merger between two investment banks of this size presents significant challenges which the new management has not altogether put behind it. It is not easy to swallow a big organization, but the acquisition of skill is so important that some obstacles look smaller. For practically any money center bank and transnational investment institution, derivatives are among the most global products in its inventory, as well as strong growth areas in business and profits. Most trades however go to triple-A banks,

- exchanging a variable interest rate contract for a fixed rate one;
- this typically be done with an AAA bank because of credit risk.

Another advantage money center banks tend to have comes from their ability to back up derivatives and other securities broking with corporate finance activities like lending. This blending increases the range of services they can offer clients. In July 1994, for example, Crédit Suisse agreed to use its balance sheet to back leveraged deals arranged in the US by CS First Boston. For its part, UBS has been working on integrating commercial and investment banking abroad. This requires that:

- bankers and corporate financiers talk to each other in the same language:
- a common language should make them more competitive on customer calls.

Combining derivatives, lending and advisory activities permits commercial banks to compete more strongly with investment banks as corporate finance advisers. As the Big Three Swiss banks found out, advising on investments, mergers and acquisitions can be an important activity which affects the bottom line.

One of the challenges is asset distribution. Though money center banks have comparable goals in their globalization drive, no two banks have the same geographical asset distribution. As an example, Figure 9.7 shows the percentage

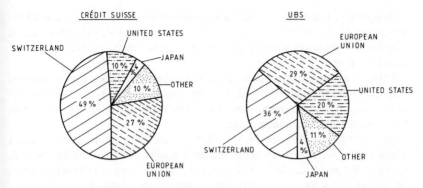

Figure 9.7 A geographical distribution of assets: notice the different percentages characterising the two banks

share in assets by major region for Crédit Suisse and UBS. Notice that UBS has been somewhat more successful in the internationalization of its assets, featuring a larger share in the United States and a smaller one in Switzerland.

Practically every non-US money center bank faces the challenge to establish a strong business in America, because this is key to forming a chain of global operations. In the underwriting and distribution of US equities, for instance, CS Holdings has an advantage in CS First Boston.

But while the global business holds the higher ground in top management thinking and in strategic planning, it would be wrong to think that domestic operations are downplayed. If anything, domestic banking can benefit from cross-fertilization. This is exactly where derivatives for retail banking come in – as we will see in section 10.

10 IS THE POPULARIZATION OF DERIVATIVES IN BANKING AND IN INSURANCE OF INTEREST TO PRIVATE INDIVIDUALS?

In August 1994, Winterthur Life Insurance launched *Windex IV*, a product aimed at its client base as well as the clients of other insurance companies. Windex IV is denominated in Swiss francs and it is based on derivatives. Its characteristics are that it constitutes an investment vehicle and a life insurance at the same time.

- It is aimed at the Swiss Market Index (SMI) of the most important Swiss stocks.
- It has a 10-year life cycle divided into five periods, each of two years.
- Its value for the holder depends 100 percent on the evolution of SMI.

Being both an investment vehicle and a life insurance, Windex IV offers all the advantages of the latter, including tax advantages as provided by Swiss law. It also features privileges which concern injury, death, succession and the case of business failure.

UBS has also launched a new financial vehicle, the *Life Index*. This is a fortune management tool of 10 years' duration, promising up to 9 percent interest per year, evidently with corresponding risks. The minimum return on investment being assured is 3.5 percent per year.

As is the case of Windex IV, the offer is based on a life insurance concept which capitalizes on movements of the stock market index. Since this approach seems to fall under the Swiss federal regulations for retirement benefits, Swiss citizen can capitalize on fiscal privileges, under certain conditions.

Key to this thrust of derivatives into private banking has been the transfer of skills from other operations, as discussed in section 8. The popularization of derivatives in Swiss retail banking started some time before the aforementioned insurance issues. The Swiss Bank Corporation was the first to develop derivative-based savings instruments for smaller investors.

• The idea has been to give the individual saver a better return on his money through an opportunity for some bigger profits.
• This means offering a chance to take a bet on a capital market the way sophisticated institutional investors have been doing for some time.

Left on his own, the individual saver does not have the culture of the complex calculations that make off-balance sheet products work. Sensing a market opportunity, in 1991, SBC offered one-year term investment instruments with derivatives characteristics, calling them *guaranteed return on investment* (Groi) securities, and selling them in units of SF5,000.

Capitalizing on the skills of its Chicago derivatives specialist partners, O'Connor Associates, SBC did a good productization job. The investor could choose from among three combinations of security and risk, the risk element being the movement of the SMI index of leading shares on the Swiss stock market over the one-year term of the fund.

• These units became popular among Swiss investors, and
• SBC had to cut off applications after taking in orders worth SF150 million.

This marketing success did not go unnoticed by other banks in Switzerland, and they soon introduced similar instruments. Union Bank of Switzerland offered the *Iglu* (the new name for the Iglu is Capital Protected Note), the index growth-linked unit, and the *Clou*, the currency-linked outperformance unit. Crédit Suisse introduced the SMI deposit. Bank Vontobel marketed the guaranteed capital index investment unit (*Kiss*) and Swiss Volksbank offered *Smile*, an SMI linked issue.

A couple of special factors have contributed to the appeal of these derivative instruments to private banking. First, they arrived on the market just as the commissions on small transactions in shares rocketed following the elimination of fixed rates. As a result, investors were attracted to securities that carried only a modest fee. Then, in the general case, Switzerland's fund managers have not been allowed to invest in pure derivatives until recently, and others have been frightened of them. The Groi, Iglu, Clous, Kiss and Smile provided an indirect way to new investment techniques.

Since its original 1991 derivatives offering, SBC has gone on to launch 60 more derivatives-based instruments for individuals and small institutions, using various other capital market indices and underliers. These offerings tend to have a life of from nine months to two years, and a secondary market has developed.

One Groi using the Nikkei index on the Tokyo stock market proved to be an object lesson on the risks of these securities. Over the period of the instrument, the Nikkei index tumbled 21 percent. Investors in the Nikkei Groi obviously got no bonus, though at least they got their capital back. The good news for them is that, if they had just been in Japanese equities, they would have lost a lot of money.

Yet, for all the initial success, there is considerable debate about how the market for these consumer-oriented derivative financial products is going to develop. It is remarkable, for example, that so far the idea has not caught on in a big way in other countries, except for France.

Notes

1. D.N. Chorafas, *Internet Financial Services: Secure Electronic Banking and Electronic Commerce* (London and Dublin: Lafferty, 1997).
2. See D.N. Chorafas, *Managing Derivatives Risk* (Burr Ridge, IL: Irwin Professional Publishing, 1996).

10 Wealth Management, Banking Contracts and Lasting Customer Relationships

1 INTRODUCTION

Chapter 6 brought to the reader's attention the nature of the marketing functions necessary to put into effect a banking strategy. It defined the sense of marketing in retail banking and outlined the common features which characterize market planning in different financial institutions. Chapter 7 extended this discussion into relationship banking, emphasizing the sales aspects and outlining the steps which are necessary to obtain

- a mirror of the activities the client has with the bank, and
- an estimate of the resulting profit and loss in the client relationship.

Part and parcel of this presentation has been the competition between computer-based communications networks and the bricks-and-mortar branch offices, as the delivery channels for banking services. At stake is the business opportunity presented by each of two major strategies which today dominate the minds of many retail bankers.

A clear manifestation of the network-based strategy, and a successful one for that matter, is direct banking which has been discussed in Chapter 8. By contrast, a good example of person-to-person relationship banking is the evolution of private banking, which was the subject of Chapter 9.

There are many other issues relating to effective banking strategies which need to be addressed in order to tie up in one neat package the function of marketing in financial institutions. One of them is the effective administration of customer relationships. Another is the internal organization necessary for the management of wealth. Within the changing perspective of commercial banking, the future management of wealth promises to be one of the most polyvalent enterprises which ever existed. Investors will still hold financial instruments such as stocks, bonds and derivatives, and also physical wealth like buildings, farms and vehicles. But wealth management will be conditioned through rigorous contracts with leading banks, while models, computers and networks will continually track these items in the individual's account.

240

One of the most challenging jobs of the coming years is research on how to make wealth virtually liquid. Some money center banks even talk of issuing individual *wealth cards* making it possible to pay for a new car by *instantly drawing* on wealth inherent in, say, a vacation house or equity in an enterprise which may be located anywhere in the world.

To consider seriously these widening possibilities in wealth management, we will start this chapter by outlining the most prominent organizational theories, which proceed by rethinking the business opportunities and functions associated with a universal sense of discretionary portfolio management. We will pay particular attention to what sort of contract should be written to provide guarantees to both the bank and its clients. We will also look into the internal controls which are necessary to ensure an effective and lasting customer relationship which is profitable both to the client and to the bank.

2 FEDERATED FINANCIAL ORGANIZATIONS AND THE CONCEPT OF VALUE DIFFERENTIATION

Given the number of issues which affect retail banking and their interrelationships, regulators are faced with unique challenges which are augmented because of the globalization of banking. Should universal banks (see section 3) be regulated in a transnational sense? How do universal banks stack up against non-banks and other specialist firms, in terms of their competitive performance in national and global markets?

A number of questions have to be answered by the top management of the banks themselves. For instance, what are the pros and cons of various alternative organizational forms of commercial banking; and of retail banking in a more strict sense? Should global commercial banks be characterized by vertical integration or through a holding structure?

Figure 10.1 shows more than 70 years of evolution in the dimensions of financial organizations and their structure. The clear pattern of a two-dimensional line and staff organization of the 1920s was first implemented by Alfred Sloan at General Motors. To a large extent, this reflected the 19th-century military organization of Clausewitz, which settled the functions of line and staff.

- The no. 1 reason Alfred Sloan gave for his organization was to make marketing skill available to all GM divisions.
- The concept of a universal bank discussed in section 3 poses precisely the same requirements in connection with marketing knowhow.

Four decades down the line, in the 1960s, the transnational corporation de facto introduced a third dimension based on its topology of operations. The 2-D model was no longer sufficient to handle the evolution of money center banks like

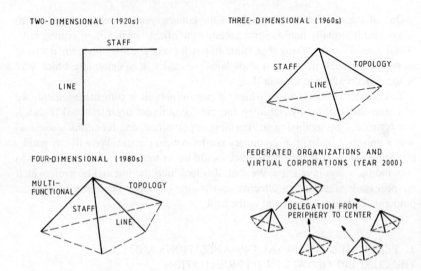

Figure 10.1   Seventy years of evolution in the dimensions of financial organization and structure

Citicorp, Chase Manhattan, Bankers Trust and J.P. Morgan. In the 1980s, a fourth dimension was added to handle multifunctional operation, as the number of channels handled by a bank both multiplied and diversified. This four-dimensional organizational model still prevails today, but with a difference. This difference comes from the *federated organization* (or *virtual corporation*). This model is currently adopted by universal banks through a holding which acts more as a coordination unit than a hierarchical line of command.

- In the federated organization, authority is not always transferred by the center to the periphery.
- Most often, it is delegated from the periphery to the center.

This type of virtual corporation increases the opportunities of competition even within the same financial holding. It is inevitable that the different independent business units in the four corners of the globe

- feel the pressure for developing new financial products,
- are obliged to automate and simplify back office operations, and
- have no alternative than to decrease the time to market in order to survive.

In a federated organization the bank's managers and professionals working for each independent business unit have P&L accountability but also more freedom of action. They can take their chances and reach their decisions without the constraints of a strict organizational hierarchy looking over their shoulders – but also without rocks behind which to hide.

To survive, the independent business units need market intelligence as well as knowledge-enriched software tools to help them in dealing with market pressures. Intelligent software is also necessary to permit the designing of novel financial products and to control risk. Both are absolutely necessary when dealing with banking instruments which are:

- innovative,
- appealing to sophisticated customers,
- characterized by fast time to market, and
- able to keep risk under control.

As we saw in Chapters 6 to 9, to stay competitive a bank must adapt quite rapidly to market changes. Quick product definitions is a 'must'; so is speed in the development-to-sales cycle. As rocket scientists and financial analysts elaborate the specifications, those in charge of trading must prepare the sales approach while computer specialists develop the intelligent software in record time.

This is why all team members should draw from the same source, visualize the same objects and speak the same language. The language has its own terms which may sound strange to classical bankers but are second nature to rocket scientists. An example is *intrinsic time*. The culture of intrinsic time is very recent. Figure 10.2 gives an example, by comparing intrinsic time with clock time *t*. Physical time is universal and has existed forever, but the awareness that it should be measured in a fairly precise manner is relatively recent, dating, in all likelihood, from the time of the Byzantine monasteries.

- Business time, however, does not need to move uniformly as physical or clock time does.
- The intrinsic time characterizing financial transactions, like securities trading and foreign exchange, may be faster than physical time – or it may be slower.[1]

Besides having a common language, so that they can understand one another, federated organizations must be able to work in unison in the design and marketing of new financial products. This is not as evident and as easy as it sounds, because of

- the differences which exist in culture between the different units, and
- the need to employ advanced technology which makes working in different time zones transparent.

The use of concurrent engineering quickly transforms design ideas into realistic models that are evaluated for technical features, market appeal, cost and risk. Banking is a deadline-oriented industry, and *there is no copyright* for

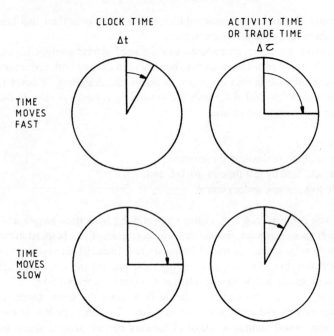

Figure 10.2 The process of time deformation: from clock time to activity time or intrinsic time

financial products. As we saw in Chapter 9, banks have to live through *value differentiation*.

- The retail bank has to come up with new solutions for problems that have surfaced during the last few months.
- This requires that all of the company's brainpower works in a focused manner to bring visible results quickly.

Like any other organization, retail banks must move fast to restructure their marketing channel. This, too, is a demanding task. A recent reorganization at Compaq, the personal computer company, provides an example. On 15 April 1995, Compaq drafted 20 managers from around the world for what became known as the *crossroads meeting* (*Business Week*, 22 July 1996). This crossroads meeting was strategic and it took place at the company's Houston headquarters. Kenneth E. Kurtzmann, vice-resident for Corporate Development, assembled five teams to

- tear apart Compaq's businesses, and
- assess each unit's strategy as well as that of key rivals.

Three weeks later, the teams presented a number of sobering recommendations: each business unit must be first or second in its market within three years, or Compaq should consider getting out of that line. Also:

- the company should no longer use profits from high-margin businesses to carry marginally profitable ones;
- each unit must show a return on investment – an advice which goes hand-in-glove with banking.

Many of the rules in retailing personal computers and banking products are fairly similar. Sales cannot be done without good products and the same is true of good marketing channels. Retail banks must offer services that sell well, with the right price tag attached to them. Differentiation is a very important marketing tool in a competitive environment. However,

- in vanilla icecream banking, it is very difficult to differentiate as the products are all essentially the same;
- but with ancillary services and derivative instruments (see Chapter 9) banks have something that stands out. There can be added value.

Borrowing a leaf from the book of the computer industry, another key way in which banks can differentiate is through a commitment to the provision of quality services. We spoke of product quality in Chapter 4, as well as of the contribution quality circles can make.

Attention to quality is more vital with federated organizations because the bank must present a *uniform high quality* to its clients no matter where it operates. Hence it must choose its salesmen, traders and account managers from people who have the skill to understand quality characteristics associated with financial products, as well as the technology that goes with them.

3 BUSINESS OPPORTUNITIES AND CHALLENGES WITH UNIVERSAL BANKING

The notion of a federated organization is just as applicable to small banks as it is to big ones. A local retail bank may divide its channels into independent profit centers, each acting as a business unit, but working in unison. Other things equal, however, the larger banks with polyvalent product lines have more to gain from independent business unit visibility.

An example is the *universal bank*. The concept of universal banking has been the subject of intense debate among practitioners in banking strategy, and also among financial analysts focusing on the performance of institutions and what they can do to improve their profitability. It has also attracted the attention of regulators concerned about stability and systemic risks.

The term *universal bank* was coined to identify an institution whose product lines ranged from retail banking to securities. Being constrained not to enter securities because of the Glass–Steagall Act in the United States and Article 65 in Japan, even some of the larger banks do not quite qualify as 'universal', though they have gone around the rules as regulators relaxed their watch on the dividing lines.

- The new dividing lines are different from those which existed in the past, and they are falling along marketing lines.
- As Figure 10.3 suggests, the rational split today follows a relationship orientation addressing a niche market or unique product – versus the mass market. (See also Chapter 6.)

The diversity of viewpoints taken by cognizant people in terms of what universal banking is and is not permits us to examine this subject from several viewpoints: what has been the experience, historically and around the world, of universal banking in terms of efficiency? What was their impact on national economic performance; on economic growth? There are also questions of principle in the financial industry.

- Should banks be in the insurance business?
- Should banks be in the securities business?
- Should banks control non-financial companies?
- Should non-financial companies control banks?

These queries go well beyond marketing, into the very foundation of banking functions in a deregulated financial industry. A good example is provided by the *insurance business.* 'Insurance services account for about 40 percent of all financial

NICHE MARKET, UNIQUE PRODUCT	MASS MARKET
• FREEDOM TO SET A PRICE	• THE MARKET SETS THE PRICE
• FEE INCOME ORIENTATION	• COST CUTTING IS A 'MUST'
• RETENTION PROGRAM IS FOREMOST	• MARKET SHARE ATTRITION IS INEVITABLE

Figure 10.3 With universal banking, business opportunity and challenges vary with the chosen strategy

services today,' Walter Wriston once suggested. 'You cannot be a truly effective financial service enterprise without offering this product.'

Citicorp, Deutsche Bank, Union Bank of Switzerland and many other universal banks are already in the insurance business. Citibank has $1.5 billion in life and disability insurance outstanding, mostly connected with its $2.5 billion portfolio of second mortgages. A Federal Reserve Board ruling has enabled the company to enter the broader business of underwriting life insurance.

In Chapter 9 we spoke of major Swiss banks, like SBC, UBS and Crédit Suisse, which not only entered the life insurance business but also introduced derivatives instruments connected with life insurance and marketed them retail. This constitutes a good example of universal banking because it points to:

- fertilization among different financial channels, and
- the cross-sales opportunities which are open in a deregulated landscape.

The more universal the product lines of *our* bank, the more management must pay attention to internal controls, as we will see in section 7. A similar statement is valid about prediction of financial conditions in each one of the markets our bank operates – and for each one of *our* product lines.

- It is not enough to ask in a general sense, 'Is our business enjoying an industry tailwind or is it facing a headwind?'
- This question has to be asked about every channel, paying great attention to each one of *our* products in each one of *our* markets.

Within this frame of reference, a number of critical questions can be asked regarding deposits and loans. For example: are we taking care to match rates and maturities? Paying attention to the mismatch problem requires clear management policies and ingenious modeling algorithms. It also costs money for

- training staff,
- establishing tighter management controls, and
- installing well-tuned computer and communications systems.

But it pays dividends. Loans books must be pruned. The same is true of derivatives books and of the books of any other product line *our* bank features. Management must be able at all times to look through risks and their aftermaths, project earnings and estimate cash flow as well as P&L for:

- any customer,
- any product,
- anywhere in the world.

Even if a universal bank offers the same products in all of its markets, chances are that they will feature different risk factors, different profitability and different growth rate market-by-market. Therefore they have to be watched individually, with senior management being always alert in planning, directing and controlling.

- Figure10.4 shows 14 channels sorted along *growth rate* and *profitability*, the way some European banks have classified them.
- The same channels along the same frame of reference but in the Asian market are shown in Figure 10.5. Notice that the positioning is quite different.

Risks, costs, profitability and growth rate are constraints on universal banking, which do not necessarily come from regulators. There are, as well, other constraints which some institutions have been able to turn into opportunities. An example is *Islamic Banking*. During the last five years there has been a competition for small but lucrative Islamic banking niches: lending money and taking deposits at no interest to comply with Islamic law or other religious principles can provide other channels for profits, both for customers and for the bank.

For example, in a curious version of a repurchase (*repo*) agreement, a Moslem customer may buy goods from a bank at one price, which he later sells back to the bank at a higher price. The difference between the two prices is amazingly close to what a deposit would earn in interest.

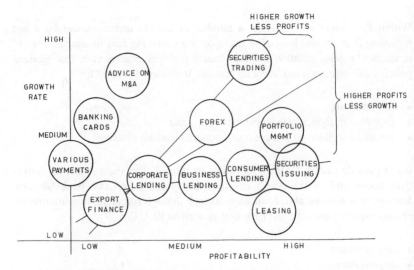

Figure 10.4   Growth and profitability of banking products as seen by European banks

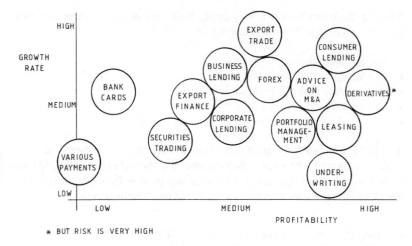

* BUT RISK IS VERY HIGH

Figure 10.5 Growth and profitability of banking products as seen by Asian banks

Also on offer are Islamic mortgages, on which customers buy their houses from a bank bit-by-bit – which is a novel approach to real estate dealing. Several merchant banks and investment banks have a dedicated business unit which does nothing but create new investment vehicles for Islamic funds.

Tradition rather than religion is behind other universal banking concepts which are at the same time constraints and business opportunities. *Reciprocity* in banking is an example. Some years ago, Franz Galliker, chairman of the board of directors of Swiss Bank Corporation, remarked that the concept of reciprocity is a key criterion entrenched in Swiss licensing procedures. Under the present banking law, a foreign bank can only operate as a foreign-controlled bank in Switzerland if Swiss banks are granted reciprocal rights to establish themselves in the other country. However, reciprocity can be interpreted in different ways.

The original intention of Switzerland's banking regulations was that the reciprocity requirement would only be satisfied if persons based in Switzerland were allowed to open a financial institution in the other country. In practice, however, the Swiss Federal Banking Commission has taken a somewhat softer line, leaning toward the interpretation that reciprocity already exists if the applicant's country treats foreign and domestic banks equally.

Correspondent banking could be seen as an extension of the concept of reciprocity, but subject to rigorous criteria of credit risk and of profitability, resulting from the correspondent's connection. Precisely for reasons of profitability, as we have already seen, there is a trend for banks to centralize transaction services, with a smaller number of banks. Over the last few years, for instance, Midland has reduced by over 50 percent the number of accounts it holds with other banks.

Some of the better known money center banks are doing the same worldwide. Business is going to those who can deliver

- the best product,
- at a highly competitive price,
- in the proper business environment,
- at the right time, and
- with solid technological support.

As will be discussed to a significant extent in Part Three, to remain competitive, banks need products that sell, which are offered at the right price and which make it possible to see through exposure because they provide the means to gauge risk. Not all universal banks are today able to fulfill such requirements.

4   DISCRETIONARY PORTFOLIO MANAGEMENT AND ADEQUACY OF FINANCIAL SKILLS

The sense of a unique product is not that nobody else has it but rather that we design it and present it in such a way that other banks cannot compete with us. This gives *our* bank the upper hand by making market entry too difficult for newcomers and/or the price of entry too high.

Banks consider *discretionary portfolio management* the most important service that the financial industry can offer to high net worth individuals, precisely because it can be packaged as a unique product. But cognizant investors appreciate that they face penalties in this process, among them:

- inadequate investment performance, which is a key reason why clients leave a bank;
- too much switching around of the portfolio's contents, to generate fees; and
- risk of changes in the portfolio which do not correspond to the investor's preferred profile.

These and other penalties are often expressed as a function of the powers the client has given to the bank in terms of managing his investments. Called in continental Europe *full powers* (Vollmacht), discretionary authority permits the bank to take the initiative in sustaining and augmenting the portfolio's wealth – but at the customer's risks and perils.

Also known as a managed account agreement, this solution authorizes the bank to administer the assets in the account, monitoring market developments and making investment decisions in accordance with instructions given by the client, but at its discretion. This gives the bank the right to purchase and sell securities on the client's behalf. The account holder can annul the agreement at any time or alter the instructions it contains.

As Figure 10.6 shows, discretionary portfolio management is one of the possible strategies which used to be quite popular but has lost a good deal of its appeal. Banks love it, but its share in terms of portfolio management alternatives has dropped below 50 percent for the following reasons:

• as clients become more sophisticated, they learn how to manage their own portfolio, and
• institutional investors do not even need the bank to execute the transaction.

The latter point describes the strategy in the second quarter space of Figure 10.6. Today this is the approach followed by many institutional investors. Tomorrow, with Internet, it may become the leading solution even for medium and lower net worth individuals.

The two strategies on the left side of Figure 10.6 differ by degree, not in their fundamentals. In both cases, the bank is executing the trades but in the lower one it has more of a say in influencing the client's decision. Some banks, for instance the General Bank of Luxembourg, charge a fee for this advice over and above the portfolio management fee.

In evaluating their relationship with the bank, cognizant customers depend on value-defining information. But while performance is one of the key issues facing asset management in retail banking, few institutions have the technology to face the market's whims without much damage to the assets they are managing.

• Ten years ago in private banking, rolling out the red carpet was the issue.
• Now the core subject is much more concerned with delivering profits and substance.

	MID-WAY CASES	EXTREME SOLUTIONS
HIGH INTERVENTION	DECISIONS BY CLIENT WITH STRONG ADVICE FROM THE BANK'S INVESTMENT SPECIALISTS	DISCRETIONARY PORTFOLIO MANAGEMENT: ALL DECISIONS BY BANK
LOW INTERVENTION	ALL DECISIONS MADE BY CLIENT – BUT BANK EXECUTES	BOTH INVESTMENT DECISIONS AND TRADING BY CLIENT, WHILE BANK ACTS AS ADVISOR

Figure 10.6 The quarter spaces in customer decisions regarding portfolio management

Simply stated, failure to provide good investment performance means losing the client. For sophisticated clients, good performance does not necessarily mean the greatest possible capital gain, because they do correlate *reward* with *risk*. Good performance can best be judged through high quality of service (see Chapter 4) and a longer-term pattern.

Patterning risk and reward through the medium to longer term brings to the fore the need to work out the risk profile most appropriate to a particular client's drives and requirements. It also makes it mandatory always to check against special private client benchmarks.

- For excellence of a portfolio management mechanism, it is necessary to understand both the product and the customer.
- The second prerequisite is the ability to find opportunities to deliver services, always betting on high-quality characteristics.

While the pricing of asset management is a factor, this factor is largely controlled by the more general product pricing set by the market, unless there is something really superior to offer. Adding value makes it possible to set the price higher, and very often what adds value to asset management is *superior performance*.

Chapter 15 will explain why tier-1 banks use technology to help in pricing their products. With technology it has become much easier to measure how much a service should cost, by simulating supply, demand and standard costing – and always keeping abreast of market developments.

Another major consideration in asset management is the *control of risk*. Many services are likely to attract a risk premium, but no two services are the same. The banks' perceptions of credit risk, market risk, legal risk, currency risk – and also a country's political and economic risk – have an important role in determining how well the clients' assets and the bank's own portfolio are managed. All this is very relevant both to asset management goals and to the type of skill needed for client handholding. It also represents a bridge between marketing (the subject of Part Two) and product design (to which Part Three addresses itself).

The problem many retail banks face in their hope to enter the discretionary portfolio management market is that they lack appropriate culture, strategy and skills. Wealth creation by the entrepreneurs of the 1980s and 1990s continues to fuel demand for asset management services, but these entrepreneurs are highly demanding investors. Even some of the former asset management specialists are losing touch with the changing market.

- As we saw in Chapter 9, private banks, many of them family-owned or controlled, traditionally provided high levels of personal service to their customers.
- But to a very significant extent these banks remained untouched by modern management techniques and most particularly by high technology. Therefore they are under pressure.

Chapter 9 also underlined that the consolidation of the private banking sector has already started, and a great moving force behind it is the urgently needed upgrading of professional knowhow. Inadequate asset management means that investment performance is stodgy and erratic. It is also out of alignment with the client's willingness to accept risk.

- In many cases, individual portfolios vary quite significantly from benchmarks.
- Even if clients do not immediately realize the difference because of the opacity of investment reports, one day they will.

Falling behind in analytical skills and in technology is way out of line with current trends where the element of performance has become quite important. At the same time, inadequate asset management means that some private banks have little idea where their costs and revenues come from.

- The result is that a small percentage of profitable clients end up subsidizing the rest.
- Inadequately managed retail banks also have difficulty establishing a proactive approach to marketing.

All the chapters in Part Two have underlined that, once regarded as rather undignified, marketing is today the cornerstone of the effort to win new customers as well as to obtain a greater share of the wealth of existing customers. The concepts underpinning this issue hold true all the way up and down the retail banking scale, and they impact on personally tailored financial services.

5   GENERAL CONDITIONS CHARACTERIZING A CLIENT'S CONTRACT

One of the subjects in which many retail banks entering private banking fail is writing up the general conditions of a contract which are fair both to their customers and to themselves. Quite often, such a contract is written by lawyers without marketing savvy, or by marketing people who are not so familiar with the legal concepts behind risk and return.

Some of the articles embedded in a contract for private banking can be considered as classical. An example is authorization, authentication and right of signature. Others are competitive, such as the type of communications from the bank to the client. Much of the discussion in Chapter 7 on relationship banking and in Chapter 9 on private banking is applicable in this connection.

Still other items entering a private banking contract are debatable, in the sense that, while they are generally written to serve the bank's interests, cognizant customers would never sign them as they stand. They will ask for alternatives and guarantees – and the bank which fails to provide them will never gain a significant account.

- An example of such clauses is what happens when securities are lost.
- The risk of this happening is non-trivial because of securities lending, repo practices and other leveraged deals.

In this and in the next section we will focus on the most important clauses a private banking contract should contain. These do not include the preliminary investigation the bank must carry out to ensure that the funds do not come from whitewashing money by drug dealers, the mafia or other forms of organized crime.

Right of Signature and Authentication

Right of signature arrangements between the client and the bank are typically established and remain in effect until such time as the bank receives written cancellation from the client. With each transaction, the bank shall verify the authenticity of signatures by comparing them with specimen signatures deposited with it.

Where more than one person has the right of signature, each party is often regarded as having the right of single signature, unless the client provides written instructions to the contrary. Usually, the bank is entitled, but not required, to undertake more thorough verification.

A controversial clause added by some banks is that the client bears all damages arising from failure to detect inadequate validity or forgeries, unless gross negligence on the part of the bank can be proved. The hinge is that it is not easy for the client to prove the bank's gross negligence.

Incapacity to Act

Banks tend to specify that the client shall bear all damages arising from his or her own incapacity to act, unless such deficiency is announced in an official publication. The same reference is valid for all damages arising from incapacity to act of authorized representatives or other third parties.

This, too, is a controversial subject because incapacity to act has many aspects, some of which might be exploited by organized crime or by members of the person's own family. Furthermore, with globalization in banking the publication 'in an official publication' is a very weak clause.

Communications from the Bank to the Client

Communications from the bank are considered as duly effected if they have been dispatched according to the client's most recent instructions. Mail which the bank is instructed to hold is regarded as delivered on the day this mail is dated.

Depending on the law of the land, mail to be held by the bank is kept for '*x*' years and destroyed upon termination of this period, unless another agreement is concluded. The bank usually charges a fee for the mail-holding service.

Many contracts stipulate that the client shall bear all damages arising from delays, loss, errors, mutilation or duplication in transmission or transportation – unless gross negligence by the bank can be proved. Knowledgeable clients do not accept this clause.

Current Account and Other Accounts Reporting

Some banks issue monthly statements and, at the client's request, quarterly, semi-annual or annual statements. Other banks issue statements by transaction or on a daily basis. Usually banks reserve the right to charge the client for any expenses, as well as for taxes or fees which may be incurred after closing of the account statement.

Also the bank reserves the right to modify its interest and commission rates shown in account reporting, at any time, in line with the general situation and standard banking conditions. In many countries the law stipulates that the bank must inform the client of such alternations by letter.

Payments and Settlements

The contract usually stipulates that, in the event of late execution of payment transactions, the bank shall be liable only for loss of interest – unless the bank's attention has been specifically drawn to the imminent risk of further damage.

This, too, is a controversial clause because the time of informing the bank about 'further damage' creates a questionable basis on which to base claims for late payments and settlements. Minor damages, however, can be negotiated with the bank after the fact.

Foreign Currency Accounts

Assets of the bank corresponding to the client's credit balance in foreign currency are typically deposited in that currency. Typically also, the client bears a proportionate part of all economic, legal and other consequences which might arise from government measures or political changes affecting the bank's assets deposited in a given country or held in its currency.

For this reason, as well as for the fact that money in foreign currency accounts should be invested immediately, company treasurers and high net worth individuals demand that account balances are reported to them immediately. Out of this requirement was born cash management in the 1970s, starting with Mars by J.P. Morgan and Marty by Citibank.

Bills of Exchange and Checks

In the event that bills of exchange, checks and other paper which have been discounted or given to the bank for collection are not paid, or the payments are reclaimed in accordance with applicable law, or should the bank be unable to freely make use of the proceeds therefrom, the bank is entitled to debit the client's account.

Typically, the bank retains all right on such paper until the debt balance has been eliminated. Collections of drafts and similar negotiable instruments at subsidiary banking places are usually handled without liability on the bank's behalf.

Safe Custody and Trust Accounts

A client's securities, precious metals and other objects are held for safekeeping by the bank, subject to custodial fees. Barring explicit instructions from the client to the contrary, the bank deposits securities and precious metals, which have been acquired or delivered abroad, with foreign correspondent banks which it regards as being of good standing.

Such deposits are made in accordance with local practices, in the name of the bank but for the account and at the risk of the client. This is a practice religiously followed by universal banks against which there is little recourse. (See also section 7.)

6   CLAUSES CONCERNING DERIVATIVE INSTRUMENTS, MARGINS AND LIQUIDATION OF POSITIONS

Section 5 has brought in evidence the fact that there are two viewpoints to be considered in a private banking contract. The examples which have been presented are, however, rather classical. By contrast, major deviations in terms of interests may be present when we talk of futures, options and other derivatives, the interpretation of margin requirements and the right of liquidation of customer positions held in custody.

Client Orders

As a matter of general practice, the bank effects the transactions due to client orders only on specific instructions by the client or under the terms of a discretionary portfolio management authorization. The client expressly acknowledges that, upon placing orders or issuing instructions over the telephone, such orders and instructions are to be carried out subsequently by the bank.

The execution is confirmed by the bank in writing. Usually, the bank executes transactions through a broker of its choice, but major clients often choose to specify the broker through which they would like to see their transactions handled.

Futures, Options and Swaps Transactions

The general norm is that the bank agrees to undertake the following derivative instruments transactions on the major exchanges and, when possible, during pre-trading periods or in the over-the-counter market. Such operations are typically done upon customer instructions for the account and at the risk of the client.

- *Financial futures*: interest rate futures, foreign currency futures, stock index futures, precious metals futures and other types of financial futures.
- *Options*: options certificates and warrants, standardized and traded options, covered options, options on futures (interest rate, foreign currency, stock index, precious metals) as well as other options transactions.
- *Swaps*: interest rate swaps, foreign currency swaps, equity swaps, reverse swaps, inverse floaters, index amortizing, index principal and other complex swaps.

The rule is that all transactions must be adequately covered. In futures, options and swaps, the bank shall only be bound by the client's instructions concerning prolongation or the exercise of options. However, such instructions must be received by the bank before the stockmarket sessions of the last day the options can be exercised or extended.

Requirements for Margins

The minimum margins are set by the exchanges but can also be set by the bank or the broker. Requirements for margins are periodically adjusted to market conditions and/or because of regulation. The margin may be increased when markets are volatile. All futures are subject to margin requirements, but not the purchase of options.

As long as a position is open, the minimum margin must be available in the form of a credit balance or a credit line. If a loss incurred on a given contract exceeds the difference between the initial and maintenance margins, the client will be required to put up additional collateral, immediately restoring the margin to its full initial level.

Liquidation of Positions

If the margin falls below a certain maintenance level and such level is not re-established by the client, and/or should the collateral decline in value, the bank is entitled to liquidate open positions. The placement of stop loss or stop limit orders is not a guarantee that a position can be liquidated at a predetermined loss, as unusual market conditions may make it impossible to execute such orders.

Positions held in contracts involving cash settlements may be held until expiry. Contracts for commodities involving physical delivery will be closed out on the date of delivery, unless the client gives explicit instructions to the contrary at least five working days prior to such first notice day.

Pledging of Collateral and Assignment

The client typically grants to the bank the rights to fulfillment of all liabilities that arise or may arise in the future from business transactions with the bank, particularly but not exclusively the following: current account(s), bills of exchange, commodity transactions, stock exchange dealings, derivatives trades, deposit of securities, portfolio management and trust transactions.

Derivatives trades include contingent liabilities such as liabilities of recourse, or those arising from other legal causes even though they are not yet validated in law. An example is possible tax claims.

The lien shall cover particularly but not exclusively the amount in principal of such claims, interest due and falling due thereon, commission, brokerage and all expenses such as storage costs, transport costs, customs duties, insurance premiums, valuation costs and rentals.

Other costs to be covered by the client are those incurred in enforcing the lien or assignments together with costs and compensation incurred in litigation and exception proceedings. The lien shall remain in force even if the liabilities of the pledgor and/or the debtor have been temporarily fully or partially satisfied.

Special Conditions

In addition to the general conditions, special regulations issued by the bank are applicable and shall take precedence over the former. Among the more classical examples are the use of checkbooks, deposits of securities and other objects, rental of safe deposit boxes and vaults, savings book accounts and deposit accounts.

More complex special conditions are those relating to stock exchange practices, foreign currency and commodity transactions. Many of these are locally regulated and the universal bank must account for such positions wherever they exist.

Approval of Statements and Complaints

The classical policy is that objections to statements of account, safe custody account or other accounts must be made within one month. Most contracts stipulate that, after expiration of this period, said statements shall be regarded as approved, even if the client has not signed a confirmation.

- The explicit or implicit approval of a statement of account implies approval of all items contained in such a statement.
- This includes any reservations noted therein by the bank.

Complaints by the client regarding execution or non-execution of orders of any description must be made immediately upon receipt of the advice concerning the transaction to which the customer objects.

Most contracts stipulate that complaint or objection by the client must be registered as if such an advice has been delivered under normal postal conditions, with the client bearing any damages arising from a delay in registering his complaints with the bank. This clause is controversial because it does not reflect the effect of postal strikes or other unusual conditions – but remedy can be provided through networks.

The Handling of Legal Risk

Typically, financial institutions include a clause in the private banking contract that, if one or more items under custody are lost and cannot be recovered, the bank will compensate with a similar item of comparable value, or through cash. This is a clause which protects much more the bank than the client, because it provides no guarantee of equal value, leaving the customer to carry the risk.

Another example of legal risk in connection to fiduciary responsibilities, where the bank is the executor, is inheritance. Some of the principal issues affecting the inheritance of estates, for which the bank includes clauses protecting its position in terms of possible damages, include the following.

- *Recognition of the will*: a will made in one country may not be valid under a second country's legal system. The globalization of finance places particular emphasis on this issue compliance.
- *Domicile and residency*: both domicile and residence are key concepts in determining which tax laws apply, but their definition is far from being uniform from one country to another – or even within the same country. In principle, a person has only *one* domicile, but he or she may have many residencies.
- *Tax treaties*: the existence of a treaty between an expatriate's home and host countries is instrumental in changing tax planning considerations. A similar statement is valid concerning the consequences of forced heirship. In the absence of a will, the relevant legal system will substitute its standard code in dividing up assets among relatives.

7 ESTABLISHING AND FOLLOWING A STRATEGY OF RIGOROUS INTERNAL CONTROLS

While the clauses of the customer contract have to be studied thoroughly to protect the bank and its interest without scaring away sophisticated clients, fencing external risk would only be a half-baked exercise unless internal risk was faced in a rigorous manner. A surprisingly large number of retail banks fail to understand this issue.

Yet the case of internal controls is unassailable. After the Barings, Daiwa Bank and Sumitomo Corporation débâcles happening in quick succession, equity investors have to inject a new risk factor, *weak management controls*, into their valuation of risk hanging over their portfolio.

- Until recently, the concept was that the main risks were external, related to entities and private individuals with which a bank is doing business.
- But now there is solid evidence that some of the top risks which can throw a financial institution into the abyss are internal.

Rigorous internal controls should be established and regularly subjected to stress tests throughout the organization, from headquarters to the branches, the subsidiaries and other independent business units. Every organization, no matter how large or how small, lives in a business environment full of recurrent and exceptional risks.

The same is true of every business opportunity we encounter. In section 2, I recommended the concept of independent business units because they tend to have a quicker response to competitors' actions, faster diffusion of new ideas, less distorted internal and external communications and a generally higher morale. They show:

- greater ability to respond to customer needs, and
- more straightforward pinpointing of individual responsibility and accountability.

This, however, is true only if we have established a very rigorous system of internal controls. Just as in Chapter 7 we spoke of the customer mirror, which makes it possible to know the profit, loss and risk associated with each customer, the top management of the bank needs to appreciate that each manager, each trader, each investment advisor and each fund manager is now the ultimate *risk taker*. As such, everything he does (or does not do) must be tracked because his actions (or inactions) may bring down the bank. The counterpart of this is that the customer has now become the ultimate profit center.

A classical issue regarding internal controls which many banks fail to observe is the separation of responsibilities between *front desk* and *back office*. When it lost $1.4 billion from derivatives trades on the Osaka exchange, which originated from its Singapore office, Barings revealed that Nick Leeson was in charge both of the front desk and of the back office. Daiwa Bank made the same statement about the man it held responsible regarding the $1.1 billion it lost out of its office in New York.

There is no doubt in my mind that clear lines regarding responsibility and accountability are the best way to avoid confused signals regarding the retail bank's financial health. Internal controls should eliminate the ability to manipulate reporting standards. In 1953, I had a professor of accounting at UCLA who taught his students that: 'If you let me choose my reporting standards, I can prove you anything.' This is today called 'creative accounting'.

On October 23, 1995, the French stock market regulator Commission des Opérations de Bourse (COB), published a warning about the half-year accounts of Pechiney. By using American accounting standards instead of French ones, the French chemicals and metals company had turned a slight loss into a good profit of FF658 million ($130 million). Pechiney was not alone in altering its yearly results in terms of direction through the use of American reporting practices. The creative accounting of Pechiney produced profits; that of other companies, such as Alcatel, Générale des Eaux and Compagnie de Suez have brought forward significant losses topped off by large provisions. All these companies used a switch in reporting practices.

- Pechiney needed profitable results because it was being privatized, and red ink would have discouraged investors.
- But financial analysts commented that each of the other three firms had recently named a new boss, whose actions would look all the better if his starting point was low.

These are on-balance sheet differences which come into perspective because the legal reporting requirements vary so considerably from one country to another. There is as well a more basic question about the meaning of *risk and return* conveyed by a company's annual report. An annual report tells its reader about cash, loans, bonds, land, machinery and buildings, but not about:

- the *risk levels* being assumed by management, and
- the *potential volatility* of the market value of assets and liabilities.

In the absence of a common language to describe risk, internal and external control of exposure becomes a very difficult task. The same is true of establishing universal reporting practices for financial, industrial and commercial companies, a subject which is very important at a time of globalization of business.

In conclusion, the way I see it, the establishment and maintenance of rigorous internal controls are a matter of ethics. Many negatives are hidden and positive aspects exaggerated when reporting standards can be manipulated. A bank cannot and should not work that way. Management must care both for survival in the large and for each one of its accounts in the present day.

8 EVEN CERTIFIED PUBLIC ACCOUNTANTS FALL INTO THE TRAP OF DUBIOUS REPORTING PRACTICES

There is nothing that can kill customer confidence as fast as the finding that the bank with which one deals takes liberties with one's account. At one time or another, every financial institution has found out that 'this' or 'that' account (which may be a client's or the bank's own) has been subjected to a certain amount of managing or manipulation. Although all banks trust their own inspection department to do an investigation, they also expect certified public accountants (CPAs) to do a clean job in reporting.

At least, this is what I learned from my professors of banking at UCLA, and believed until fairly recently. But 44 years down the line I am not sure this principle holds because of major CPA troubles in connection with reporting practices. *Event risks* have recently hit CPA for allegedly not having done the job they were paid to do:

1. Barings liquidators versus Coopers & Lybrand: the Court-appointed joint administrators of Barings started proceedings against Coopers & Lybrand, in London and Singapore, as well as against Deloitte & Touche in Singapore, to the tune of $1billion (*The Times*, Wednesday 24 January 1996). The Bank of England also criticized and questioned the actions of both firms of auditors.
2. A High-Court judge in London found an accounting firm liable for negligence in permitting a loss-making Lloyd's (the insurer) to close its accounts. (*The Economist*, 4 November 1995.)
3. British accountants (Deloitte & Touche) called in to wind up the Bank of Credit and Commerce International (BCCI) allegedly overcharged by 40 percent for their services. (*Financial Times*, 23/24 March 1996.)
4. In Germany, Price Waterhouse has been seeking an out-of-court settlement with the creditors of Balsam and Procedo, two failed companies.

German banks, which faced losses of DM2.3 billion as a result of the Balsam and Procedo collapse, claimed that Price Waterhouse auditors were guilty of intentional misconduct by:

*   not qualifying the accounts of both Balsam and Procedo, and
*   failing to blow the whistle on long-standing fraudulent deals between the two companies.

Price Waterhouse had originally rejected the creditors' allegations and refused to enter into talks of any kind until it was fully aware of the facts of the case. It changed its mind after being presented with a draft written by the creditors, which seems to have included evidence PW had not seen before. Also critical was the fact that, given the enormous complexity and volume of the material, a court case would be extremely costly and could last for years.

Price Waterhouse also faced significant problems of a similar nature in the United States. As an American analyst commented, this is neither the first nor the last case of that kind with CPAs. Neither will it be an exceptional case if people in responsible organizational positions both at operating companies and their auditors falsify official accounts and, up to a point, do so with impurity.

As attested by an article in the *Financial Times* (19 June 1996), in October 1991, Yasuo Hamanaka – a senior executive and top copper trader of Sumitomo Corporation – in a handwritten note asked his counterpart in London to falsify the accounts by issuing a backdated invoice for a fictitious copper deal worth $225 million.

- One of the troubles with Sumitomo Corporation is that Hamanaka remained in his senior job for nearly five years after this scandal.
- He was discharged only in mid-June 1996, when Sumitomo lost $1.8 billion because of long positions in copper derivatives.

For a Japanese company it is very difficult to make the case that top management was unaware of scandals (which is not, however, altogether excluded) because the hierarchical structure is so strong. Whether a financial institution or industrial company, the Japanese-type organization moves only on the basis of intensive consultations between successive management strata, up and down the hierarchy.

As a matter of principle, there is nothing better than a good case study to help in explaining what goes wrong with the system of internal controls. After the $1.1 billion losses by Daiwa Bank and the $1.8 billion losses by Sumitomo Corporation, many people started asking, 'Why made in Japan?' Among the answers are the following:

- The Japanese culture tends to discourage investigatory activities and disclosures, which are an integral part of management.
- At the same time, Japan's regulatory mechanism has not kept pace with the country's extraordinary economic growth.

An integral part of Japanese values is that an embedded bureaucratic system places more importance on harmony rather than looking at things for what they are. American practice is often different. 'Scare them to death,' Henry F. Kaiser used to tell his assistants regarding the way they should report their findings, 'Tell them the truth.'

Japanese are neither more likely nor less likely to make trading errors than other people, but they are less likely to uncover them until great damage has been done. This is the case because in Japan societal factors play a significant role in the way corporations operate – more so than they do elsewhere. As a result, various cases of staggering losses are now coming up as offshoots of decades of phenomenal economic growth since the end of World War II. The trouble for Japan is that this fast and significant economic expansion was built upon an archaic structure of:

- regulations,
- business customs,

- codes of protection, and
- weak internal controls.

In most Japanese banks and commercial or industrial companies, internal controls did not change sufficiently as the country's postwar economy accelerated. For instance, while traders registered losses, as happened everywhere in the world, accounting practices in Japan did not capture them or, when capturing, did not report them because

- accounting rules are outdated,
- risk management systems are vague, and
- controls are not always strictly enforced.

Cognizant financial analysts suggest that Japan's opaque accounting system does not exert sufficient discipline in bookkeeping. Assets are stated at their acquisition price rather than at their market value, no matter how long ago they were purchased or how much their value has changed.

As elsewhere in the world, a rigid corporate hierarchy and inflexible compensation systems also contribute to this problem of unaccountability of exposure. Faulty compensation and personal prestige are putting uncommon pressure on star performers to derive rewards from reputation. Not only anyone who is successful is admired, but also it is considered rude and a sign of jealousy to check and double-check whether achievements are solid, or tricky business is the rule.

Furthermore, as in many other countries and in a myriad of companies, there is no real wall between the front desk, which trades, and the back office, which processes the transactions. As the Barings bankruptcy has shown, this failure can be lethal. Daiwa Bank and Sumitomo Corporation have added their names to the roster of companies in which internal controls are wanting and certified public accountants do not seem to have done the job for which they were paid.

Note

1.   Dimitris N. Chorafas *How to Understand and Use Mathematics for Derivatives, volume 1: Understanding the Behaviour of Markets* (London: Euromoney, 1995).

Part Three
Product Pricing, Profitability, Security, Credit Risk and Market Risk

11 Setting a Pattern of Products, Markets and Bank Profitability

1 INTRODUCTION

'*Strategic*' is the product on which *our* bank depends for its survival and for its future profitability. 'Strategic' as well is a pivot product through which other financial services have to transit. I always advise that a current account is opened for each customer, even if he only does export credit or only fund management with *our* bank. This makes the current account a strategic node in the network of services.

The concept underpinning product management is that more attention should be paid to strategic services than to all others. Typically, strategic financial products are longer-range; they view future needs, not only present ones; and there is a commitment to their continuation and further development. The evolution of new products and services as well as the upkeep of those already in the product line is part of the future cost of staying in business. This contrasts with day-to-day expenses which are part of the cost of doing business. No retail bank can avoid the challenge of the cost of staying in business.

As contrasted to a strategic product, a *tactical* product is shorter range. It may be able to help today in doing business but nobody is really sure of its survival and longer-term perspective. Tactical financial products, like a bread-and-butter type of savings account or of loans, are part of the current cost of operation – as well as of current profitability.

Notice that bank profitability plays a key role in the case of both *tactical* and *strategic* products. There are as well what I call *free-ride products*. These are typically services which for a retail bank do not necessarily represent significant money-making opportunities. But we may need to have them in order to present a full range of products to our customers.

Products which are 'free-ride' for one institution may be tactical or even strategic for another. There is no unique way of classifying *a priori* retail banking services. In terms of an accurate way of looking at product range, much depends on

- the history of the financial institution,
- the profitability goals it has set for itself,
- the market's conditions and drives, and
- innovation and other variables.

Let me take an example. In early 1995, one of the large Italian banks asked a consultancy to examine its product line and the general characteristics of its market as well as its organization. Following this, the consultancy was expected to come up with recommendations. A point stressed by top management was what to do in terms of personal banking.

A year later, the consultancy deposited its report and gave thumbs down to the personal banking proposition. The reason was not that this is not a flourishing business among Italian retail banks but, rather, a couple of basic facts of life which conditioned the expected profitability.

The financial institution in question was (and it still is) controlled by the Italian government. Afraid that there may be a conflict of interest between the nationalized Italian banks and the tax authorities, high- and medium-net worth individuals prefer to have private banks as assets managers. Equally important is the fact that the culture of the bank in question is totally alien to private banking and, curiously enough, management would not care much about fee income.

2   THE CHANGING NATURE OF FINANCIAL INSTRUMENTS AND THE TECHNOLOGY THEY REQUIRE

Financial instruments are a means of *buying and selling risk*. Used in an able manner, they can serve in trade-oriented transactions, contribute to market liquidity and provide protection against an unwarranted exposure. We design and sell financial instruments in order to *make profits*. This is feasible if risk is kept under control through:

- appropriate policies,
- a valid methodology, and
- high technology.

Profitability will never be the sure outcome of trading in financial products, whether these are simple loans or complex investment vehicles. Apart from the risk the bank assumes, which is always present, there are also costs in developing and delivering banking services, as well as in managing the customer relationship.

While everybody says that banking is a labor-intensive business, and this is valid up to a point, it is no less true that product profitability highly correlates with the level of technology which we use. Some years ago, when product innovation in banking started going strong and technology made a big difference in the profitability of services, Bank of America did a study whose results are shown in Figure 11.1. The core of this profitability study has been to gauge, not just market response, but also what the commercial bank gains and loses from a product, as well as from a homogeneous group of services requiring a *production system* to be brought to market.

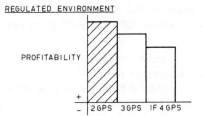

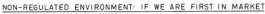

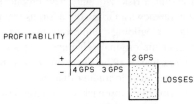

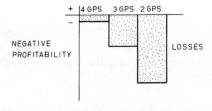

Figure 11.1 Product profitability and information systems support

- A second generation production system (2GPS) is one based on a centralized mainframes working batch and snowed under with paper (a 1960s–1970s approach).
- A third generation production system (3GPS) utilizes a distributed computer environment assisted through networks – a sort of early 1980s solution.

By contrast, a 4GPS is a fully networked solution, from point of origin to point of destination, assisted through knowledge engineering artefacts. This is the computers, communications and software technology characterizing interactive computational finance, of which we have spoken on several occasions. Note that:

- In a regulated banking environment 2GPS has a better profitability even if the competitiveness of such solution is lower, because vanilla icecream banking requires no new investments.

- But in a deregulated environment the pattern changes radically. Only 4GPS presents an opportunity for profits: 2GPS and 3GPS mean deep red ink.

Bankers who persist in using old technology, because of inertia or other reasons, should not fail to notice that the nature of financial products has changed tremendously since the Medicis or since Simon W. Straus originated the first mortgage real estate bond in 1909 – and it continues to change. The same is true of market characteristics.

The evolution in products, markets and technology has a great impact both on the P&L and in terms of assumed risk. Not only new products but also restructured old ones present many unknowns. Originally a Straus real estate bond was a security with a senior claim on a building – and Straus became a leading financier of skyscrapers. However, after the original self-imposed rules were relaxed, the edifice tumbled and finally crashed in 1929. There are lessons to be learned from the Simon Straus experience in regard to trading financial instruments. For nearly 10 years the real estate securitization approach was conservative. But with time, by the middle of the 1920s, it became risky. This evolution is in fact telling, not only for the 1920s but also for what might be anticipated in terms of off-balance sheet business (see Chapter 9) in the 1990s and beyond.

- The problem is that, in the gathering prosperity, lending standards and trading standards are generally softened.
- Being caught off-guard is not something that happens only once in life. It can take place time and again.

The easing of prudent rules can lead to a precipice. After 1924, for example, Simon Straus dropped his opposition to junior liens. He began to securitize and offer second and third mortgage bonds as well as a mix of them pledged as a security. This predated by 60 years the junk bonds market.

Like a significant number of present-day derivative instruments, Straus bonds were safe only as long as their issuer remained solvent. But, as the quality of these bonds deteriorated, this became a kind of Ponzi scheme which was destined to go under. In effect:

- Each new wave of investors paid for the exceptional gains collected by the preceding wave.
- In a similar manner, many new but ill-studied financial instruments seem to promote (and prolong) the life cycle of the security on which they rest.

Typically, the asset that secures a derivative instrument is the other bank's debt. This sees to it that there is really no connection between the asset and the corresponding liability. Hence the need for rigorous risk management solutions which are technology-intensive[1] and cannot be served, let alone controlled, by anything less than 4GPS.

High technology is necessary to explore business opportunity, to be able to sustain innovation, calculate profitability and control risk. The problem is that most retail banks do not have the 4GPS derivatives require, and some do not even have the necessary culture to appreciate the risks which they are taking.

Contrary to the classical spot transactions, the new financial instruments permit taking a position on a future price change of currencies, interest rates, agricultural and other commodities. But off-balance sheet derivatives are geared instruments, offering a much greater market exposure for a smaller outlay than the more classical financial tools. This has evident consequences for the bank's survival – and therefore backward technology and inadequate culture should not be taken lightly.

3   WHAT IS MEANT BY NEW PRODUCT PLANNING?

Product planning is a process which was first introduced in manufacturing. Its usage in banking rests on the fact that today the most competitive bankers think both product and market and see themselves as innovators (or investors) and sellers of *financial solutions*. In retail banking, innovation

- produces a stream of new services,
- generates income which improves the bottom line,
- stimulates alternatives to conventional debt, and
- opens up new investment opportunities.

Innovative forces in the international financial industry are currently creating a steady stream of new instruments which increasingly operate cross-border. This is significantly assisted by the spread of communications, computers and sophisticated software. Innovative information technology solutions can bring forward unprecedented opportunities.

As section 2 has underlined, information technology is both an ingredient of financial strategic products and a strategic product itself. Sam Armacost, former president of Bank of America, said in the mid-1980s, 'We are an information processing company.' Since that time, hence for over 10 years, the trend has been toward introducing more technology-driven financial products to meet expanding market demands.

The bank benefits from networks that tie together foreign exchange dealers on five continents, models able to serve capital market needs, and capillary 24-hour networks reaching every office and every home, as exemplified by the Internet. New financial products and services ride on these networks but in essence the evolution of innovative banking services is not a concept of the 1980s and the 1990s.

- In the 12th century, *lettres de faire* were introduced, specifying the delivery of goods at a later date. They were first used at fairs in Champagne, France.
- In 1570, the *Royal Exchange* opened in London. This was the first place in the world at which contracts for goods could be bought and sold all year round.

During the 17th century, organized *futures trading* began in Japan. American Express (AMEX) was established in 1850, and in 1882, AMEX issued its successful *money order*. In 1891, the AMEX *travellers check* was born. Diners Club was incorporated in 1950, promoting the principles of the *worldwide credit card* industry. VISA was launched in 1958, evolving from BankAmericard. In 1966, Bank of America began to license VISA credit card accounts to other banks, creating in the process the largest financial network that has ever existed.

Comparing the example in this last paragraph with those preceding it, we observe that the frequency of innovation in the financial industry has increased. It accelerated over the last 10 years with derivative financial instruments, which started to resemble the life cycles of products in the electronics industry.

As an example, Figure 11.2 presents the contribution of innovation to Hewlett-Packard's bottom line over a five-year timeframe. Each successive shade identifies the sales, from a year's new product and their subsequent decay. Similar life cycle studies start now being developed by commercial and investment banks.

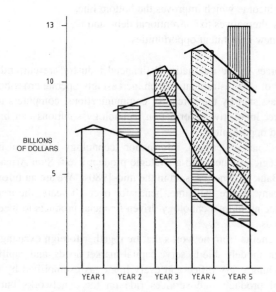

Figure 11.2   Rapid product life cycles: an example from the sales of Hewlett-Packard's products introduced to the market, by year

Like technology companies and like investment banks, retail banks, too, need not only to steadily innovate and revitalize their product line but also to face the competition from non-banks. For this purpose, they enter into *ancillary services* which need to be managed in a product line fashion. Typical ancillary services include sales of:

- insurance policies,
- mutual funds,
- safe custody,
- real estate, and
- travel agency chores.

Product planners and product managers are necessary to plan, schedule and coordinate the retail bank's activities regarding its strategic and key tactical products, to look after the development timetable and to solve product launching problems in close collaboration. We will be talking of time-to-market in section 6.

An integral part of product planning in the banking industry, and anywhere else, is looking after details. The Mies van der Rohe dictum is *'God is in the detail.'* Detail is necessary because the products and service offered by a financial institution to the market are its lifeblood. Hence the need to ask a lot of questions which go beyond 'What's our product line?'; for instance:

- Do we know the strengths and weaknesses of our products?
- Are we aware of where we lag behind?
- Are we capitalizing on our strengths?
- Which is the direction the market takes?
- Can we move as fast as the market grows, shrinks or shifts?

Part of the job of the product planner is to give a documented answer to the following queries: How well can our products face the competition? Can they respond to new market requests? Where should the modernization drive be? What constitutes an affordable cost?

True enough, neither the designer of a new propduct nor those who market it can properly estimate its future impact at the time of its original inception. My favorite example is that of Hiram Maxim (1840–1916), an American engineer working in London, who in 1895 harnessed the power released by the firing gun to load and fire again in a repeating cycle. At the time, the advent of a *machine gun* was a military curiosity rather than the evident start of a new period in warfare. Its wide acceptance as a weapon of defense and offense came 20 years later. Maxim's machine guns accounted for 80 percent of killing in World War I. Time and again, the machine gun has shown that, in three minutes, it could decimate a batallion of 600. (Reference from the British War Museum at the Tower of London.)

Table 11.1 A bird's-eye view of the responsibilities of product planning

---

1. Establish a product development strategy and programs consistent with the bank's overall objectives.
2. Define product scope, characteristics and timing as well as correlation with marketing and cost improvement objectives.
3. Project cost changes by product due to design or process changes necessary to upgrading existing products – always with an eye on sharply reducing costs.
4. Relate proposed expenditures to market offense/defense and risk factors, by product and market segment relating to business opportunity, in collaboration with marketing and the chief executive officer.
5. Together with the chief risk management officer and the operating department handling the product, elaborate a plan to control exposure.
6. Establish proposed technological requirements by product and process, both for new products and improved products; likewise for processes.

Similar feats happen in banking, particularly with derivatives. It is the job of the product planner working together with the chief risk management officer (CRMO) and the department which will do the marketing to evaluate the product's risks. This three-party collaboration is very important at a time when developing and trading new financial instruments has become an ongoing business even in retail banking.

If I was asked to define in a nutshell the mission a product planner should perform in the banking industry, and by extension what is meant by new product planning, the highlights presented in Table 11.1 would have been the answer. Purposely, I have kept these references generic. Every bank should adapt them to its own market, culture and product requirements.

4 BASIC FACTORS CHARACTERIZING STRATEGIC PRODUCTS AND THEIR PROCESSES

As the Introduction has explained, a strategic product is longer-term, high-efficiency, low-cost and with good profit margins. Typically, it is innovative, projected on the basis of market demand not in the abstract, and it should be kept dynamic through steady research and development.

To a substantial extent the bank's strategic plan reflects the nature and the appeal of its strategic products. Practically all financial institutions with strategic planning take this road, but while they bet on projected profits, many fail to account for probable losses. Yet all products and all markets have both upturn and downturn.

An example from derivatives hedging by Japan Airlines (JAL), explains the reference made in the preceding paragraph. It shows how financial instruments can affect the treasury and P&L in a profound manner. Since the mid-1980s, JAL has taken out forward currency contracts to buy dollars for yen to hedge the future purchase of aircraft.

- But, as the dollar weakened against the yen, at the end of 1994, the hedging resulted in a loss of 176.3 billion ($1.7 billion).
- These losses were being ignored until the aircraft were purchased, and then spread over the life of the assets through higher depreciation.

Nobody at JAL was ready to admit that $1.7 billion was lost as a result of currency speculation thought to be a sort of hedging. However, an accounting change in Japan brought the red ink to light, with JAL added to the problems of Orange County, Metallgesellschaft, Procter & Gamble, Mitsubishi Motors, Sumitomo Corporation and many others. This example is telling because derivatives satisfy the criteria outlined in the first paragraph of this section in terms of what makes a strategic financial product. JAL's oversight was in *risk management* – and this is also the most widespread weakness in the banking industry today.

Derivatives is by no means the only strategic product for the 1990s in the financial industry. There are many others, such as the securitization of mortgages, and more generally debt productization in the investments field, as well as credit cards/debit cards in classical banking. Some of these products correlate: receivables from credit cards can be securitized.

As we saw in section 2, behind every product there is a productization system which will handle the back office chores. The sophistication of this production system will propel the financial product in the market, or it will inhibit its sales. It may even make its offer unadvisable because

- high production cost do not allow any profit margins, or
- low technology results in an unbearable product risk.

Some financial products are considered to be *procedure-oriented*. Other things equal, these might be classified as less risky than those which are *innovation-based*. In the first category belong:

- *integrated account management*, in a global banking sense,
- *private banking*, including investment advice for high net worth and corporate clients, and
- *direct banking* through the use of 4GPS technology.

Notice that all three examples are neither purely market nor purely product. As Figure 11.3 suggests, they are product-and-market-oriented, though the

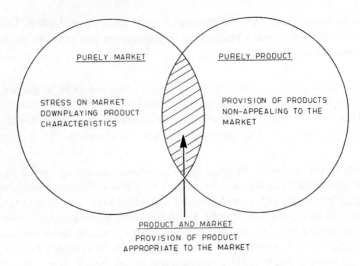

Figure 11.3   Product and market orientation

market component is the stronger. By contrast, innovation-intensive product examples are:

- *dynamic interest rate trading* based on models and high-performance computers,
- *currency exchange dealing* cross-time windows, backed by simulation and knowledge engineering, and
- *other treasury operations* integrating volatility and liquidity and profiting from experimentation.

Whether we talk of procedure-oriented or product innovation-based solutions, we must keep in mind the type of market we appeal to and the kind of technology required for production and distribution purposes. Table 11.2 reflects this argument by combining the references made in Chapter 6 with what section 2 above has said about technological supports.

Table 11.2   Type of market, type of production and objectives to be reached by technology

Type of market	Type of production	Goal of technology
Mass market	Mass production	Low cost
Unique product	Series production	Sophistication
Niche	Job lot	Personalization

Another basic issue which was introduced in Chapter 4, but to which we must return from a strategic products viewpoint, is *quality of service*. Always, in any financial or industrial activity, quality is a function of the relation between provider and client. In terms of product and process design, quality encompasses the human interfaces, the distribution channel, production facilities and the functionality of the product as such. For pricing purposes regarding niche and unique products, quality must be negotiated upfront, between provider and buyer of the service.

For this reason, quality must be addressed before the product comes off the drawing board. A similar statement can be made about product life cycles, and therefore *sunset* clauses. Like people, products die. Said an article in the *Institutional Investor*: '[At Bankers Trust] they are first in. As the profit margins begin to decline, they get out' (August 1992).

Banking products may not die a natural death, but rather one induced by competition or, in some cases, by the central bank. Too many entrants thin the margins and kill the business opportunity. Therefore the management of key products presupposes an evaluation of the strategies of the competition beyond the drives, location and extent of the market in terms of wants and needs. Retail banks should always do a competitive analysis of what their competitors (and they themselves) have available to fulfill market requirements – including not only new product development but also a steady training of their sales force, as already discussed.

Because strategic products are dynamic, retail banks should be flexible in order to change their strategic plans as the market conditions evolve and technology advances. This is a cultural issue to be supported by appropriate policies as well as human and financial resources.

5 CUSTOMER GATEWAYS AND THE DEMANDING JOB OF PRODUCT FORMULATORS

Both product design and product marketing change as a function of time and of the characteristics of revamped services as well as their product appeal. The same is true of funding sources. As an example provided by the Abbey National Bank helps document, new mortgage types such as fixed rate at, say, 5.9 percent for two years are not funded from the retail market but from the wholesale market.

- The bank gets a few hundred million pounds at that rate: for instance, £200,000,000, which represents about 1,000 mortgages.
- Through a joint treasury–marketing operation, the 1,000 can be launched in the morning and sold by noon.

In the UK, as of 1993, such offerings have been capitalizing on good rates that exist in the money market, but the whole issue has become very competitive, hence the need to react very quickly. 'We cannot afford to take two years for software development,' said a cognizant executive at Abbey National. Not only must the product itself be developed very fast, but also the targets must be reviewed, and this too requires rapid production of computer software. Such review may concern:

- product specifications,
- booking fees,
- terms and conditions,
- margins and other issues.

The majority of rapidly developed financial instruments are niche products, but they can be lucrative if the bank moves fast. For instance, through an initiative which was rapidly implemented, Abbey National was able to gain 36 percent of the new mortgage market in the UK: a very significant increase from the 16 percent to 17 percent it used to have.

This sort of trend toward greater market competitiveness through innovation will continue. In many financial institutions, for important customers, marketing wants to offer at any time between two and five new products, at a rate of at least 10 to 20 new financial products per month. Such a strategy brings into perspective a new concept in banking, that of *product formulators*, whose job is to focus on structuring new financial products out of existing services such as mortgages or savings accounts, for delivery either direct to clients or to intermediaries. Product formulators are market planners such as those we have examined in section 3, but with a difference:

- their responsibility is to take the proverbial long, hard look at the product line and find gaps which must be filled while avoiding overlaps.

Figure 11.4 provides a good example of this concept with a reference to General Motors in the 1920s. When Alfred Sloan took over as general manager, he found a company made of mergers and acquisitions whose products overlapped each other in terms of price and market appeal.

- Sloan restructured the company's product line by reformulating the mission of each GM division, so that all different price ranges were covered.

A new marketing division was established to help coordination among the GM divisions and their product range which was differentiated. A similar concept is applicable in banking and can best be followed by major field of activity. Direct banking and private banking, which were the subject of Chapter 8 and Chapter 9,

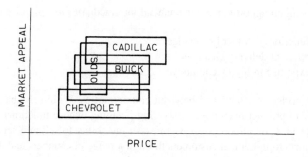

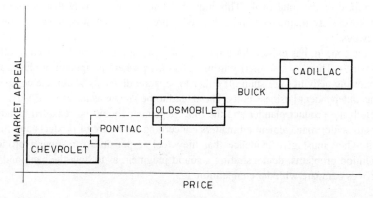

Figure 11.4 Restructuring a product line is no easy task, but it is feasible

respectively, provide a good example both in terms of pricing and of market appeal.

• Market appeal increasingly calls for generic studies in finance for which banks employ rocket scientists,[2] whose work is akin to that of physicists and design engineers in manufacturing.

Major universities have got the message and are retooling to produce this type of scientist. In Paris, the Ecole Normale Supérieure, one of the best technical universities in Europe, has created the *Phynance* department – a merger of Physics and Finance. The University of Zurich restructured its School of Economics to emphasize mathematical finance.

New financial products must be sold aggressively, which calls for the creation of efficient customer gateways. The concept of *customer gateways* is new in banking. It constitutes a bridge between product planning and marketing, focusing on opportunities for financial intermediaries to capitalize on

- superior customer knowledge,
- efficient delivery channels, and
- expertise in high technology.

This bridge is established between counterparties. Within the bank the counterparty to product planning is marketing planning, whose functions are outlined in Table 11.3. Its mission is *cross-sales*, or the ability to sell and service a range of products to individual customers through a range of channels and their gateway.

The concept is similar to virtually dividing the bank into specialized mini-banks able to provide the support functions which are at present woven into the fabric of the total bank. This must be done in such a way that cross-sales capabilities are maintained and enhanced – precisely through common customer gateways.

This concept has existed for a number of years and is being practiced in other industries. There is a similarity in manufacturing where peripheral products and supporting activities are spun off either to separate divisions within the company or as independent business units. These tend to be known as *industry servers*.

Both the product planner and the market planner should be regarded as advisors to senior management on matters concerning the future of products and markets. They must give evidence that they feel responsible for solving product evolution problems, demonstrating a sound judgment as to how the bank and its services compare with the competition.

- What kind of products will customers be asking for?
- Which characteristics must these products have?
- What is the quantity of the product that can be sold, at which prices, over which periods?

Table 11.3   The main functions of marketing planning

1. Identify market requirements and schedule the introduction of new and improved products.
2. Analyze each customer segment in terms of market potential by product, down to the individual customer, for the top 2 percent of customers.
3. Establish support programs to increase sales volume and share existing market between channels.
4. Emphasize specific activities for better market penetration and cross-selling.
5. Establish marketing communications, sales promotion and sales quotas by product.
6. Establish manpower requirements and other marketing expenditures by division and individual product.
7. Steadily test cost of good, including sales expenditures, against turnover, cash flow and profits.

Not only must product planners and market planners establish where the competitive situation stands now, but they should also define the kind of competition *our* products will face in the years to come.

Product formulators will do a half-baked job without providing answers to the following queries. Which other banks are likely to enter the market with a similar product? Can they bring out a seriously competitive item quickly? Can our product compete favorably on a price basis with similar products to be introduced to the market? Factual and documented answers to such questions bring into perspective a price policy, of which we will talk in Chapter 13. Through a methodological approach to the identification of business opportunity, product formulators should be capable of developing a comprehensive view of projected business opportunities, competitive factors and expected benefits.

6 WHAT CAN BANKS LEARN FROM THE MANUFACTURING INDUSTRY IN TERMS OF TIME-TO-MARKET?

Clear-eyed banks have learned a great deal from manufacturing, applying its lessons to their advantage. As we saw in Chapter 1, strategic planning is such an issue, and the same is true of standard costs. Product and market planning is another example, and with it time-to-market.

In business and industry today, time-to-market has become a crucial issue for profits and for survival. It is also a competitive weapon. But short time-to-market has prerequisites, the most important being *design reviews* which weed out moribund projects as well as those which – while still in the laboratory – have lost their competitive punch. There are as well complementary processes, for example:

- in the manufacturing industry, just-in-time (JIT) inventory management;
- in merchandizing, fast flow replenishment (FFR); and
- in banking, global risk management, to be executed in real time.

How fast should the new product development and marketing cycle be? The Japanese auto manufacturers answer this query by suggesting that their goal for the year 2000 is to be able to deliver a custom-made car in three and a half days. The forecast is that, in the years ahead, the time-to-market will shrink to the level of days. This requires not just rethinking but turning inside out the information technology which is supporting *our* bank.

A growing number of financial institutions are looking at time-to-market very seriously; their management is keen to improve performance the way manufacturing industries did. In August 1995, the reorganization at General Motors had the goal of

- speeding up development of new models by 25 percent, to 36 months,
- slashing engineering costs by 30 percent, and
- restoring pizzazz to GM's brands.

But on Wall Street financial analysts were quick to point out that neither of these goals pleased them. GM is targeting 36 months time-to-market, while Toyota already has 30 months and is trying to shrink them to 20. Even if the 36 months period is three-quarters of GM's current average of 48 months, it is silly to target 36 when competitors do better than that. The target should have been 20 months or less.

Similar references are valid in the banking industry. There are financial institutions which, by the time they bring out a new product, are way behind the competition. Nothing short of a thorough reorganization enriched with cultural change can change things for the best. Even a reorganization may prove not to be sufficient. In the case of General Motors, for example, Wall Street is not pleased with the reorganization. 'GM has too many cooks making the stew,' said the Morgan Bank analyst David Bradley. 'It's a disaster.' Why did they have to make it so complex?' (*Business Week*, August 14, 1995.)

Wall Street does not evaluate only manufacturing companies. It also keeps a sharp eye on banks, including their management, their structure and their products. Figure 11.5 illustrates the best advice which can be given for product planning purposes: 'Avoid being boxed in.'

- Boeing's original 707 was a good product because it shrank to become the 737 jetliner and it expanded into the 747, 757 and 767.
- Aérospatial's and British Aircraft's Concorde was a poor product. It was monolithically designed for a market which did not exist.

Intel's microprocessor is another example of a good product, both in terms of flexibility towards its own evolution and in regard to time-to-market. More than 20 years after the original 4-bit chip was brought to the market, by early 1995, the

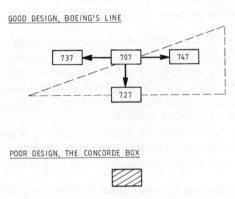

Figure 11.5 Good design and poor design of advanced aircraft: a concept for financial products

world's biggest chipmaker had adopted three major strategies which created a winning pattern:

- cranking up production of the new Pentium processor,
- spending $150 million on a television advertising blitz, and
- chopping prices by as much as 40 percent.

The result was that Pentium sales grew eight times faster than did sales of the previous-generation 486 when it was young. Then came the manifestation of the fourth strategy: fast time-to-market.

In mid-February 1995, Intel presented its sixth-generation chip, originally code-named P6 and now known as Pentium Pro. This microprocessor is the company's biggest technical advance since the third-generation 386 was unveiled in 1985. And the P6 headed to the market at an all-out sprint, with small-volume shipments starting in the fall of 1995.

- The Pentium Pro succeeded the Pentium as Intel's most powerful chip in just over two years.
- This is a year less than the gap between the 486 and the Pentium.

At the time, industry analysts said that, from there on, it would get a lot tougher. This, however, was also stated after the introduction of the 486 and the Pentium. The fact that the P6 is very complex, featuring 5.5 million transistors (nearly twice as many as the Pentium) posed major challenges. One of them has been that Intel also had to develop new applications that require its chips powerful features, such as:

- voice recognition and videoconferencing at PC level, and
- new top-end systems, for engineering workstations, computational finance and network servers.

At the same time, to keep its pace Intel had to thrust resources into P7 R&D, with the new chip expected to make its debut as early as 1997. This is a self-imposed deadline because rivals are picking up the pace. This is also a first-class lesson which bankers must learn. In a deregulated environment, nobody and no institution is immune from toughening competition – and survival greatly depends on our speed.

7 PRACTICAL VIEWS ON THE ESSENCE OF PROFITABILITY IN BANKING

Boeing's products were kept very flexible and Intel steadily shrank the time-to-market because of the same concern: *profitability*. Also for bankers the financial events of the mid-to-late 1980s underlined the need to pay attention to profitability. This has been translated into

- strategic withdrawals from low-yielding businesses,
- new product offerings, and
- tough cost control.

Both cash flow and profits have become focal points, and this not only in banking. All industries today face similar challenges, but banks are particularly shaken because fat margins in some products were for years hiding the bleeding in others.

As the protective cover of fat disappears, banks are becoming cost-conscious and at the same time more profit-oriented. The chief executive of a leading European bank stated in a meeting I had with him in the late 1980s: 'We are losing money with 35 percent of our customers.' The fact that top management recognizes the magnitude of the losses is indeed a change in culture. 'Banks and their customers have changed,' said Willard C. Butcher a short while after he succeeded David Rockfeller as chairman of Chase Manhattan. 'In the late 1950s, 90 percent of all loans went to the large American companies. Today, that figure is 4 percent.'

The sustenance of profitability in commercial banking is one of the present day's strategic challenges, as well as a key issue to which product planners and market planners should address themselves. Here again lessons can be learned from other industries.

In the mid-1980s, American Airlines commissioned a study of its business future during the next 10 years: 'Who would be the no. 1 competitors of American Airlines in the mid-1990s?'

- The conclusion was that the challenge will come from telecommunications – not from another air carrier.
- To enter this new industry, American Airlines developed a sophisticated reservations system which is today the largest online network in the world.

Wall Street analysts suggest that American Airlines makes much greater profits from its network than from air transport, while at the same time the network constitutes a major competitive advantage for the carrier business. American Airlines knew how to capitalize on a changing market. All industries find themselves in the midst of transition. Those most successful and most profitable know how to capitalize on change.

General Electric today derives about 50 percent of its business from GE Capital, which is essentially a non-bank bank. Siemens has seen in 20 years a major transition in its products: in 1975, electromechanical wares represented 75 percent of the company's business, with electronics accounting for the other 25 percent. As shown in Figure 11.6, by 1995 these ratios had been turned on their head.

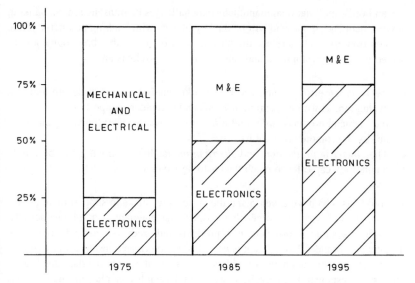

Figure 11.6 Evolution in yearly business of Siemens AG

Because new products development is expensive and product life cycles have been shortened as a result of global competition, companies in the manufacturing sector and in banking try to devise and sustain global products, thus spreading the R&D costs over a broader user population.

- In banking, this is attempted through product planning coordination leading to the development of software which is valid for all of the bank's operations abroad, particularly in the mass market.
- In auto manufacturing, this takes the form of a global, economical small car of standardized design, capable of being assembled in any country of operations with components produced around the world.

These components must be suitable for a variety of environments, as the industry moves towards a 'world product'. In the case of Ford's Escort, for example, nine countries besides the US supply parts for this auto – in alphabetic order: Brazil: rear brake assembly; Britain: steering gears; France: hub and bearing clutch assembly; Germany: valve-guide bushing; Italy: engine cylinder heads; Mexico: door lift assembly; Taiwan: wiring. Other parts are made in Spain and in Japan. This multinational manufacturing underlines the planning challenges, from the product, production and distribution viewpoints. The Escort is assembled in three countries, and the US version contains parts from the aforementioned nine different origins.

Can Ford's multinational manufacturing challenges be translated into a banking environment and, if so, who will be the key players with banking products? While the contributors, and therefore the players, will be many, the three topmost connected with the development and sales of banking products are

- the *research* effort, which involves market analysis, product design and risk evaluation, as well as communications and computers support;
- the financial products' *sales* and *relationship management* functions, and their ability to promote profitability;
- The *low-cost production* and *distribution* facilities, utilizing the best high technology can offer to reach the customers online.

The products which we develop and the systems we make to support them are for the market. Let us never forget that product management is a *support* activity, necessary for strategic products, new products and products widely distributed in the network. Product development is no staff function created just to employ people.

But product management should not be a profit center overlapping branch offices. If responsibilities overlap, we should establish a plan to share quotas and commissions. We should never use product management to do internal sales. This works against the bank's profitability and leads to an introvert culture which precipitates the bank's downfall.

8   WHY PROFITABILITY IN BANKING IS INDIVISIBLE FROM COST CONTROL

A number of studies have explored short-run earnings performance at retail banks, in an effort to establish links between *profitability* and various aspects of *operating characteristics*. The consensus is that tough cost control is the most important factor in achieving high bank profitability.

Focusing on a relatively long period of time which spans the decade of the 1970s and the early to mid-1980s, some of my own studies with Banca Provinciale Lombarda, Istituto Bancario Italiano and Credito Commerciale have permitted the testing of expense control as a long-term determinant of profitability. This type of test is useful because economic theory suggests that information flows and competitive pressures should reduce operating efficiency differences over time. On the other hand, there is a persistence of differences in operating efficiency which contradicts economic theory. The difference is made up of the fact that,

- while some inefficiencies are being corrected others come up to take their place;

- at the same time, market forces constrain relatively inefficient banks into restructuring, or push them out of business altogether.

In one of the studies which took place in the 1990s, high- and low-profitability banks were selected, based on return on equity (ROE) which persisted in the highest and lowest 30 percent of all listed banks for at least seven out of 10 years. This criterion was chosen to ensure samples of banks characterized by an earnings performance which was relatively consistent, but distinctly different.

This research project established that high earnings banks are significantly less leveraged than banks in the low-profit sample. But much more consistent has been the fact that higher operating expenses were recorded by the low-earnings banks. It is quite interesting to note that no differences have been observed in the ability of the two bank groups to utilize the tax laws in an optimization sense.

High-profit banks tend to record lower operating costs as a percentage of total revenue than their low-profit counterparts across a number of expense categories. In particular, the high-earnings banks

- spend less on salaries, wages and other expenses, and
- register lower ratios of interest on subordinated notes and debentures, as well as provision for loan losses to total revenue, than low earners.

Table 11.4 shows some American statistics. They represent selected ratios listing in the nominator different operating expenses – all being divided by total revenues. These ratios suggest that operating cost differences, particularly in salaries and wages, are a principal discriminator between high- and low-profit banks.

Table 11.4 Statistics on selected operating expenses divided by total revenue (average ratio per year)

	High-earnings banks	*Low-earnings banks*
Salaries and wages/total revenue	15.0	20.0
Interest on deposits/total revenue	31.7	32.5
Expense of federal funds purchased total revenue	7.4	9.6
Interest on other borrowed money/total revenue	0.8	1.2
Interest on subordinated notes and debentures/total revenue	0.2	0.9
Provision for loan losses/ total revenue	2.3	3.8

While, when raw statistics are examined, observed cost differences reflect variation in management expertise, product range and innovation, marketing savvy or asset and liability structure, a carefully selected sample and the ability to keep some of the variances constant point toward cost control as a key determinant of profitability. This is my experience at least. Contrary to other researchers, who somehow tend to leave risk management out of the profitability equation, it is my policy to closely follow the control of exposure. This comes from the belief that differences in risk preference between the two banking groups, high earners and low earners, need to be properly addressed.

In Holland, in 1988, a study by Staal Bankiers demonstrated that, among the three biggest and three of the smaller Dutch banks, a third of the would-be profits during the preceding five years were consumed by the write-off of bad loans. In the last analysis risk, too, can be monetized and treated as a major cost element.[3] Among other findings of my own and similar studies is the fact that low-earnings banks hold a higher percentage of capital in subordinated debt, though this may simply reflect greater difficulty on the part of the low earners in raising equity. High-earnings banks tend to pay out less interest than their low-earnings counterparts, owing to a different deposit mix and/or lower rates paid.

- This finding, too, suggests that managerial ability is key to the long-run earnings performance.
- An interesting hindsight is that the economic rents provided by regulation may be sufficient to secure the long-run position of relatively incompetent management.

The proof of this statement is that, when such stiff regulation is significantly relaxed, as part of a substantial precompetitive deregulation of the banking industry, the low-profit banks and their managers are forced out of the market by competitive pressures – or they are obliged to merge.

This last issue brings our discussion back to section 2 and Figure 11.1. The careful reader will remember the very different profitability patterns of 2GPS, 3GPS and 4GPS between a regulated and a deregulated environment. The fact that every banker should record with care is that, in the Group of Ten countries and many others, the regulated financial industry in terms of products and services is something of the past and it will not return in the foreseeable future.

Though new regulation is forthcoming, in all likelihood it will focus, not on product, services and technology, but on the management of risk: from derivative financial instruments to the follow-the-sun overdrafts and reporting practices. An example of such regulation is the 1996 Market Risk Amendment. This does not protect banks from competition, like the old regulation. It only maps the effects of exposure and of off-balance sheet risks in the bank's balance sheet.

Notes

1. See D.N. Chorafas, *Managing Derivatives Risk* (Burr Ridge, IL: Irwin Professional Publishing, 1996).
2. See D.N. Chorafas, *Rocket Scientists in Banking* (London and Dublin: Lafferty, 1995).

12 Managing Research and Development in Retail Banking

1 INTRODUCTION

Research and development (R&D) is a key phrase at Morgan Stanley. Management firmly believes that since the mid-1980s the real money has been made in developing innovative products, packaging services for a wider clientele and personalizing them for a single important customer. All this calls for research in banking which is product and market-oriented:

- focusing on market drives, on customer wishes and on the ability to continue producing innovative services;
- being greatly concerned with production and distribution, as well as the resulting profitability; and
- including a great deal of high technology to gain competitive edge, control costs and maintain market lead.

Heavy duty R&D is becoming a hallmark of modern banking. 'You cannot divide trading, execution, control from R&D activities,' said Nunzio A. Tartaglia, managing director at Morgan Stanley at the time our meeting took place. His division, Advanced Systems Group (ASG), was a research laboratory like a miniature Bell Labs.

Figure 12.1 brings to the reader's attention the fact that the R&D effort requires a close coordination with strategic planning. In banking, as in all other dynamic industries, the able implementation of strategic perspectives rests on five pillars:

- business opportunity analysis,
- business architecture,
- product architecture,
- policies and standards,
- technology planning.

These pillars support *one system* which propels innovation in commercial banking, but keeps product development subordinate to market trends and drives.

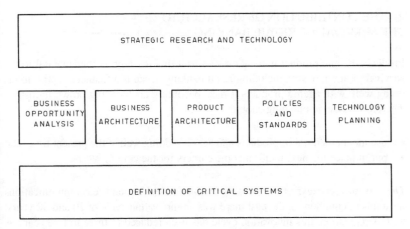

Figure 12.1   A bank's research and development effort and its technology must work hand-in-hand. This is particularly true with mission-critical issues

Notice that the common ground on which rest all five pillars is that of mission critical systems which must be rich in high technology. The most competitive commercial banks invest in research and development.

- They have their own research laboratories or at least a team of rocket scientists.[1]
- They sponsor research in the best known universities, such as MIT.

The way it will be treated in this chapter, research, development and implementation (R,D&I) should not be confused with studies in economics which banks have been classically doing for investment purposes. This goes beyond the more classical economics research and associated financial studies.

R,D&I is a comprehensive new product development effort. In many banks, the R,D&I staff is growing both in importance and in number. In the mid-to-late 1980s, it was unique to find 30 or 40 people in the research laboratory of a bank. Today the rocket scientists, who constitute a growing breed, have become a most precious source of brainpower, particularly in connection with derivative financial instruments.

Because of its concern about strategic products, the bank's strategic planning department both promotes R,D&I and plays the role of 'devil's advocate' on current research plans. In several commercial and investment banks, management has made R&D a profit center which, year in and year out, contributes significantly to the bottom line.

2   THE CONTRIBUTION OF RESEARCH TO
THE SURVIVAL OF RETAIL BANKING

Products die and product innovation sees to it that research is fundamental to the survival of any industry, including retail banking. Even if a financial institution is doing well, with ageing products it risks becoming another 'big brown industry'. Therefore strategic planning should

* use the momentum of products and services doing well at the present time, and
* put in place the next major income earners for the coming years.

There is no copyright in the banking business. Banking and telecommunications have this in common: in the past there was an innovation cycle of 20 and 30 years; with deregulation, this innovation cycle has been reduced to three to five years. A recent American study found that, for a high-technology company to survive, it must *reinvent itself* every two and a half years. As a result of R&D and innovation

* in the communications, computers and software industries, some *80 percent* of the revenues come from products that did not even exist two years ago;
* in banking, over *50 percent* of the profits, and about *30 percent* of the business, come from products which did not exist two years earlier.

R,D&I, however, requires new images and new departures. It also calls for cultural change. Solutions must be cross-departmental and the time-honored unity of command will not be observed, as it is demonstrated in Figure 12.2, which gives in a nutshell an example from Bank of America. In the re-engineering of its structure and its services, which it did in the late 1980s, Bank of America departed from the old policy that every department head should have one boss to whom to report. It made its newly created *research division* dependent both on marketing and on BASE (Bank of America System Engineering), hence computers, communications and software.

The rationale for the structure shown in Figure 12.2 was that any new product launched on the market which does not have a significant high-technology content will have very slim chances of success. The market would not like it because:

* its flexibility is low,
* its appeal is limited and
* its cost is high.

As Chapter 11 has demonstrated in regard to profitability in banking, and its prerequisites, the new retail activities are not just financial. They are also demanding

Figure 12.2 The computers and communications reorganization at Bank of America created a research activity co-managed with marketing

a great deal of market and product awareness. The search for new opportunities is closely tied to:

1. refining current market plans,
2. developing new products, and
3. capitalizing on market growth.

To be executed in an able manner, all three goals demand a good deal of forecasting: anticipating innovations and oncoming changes, projecting and supervising the profitability of available financial instruments, and guiding the hand of management on the basis of early indicators.

In terms of brainpower, the rocket scientists are the no. 1 human asset working on research, development and implementation (R,D&I) in the banking environment. The no. 2 asset is the technologists who will develop and mine large databases on clients, markets and market movements, establish intelligent any-to-any networks;

and provide expert systems and agents[2] to analyze in real time available information.

Research in banking is part of the money spent on R&D in the more general context of business and industry. In every country, investments in science and technology have a longer-term payoff period. In the United States, business and industry has boosted spending beyond the $200 billion mark industry-wide. However, a report by Battelle (*Communications of the ACM*, vol. 38, no 8, August 1995), of Columbus, Ohio, acknowledges that, while funds continue to grow in applied research, money going to basic research is tapering off or in decline.

Also in the manufacturing industry there is an increased reliance on cooperative research, often with other companies but also with government and non-profit labs. By contrast, in banking the foremost institutions tend to work on their own, though eventually they may license some of the products they develop – particularly software.

Also in banking, while the director of research as well as the rocket scientists play a vital role in the success of the R,D&I effort, the top ingredient is the ability of senior management to conceptualize new developments, actively search for new challenges and come up with new goals. The R&D effort may be the motor behind innovation in banking, but management is the vehicle.

Regarding the products which propel innovation in banking, their origin is diverse and they also vary from one institution to the other. But if we were to make a general comment on the banking industry this would particularly underline five origins:

1.   demands posed by sophisticated clients,
2.   the results of market research by the bank,
3.   products already launched by the competition,
4.   new ideas from senior management and specialist departments, and
5.   strategic planning considerations about the next income earner.

Strategic planning is well positioned to appreciate that financial investments and other banking activities pay dividends *only if* the institution can come up with bright new ideas for which it is paid a premium. It is part of the responsibility of strategic planning to explain to other departments that

- the life of financial products has shortened dramatically, and
- a commercial bank can move ahead only if innovation is continuous.

The role of R&D in banking can be better appreciated when we realize that we live in an age in which knowledge holds the key to our future – and to our jobs. Research, development, implementation and technological leadership determine who wins the next round of global competition and which bank may lose its independence because its management did not know how to plan for survival.

3 IS RETURN ON INVESTMENT AN IMMEDIATE PREOCCUPATION WITH R&D?

In some of the consulting assignments I have in the banking industry, members of the board and other senior executives often ask questions regarding return on investment (ROI). R&D money is part of the cost of staying in business. Therefore it is not an investment from which immediate financial results should be expected.

While every effort must be made to steadily shrink the time-to-market (see Chapter 11) and pass from development to implementation, there is a difference between the cost of doing business and the cost of staying in business. An example is given by Johnson and Johnson, where

- management policy sees to it that not every new product has to be a block-buster;
- but the hundreds of new products that were introduced during the previous five years accounted for about 25 percent of J&J's sales in 1996.

Another one of the industrial companies which, year in and year out, generates 25 percent of its sales from new products, is 3M. Both in J&J and 3M, management encourages its people to take risks, creating a corporate culture where even mistakes could be a badge of honor – because mistakes are an inevitable by-product of innovation.

A third industrial example comes from Digital Equipment, specifically from the major successes the company had in the 1980s. When, in mid-1986, DEC engineered a new assault on the market through minivaxes, published statistics indicated that

- 85 percent of the company's sales came from products introduced in the previous 18 months;
- this contrasted highly with the IBM record which showed that only 40 percent of sales came from new products introduced over the same time period.

As every supermarket is filled with shelf after shelf of not so successful brands, every bank tries to market 'me too' services in the hope that it can develop a sort of client loyalty which will lift dumb products into winners. Instead of examining the patterns of customer acceptance, of costs and of profits, many financial institutions fall into the old glory trap – and they pay the price. Few banks learn from experience and become star performers. Keep in mind that experience can be acquired from all walks of life and from all industries if one tries hard enough to understand what has taken place, and what may come next.

From computers to banking, other things equal, lower percentages tell a story of sluggishness in an ever-accelerating computer marketplace. As cannot be repeated too often, like the computer industry banking has become a technology-driven business, and therefore management must always be making investments in *the next product(s)*.

Creating a basic innovative capacity makes sense if we are indeed capable of producing a steady flow of new products and services. This is closely linked with the ability of management to change which, to be sustained, requires the assurance that

- the board and the CEO stand solidly behind the management of change;
- all managers in the organization are measured on how much innovation they induce in their area of activity; and
- there is in the bank an adequate number of passionate and at times disruptive champions of change.

The management of change, of which we have spoken in Chapter 5 and on a number of other occasions, is closely connected to return on investment from R&D. By definition, change means disruption, and disruption has its costs; but it also leads to major improvements.

Some Japanese banks maintain that every executive should spend at least 50 percent of his time on improvements, creating a corporate capacity for constant innovation. This is a staggering task, but it is feasible, provided we appreciate that innovation

- is the antithesis to bandaid approaches, and
- requires skill, intelligence and persistence.

Statistics from the manufacturing industry indicate that in the long run about 85 percent of new product projects die in the laboratory or right after they are introduced to the market. Another 10 percent more or less survive the market test, but they just break even. But the 5 percent which become hits produce the company's cash flow in the coming years.

- Return on investment comes from this successful 5 percent, with profits so abundant to justify all 100 percent of R&D.
- Eventually, however, even successful products die. The graphic in Figure 12.3 serves as a reminder of this fact.

Section 2 made the statement that there is no copyright in banking, I do not believe that survival can be assured by hanging onto old connections and by maintaining secrecy. Rather than staying defensive, I would advise forging ahead – and let competitors copy our dying products.

In the 15th century, Christopher Columbus made the mistake of trying to keep his discovery more or less a well-guarded secret. By contrast, Amerigo Vespucci

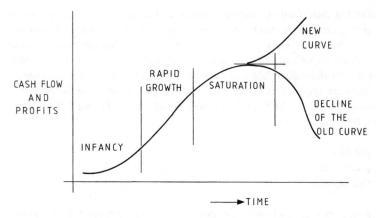

Figure 12.3   Every strategy that works has a life cycle: the same is true of product cycles

not only established the new world as a separate continent but also wrote extensively of his discoveries. Quite interesting is the pattern of dissemination of information and its results. One of Amerigo Vespucci's letters was translated into 40 different languages and in the mind of people established its author as the discoverer of the new world.

- The Americas is the name of the whole western hemisphere.
- Colombia is just one country whose name is closely linked to drug cartels.

Entrepreneurial banks succeed largely because research, development and marketing people talk to each other and to their customers regularly, and often informally. Valuable lessons in financial R&D can be learned from other industries. In pharmaceuticals, for example, value is added primarily by

- service activities like drug development in carefully constructed patent and legal defenses;
- clinical and regulatory clearances; and
- effective drug retailing and distribution systems.

With production costs a trivial portion of a drug's value, the strategies of leading companies concentrate on specialized activities within the value chain. Merck, for example, focuses on a powerful research-based patent position; while Glaxo targets rapid regulatory clearance of drugs.

Business success is the result of sound, professional management of long-term investments and well-established relationships with customers who have committed their funds to the bank because it is an *innovator* and a *leader* in providing services its clients need. This is the strategy of Amerigo Vespucci.

In world money markets, a bank's reputation as a leading financial trader is often built on its capability to arrange sophisticated currency and interest rate swaps with innovative debt instruments. But success would not last unless new products are implemented in parallel with tough internal controls and risk management standards. As Chapter 11 underlined, in any financial field, there are three types of innovation:

- product,
- process and
- risk control.

As a rule, new products offer the institution which developed them competitive advantage only for a short time. Hence opportunities to excel have to be found and exploited without delay. Simultaneously, however, great attention has to be paid to the risk new products implicitly or explicitly imply. Otherwise exposure may outstrip the benefits.

In conclusion, unless we always keep our mind dynamic events will crowd one upon another. Risk will grow out of proportion and profitability will deteriorate. Unless we exploit the factors of *time* and *space* to our advantage, our forces will be ill-balanced. Resources scraped together at the last minute have never achieved commendable results.

4   NON-TRADITIONAL RESEARCH IN FINANCIAL INSTITUTIONS AND MARKET INEFFICIENCIES

Financial institutions like Morgan Stanley and Fidelity Investments are funneling funds into research departments. Their rocket scientists build proprietary models that search for patterns through market data, using such tools as non-linear financial models, genetic algorithms and fuzzy engineering.[3] Commercial banks like J.P. Morgan and merchant banks like Bankers Trust have funded research at MIT and other major universities, which is non-traditional. An example is time series based on *intraday* data streams, as contrasted to the classical *interday*.

The world over, in first-rank banks, top management has come to realize that interday financial time series are too coarse to permit effective decision support. The opening and close of a stock price or of an index tell precious little about market behavior that particular day.

- Even intraday five-minute intervals on prices, which is within current technology, provides a wealth of information.

Figure 12.4 gives an example of intraday trading volatility from the Standard and Poor 500 index. The prices are mapped into the figure at five-minute intervals. Slowly but surely, we can do better than that.

- Cognizant financial analysts now believe that eventually even the five-minute intervals will be coarse. Subminute data streams will be the next goal.

The reason why we are interested in five-minute and in subminute recording intervals is that a top goal of non-traditional financial research is *prognosis*. Among the leading financial institutions the rationale behind R&D investments is the search for predictability. This task is challenging and complex.

- By the time a model is perfected, market conditions or the variables that feed into this model have changed.
- Sometimes such changes come subtly, but other changes are brutal and the model is rendered ineffective.[4]

Since nobody has figured out a model which can withstand market shocks for very long, and because there is a chaotic pattern in trading, rocket scientists are needed to exploit market inefficiencies. But at the same time, inefficiencies which already existed may no longer be sustainable. In general, market inefficiencies and our ability to exploit them tend to be time-limited.

A good part of market inefficiencies which are the object of non-traditional research, and present considerable business opportunities, have to do with the way investors, treasurers and bankers trade. Behind market patterns are persons, egos, experiences and time horizons:

- each investor or trader acts and reacts according to his own frame of reference;
- the time horizons of different players are not at all the same.

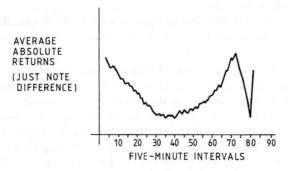

Figure 12.4 Volatility characteristics in intraday patterns: an example from S&P 500

The more traditional economic and financial research, of the type we consider in Chapter 13, has no use for investor's time horizons and of intraday data streams, because it does not have the tools to exploit them, and sometimes it even lacks the concept(s). To the contrary, intraday information and investor time horizons are two of the pillars of non-traditional research.

For instance, arbitrageurs and market makers trade on a time horizon of a few minutes. In contrast to this, central banks trade on horizons of a few years. Every pulse of the market is interpreted by each participant according to his own frame of reference, therefore giving rise to different reactions to the same market event.

Some of the analytically oriented financial institutions, like Morgan and Bankers Trust are looking into market behavior patterns and their timely detection, using genetic algorithms and nonlinear regression analysis. Through modeling:

- they try to better their understanding of the trading system and they 'guesstimate' what might be the next move; but
- they also appreciate that interactive computational finance offers a certain amount of discipline to the human trader.

Some institutions now use the *breakout theory*, which rests on the hypothesis that there is going to be some driving force that pushes a price up or down. When that happens, there will be some momentum, or persistence, in the direction being taken – even if it is short-lived. The challenge is the timely prediction of the right direction.

Using established mathematical tools from engineering and physics, a rocket scientist looks at price as the output of a nonlinear system. Because of his background he appreciates that financial markets are nonlinear in their characteristic behavior.

- The lens of nonlinearity opens up a whole series of market inefficiencies, which can be exploited.
- These are best detected through high-frequency financial data (HFFD), which records real-time, tick-by-tick market response.

An example is the intraday models for currency exchange currently in use. They include proprietary techniques of measuring absolute and relative changes in market volatility by means of studying the market's *microseasonality*.

Once established, microseasonality can be employed to unearth business opportunities but also to evaluate risk embedded in the trading book. It can also be instrumental in risk assessment in regard to the banking book's volatility, as well as in the asset allocation processes at the level of a given portfolio.

A great part of the skills and of the tools possessed by rocket scientists comes from nuclear engineering, aerospace and weapons systems; also from physics, astrophysics and biology. The parallels between weapons systems and investing are uncanny.

- Both have lots of HFFD and a poor signal-to-noise ratio.
- Both require quick decisions based on robust models of what is going on.
- Both punish wrong decisions with losses, and sometimes with a total loss.

Adapting the existing rocket science technology to problems in economics and finance means swapping tanks and aircraft for shares and bonds, trying to map a trader's or fund manager's chain of thought into a model. Processed through high performance computers, this model assists the trader in his decisions.

As non-traditional financial research progresses, models tend to go beyond, say, evaluating mortgage applications into more complex domains. For instance, predicting currency fluctuations, aiming to tackle the challenge of different levels actively prevailing among financial markets, and evaluating whether investments should be in assets or in debt.

The aim of projects in non-traditional financing research is to exploit the fact that computers have an advantage of speed and comprehensive evaluation over people. High-performance computers can simultaneously follow more markets and many more economic variables than traders. But, as we have already discussed, models are always subject to failure – just like the people who make them.

5   CAN THE GOAL OF STEADY INNOVATION BE SERVED BY PRECOMPETITIVE RESEARCH?

Chapter 11 has documented 'how' and 'why' the spirit and policy of steady innovation is the way to gain a competitive edge in the last decade of the 20th and well into the 21st century. This involves constant research in discovering, structuring and marketing new products and services, and in finding better processes for running the banking business.

But analysis and experimentation also involves costs. Therefore some of the banks with which I work as a consultant, or which come to my seminars, are asking whether it is advisable to co-sponsor R&D Typically, this is done through common precompetitive research with other banks, while thereafter each partner is free to exploit the product. My experience has made me a non-believer in precompetitive research. The reasons are very practical. First and foremost, precompetitive research is a collaborative effort which has neither a body to kick nor a soul to blame.

- It is characterized by funding without precise goals, strict timetables, and tough design reviews.

- There is no urgency to produce results – as the Esprit I, II and III projects of the European Union demonstrate.

Second, as Figure 12.5 explains, any project in new financial product development has three major components: research, design and packaging. Precompetitive research takes place in the first stage, and even in this the results are wanting. Most particularly, the technological support is ill-defined and heterogeneous.

There is a third negative reason which characterizes such projects. Precompetitive research is run by the book, and many of the essentials of a fertile, creative environment are anathema to an organization which is run by the book. Stifling innovations is a policy which time and again proves to be deadly wrong. To flourish, innovation needs a free rein and the freedom to take alternative paths. Marvin Minsky says that you do not know something until you know it in more than three ways. Only *after* you examine all alternatives,

- innovation comes by focusing and it shows up in big leaps;
- it does not come in small steps and in diffused sense.

R&D projects financed by the European Union have stressed precompetitive research. In Japan, too, corporations and government have long pooled their funds to subsidize precompetitive research. Both efforts proved to be dry holes because they spread the costs but did not spark innovation. And besides, no self-respecting company sends its best people to these projects.

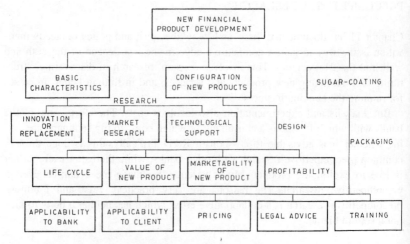

Figure 12.5 In finance, as in manufacturing, new product development has many prerequisites – this figure shows the most important

Therefore banks, companies and governments should question spending large amounts of money from one precompetitive program to another. The facts of industrial life see to it that there is no industrial application worth talking about. Instead of putting in seed money without a clear vision, the goal must be:

- to bring innovative and competitive financial products to the market, and
- to target servicing real needs, doing so in a short timespan.

To be successful, R&D projects require both imagination and cross-fertilization. 'My advice to graduates,' says MIT's Nicholas Negreponte, 'is to do anything except what you are trained for. Take your training to a place where it is out of place. Stimulate ideas, shake up establishments, and don't take "no" for an answer' (*The MIT Report*, March/April 1996).

In a way which is not too different from what happens in the manufacturing industry, R&D in banking is not only about products which never existed before. Whoever says that R,D&I is only about products simply supports a hype. Fundamentally, there exist three types of innovation.

1. New products or vastly improved existing products.
2. The redesign of a business process to improve efficiency.
3. Paradigm shifts, including changes in the rules that govern a particular activity.

All three types can give results if we are able to anticipate developments and predict customer needs. Anticipation is necessary in order to be in the right place at the right time with innovative products and services. The ability to anticipate dramatically enhances the chances of success. It also makes easier the needed paradigm shifts.

Most businesses and their managers today work predominantly in a reactive mode. After a problem arises, they try to solve it, but have no experience because they have not been trained as trouble-shooters. Therefore they have no interest in anticipating the future, because this makes their job more complex. This inability to plan is much more pronounced in precompetitive research. To a significant extent, it is due to inertia and to the tendency to follow the beaten path. When we are in the middle of a known paradigm it is hard to imagine any other paradigm.

- The set of rules which we follow establishes boundaries for behavior.
- Those boundaries confine us to viewing a problem from only a single viewpoint.

Defensive attitudes reinforce this staying behind because new paradigms put the old and known paradigm at risk. The more successful one is at practicing the old way of doing things, the greater the inertia in accepting a paradigm shift and changing one's ways.

When, in 1930, Hollywood's studios faced the challenge of switching from silent movies to sound, most took a defensive attitude and with this they lost their clout. But, at MGM, Louis Meyer saw sound movies as a challenge. He tore down part of his studios, invited sound experts from New York and was the first to introduce the new technology, making MGM a premier film producer, and with it surviving the negatives of the Great Depression.

Staying put amounts to loss of opportunity because paradigm shifts change the rules, dramatically altering the solutions already in place. However, a valid system of anticipation requires a first-class strategic exploration. Rather than waiting for a trend to develop, we should constantly monitor paradigm shifts through early indicators. That is the work rocket scientists are paid to do.

Early indicators on impending changes permit capitalization on lead time. Typically, new paradigms start out slow because the rules are not so well known or understood but, if successful, they move quickly to center stage as the rules become better known. Then they slow down again at the end of their life cycle, according to the lifespan which we saw in Figure 12.3.

6 NEVER FORGET MARKETING'S CONTRIBUTION TO THE SUCCESS OF BANKING PRODUCTS

One of the pillars supporting the success of new banking products in a competitive marketplace is close collaboration with marketing. This collaboration contributes both the salt of the earth and the specific orientation product sales should take. Market, R&D project and final product design closely correlate. The market opportunity is not made just out of the specifications of the product or services, or the amount of R&D effort invested in development. As Figure 12.6 suggests, market, project and product are closely linked. If one of them is weak, the result will be wanting.

Great attention must be paid to structural relationships which support successful products. Project after project documents that the no. 1 reason for bank failures is weak products. Research and development aim to bring new products to the market, but to sell them we must have a first-class sales force.

- As I have already underlined in Chapter 10, no two salesmen are the same.

Besides this, the marketing budget often amounts to four times the R&D budget. If marketing is going to be substandard, there is no reason to spend R&D money in the first place.

- Both the R&D effort and budgeting for marketing reasons have often been underestimated in banking.

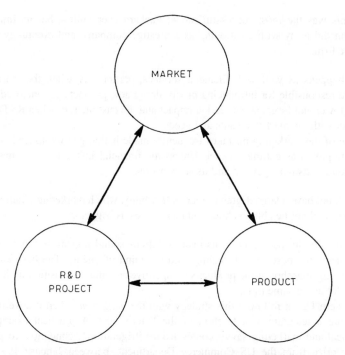

Figure 12.6 Pillars of success with new banking products

Even manufacturing companies often fail to appreciate the importance of marketing and its budgeting. In banking, in a deregulated environment, the marketing effort is very much capital-hungry. To the contrary, in a regulated environment huge back office expenditures may, and often do, exceed those of marketing and R&D taken together.

Marketing is like the crust of the cake which hides and often presents an illusion of product characteristics. IBM did not buy Univac when it was offered for sale and therefore it did not become the first punched card company to move into computers.

- Remington Rand bought Univac. But, through marketing, IBM was the first company to build a computer concept in the mind of its clients.

Without marketing savvy, product planning can make major mistakes. Prior to World War II, Packard was the premier car in America, more of a status symbol than Cadillac. Like Rolls-Royce, Packard declined the annual model change policies by positioning itself above the pack. Then, in the mid-1930s, Packard introduced its first step-down model, the relatively inexpensive Packard Clipper.

- This was the most successful model Packard ever built – but its introduction did away with positioning as a prestige company, and eventually killed the firm.

This happens as well with financial services, particularly when the marketing people responsible for introducing or sustaining new products get enclosed in an ivory tower and forget about market impact and the customer, or when R&D loses contact with the market's wants and needs.

One of the marketing mistakes frequently made is that getting noticed is often misinterpreted as getting tougher. Unless the financial institution is a master in positioning, its management and its sales people

- will not have a large degree of mental flexibility, which marketing requires; and
- they will not be able to choose and use words as triggers.

Superficially, in marketing terms many solutions sound logical, but they are not necessarily the best way of dealing with the mind of clients. The best way is a convincing snapshot of the product's competitive advantages, positioning it in the right slot at the same time.

Western Union followed this strategy with the *mailgram*, when it advertised it as being a telegram at a fraction of the latter's cost. A practical example of technical-and-marketing savvy comes from refrigeration technology. To gain a major prize from the US Commerce Department, between January 1994 and July 1997 the winner had to manufacture and sell over 250,000 refrigerators free of ozone-depleting chlorofluorocarbons (CFCs) and at least 25 percent more energy-efficient than the 1993 federal standards. Three criteria were established:

1. 75 points for kilowatt hours saved.

The evaluation was determined by energy-efficiency gains per refrigerator, multiplied by number of units sold. Fuzzy engineering was the technology chosen by most competitors to permit this breakthrough. Using fuzzy logic to adapt to temperature changes, a defrost control saved energy by judging exactly when a freezer needs defrosting, not simply doing it at regular intervals.

2. 21 points for a tracking system that pinpoints who buys the new refrigerators and where.

Correctly, this project matched R&D and marketing by seeing to it that information flows ensure that sales are within the sponsoring utilities' market. Here the competitive advantage was obtained through database mining.

3. 4 points for vigorous sales and marketing strategies.

Here, too, database mining was instrumental in providing the documentation necessary to win the prize, while *re-engineering* made it necessary to rethink and redesign basic business practices like product development and customer service.

The lesson is that radical change is impossible unless managers know how to organize, deploy, enable, measure and reward the value-adding operational work, and also how to break resistance to change. The lack of these skills has been a stumbling block to nearly every re-engineering initiative – or, for that matter, every R&D effort.

7 USING TECHNOLOGY TO SOLVE PROBLEMS AND GAIN MARKET EDGE

One of the most powerful tools marketing uses is technology (see also section 9). Technology, particularly sophisticated software and real-time systems, has played a major role in shaping the new financial market. Notable is the impact of computers and communications on those sectors of the banking industry I have outlined in Part Two, leading to

- new financial products,
- faster product innovation,
- higher speed of transactions,
- the handling of larger volumes,
- much wider reach of messages,
- increased competition, and
- successful global marketing.

With the mounting capabilities of computer networks has come the birth of larger and broader markets in options and futures, in swaps, in interest rate products, in currency exchange – but also in direct banking and in personal banking, with the result that the whole retail industry has been revamped.

Banks, however, are not always prudent in the use they make of technology. A recent example is the preparation necessary for the coming implementation of the Euro. The *European Currency Union* will require banks to make huge investments in technology:

- from advanced software telecommunications systems.
- to the heavy costs of retraining staff and reprinting product literature.

Estimates given to the European Banking Federation in Brussels suggest that European banks could need to pay over 2 percent of their annual operating costs, for three years, to make the necessary changes in technology, procedures and human capital. The introduction of the Euro is likely to open another front in the ongoing banking revolution.

The new channel may also prove to be quite profitable, for technical reasons. The repackaging of bonds whose principal coupon payments will contain Euro fractions is projected to be too costly. Therefore it is not being planned. Because of this, several banks advance the idea of a market convention of quoting in hundreds of Euros. In my judgment, this is worse than inadequate: it is a Euro conversion loophole. Even quoting in thousands of Euros will open the gates for:

- very significant losses to investors, and
- a windfall of profits to those banks which apply that convention.

This ECU-Euro conversion loophole is another example of the way in which poorly studied solutions and measures are executed. We must face it: governments are generally low performers because they think they have the luxury of being mediocre. This unpreparedness is, of course, quite a pity because

- a single currency will make it easier for banks to cross borders to sell products such as loans, mutual funds and insurance to retail customers.

This requires significant R,D&I effort to get ahead and stay ahead of the pack, as all banks will be struggling with the problem of compliance.

- The Euro will also make it easier for big corporate clients to shop around the multinational banking industry, to find the best deal.

Within each one of the 15 European Union countries, until now banks have had a strong franchise in their domestic market. But with the introduction of the Euro, even the bigger national banks will have to face international competition without being able to hide behind national protective measures.

- Technology breaks down barriers: from frontiers to legislation made to protect certain industry sectors.

An example where banks fail to take advantage of technology, in spite of the huge expenditures it entails, is in their internal information systems. All over the financial industry, there is a proliferation of incompatible management information systems (MIS), executive information systems (EIS) and data warehouses – but very little support for senior management.

Figure 12.7 gives an example of what I would consider an able decision support for senior management in terms of bank profitability as it has been discussed

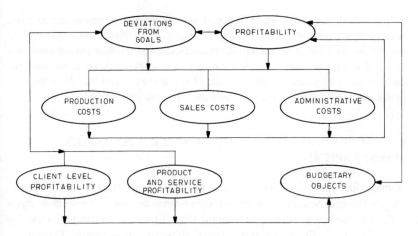

Figure 12.7 Management decision support to evaluate profitability should benefit from modeling and work in real time

in Chapter 11. To be effective, it must most definitely operate in real time:

• integrating parochial information carried by different MIS-EIS,
• using algorithms and heuristics for online database mining, and
• benefiting from sophisticated models which are always kept dynamic.

While today modeling is a cornerstone of decision support, bankers should appreciate that any mathematical model is based on abstraction and hypotheses. We may err on both counts. The abstration might be too coarse grain and one or more of our hypotheses might be wrong. Rocket scientists know by experience that testing is an integral part of model development.

Testing is also an integral part of model usage. This is starting to be being generally appreciated. In January 1996, the Basle Committee of Banking Supervision of the Group of Ten countries published the Market Risk Amendment. This follows the line established in the United States by the Federal Reserve and promotes marking-to-model of a bank's trading book. But it also specifies *backtesting* throughout the life cycle of the model.

Another major technological failure by the majority of banks, because of old rusty ideas and concepts under the old name of 'EDP' often renamed 'IT' without change in content, is the presentation of information to the end-user. Tier-1 banks have top systems, but the approach followed by the large majority of banks leaves much to be desired. Object databases and object programming are indivisible. Similarly, the concepts of *visual programming* and *data visualization* and *modeling* cannot and should not be separated from one another. There are as well differences between standalone and networked solutions – each with its own costs and benefits.

In conclusion, whether we look at new tools as languages, processing routines, horizontal software, methods or all four together, their contribution will be limited unless we change our culture. Computers and communications are tools, *not* goals. Though our tools may be wearing out and therefore be ineffectual, the greatest stumbling block to the able use of technology is cultural. As with every bottle, the bottleneck is at the top – and the top is our culture.

8   DO NOT UNDERESTIMATE THE SMALLER BANK AND ITS MARKET APPEAL

A study done in the early 1990s by the National Science Board, which is part of the US National Science Foundation (NSF) reveals that only 34 percent of major technical innovations have come from the larger firms. This is the more suprising as NSF has put in the 'larger firms' class all those with more than 10,000 employees. If the share of industrial output is taken as the basis of comparison, the smaller American firms produced:

- four times as many innovations per R&D dollar as middle-sized companies, and
- 24 times as many innovations as the very large firms.

Smaller firms perform better not only in absolute R&D return on investment, but also in terms of R&D–Marketing collaboration, as discussed in section 6. The same NSF study revealed that smaller companies which try hard to survive are more successful in focusing on time-to-market as a critical factor, reducing product development cycle time by 75 percent or more as compared with larger firms.

These references from the manufacturing industry have a direct impact on product development and innovation in banking. Senior bankers who participated in the research which led to this book estimated that, by the year 2000, product development cycles in the financial industries will be measured in weeks or months, not in years. Therefore these cognizant executives suggested that the time has come for the creation of new organizational philosophies to tap the full potential of technology in reaching the financial markets. But they also emphasized that, at the same time, an integral part of the new landscape is product variety:

- the 1990s are the era of customized production and online distribution.

The personalization of financial products as well as sharp reductions in lead times are made possible through simulation prototyping and sophisticated software, as suggested in section 7. Because one of the prerequisites of high technology is large investments, knowledgeable bankers advise the use of a sharp knife in

- cutting down company fat,
- by radically reducing management layers.

Well-managed smaller retail banks (see also Chapter 8, section 9, on the Danish Lan & Spar bank) are better able to apply these principles efficiently because they suffer less from bureaucracy. They tend to appreciate that a solid client base increasingly reflects a three-dimensional frame of reference, like the one in Figure 12.8. And smaller banks can see more clearly that, while the general tendency is to orient R&D to the most sophisticated future product, no banking service should be really excluded from the spotlight, from the simplest short-term credit to the most complex project financing offer.

In terms of markets and products, some of the areas to be included in the research effort will be *trading* and the bank's *distribution functions.* But smaller banks cannot afford to spread themselves thin by competing in many domains. They would rather capitalize on the rapid transition from R&D to sales. To do this in a successful manner, the retail bank should be listening most carefully to its customers, adjusting rapidly to their wishes and testing the current limits for new opportunities. This requires not only first-class technology but also well-trained and very flexible bankers able to deliver:

- innovation,
- quality,
- low cost, and
- productivity.

All four goals should be pursued, not sequentially but in parallel. A market-creation strategy is very different from the one oriented to market sharing. The bank has to generate new ideas and turn them into value-added products; and it has to do so at a very rapid rate, without delays and bureaucratic obstruction.

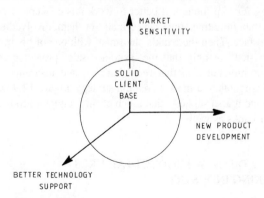

Figure 12.8　Marketing, new product development and technological support constitute the frame of reference of competitiveness

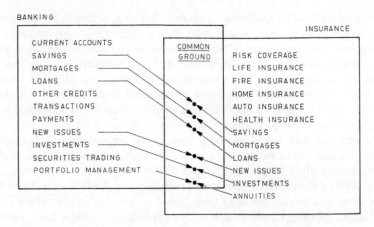

Figure 12.9   Common ground in financial industry products

An example from the manufacturing industry helps to explain what I mean. Some years ago, Lee Iacocca, then Chrysler's CEO, wanted to add a convertible to his company's product line. Following existing operating procedures, he asked his chief engineer to design a model in the shortest possible time. 'Yes,' the chief engineer answered, 'we can put together a prototype in nine months.' 'You just don't understand,' slapped back Iacocca. 'Go find a car and saw the top off the damn thing.' This being done, the chairman himself drove the prototype in down-town Detroit and when a sufficient number of people expressed interest he ordered the car built – with a big market success for that matter.

In a similar manner, in one of the retail banks I worked with as consultant to the board, the chairman wanted to add insurance as an ancillary service. But the people working for him thought it better to work this concept of cross-selling to death – rather than initiating something which, for them, involved unknowns they did not wish to face. Then the bank's chairman, with one of his immediate assistants, demonstrated not only that the insurance sales project presented a good business opportunity but also that retail banking and insurance have common ground which amounts to a market creation strategy. Figure 12.9 helps to explain this reference and it also suggests that much of this common ground can be found among smaller banks as well.

9   HOW TO AVOID NEW PRODUCT FAILURES IN THE BANKING INDUSTRY

When the retail bank moves from order taker to salesman, its management needs to establish new work habits, hire and train extrovert people and follow up on their performance. One of the ways of doing so is quality circles, of which we have spoken extensively in Chapter 4. Senior management must also follow very closely the R&D work through *design reviews*. Two types of design reviews are necessary:

- *regular*, whose frequency depends on the project (but I strongly advise that they are done weekly, on Friday afternoon); and
- *major*, which can be periodic or ad hoc – and may well lead to killing the new product project.

One of the weaknesses of R&D at large, whether in the manufacturing industry or in banking, is that projects tend to skid in the laboratory and they never come out to meet the market and earn an income. Management is often too lenient with different projects, and most particularly with those it does not understand very well.

- When a project has all the financing it needs and is assured of continuing support, the people behind it have every reason to keep it in the laboratory.
- This is no longer research. It is money thrown at the problem to feed the unable who have been asked by the unwilling to do the unnecessary.

But even well-managed new product projects may have problems which make it unwise to continue them. One of the reasons for oversight is that project evaluations are made without considering changes in the marketing environment – those which have been and the others which may come.

Another reason for failures with new banking products is that, because they involve so much complex software, the project becomes people-dependent rather than market-dependent. Progress advances as in a convoy, at the pace of the slowest person. Still another reason is *poor timing*. There are also other aspects of bad management.

- Many projects I see in banks are a response to competitors rather than representing fundamental research.
- Others have meager marketing budgets and pay little attention to training salesmen and users.

Lack of adequate training results in lack of sustained sales effort. In some cases, while senior management has a good idea about what it wants as a product, its vision of how the product should be sold is blurred.

Management without clear objectives is the sign of a business in trouble. Retail banks that do not provide for thinking and planning have fallen behind the times. If we cannot measure the efficiency of our service(s) then we cannot

- establish and follow quality measures,
- provide for steady upgrading of products and skills, or
- revamp and restructure our front desk and back office.

As a result, the services our bank offers have run out of control. This is the time of downturn. Alert management would not allow such things to happen. The chairman of National Life Insurance whom I met at Burlington, Vermont, following one of my seminars, was to remark: 'After we examined the course of technology and its effects on us and our competition, we decided to get in high gear, or we may not be around for long.' (See also section 7.)

The first decision by top management was to train itself to become computer-literate. It then defined the guidelines involving three paths: (1) automate what you do, but do it in a homogeneous way throughout the company; (2) improve the operational aspects by revamping current methods; and (3) as new technology comes along change the whole method. Said the chairman: 'You can do no. 3 if you master your own business, know well the technology and have a vision. Otherwise, forget it.' Hence the idea of top management training. Well-trained top management will easily detect whether the R&D and marketing proposals which it gets show the proper attention to both business and technology. Short of this, the new banking product(s) will be failures.

I am surprised how often senior bankers fail to understand that the proposals they get for new product development and marketing have an interest only in funding. In many projects I have been asked to audit by banks I work with, there has been an absence of business-oriented culture. While rocket scientists are today a 'must' – from new product development to risk management – this does not mean that they should be left to turn the bank into a minor academic campus. Without clear top management guidelines,

- few projects will focus on the target market, and
- even fewer will value the final customer and the income stream.

In other cases, even when senior bankers get involved in project planning, return on investment is non-existent, the market analysis is weak and business opportunity has been put on the backburner. If more than one department has an interest in the project, they will typically follow different agendas. And the involvement of market oriented skills will come too late to influence the product's characteristics.

People are asking for funding but they count neither the cost of staying in business nor the cost of goods sold. Neither do they have a concept of the cost of sales. The real cost of distribution includes much more than what most banks consider when they attempt to deal with distribution costs.

Any major distribution decision can affect the cost of doing business and also relate to other cost issues. From electronic banking to bricks-and-mortar branch offices, many elements may prove critical in evaluating the impact of alternative distribution approaches on total costs and profits. Banking products can neither be warehoused nor inventoried. Yet they are subject to:

- obsolescence,
- supply alternatives, and
- cost concessions,

The channels of distribution and of back office facilities must definitely account for this fact. And, like any other product, the new banking services which we develop must target both cash flow and profits.

Yet, even if there is some thought given to profitability, most often cash flow is nowhere reflected and even simple accounting is wanting. Few proposals for funding really think of value to be created for the customer. Yet, without this basic ingredient, a banking product will be a flop.

Notes

1. See D.N. Chorafas, *Rocket Scientists in Banking* (London and Dublin: Lafferty, 1995).
2. D.N. Chorafas, *Agent Technology Handbook* (New York: McGraw-Hill, 1998).
3. See D.N. Chorafas, *Chaos Theory in the Financial Markets* (Chicago: Probus/ Irwin, 1994).
4. D.N. Chorafas, *How to Understand and Use Mathematics for Derivatives, volume 1: Understanding the Behaviour of Markets* (London: Euromoney, 1995).

13 Pricing Financial Products and Services

1 INTRODUCTION

There are no formal, absolute rules about pricing financial products. Diversity in prices characterizes the banking industry, and this diversity is what makes the market, as well as offers a business opportunity to clients who know how to optimize their financial costs.

Diversity even prevails within the same bank when branch offices operate as profit centers and therefore are allowed to establish their prices for deposits, loans and other services in a way that will improve their P&L. Yet, in spite of such diversity senior management appreciates that banking products must be properly priced because:

- competition intensifies,
- margins have been reduced, and
- costs often escape control.

Faced with the rising operating costs, deregulation of interest rates and the loss of cross-subsidies among accounts, the financial services industry is now increasing its fees for a range of services, charging for some products that were previously free. The word *free* is, of course, inexact.

In retail banking, prices were *implicit* in the interest margins between deposits and loans, while some of the deposits were interest-free – as, for instance, in America under Regulation Q. In wholesale banking, some would-be charges were offset against compensating balances rather than *explicitly* debited to the customer account.

But times have changed. Bankers do understand that, in pricing policy, as in driving a car, we must conduct ourselves defensively. We must take into account the possible and likely *wisdoms* or *faults* of others. Other banks' strategic moves build barriers, while their faults provide us with profit opportunities.

Very little is 'unique' in banking in a pricing sense. The issues coming up are quite similar to the problems manufacturers and retailers encounter. This is true all the way to the fact that a few large customers account for the largest percentage of *our bank's* income, as we have clearly seen in Part Two. Furthermore:

- bank services are seldom independent of one another,
- customer demands for banking products are often highly interrelated, and
- cost pressures are causing many bankers to price non-credit services.

At the same time, there is no financial institution with the clout of a General Motors in the 1950s, when it controlled 53 percent of the US auto market; or an IBM in the 1960s and 1970s, when it controlled 62 percent of the world's computer market. There is no monopoly in banking.

In 1953, at UCLA, I had a professor of production management who had been a senior Ford executive. One day, in the graduate seminar, a fellow student asked him how Ford established its price list. 'At Ford we don't do a price list,' answered Ralph Barnes. 'We read the price list of General Motors and we try to do better. Otherwise, we would not sell cars.' The Barnes dictum applies fully in banking.

2 FINANCIAL PRODUCT LINES AND THE PRICING OF DIFFERENT INSTRUMENTS

The product line of a financial institution can be built up in several different ways. One is to distinguish between breadth and depth of the product line *our* bank offers to the market. *Breadth* of product range represents more and more alternatives. *Depth* focuses on greater, better thought-out options within a given banking line and the products it contains.

Another way of looking at the same issue of product line differentiation and its competitive characteristics is that pricing mechanism should be used in a way to sustain and promote *our* bank's strategic moves. For every product line and every service, our pricing should be commensurate with the strategy we have chosen:

- *specialization* provides greater depth, clarity of offer, higher quality of service and differentiation style, allowing premium prices.

Specialization can also address selected clients who must be served on an individual basis and handled with great care by skilled professionals able to act as personal problem solvers. We have spoken of this in Chapters 7 and 9, when we discussed relationship banking and private banking, respectively.

- A *superstore* type of marketing financial services offers massive choices and shows assortments – but also calls for cut-throat price competition. (See also Chapter 6 on niches, unique products and the mass market.)

This contrasts with specialization and it addresses all other bank customers who, by and large, may be nameless to the institution. Though it is a modern service, and largely oriented to a class of clients, direct banking (see Chapter 8) falls into this class. To the contrary, high net worth clients cannot be nameless – neither can they be successfully served as part of the mass.

Whichever pricing strategy we choose, it should not escape our attention that the first and foremost duty of management is to sort out market and product priorities. Let me explain this statement through an example from the computer industry. Many years ago I was working as a consultant to the board of a computer manufacturer offering to the market seven different model ranges whose positioning was not done with the greatest care. Figure 13.1 shows what is meant by such a disorderly product line.

- 'Upscale model' was company jargon which essentially meant a higher price tag.
- But the market appeal of this product was relatively low, because it was obsolete.

Setting aside the fact that 'upscale' was just a marketing gimmick, as shown in Figure 13.1 the organization of the product line was disorderly. Quite often, this also characterizes banking services. Even when management has a fairly good idea of the market segment it wants the bank to be, it has not thought out the overlaps and contradictions in the product line.

In the case of the computer manufacturer (and frequently this is true in banking) the first priority was to restructure and re-engineer the products and services, as indicated in the second half of Figure 13.1. Five product lines were retained, two product lines were dropped. Those retained were offered a specific market segment to which to appeal, with L3 and L4 partly overlapping within the market segment to which they addressed themselves. This was a deliberate management choice, largely dictated by competition.

Not only was I personally involved in this product line restructuring, but also some years ago I performed in banking a project on product line organization very similar to the one just described. The first major product range to be restructured was loans, which were organized into:

- personal (other than mortgages),
- mortgages,
- partnerships and small companies,
- business (medium-size companies), and
- corporate.

One of the options being considered was the creation of a fully owned retail subsidiary with extremely low overheads, to handle the first three types of loans. Sophisticated models were developed to support these functions at minimal costs as far as technology permitted. For the latter two classes, which were handled by the parent bank, the key phrase was *relationship banking*. (For marketing references, see Chapter 7; for loans, see Chapter 14.) Personal banking and loans relationship strategies have been used as the instrument for attracting and keeping

DISORDERLY PRODUCT LINE

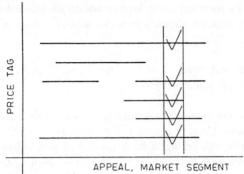

ORDERLY PRODUCT LINE
WITH MARKETING GOALS

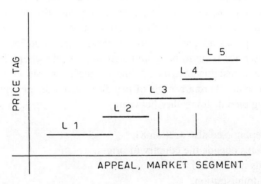

Figure 13.1 Restructuring a confused product line in a way appealing to the market

a bank's best customers. This approach influenced the structure and way of selling of fee-based services, since these loans customers were also investors.

3 PRODUCT PRICING AS A DYNAMIC STRATEGY AGAINST COMPETITION

Over the years, sophisticated technology has been employed as the way to up the price of financial services as compared to those of competitors. This has been achieved through a sensible response to a significant level of personalization, a matter which, as we saw on other occasions, required a change in the bank's technology culture as well as in top management commitment.

Whatever may be its strategy in setting and in revising prices, no bank can afford to take a static approach. Instead, senior management will be well advised to conduct periodically for each product line (and in cases of individual products within the main line):

- market research, and
- competitive business analysis.

Revamping prices to meet competition is not necessarily a one-way street, leading to lower income. Creative approaches might make it exactly the opposite. Using a gimmick like unbundling, a bank could lead to a higher price for financial services, as solutions followed for private banking document.

Because the market is dynamic, focused studies are instrumental in revealing weaknesses existing in the bank's pricing structure in response to market moves. Said a recent letter from a money center bank: 'Several client surveys have shown that our current pricing system no longer reflects our clients' needs. As a result, we will be introducing new service prices for custody and administration, stock exchange transactions and portfolio management.'

The new prices advanced by this bank are structured in such a way that the costs of a service seem to be more transparent for the client. Senior management has been emphasizing that, depending on the composition of the client's safe-keeping account, there are ways of benefiting from the new price structure. This new pricing plan distinguishes between:

- safekeeping (see also section 8),
- custodians outside the country of origin,
- precious metals, and
- asset administration.

The foreign custodian cost is added to the safekeeping price. It is a surcharge for securities held in safekeeping outside the country of origin, or in clearing organizations. Precious metals also have a surcharge.

This, of course, is no universal practice, which suggests that inquisitive clients can get themselves a deal. With client loyalty waning, the management of financial institutions should appreciate that the knowledgeable customers are willing and able to shop around.

In the foregoing example of unbundling, the asset administration price is a flat fee covering all transactions done on behalf of the client. This charge is waived only on securities in investment funds by the bank, the bank's own shares and the bank's medium term notes. In a way, this charge replaces the charges levied in the past for some transaction on an individual basis.

Altogether, the unbundling has been presented as a reduction in costs paid by the client, but in reality it is an increase – particularly so if compared (on a percentage of wealth in safekeeping basis) with charges effective in the late 1970s by the same bank.

- Twenty years ago, the charge was 1.25 per thousand of the deposited value of securities for safekeeping.
- Slowly, over the 1980s and 1990s, the charges reached almost 2.0 per thousand.
- With the unbundling, they have become 2.2 per thousand, plus the outside custodian surcharge.

If the customer does not react, these surcharges bring the total to between 3.0 per thousand and 5.0 per thousand depending on the country in which the securities are held. Some banks bet on the fact that many clients do not see the difference until the bill comes home at the end of the exercise year. Even then the customers may not be attentive enough. But those clients who know how to calculate, revolt. (See also the discussion on sophisticated private banking clients in Chapter 9.)

Knowlegeable investors start shopping around, they put different banks in competition, and they negotiate the charges: 50% reduction in fees used to be rare. Now they are not so unusual. By switching banks, in 1997 I reduced the fees for my portfolio from 2.5 per thousand to just below 1.0 per thousand. The next bid was 1.2 per thousand.

Notice that, by applying percentages on the client's net worth in order to compute their charges, banks avoid the pricing problem hitting other industries because of *currency* revaluation or devaluation. Typically, a manufacturing company must defend its market share worldwide. This

- induces exporting enterprises to refrain from immediately passing on an appreciation of their currency in their prices;
- instead, they absorb the effects themselves by reducing their own profit margins – even if these are already thin.

Such a strategy appears advantageous if the cost of regaining market shares later on is thought to be higher than the resultant reductions in profits, which may be only of a temporary nature. Among the costs of market entry are advertising and the creation of a marketing and after-sales service infrastructure.

Indeed, recent contributions to the debate on entrepreneurial pricing emphasize the significance of exchange rate expectations in the pricing-to-market strategy. Irreversible *menu costs* include all unrecoverable costs of adjusting prices. Therefore, quite often, manufacturing companies prefer the selling prices not to be adjusted until the lower earnings expected for the following periods exceed the menu costs.

- Banks, typically, do not have this pricing problem, though exceptions are always possible.

- By using as the basis of their charges for safekeeping a percentage of the client's net worth, they also escape the devastating effects of *inflation* on their income.

There is, however, an issue which manufacturing companies and banks share. This is the impact of quality on products and services, and therefore on the pricing strategy to be chosen.

'When we charge for our services, the prime criterion is the *quality* which we offer,' said the chairman of a financial institution during our meeting. Some banks solve quality of service problems through *differential pricing*, by having two different banks (under the same ownership) offering higher and lower net worth services. In the general case, however,

- this sense of prices to be commensurate with the service quality which we support has not yet entered the banking culture;
- therefore many mistakes are made, leading to the overpricing or underpricing of financial instruments because of the law of averages.

As I have the opportunity to underline on many occasions, in relationship banking the emphasis is on selling and servicing high-quality banking products to a selective group of clients. With the right product range in terms of organization and sales, which we have discussed in this section, the no. 1 aim is not volume but *control* of the most profitable part of the market.

4   A DOUBLE-EDGED SWORD: PRICING PRODUCTS EFFICIENTLY AND CUTTING COSTS

Unregulated by government, the market-based pricing system is the most efficient indication of whether an economy's financial resources are put to their most productive use. When he was chief economist of Prudential Securities, Edward Yardeni often used microeconomic theory to identify under which prism financial institutions shape the market price of their products.

Ford Motor Company's Mustang was not designed to be a sports car, with all the preconceptions of what a sports car should feature. The Mustang was originally conceived as a model able to cover costs and a targeted return. Then, through market research, Ford discovered that a market segment existed which valued sportiness in a car, but was unwilling to pay the high price on a sports car's tag.

- The task Ford successfully completed was to project a car sufficiently sporty to satisfy this market segment.

- The product purposely missed those elements of a sports car trade which would drive costs up.

Ford's strategy was customer-oriented. It was also market-centered. With the target buyer in mind, the firm anticipated a price even before the Mustang's specifications were finally closed. This was done by evaluating proposed product benefits versus affordable price – a challenge also answered through market research.

Whether in manufacturing or in banking, in a situation characterized neither by monopoly nor by oligopoly, there exist three main ingredients which first enter into the system to produce the price:

1. prices of the same or similar products by competitors,
2. projected volume of sales, and
3. the fuzzy notion of 'what the market will bear'.

Costing is not even part of this first phase – but it is part of profit and loss, as Figure 13.2 underlines. This is the opposite of what many companies think should be practiced when pricing their products: writing the price tag on a 'cost plus' basis.

A market-centered product pricing may be devastating for our current cost structure. If so, it is our costs which are awfully high rather than our prices which are too low. Figure 13.3 shows that, in a P&L sense, our costs should include the monetization of risk, general management overheads, direct labor and direct material. The last two elements constitute the classical costing. Interest expense as well as exceptions and discounts are also part of the picture.

Figures 13.2 and 13.3 should be taken together. The careful reader will appreciate that one of the key components in Figure 13.2 is realized sales, as contrasted to projected sales. If the product succeeds, then the underestimation of projected sales will be a 'good failure' because the bank will experience a windfall of profits. Such lucky failures do happen.

- In 1954, IBM estimated that its 650 computer, one of the first brought to the market, would sell 50 units at best.
- Before the product was dropped, six years later, sales exceeded 2,000 units, with the 650 becoming a gold mine for its manufacturer and vendor.

Generally, at the original product-pricing level, prices are only tentative. After each step in the development process they should be re-evaluated on the basis of market surveys, reflecting market changes as well as new features the product will be endowed with. This is a totally different ball game than classical pricing procedures, which are fixed and monolithic. Dynamically maintained tentative prices are an important guide to life cycle product development, since they can

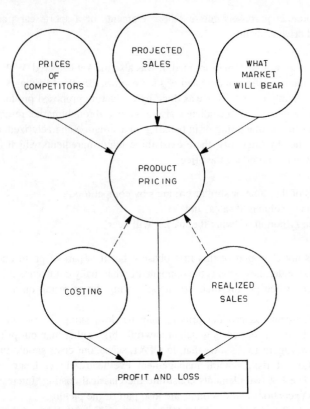

Figure 13.2   Elements entering the definition of a product's price

mark products, as well as potential products, as candidates for sunset clauses or redesign to increase their market appeal.

By early recognition of those products for which tentative prices are too low, or too high, relatively to additional development(s), sales costs and production costs, a bank can manage its product line much more profitably. Among the great advantages of a buyer-oriented price structure is that:

- market research flashes out in which way clients value different benefits on a product, and
- fine-tuning of pricing leads to an early detection of differences as compared to the competition.

One of the challenges of market-centered, buyer-oriented pricing is to identify different consumer segments to which the product can appeal. This helps to develop a marketing strategy that effectively distinguishes the key pricing issues

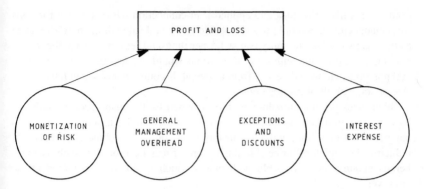

Figure 13.3   Major cost items in bank's profit and loss

being involved. Airlines, for example, successfully sort out market segments simply by requiring a long lead time to reserve a low price fare.

- Vacationers are price-sensitive, but they are able to anticipate their demand for air travel as well.
- Business travelers are much less price-sensitive, but require flexibility in their travel plans.

By offering lower fares with inflexible scheduling, airlines can attract enough price-sensitive travelers to support the frequent fliers as well as the numerous destinations that the business travelers demand.

Rarely, however, are markets so easily separated. Rigorous market differentiation requires creative efforts in product design and/or distribution, which explains why development of a pricing strategy should begin early in the product development process. The market for photocopiers offers a good example.

Xerox Corporation developed a valid approach to monitoring and measuring not only intensity but also type of use. When this method was put into effect it built a pricing schedule for a popular Xerox copier which included a usage charge for the number of copies made, in addition to a monthly fixed charge for renting the hardware.

- Through this approach, customers who use the machine more intensely pay more to have it.

But the charge also differed according to the type of copying the customer would be doing.

- The more copies made of an original, the lower the charge for a copy.

Some banks liked this idea and applied it in connection with their fees for portfolio management. Not only was the absolute size and value of the portfolio taken as the basis on which to apply (say a 1.5 per thousand fee), but also a client with a $10 million portfolio with only 20 positions would pay less than one with 50 to 100 positions. He would benefit from a special discount connected with the larger size of some or all of his positions.

Other sales promotion solutions, too, invented by the manufacturing industry have passed into banking. In Xerox's case, for example, a strategic approach has been that of selling collators cheaply with copying machines, appropriately reducing the collators' price. Similarly, some financial products, such as numbered accounts, are cross-sold with others which lie lower in the food chain. However,

- *creative pricing* calls for creative insight;
- such insight should be based on differences in buyers, not differences in production costs.

A valid pricing solution requires that customer differences be identified early in the product development process. Also early in the development process should be made decisions about bundling or unbundling product features in terms of pricing.

In conclusion, like design features, imaginative pricing decisions are integral to product strategy and they can also be used to segment markets. Companies using creative pricing have discovered numerous ways to do so, and have obtained interesting results.

- Kodak traditionally designed cameras to take only Kodak film.
- IBM leased its early computing machines requiring that they be used only with IBM cards.

Both firms charged a lower explicit price for the durable product. The price of supplies, however, carried a substantial margin, resulting in higher prices than those charged by competing sellers. The true price of the durable good was not the low explicit price, but the low explicit price plus the extra cost of required supplies.

This, too, is an ingenious pricing strategy which finds its counterpart in banking. In some of the retail banks I worked with, we offered a slightly lower interest with loans if *our* bank would also do the payroll of the borrower company as well as the export trade routines. There are significant profits to be made in documentary export credit.

5   REDUCING PRODUCTION COSTS BUT ALLOWING FLEXIBILITY IN MARKETING

The point was made in Chapter 11 that wise bankers differentiate between the *cost of doing business*, which is the main component of current costs, and the *cost of staying in business*, which essentially concerns research and development expenditures. If I were to use a sharp knife, I would cut to the bone the cost of doing business.

Figure 13.4 says that much, but in a different way. Its point of reference is statistics from five commercial banks with regard to retail financial business. Accounting data have been divided into three main classes:

- R&D and sales (frontdesk),
- general management (overheads) and back office (production),
- the bottom line: profits and losses.

The bank with the lowest overhead and production costs was also the most profitable. It is interesting to note that the more the general management and back office expenditures increased, the less profitable the bank was. In two cases, including the loss-making bank no. 5, management cut costs at the wrong end: the front desk and the research effort. The more this happened, the worse were the end results.

While, as a matter of principle, the right pricing of financial products and services is one of the pillars on which bank profitability rests, we should never forget the importance of tough cost control in the right places. This is valid all the way from the handling of classical bank accounts to securities and fund management.

Innovative solutions help promote profitability by providing more leeway in regard to product pricing. In October 1988, Merrill Lynch offered a new pricing structure for 22 of its existing mutual funds and all funds it projected for the near future. This plan permitted investors to choose whether to

- pay a sales charge when they first buy shares, or
- pay annual marketing and distribution fees and a withdrawal charge for redeeming shares in less than four years.

Such a move by the second-largest US fund group came at a time when industry sales were down and competition to attract investors was keen. It also coincided with increased scrutiny by US regulators, who wanted to tighten controls over fee structures.

Merrill Lynch took the right initiative after its management appreciated that the offering of options in terms of sales charges helps to sell different fee schemes by bringing the customer into the picture. Similarly, fee options is a good pricing strategy in regard to the features the customer would like to buy.

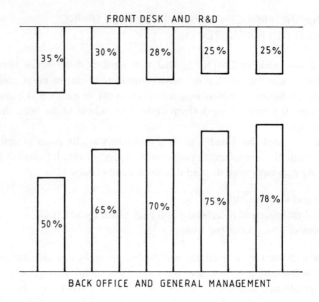

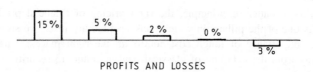

Figure 13.4 The cost of doing business needs a profit and loss perspective

This approach may be new in banking but not in consumer goods. Manufacturers of motor vehicles follow this strategy: they are constantly developing new product benefits in the form of style, technical improvements, and options.

- The initial temptation might be to identify buyer groups and combine benefits.
- But if this results in a much higher price, some groups of buyers would be priced out of the market.
- Therefore the basic price is kept low and over it come the extras – at the customer's choice.

This strategy is polyvalent. If prices were altogether set low enough to attract lower income buyers, they would be insufficient to cover costs. By deliberately designing benefits that different buyers find attractive for *their* car model, such as accessory packages, auto companies can price their products to earn more on each model run.

Still, as I will never tire of repeating, the other side of imaginative and aggressive pricing is cost-cutting. Over a number of years, Japanese car makers have been earnestly cutting costs on all their models. As Toyota redesigned its Camry for 1997, it aimed to squeeze out 20 percent of its cost.

Whether we talk of financial instruments or of motor vehicles, belt tightening is becoming a global strategy. In the auto industry, for example, it has already shown up in US-built models such as the Camry. Even penny pinching has become a competitive move which means that Detroit must follow to stay competitive in the American market.

Faced with a tremendous increase in *personnel costs*, which see to it that only low-cost producers and distributors of financial services can survive, banks and other service companies find it difficult to capitalize on the manufacturing abroad strategy which automakers, computer vendors and many others can use. Top-tier banks never forget this cost issue, and they are always careful in trimming their waistline. Dutch ABN Amro has concentrated on cutting costs at home, expanding its core business abroad and moving only cautiously into investment banking.

'Like our competitors, we want to build on our strengths and become a global universal bank,' says ABN Amro Chairman P.J. Kalff. 'But we have a different way to get there' (*Business Week*, October 28, 1996). This different way is seen in the 17.3 percent 1996 return on equity (ROE):

- this ROE is nearly seven percentage points higher than Deutsche Bank's, and
- almost 600 percent higher than the meager 2 percent ROE of the investment banking division of the Swiss Bank Corporation prior to Marcel Ospel's radical restructuring.

As we have seen in section 3, there are several ways in which to restrucure the pricing of safekeeping and investment advice. More linear, therefore subject to less degrees of freedom, is the approach to be taken to costing and pricing retail banking services. (See also section 6.)

- Services must be produced where they are consumed.
- They are not subject to the same rules of import/export as manufactured goods.

This is an area where auto manufacturing and banking significantly diverge. In BMW's new factory in the south-eastern United States (Spartanburg) each worker costs BMW $40,000 a year. This is an impressive 33 percent less than unionized workers at General Motors or Ford cost in Detroit. It is also 50 percent less than what BMW employees earn in Munich, Germany.

BMW forecasts that, in the longer run, with the most likely exchange rates, production costs in America will be 30 percent below Germany's – and it hopes the lesson will not be lost on its workforce back home. The company aims to improve productivity there by 4 percent a year, by switching to the flexible working system it is now using in Carolina.

- In the worst case in connection with German wages, BMW can always manufacture in the United States and export to Germany, or anywhere else in the world.
- A bank cannot do so, at least for most of its product lines, such as the handling of current accounts and savings.

For this purpose Table 13.1 advises some administrative planning duties which, when properly executed in a banking environment, will help to reduce personnel costs, or at least to contain them. There are no miracle solutions in cost control. Steady senior management attention is the answer.

Similar arguments apply to other industries which have gone through stress because of rapidly shrinking profit margins. Figure 13.5 provides an example from computer firms in the 1981 to 1995 timeframe, which to survive have to espouse a policy of reinventing themselves every two and a half years. Exactly the same trend shown in Figure 13.5 in regard to profit margins of semiconductor companies characterizes the prevailing margins from loans in the banking industry. Banks, however, find it more difficult to capitalize on reinventing themselves as the go-go computer companies do.

Table 13.1   Administrative planning duties

---

1. Define scope, objectives, timing and responsibility for front desk, back office and overheads.
2. Establish in an objective manner manpower requirements, based on standard costing.
3. Make monthly employee and payroll forecasts and experiment on them to cut down labor content.
4. Include approved recommendations in management, professional and administrative personnel individual budgets.
5. Establish next year's merits increases by cost-cutting function and evaluate its aftermaths on the bottom line.
6. Determine cost improvement goals and steadily follow up on them.
7. Project proposed manpower expenditures and cost reduction benefits versus the new technology investments.
8 Determine depreciation and investment tax credit for proposed technological facilities, programmed by country and branch office.

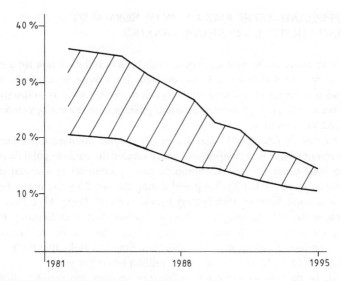

Figure 13.5 Range of profit margin among American computer firms, in the 1981–1995 timeframe

In order to improve the level of profitability of its bank, able management always strives to ensure that costs do not get out of line and that benefits exceed costs by a steadily greater margin. *High-quality management* is keen to institute:

- objectives which should be followed;
- measuring systems for productivity evaluation;
- efficient means to detect deviations from goals;
- advanced technology to cut employment; and
- factual manpower budgets which are steadily reviewed in terms of profitability.

Personnel costs can be further reduced through expert systems support – not just computers – and the assurance of well documented controls which are always kept up to standard in order to detect deviations. Few financial institutions have the culture and guts needed to do this.

In conclusion, the sustenance of bank profitability requires that *corrective action* be taken immediately. Instead of letting the financial organization believe that top management condones the slogan, 'Beware! Sacred Cows', the chief executive officer should leave no doubt that his motto is: 'Sacred Cows – Beware!'

6   APPRECIATING THE EVOLUTION OF NORMALIZED PRICING STRATEGIES IN RETAIL BANKING

The fee structure in the banking industry has been in full evolution for a number of basic reasons which are not that different from those which have induced tremendous changes in financial products and markets. As has been discussed on many occasions, topmost are deregulation, globalization, technology and associated product innovation.

As we saw in Chapters 11 and 12, steady *product innovation* has been promoted through increased competition, which created the banking public's appetite for more and better services. The normalization of a number of financial services also played a role. What has happened during the last 20 years in the financial markets is reminiscent of 19th-century experience with *Penny Mail*. Few people have taken the time to study the effect of uniform letters in England. Prior to 1839, there were some 76 million letters per year. This was before the introduction of a uniform format and cost for letter handling. But right after normalization was established, in 1840, there were 169 million letters per year.

Similarly, there is an explosion in banking services and therefore a need to structure them and price them in a fairly uniform way. The opposite argument is also valid: differentiation in prices presents the banking community with alternatives from which to choose.

Superficially, the two statements made in the preceding paragraph may seem to contradict one another. In reality, this is not the case. Prices may differ, but within each class they may be normalized. As far as current account pricing structures are concerned, the most popular alternatives are as follows:

1. *Implicit pricing* (still practiced in France). There is no interest on current accounts and no check charges.

Implicit pricing essentially means that the bank covers its costs and earns its profits from other sources, such as the difference between negative and positive interest rates in loans, and the balance on current accounts on which it pays no interest.

2. *Semi-implicit pricing* (as practiced in Germany). This features very low interest on current accounts and account pricing is below cost.
3. *Rebate strategy*. The bank levies charges but rebates them on the basis of a minimum balance. This is popular in the US.

No two fee schemes practiced by American retail banks are the same but, in general, a balance of XXX dollars will allow two free deposits and three withdrawals free of cost. Whatever is above that is usually charged at cost level. XXX may be an escalating clause with greater numbers of free transactions.

4. *Cost-free banking*, but with heavy charges on negative balances. There are no charges if the customer does not overdraw his account.
5. *Salary account*. To attract customers, banks are paying interest on salary deposits, but they distinguish between accounting date and value date. Likewise for student accounts.
6. *Symmetric account*. This pays interest in function of minimal or average balance.

The concept behind all these alternatives, as well as three more we will see in the following paragraphs, is to devise a normalized pricing procedure for current accounts which serves well the reporting frame shown in Figure 13.6: the underlying notion is that of establishing the cost of elemental operations, mapping them into the profit center account and developing a profitability evaluation, which helps to tune product pricing.

7. *Explicit pricing*. The fee schedule is based on 'costs plus', the plus being the bank's profits as far as competition permits.
8. *Relationship pricing*. For instance, if the customer has more than one account, he gets a better price break.

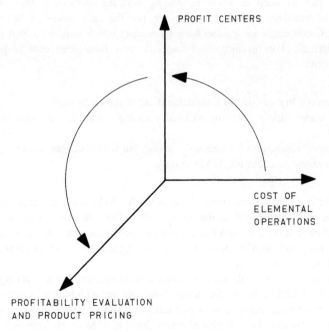

PROFIT CENTERS

COST OF
ELEMENTAL
OPERATIONS

PROFITABILITY EVALUATION
AND PRODUCT PRICING

Figure 13.6 Developing and implementing a pricing procedure

Relationship pricing may involve no specific charges if combined balances give the bank a good profit, as specified in the fee structure. The aim is to encourage customers to concentrate their main banking business with *our* bank. In corporate banking, cash management has a similar goal.

9.   *General account.* Instead of many alternatives, there is one account (AllKonto), a concept practiced by Swedish banks.

The AllKonto account pays good interest but it also charges a low fee per transaction. Therefore customers with many transactions will not make more money than with other fee alternatives. Introduced in 1979 by Svenska Handelsbanken, the General Account offers checkbook facilities and ATM card services. It requires no notice of withdrawal. But, while it pays good interest, each withdrawal is subject to a flat one per thousand fee, as service charges.

All nine examples address the different varieties of current accounts. Other schemes exist for savings accounts, time deposits, negotiable orders of withdrawal (NOW) accounts, money market instruments and so on. Sometimes it is competition in the financial industry which structures the fees of these accounts. In other cases, the law of the land is the moving force.

The fact to keep in mind in pricing banking services is that, in terms of retail banking, current accounts are not the only issue to be carefully priced. Credit cards are another banking product which requires a well-balanced fee approach. For instance, in France the new blue-green card is priced at four levels:

- there is a higher cost for international use of the credit card,
- an upper-middle cost for national retailing, charged with end of month billing,
- a lower-middle cost for national retailing, but with instantaneous charges, and
- the lowest cost fees for ATM use only.

Whether retail customers should be charged for ATM usage is, however, debatable. In my judgment this is the wrong policy. The cost to the bank of a simple transaction at teller level is $3 to $4, as a number of internal banking studies document. Provided the ATM network is fully used, the marginal transaction carries a small fraction of this cost.

Therefore the Swedish savings banks and commercial banks, among others, charge for withdrawals at teller level about 1Kr per withdrawal, which does not cover costs but discourages the use of tellers for simple transactions. By contrast, cash withdrawal is free of charge when done at ATM level. This is a rational pricing approach.

7 USING COMPUTERS AND SIMULATION TO EVALUATE ALTERNATIVE PRICING STRUCTURES

As we have seen in section 5, there exist different pricing structures even for basic financial instruments such as current accounts. Some focus on charges per transaction, others center on minimum deposits, still others target overdraft. There are significant differences in fee solutions.

Other norms apply to account management, fiduciary and other fees, as we will see. Though different among themselves, all fee structures have to do with relationship pricing, and therefore require a finely tuned mechanism which permits optimization of fees without losing customers because of overcharging. The principle behind fine-tuning is *optimization*. Much depends on our ability to evaluate the charges from different perspectives. A fee structure will be that much more successful if it is examined from a number of angles rather than just one. This statement is valid in terms of charges on transactions and all other issues we have been discussing.

- Sophisticated banks experiment on pricing because they recognize that brute force pricing has limits.
- Competitive pressures make the need for optimization most evident; no bank has free rein on its prices.
- Sprawling costs must be controlled internally. They cannot keep on being recovered through increases in fees.

Modeling is a good way to observe the constraints implied by these three points, setting the stage for optimization. Through computer simulation we can study alternative fee structures, make projections which affect the bank's income from services and rationalize the price structure.

One of the financial institutions I have been associated with developed mathematical models and a fee database with the goal of examining industry practices. The models made it possible to preview the effects of *paying interest* on checking accounts but also to levy a *fee on transactions*. Subsequently, this system was upgraded to permit

- experimentation on service fees in different banking channels, and
- improvements in pricing, including alternative fee structures versus what was offered by the competition.

The model a bank develops for experimentation reasons on product prices and fees should pay a great deal of attention to the customers' management targets as the prime clientele, their current account practices, investment objectives, loan policies and the supports necessary to meet their needs. Generally in investments the customer wants:

- return on capital combined with a reasonable level of capital safety, and
- a balanced capital growth, accepting a certain degree of risk.

Another customer requirement is quality (see Chapter 4). Therefore the bank should position itself to provide first-class services to the customer: advising on investments, detailing the transactions, providing information on market developments and handholding in a way which gives the customer confidence that his assets are looked after.

For these services the bank earns a fee, and the object of the experimentation is to maximize this fee commensurate with the quality of service the customer gets. Known as *product pricing by computer*, this approach can lead to an efficient evaluation of the bank's products and services along the three-dimensional frame of reference shown in Figure 13.7.

In the application to which reference was made in the preceding paragraphs, the model designed for current accounts has been based on a sample of the bank's customer base. It employs data about

- demand deposits activity levels,
- customer/account make-up and maintenance,
- transaction by type of account and customer bracket, and
- average and minimum balances by account.

The model receives input from costing, analyzes existing service charges and integrates competitive fee levels as well as other relevant information. The end product is an interactive computer output which shows alternatives and their aftermaths in the most likely P&L sense.

One of the interesting outcomes of this experimentation was the evidence that the bank loses its efficiency once it spreads out its service fee structure to cover every contingency. It can no longer see clearly its costs and income, in spite of the support provided by the simulator. Another interesting finding was that, even if it is theoretically better to adjust the fee structure dynamically, practical considerations make this unwise. After deciding to change the price of a service, management should implement the change in a manner that reflects positively on our bank. It is important that not only the customers but also everyone in our institution

- understands the reason(s) behind the price change,
- appreciates why it is fair both to the bank and to its customers, and
- sees how *our* price structure compares with others'.

Such understanding will help in following the projected changes, as well as in discussing them intelligently with our customers. Depending on the channel and

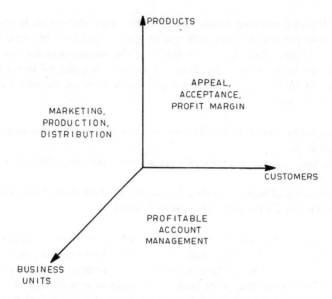

Figure 13.7 Profitability evaluation along three axes of reference

the complexity of the fees, training sessions will be necessary for relationship management personnel.

Not only should the people who directly produce fees for the bank be steadily and thoroughly trained, but also those who plan, organize and staff the fee-generating function, such as investment advisors, account managers, cross-sales personnel and other functions in direct contact with the customers. Even the best simulators for the evaluation of alternative pricing schemes will not make up for the fact that the contact element is not of a high standard or irritates rather than truly serves the customer. One of the irritants is the rapid change of personnel in investment advising and account management functions, obliging the customer to repeat his explanation about his investment goals and horizons, as well as destabilizing the bank-to-customer connection.

8   PRIVATE BANKING OPERATIONS AND FEES FOR PORTFOLIO MANAGEMENT

Typically in private banking, the portfolio management charges include a management fee and an advisory fee. There are as well trading fees calculated on the basis of trading activity. The management fee is a percentage of net worth and is typically but not exclusively charged on a yearly basis covering, among other services, client handholding.

Not all banks, however, follow this algorithm. Some distinguish between the *management* fee, which varies with type of mandate and level of accounts, and the *advisory fee*, which is flat. In this case the management fee essentially concerns administrative services. This is a way to distinguish between advisory services and the management/administrative functions connected with the client portfolio's net worth.

• Some banks choose to bundle their services into one fee structure; others detail them.
• Most banks charge the customer's account once per year; others do so every trimester.
• The majority of banks debit their fees at the end of the elapsed year; others do so in January for the year which has just started.

There are no uniform rules in private banking services in terms of charges. Some banks vary the level of administrative fee according to the services the customer buys: for instance, in Switzerland, whether he has a numbered account or/and he wishes his mail to be held at the bank. Other banks have an all-inclusive flat fee which incorporates the cost of numbered accounts and held-back mail, whether or not the customer chooses to use these services.

Generally, the charges in question apply to the value of the entire portfolio. The fee schedule forms an integral part of the management mandate the client signs with the bank. The bank also assesses individual surcharges on, especially, labor-intensive mandates.

• Table 13.2 presents the portfolio management charges at bank ABC, a Swiss financial institution.
• Table 13.3 gives the all-inclusive advisory and management fees of bank XYZ, also a Swiss institution.

The all-inclusive management fee shown in Table 13.2 includes in-house safe-keeping charges, external safekeeping charges, coupon collection commissions, charges for securities administration, charges for account maintenance and balancing, charges for payment transactions and postage.

Also included in this fee are foreign exchange commissions (cash transactions), travelers check commissions, commissions for bill collection and check cashing, all fees and charges in connection with EC credit cards, guarantee commissions for credit card guarantees and charges for portfolio deposits.

There is nothing unique about the portfolio management fee structures in Tables 13.2 and 13.3. Neither of them is a norm. But the differences characterizing them are interesting. Both are alternatives worth considering.

An example of still another fee structure for portfolio services is that provided by a Luxembourg bank which applies a percentage on the value of the portfolio

Table 13.2 Portfolio management charges and transaction fees per year at bank ABC (Swiss franc charges converted into dollars)

Management and advisory charges	
Securities by bank ABC	0.08%
Other investments	0.12%
Minimum charge	$3,500–$7,500*
Transaction fees	
All-inclusive fee per settlement	$170 plus third party charges

Notes:
There are, however exceptions. Transactions in the bank's own investment funds are net of charges. Transactions in the bank's money market funds are charged $85. But transactions on non-primary markets are charged $340.

*Depending on account credit balances and other factors.

Table 13.3 All-inclusive management fee and transaction fee per year at bank XYZ (portfolio value expressed in dollars converted from SF at SF1.12/$)

	*Fee p.a.**
Up to $450,000	0.400%
Up to $1,350,000	0.375%
Up to $1,800,000	0.350%
Up to $4,500,000	0.325%
Up to $6,750,000	0.300%
Up to $9,000,000	0.275%
Up to $22,500,000	0.250%
Over $22,500,000	Special conditions

Note:
*There is a minimum charge of $250 to $700, dependent on the share of the bank's own securities and account credit balances.

for management/administrative services and a lump sum for advisory functions:

- the management fee which ranges between 0.1 percent and 0.175 percent of the net worth, depending on the net worth of the fund;
- the consulting fee is $3,000 per year and is independent of the net worth of the portfolio.

If the two fee chapters: consulting and account management are lumped together, then for the majority of cases the yearly fee tends to vary between 0.15 per thousand and 0.25 per thousand. But as it has been explained, there are special conditions made for large portfolios under custody.

Notice that, in many cases, the transaction fees which represent the bank's own and third party charges – such as commission, brokerage fees, stamp duties and the like – are passed on to the client. Physical deliveries from portfolio, per security position, are also being charged. A sample value is $170.

- An example of charges for non-physical deliveries from portfolio, also per security position, is $85.
- But, in terms of non-physical deliveries, there is a cap to the total amount charged, $800 representing a mean value.

Some banks charge an all-inclusive fee of $200 per year, per position, for the safe custody of special assets such as envelopes, documents, non-valuables and so on. With the introduction of value-added tax (VAT), for clients domiciled in the country where the bank resides, the management fee charged by Swiss banks is subject to value-added tax. For clients domiciled abroad, the portfolio management charges are usually free of VAT.

There exist many other different fee schedules, such as minimum brokerage fee, transactions made in the home country of the bank and abroad, the bank's own investment funds, fiduciary investment in the Euromarket and fiduciary investments in the call market; also for money market investments which, in some countries, like Switzerland, are taxed quite heavily.

Regarding Swiss financial institutions, the minimum brokerage fee for transactions in Switzerland or primary stock markets abroad tends to be $180 per transaction, while for transactions on other stock markets abroad it goes up to $360 per transaction. The fee schedule for transactions in Switzerland and abroad is:

- 0.10 percent to 0.80 percent for bonds, and
- 0.20 percent to 1.10 percent for equities and external investment funds.

Here again third-party charges and fees are passed on to the client. Fiduciary investments for call money feature a minimum commission as well as a fee per year. Charges for money market operations vary, according to maturity and type of transaction, from 0.125 percent to 0.500 percent of invested amount, with a minimum commission which tends to be $180. The exact minimum commission depends on currency and investment instrument.

Practically all banks also offer other services to private clients, for which they apply a fee schedule. Examples are: safe deposit box rental, securities tax statement, tax refunds, short-term investments, special reporting practices, legal counseling, estate planning, trust services, securities lending and borrowing.

9 QUESTIONS REGARDING FEES FACING THE BROKERAGE BUSINESS

Though they work together in the stock market and they collaborate in equities investments, banks and brokers do not see eye-to-eye when it comes to customer handling and fee structure. This is changing, however. Strategic planning considerations bring up some key questions facing brokerage houses in terms of market opportunity which now center on advice-dispensing to the client base and the pricing of such advice.

Fees will present a contrast to past policies of brokerages which came with the motto: 'I can do it cheaper'. Other questions which now rank at the top of the list of investment banks, and require a significant amount of focus, are:

* how to find out about their clients' *tolerance to risk*, and
* the underlying *asset base* which could be brought in-house.

Able answers to these queries are an important ingredient in fine-tuning the investment advice the broker gives to his clients, as well as deciding if fees should be charged and, if so, how much.

Several brokers are currently contemplating changing their policy of charging minimal or no fees. Present policies generally depend on transaction commissions for their profits. Applying anything above minimal charges will require that brokers outperform the banks in terms of asset management.

To help themselves to do so, some brokers have developed expert systems[1] focused on serving investor needs. Table 13.4 gives a snapshot of some of the knowledge artefacts currently active in portfolio management. The use of knowledge

Table 13.4 Implementation of expert systems areas of interest for portfolio management

Knowledge artefacts for investor needs	Basic economic factors
1. Capital gains at a given level of risk	Financial market performance
2. Investor's inclination to risk	Volatility, liquidity, other risk factors
3. Expected rate of return from an investment	Prime rate, inflation rate, other economic conditions
4. Investor's time horizon	Market prognosis
5. Tradeoffs between different types of investments	Capital markets, money markets, commodities, derivatives

engineering helps in targeting the customer base in a more accurate manner. This is very important inasmuch as:

- at Merrill Lynch, 2 percent of the clients bring in about two-thirds of the company's profits;
- at Prudential Securities, about 90 percent of revenue comes from 10 percent of clients.

The first important module for each of the expert systems shown in Table 13.4 is the investor's profile analyzer. Said a senior Prudential Bache executive during our meeting in London: 'Targeting is for us a key question which goes beyond choosing an advertising agency and an advertising strategy. Should we focus on this 10 percent or go for the 100 percent hoping to find in it the 10 percent?' This query, and the answer which it will receive, speak volumes about the guidelines which should be developed in connection with a fee structure by brokers, and also in regard to the charges for transactions the broker undertakes for his clients. Over the years, the portfolio investment themes have changed significantly.

- In the 1950s, the passive fixed income portfolio concept carried the day.
- In the 1960s, emphasis was placed on active equity portfolios.
- In the 1970s, real estate investments and active fixed income management became the focal point.
- The 1980s, were the decade of leveraged buyouts, junk bonds and stock market indexing, followed by the introduction of derivatives.
- In the 1990s, derivatives trades boomed and emphasis has been placed on global investing, as well as the experimental evaluation of alternative investments.

These alternative investments have addressed both financial assets and real assets. While portfolio objectives have broadened, time horizons now vary from short-term to long-term. The contents of a portfolio vary from narrow to broad-based, and from static to dynamic. Just like banks, brokerage houses are massaging their fee structures and making them more flexible to fit a range of investor drives and goals. The same is valid for fund managers.

During the late 1980s and early 1990s, a number of fund management organizations introduced alternative pricing schemes when launching new funds. Merrill Lynch seems to have been the first to offer a 'pay now or pay later' arrangement. It is doing so

- to attract new investors by lowering the front load, and
- to retain those that have been its clients for a number of years.

Because of its worldwide marketing capability, Merrill Lynch has a broad influence on the industry. Every one of its newer fee structures obliges other fund management institutions to review their pricing schemes, if they want to remain competitive.

From the investor's and the depositor's viewpoint, however, not everything which looks like a low-cost product offering may remain so under scrutiny. Therefore experts caution investors to review carefully the long-term implications of the various new pricing terms, even when they promise cost savings.

Because a growing number of institutional investors buy this advice about the wisdom of greater scrutiny, banks, brokers and funds managers should do a lot of homework. Competitive forces see to it that, while the better managed financial institutions experiment beforehand on new fee structures in order to maximize their income and attract more investors, there are limits to the level of fees. As underlined on many occasions, fee structures are established by the market as a whole and its thresholds impact on pricing. Smart investors take advantage of this fact. Shopping around, spreading accounts and switching accounts are today important aspects of fund management.

In conclusion, when it comes to investments, trading and assets management, different segments of the financial industry follow different paths in product pricing. Brokerages and banks are in competition regarding the management of wealth and this leads to different structures with regard to fees they receive for their services.

• Banks classically have focused on gaining control of their clients' asset base, and their income planning has been turned in this direction.
• Brokers have been particularly interested in trading fees for commission-generating business, but now they realize that they have lost control of the asset base.

Because financial markets and financial products are in full evolution, this line of distinction between the two types of services, banks and brokers, is no longer as clear as it used to be. Banks are keen to develop a fees and commissions business. At the same time, as a good part of the banking public has become more wealthy, brokers are after a chunk of its assets base. Apart from the fees this provides, there is as well the realization that whoever controls the clients' assets also controls the profitability of the account.

10   STRATEGIC PLANNING AND THE ELABORATION OF A PRICING SCHEDULE FOR BANKING SERVICES

Strategic, organizational and procedural prerequisites should be observed with all fee income services. As the first nine sections of this chapter have demonstrated, an important first step in establishing and controlling fee income is to elaborate a pricing policy. Every bank should study and steadily re-evaluate its fee policy via a small team working in close coordination with strategic planning. The job description of this team should state the mission of

- assessing the bank's pricing position compared with its competition, for all fee-based services;
- analyzing the prices of existing products and services, comparing them to their costs and their profit margins; and
- evaluating fee arrangements for all new products, before they are introduced to the market and offered to customers.

The bank's chief executive officer should expect strategic planning to make recommendations concerning amounts and timing of price changes, based on simulation and experimentation, and also to monitor results of implementing fee structures and price changes, evaluating the bank's competitiveness and reporting on it. All this requires expertise in strategic planning.

- While contemplating a *new service*, the bank should first determine whether what it represents is an integral part of its strategic plan for the future.

It should evidently evaluate the potential market for the service, the number of competitors and their punch. Nothing should be taken for granted when analyzing market potential, costs, prices, fees and margins.

- Both for *new products and for existing products*, the bank should know in depth its competitors, their strategies and their prices.

This includes present prices charged by competitors, recent price increases or decreases, the most likely direction of the competitors' plans, new marketing programs and the like. This is essential information for developing both product strategies and price strategies. Many banks fail to realize that much information can often be obtained from annual reports, news items, speeches and publications, and also from banking meetings and other public pronouncements. As we have seen in Chapter 1, a strategy is never published black-on-white, but it can be deduced through the fine print of actions and reactions which are public knowledge.

Let me once more repeat what Sun Tzu, the statesman and general of ancient China, said 25 centuries ago. If we know ourselves and know our enemy, we do not need to worry about the outcome of 100 battles. In line with this dictum, a successful pricing effort requires careful evaluation of market strengths and weaknesses – as well as of those of our competition. Every well-managed bank should

- study the benefits of the products and services it offers to customers, and
- analyze what customers really want and need beyond the current offerings.

The first crucial question is: 'Will they pay for what we give them?', followed by the query: 'Why should they pay?' The answers can be found by establishing what *we* offer in terms of value differentiation. Does our service meet *our* customers' needs? Where should it be improved? Or should it be fully modified?

It is not enough that promotional materials state the benefits to the customers. It is also important that *our* salespeople, from tellers to the bank's account managers, are trained in the service, that they know how to explain it to the customer, as well as how to demonstrate its advantages. In terms of products and services, I have found it rewarding to consider *value pricing*, based on value analysis of the products offered by competition. Banks which base themselves only on calculating costs and adding a percentage for profit are in for rude surprises.

Section 6 has underlined the importance of computer modeling in studying fee structures. No self-respecting financial institution should charge the same prices as competitors without regard to the intrinsic value its own service offers. *Intrinsic value* is a term introduced by Warren E. Buffett. It is a cash flow concept leading to a logical approach to evaluating the relative attractiveness of investments (*An Owner's Manual*, Berkshire Hathaway, Omaha, NE, 1996). A similar notion can be used in connection with other banking products and services.

- Intrinsic is the discounted value of cash that can be taken out of a business during its remaining life.
- It is an estimate rather than an exact figure, and it must be changed in function of interest rate volatility or the revision of cash flows.

The concept of intrinsic value applies to an investor's portfolio, or to the portfolio of a bank. It permits the calculation of a fee structure, because it helps to demonstrate to the client how much the intrinsic value of his portfolio has grown, as a result of sound investment policies. The successful banker uses a more informed method in setting prices than the imitation method. I also advise the use of simulation and experimentation.

- Wise banks make pricing decisions within the perspective of long, medium and short-range goals.
- They answer in a documented manner questions such as: How will this price affect *our* banks's business?

If our bank is here to stay, we should not be concerned only by the short run. How will the pricing scheme affect our client base in the long run? Are we building for the future? Are our products and services designed to attract and keep the kind of customers we are interested in? Is our fee structure fair to all parties?

We should look at our products as a system. Is the product we price standalone, or is it part of an integrated group of financial services? Will the new or revamped product help establish and retain relationships with target customers? It is important to answer these questions prior to setting pricing policies. Fees are an integral part of the strategy we have established for our survival in a market more competitive than ever. But fees should work *for* our bank. They should be friends – not foes.

Note

1.   See D.N. Chorafas and H. Steinmann, *Expert Systems in Banking* (London: Macmillan, 1991).

14 The Choice of a Strategy for Loans

1 INTRODUCTION

We have spoken about the strategic prerequisites for new financial instruments as well as the role research and development plays. The subject of this chapter is the choice of a strategy for loans and consequently the profit and loss which may result from the retail bank's loans policies.

Should the primary emphasis be on the manufacturing industry, the merchandising industry, agriculture or the consumers? If all of them, what should be the mix? Also, what kind of a balance can be found between loan origination and loan servicing at the branch office – and what about central control?

Even after one industry has been chosen as the target for the loans business, chances are top management will come up with more focused questions. If it is manufacturing, should it be rather small, medium-sized or large firms? If it is merchandising, should the loans orientation be to retail or wholesale? And if retail, should it be proprietorships, partnerships or corporations?

A number of queries would be posed if the choice of orientation was agriculture. Should we target cooperatives, large firms, smaller firms or family firms? As for professionals, which could be the best sector: lawyers, accountants, architects, engineers, medical doctors or others?

The consumer loans market, too, is diverse and therefore requires choices to be made. Should we favor mortgage loans, house improvements, appliances, autos, loans for the education of the children or personal loans required for the solution of short-term family problems?

These lists are just examples and the careful reader will observe that there are as well many other loans channels to be exploited, such as real estate developers. Other examples are bridging loans for mergers and acquisitions, syndicated loans and sovereign loans. Each and every one of them requires experienced lending bankers, risk managers and senior executives responsible for strategy.

- The lending strategy *our* bank establishes should see to it that rational risk/reward decisions are being followed.
- These should be clearly stated to help in solving the problems loan managers face in evaluating the borrower's financial risk.

Policies are also necessary to compensate for pricing risk in a highly competitive banking environment. Able answers to risk and reward questions will be

347

instrumental in providing our bank with superior skills in a particular industry or region we have targeted. We should also keep in mind that

• as a bank builds expertise in a given field, it tends to increase its exposure in that area; and
• the lender is vulnerable to pricing that does not compensate for the full risk, and to over-concentration in a certain market.

Therefore bankers should be keen to develop knowledge-enriched approaches to managing their loan book, using statistical tools, risk models and hedging techniques. Many of these tools are similar to those used in fund management. They can be combined with specialized credit rating frameworks, to allow tracking of expected default frequencies and managing exposure, and also to permit weeding interest rate risk out of the loans book and into the trading book – where it is hedged.

2   RELATIONSHIP BANKING, LOANS AND COVENANTS

The no. 1 problem with loans today is that too many banks with too much money are chasing too few loan transactions. This characterizes the whole banking industry, from local individual loans to the global syndicated loan market.

There are plenty of signs of bitter competition for business. One of the more interesting came in September 1995, when America's Chemical Bank and Britain's Lloyds Bank brought to market a $700 million five-year loan for BTR, the British conglomerate, priced at just 11.5 basis points above LIBOR.

• This, like many others, was a cut-price transaction.
• That is the rate at which AAA banks can buy money from their peers in the interbank market.

In the London syndication market, which is the largest in the world, banks are lending to blue-chip industrial companies about 15 basis points above LIBOR. To appreciate how low this margin is, it is sufficient to recall that in 1991 the mark-up was 140 points.

There is another reason why the cut-throat loan to BTR caused so much concern to other bankers: the merger between Chemical and Chase Manhattan, announced on August 28, 1995, could create a huge force in syndicated lending. Together, the two American banks have about a tenth of the overall market.

• With margins between positive interest (the rate charged to the client) and negative interest (the cost of money to the bank) at rock-bottom, banks are using their loans as a strategic weapon.

- They expect to win other business from the companies to which they are lending, like cash management and the handling of their foreign exchange needs.

Toughening competition is also weakening *loan covenants*: the contracts detailing financial targets, like debt–equity ratios and cash flow. In the past, banks were turning their backs on a number of deals because the borrower would not grant sufficient convenants – which was seen as an indicator that the quality of their borrower was not truly high.

One of the problems with toughening competition is that, whenever blue-chip borrowers get better terms, this has a domino effect, reducing margins for less creditworthy firms too. A borrower's market sees to it that banks cannot dictate their own terms to lenders, as used to be the practice.

Yet there is a declining credit quality of many industrial companies as well as financial institutions. In the case of banks, the loss of AAA and, in some cases, of AA status has proved a severe handicap in the lucrative derivatives market, since many potential clients are unwilling to deal with institutions rated less than double A.

Similarly with loans, where corporations with AAA status are able to obtain many more concessions from banks than their brethren with AA or A only. Lenders justify their leniency as being a function, not so much of tough competition as of the fact that they can acquire much more business from multinational, well-known firms. There is a grain of truth in this statement given that, profits aside, the acquisition of business leads to better information about credit quality by lenders. This is much more problematic for small firms than for large ones. It is not surprising, therefore, that the ways in which small and big companies obtain credit financing differ significantly.

The able management of loans, like that of any other business, is very sensitive to the quality of information which is available regarding the borrower. Banks employ a variety of mechanisms to address the information-related problems associated with lending to small firms, including:

- intensive borrower monitoring through loan covenants, and
- loan contracts tailored to the financial conditions of the loan firm.

The bank loan market for small business also differs from the corporate market in its emphasis on the lender–borrower relationship. Through the bank–borrower relationship, banks may acquire private information over time and use this information to refine the contract terms which they offer.

The best managed financial institutions use data on loan rates and collateral requirements on lines of credit issued to businesses to test the dependability of the relationship as it progresses. Then they adjust the contract terms. Well-organized lenders also examine price and nonprice terms of the commercial bank's *lines of credit* (L/C). Companies which establish a good dependability record tend to pay lower interest rates. Some research projects estimate this differential at about 60 basis points over a 10-year relationship. They also find that small businesses with longer banking relationships are less likely to pledge collateral.

On the basis of these findings, some banks have formulated the hypothesis of *relationship lending*. (See also the discussion on this concept in section 5.) It suggests that it is possible to limit the decline of bank lending – in spite of the fact that commercial paper and non-bank competition are reducing the share of loans held by banks – by developing a long-term relationship which ties the company closer to the lender. A similar relationship lending strategy can be used with personal loans.

Where, however, many commercial banks fail in their strategy is in the knowhow necessary to master interest rate risk. Brandon J. Davies, the treasurer of Global Corporate Banking, Barclays Bank, is right when he says that the whole area of interest rate risk management in retail banking is not well understood. This is evidenced by

- the often poor hedging decisions made by bank treasurers, and
- the rather meager literature available on loans' interest rate exposure.

Another domain not yet properly mastered by commercial banks is the recovery from a shower of non-performing loans. In my book, the best example of a wise strategy has been Securum, a 1992 to 1997 project, that can be seen as a good way to resolve the worst crisis to affect the Swedish financial system since the Kreuger crash of the early 1930s. (See section 8.)

3   THE PERSONAL LOANS PORTFOLIO OF A RETAIL BANK

In the general case, a consumer loan can be defined as a personal loan to one or more individuals which is either indirectly secured through the borrower's paycheck or directly secured by consumer goods bought primarily for personal, family or household use. Personal loans can also be unsecured. Whichever is their type, they may be distinguished in several ways:

- purpose of the proposed expenditure,
- method of acquisition and collateral,
- contract provision and sunset clauses, and
- treatment of interest and other factors.

Consumer loans, classified by purpose, would include automobile loans, home improvement loans, home equipment loans, mobile home loans, marine loans, education loans, recreational loans and other types of personal loans. Many banks look on credit card loans as a separate class, but because the use of credit cards enters into many commercial transactions I would integrate them into this list. Credit cards are today a very important class of personal loans. They also provide an excellent customer database on which merchandising firms and other non-banks capitalize in order to enter the banking business. A well-managed bank would be keen to mine its credit card database in order to obtain factual and documented information on:

- the buying habits of its customers, and
- the opportunities which exist for cross-sales.

All types of loans have to be monitored very carefully, with a view to a more or less permanent lending relationship. Because personal loans are part of a mass market, as defined in Chapter 6, the efficiency of the operation, its low cost and the image the lender presents to the market are critical elements of success.

An article in the *Financial Times* (27/28 July 1996) focused quite well on the strategy of personal loans by elaborating on the way in which it affects Lloyds TSB's share price. Revenues are growing and the bank's cost–income ratio is being rebuilt thanks in large measure to personal loans. Part and parcel of looking at consumer loans as a strategic product is the assurance that barriers to new entrants in this market become formidable. Lloyds, the *Financial Times* article says, has two big advantages over its main competitors:

- the cost savings from its merger with TSB, and
- its heavy weighting towards high-margin retail lending which is at the core of its strategy.

While competition is getting sharper in retail banking, retail customers are always likely to be a softer touch. 'Even if Lloyds' returns on its fast-growing capital base are bound to fall, its edge over its competitors looks secure,' suggests the article in question. What makes the edge look so secure?

Starting with the fundamentals, I would say that the front line is management's attention to building defenses, along with an understanding of the types of personal loans which can provide competitive advantages. Not all consumer loans are the same in their fundamentals. Then come the marketing aspects, cross-sales and customer handholding: that is, the relationship banking culture to which reference was made in section 2. Next are the accounting principles and procedures applicable to all types of consumer loans, but used in a way which permits distinguishing between their purposes from a management accounting viewpoint.

Accounting for consumer loans written on a simple interest bearing basis is essentially the same as the accounting for direct reduction mortgage loans. Some lenders charge interest on a daily basis, as opposed to the monthly basis for most mortgage loans.

- When interest is charged on a daily basis, the amount of the last payment can be scheduled, assuming that all payments will be received on the due date.
- It is probable, however, that payments will differ from that schedule, since they are seldom received exactly on due date.

There is no difference in accounting for loan fees and late charges between simple-interest loans and loans with precomputed interest. A *refinance* of a loan is the repayment of an existing loan from the proceeds of a new loan to the same borrower. The accounting for a refinanced loan involves two entries:

- the recording of a new loan, and
- the repayment of the loan being refinanced.

Accounting entries reflecting these two transactions are fairly straightforward. An *extension* of a loan occurs when a borrower is permitted to defer the scheduled payment dates, thus extending the final payment of an extension fee which represents compensation for the deferral to future periods of interest. The accounting treatment of extension fees should be consistent with the accounting used for unearned discount. If extension fees are not significant, they may be credited to income when collected, irrespective of the accounting method used for unearned discount.

Differences exist between banks in the way they handle *bad debts*. Usually, when it is determined that a loan is uncollectable, and the loan is not insured or guaranteed, the unearned discount is credited against the loan.

- The balance of the loan is then charged to the appropriate account.
- The amount charged will depend on the bank's method of accounting bad debt.

For accounting purposes, many banks follow the reserve accounting method. Where bad debts are not significant, the charge-off method is often chosen. A better strategy is that of a dynamic calculation of reserves for bad loans, as Swiss Bank Corporation is doing with its Actuarial Credit Risk Accounting (ACRA) model for major corporate loans.

When a loan with precomputed interest is paid off prior to maturity, accounting adjustments may also be required for *insurance premiums*. There are, however, some insurance premiums which do not require accounting adjustment since no portion of such premium is returned to the lender if the loan is paid off prior to maturity.

For other types of insurance premiums, like credit life, credit accident and health, fire and casualty, the accounting in the event of a payoff to maturity depends on the original accounting for the payment of the premiums to the insurance company or agent. It is also a function of the agreement between the association and the insurance company or agent. In many cases, a portion of the premium paid to the insurance company or agent is rebated to the borrower in the event of a payoff prior to maturity.

4 DIRECT THIRD PARTY PARTICIPATION AND POPULAR ACCOUNTING METHODS

In addition to borrower and lender, consumer loans frequently involve some degree of direct or indirect participation by third parties. Such participation may be only incidental, or the third party may be a basic part of the lending process.

In many cases, retail banks will use a third party, such as a dealer, insurance agent or merchant, as a source for consumer loans. This is a virtual extension of the bricks and mortar network of the retail bank. It is creating business for both the bank and the dealer because:

- it gives the financial institution a new source for originating consumer loans, and
- it assists the dealer in making sales by providing his customers with a means of financing the transaction.

An example of this type of arrangement occurs where the bank finances sales of automobiles, boats, home electronics or home appliances. The retail bank might also be financing the dealer's inventory of unsold stock through floor plan or wholesale loans.

Wholesale or floor plan financing centers on a dealer's unsold inventory. Such financing is usually under a trust receipt arrangement wherein individual units are purchased by the bank directly from the manufacturer and held in trust by the dealer. As a matter of usual practice, floor plan loans are made as demand or 90-day notes. Interest is computed on the average daily outstanding balance.

Another type of third party involvement is that of servicing corporations, whose primary business is to solicit, originate and service loans for the portfolios of participating lending institutions. There may as well be other types of loans bearing similar third party arrangements, subject to the bank's strategic plan for personal loans.

As a matter of good accounting practice, fees paid at the outset to the dealer, or the service company, should be shown separately as assets on the simple interest loan. But they are netted against the unearned discount on the precomputed interest loan. The chosen method should follow either of the three principal costs associated with a consumer loan:

- acquisition costs,
- collection and servicing costs, and
- cost of funds.

Acquisition costs are incurred at the time the loan is made or acquired. Collection, servicing and operating costs are spread in generally equal monthly amounts over the life of the loan. The cost of funds is incurred in declining amounts over the term of the loan, as it is repaid. Therefore, when earned discount is amortized on a pure straight-line basis, it is not credited to income at the same time that the related costs are incurred. There is, however, a variation of the straight-line method, known as the pro rata with transfer, which under certain conditions may be the better alternative.

Under the pro rata method, a portion of the unearned discount is transferred to income at the time the loan is made or acquired to match the related acquisition cost. For instance, the bank could transfer 5 percent of the unearned discount to income, and amortize the remaining 95 percent over the term of the loan.

Another method is known as the effective yield with transfer. Still another option is the combination method which, as the name implies, is a combination of other methods. It recognizes as income unearned discount on loans written on an add-on basis. Many accountants believe this is the best approach since it results in the matching of costs with revenues.

Whichever method is being chosen, it is very important to standardize what enters into direct and indirect costs in lending; also, in collection, servicing cost of funds and other expenses. The fact of involving third parties in the sale of consumer loans – which can be seen as another form of relationship lending – leads to acquisition costs. These consist of

- *direct costs* which are identifiable out-of-pocket money such as filing fees and costs of credit investigation paid to third parties;
- *indirect costs* consisting of portions of salary costs, advertising, and other operating expenses related to acquisition of loans; and
- *provision for loan losses* involving an estimate of uncollectable loans often expressed as a percentage of loans made or deferred finance income.

The provision for loan losses would be based on such factors as prior experience and current economic conditions. A portion of deferred finance income which represented reimbursement for or matching of acquisition costs would be transferred to income at the time the loan was made, assuming all such costs were charged to expense during the same period.

Collection, servicing and other operating costs represent an amount of deferred finance income equal to the estimated cost per loan for the period. This is usually calculated on the basis of budgeted expenditures and the projected number of loans. It is often transferred to income on the straight-line or pro rata method.

- The cost of funds and profit before taxes is also an element of deferred finance income.
- These elements are credited to income over the loan term by a chosen method which, once chosen, should be consistently followed.

There are two methods used to account for bad debts in connection with third party participation in consumer loans. One is the *specific charge-off*, whereby the expense of the uncollectable loan is recognized when the loan is written off. This approach is simple to use and may be appropriate where the losses are not significant, but, from the standpoint of sound accounting principles, this is usually not an acceptable method.

A more rigorous accounting approach is known as the *reserve method*. An allowance for losses, sometimes called a reserve, is established by a charge to expense. Losses on loans written off are charged to this allowance. This is more appropriate for personal loans since a consistently recurring pattern of losses can usually be expected on this type of loan.

Generally speaking, all methods of computing earned income will amortize the same amount to income over the life of the loan. However, the amount that will be recognized in different periods may vary. The method which produces the largest amounts of income in early life of the loan also results in the lowest amounts of income in the latter portion of the loan term – but the *yield* on the loan is generally constant.

The reverse is true with respect to the straight-line or pro rata methods. Outside the initial transfer, the amounts are constant but the yield declines. While these accounting principles have focused on personal loans, similar methods exist with wholesale loans – each with its aftermaths on the bank's bottom line.

5 EXPERIMENTAL AND PRACTICAL RULES FOR THE MANAGEMENT OF LOANS

There is a whole list of prerequisites in establishing and maintaining relationship banking for loans. Only a few of the rules are theoretical. The large majority are practical, while some are experimental, relating to a systematic approach to the assessment and presentation of loans risk.

To be able to maintain relationship lending in the way described in section 2, bankers should develop a good understanding of the more complex credit analysis techniques and their place within business lending (mid-sized loans portfolio) and corporate lending. They should also

- learn about sensitivity analysis,
- enhance their knowledge of cash flow prognosis,
- identify some of the problems encountered by company loans, and
- learn about competitive positioning and business risk techniques.

A rigorous approach along this line of reference will sharpen the bankers' skills in identifying a company's or a private person's financial needs as well as mastering workout issues. Lending is no longer the relatively simple business it used to be.

In terms of competitiveness, very important is the ability of monitoring client and loan behavior at varying levels of seniority, depending upon the complexity of the local banking environment. This is not only a cultural issue but also one which depends on the level of technology the bank uses.

Technology can be instrumental in providing management with real-time information as regards the limits to credit risk, whether this concerns classical loans or derivative financial instruments. Figure 14.1 presents in a snapshot what is wrong with credit limits today. Deficiencies range all the way from client relationships to internal controls.

Some statistics derived from experience can be important in creating a concept of loan management. There is for example the '80–20' rule, which follows Pareto's law and states that in terms of business and corporate lending:

• 80 percent of the loan dollars lent by a bank are borrowed by 20 percent of its customers.

This underlines the wisdom of analyzing on an individual basis the bigger borrowers. The lending population should be subject to stratified sampling, focusing on lending habits, lending reasons, dependability of borrowers and profitability of the different strata.

A thorough analysis of the top 20 percent and the profiling of the other 80 percent of loans clients will permit identification of the complete *customer relationship*, along the line outlined in section 2. A rough but fairly accurate definition of

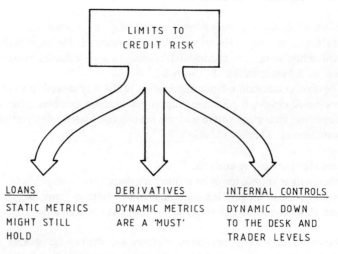

Figure 14.1   The concept of credit is important, but in connection with new financial vehicles the bank needs market risk limits

relationship lending is 'all the business a customer could take away from us if he got mad at our bank'.

What was said about marketing in Chapter 6 and relationship banking in Chapter 7 can be repeated with loans. The able management of loans relationships requires a great deal of information technology support, from real-time networking to database management and expert systems. Interactive computational finance makes it possible to look for

- deposits by the client in all of the accounts he has with *our* bank;
- loans related to these different accounts, and the conditions which were made;
- commercial paper handled on behalf of the client in one or more markets;
- foreign trade business generated by the same client and its subsidiaries;
- stock exchange transactions and portfolio holdings;
- derivative financial instruments traded with the client and resulting risk.

As this short list helps in documenting the able handling of the loans relationship with the client, and its exposure, does not end with the loan *per se*. Wise bankers look at the pattern of transactions and the inference which it provides in terms of risk management.

The total pattern should be seen from the viewpoint of a partnership between the bank and the client, which works both ways. Bankers Trust was mentioning in a meeting that its exposure to Digital Equipment Corporation (DEC), because of hardware and software used in its information system, was five times the loans the bank had given to DEC – and the whole amount was at risk if DEC went under.

Within this broad range of partnership reference characterizing the bank's clientele, risk control and profitability analysis bring together in one place all the facets of a pattern necessary for management to make factual and documented decisions. Hence the need to present management with both a detailed and an integrated picture of client account(s). Similarly, we should determine the servicing costs of the entire relationship, then project these statistics for the year ahead. The critical question is: What will we do for the customer and what will he do for us the next year, in the next two years, the next five years? The following are essential for providing an integrative decision-making tool:

- future cost of funds,
- future profits goal(s), and
- future risk exposure.

If we use historical costs and historical loans data on the relationship, all that we can find out is that we made a mistake when we last priced the loan or, alternatively, that we were lucky and priced it right.

Correct loans pricing, however, cannot be based on a hit and run basis. It should involve the future perspectives of present decisions, not the past, because the customer will pay in the future and the profits will also be earned in the future. The factors used in the analysis must relate, quite definitely, to future business. Though service costs are a vital input into a profitability analysis, as section 3 has underlined, with loans the big expense item is the *cost of funds*. Many approaches can be used in calculating client profitability, but they all come down to an analytical income statement for the borrower's relationship with the bank.

- The profit is compared to funds used, or capital allocated, to determine a profitability index.
- The index allows loans of different sizes to be compared with each other and with a profit goal.

It would be wrong, however, to calculate *profits* without accounting for *risks*: both credit risk and market risk. The best policy is to follow the July 18, 1996 discussion paper by the Accounting Standards Board (ASB) in the UK, which requires that the loans portfolio be marked-to-market.

One of the best models is to consider the loan as risk capital and to apply the return on risk capital (RORC) algorithm,[1] to a similar function like the risk adjusted return on capital (RAROC). Though RORC has been developed for derivative financial instruments, the fact that it integrates both market risk and credit risk makes it a good candidate for applications with loans.

An alternative strategy favoured by many banks, and by the British Bankers Association, is internal interest rate swaps. These weed interest rate risk out of the banking book and switch it to the trading book (where it is marked-to-market or to model), thereby exchanging fixed interest rates for floating interest rates.

- The Bank of England prompts banks to do internal interest rate swaps for management accounting purposes.
- But the Bank does not accept internal interest rate swaps for regulatory reporting.

Internal swaps is not the only means. Since the early 1980s, retail banks have been liquefying their portfolio of mortgages through *securitization*. Typically, a savings and loans or building society will ask an investment bank to make it an offer for a pool of mortgages, which will be repackaged and sold to investors.

However, securitization has not been successful with corporate loans. In America, it has only addressed 2 percent to 3 percent of the corporates market. Quite recently, however, *credit derivatives* may have begun to break this bottleneck which is largely due to resistance by investors in terms of depending too much on a small population of corporate borrowers. Credit derivatives are not a subject covered by this book.

6 CAN WE MARK-TO-MARKET THE LOANS PORTFOLIO?

The whole business of loan valuation rests on the ability to estimate correctly the expected value. On the credit risk side, critical references are the rating of the lender by an independent agency and the covenants. In regard to market risk, attention should be paid to interest rates, exchange rates, settlement risk, legal risk and other risks, and also to the cost of capital, which plays a key role in the bottom line. This analytical approach is today at a premium, not only because quantitative approaches and knowledge engineering solutions have proved their value in lending, but also because analytics has become the cornerstone to the valuation of the loans portfolio.

On the basis of its experience with RiskMetrics, which is a parametric value-at-risk model, the Morgan Bank introduced in 1997 CreditMetrics. The new model goes beyond the quantification of credit risk because it is based on a sound mathematical approach and policies which permit building up reserves by distinguishing between:

- losses expected because of credit risk,
- unexpected losses which have a lower frequency but are still present, and
- relatively rare cases of supercatastrophes in lending.

Swiss Bank Corporation has recently developed the Actuarial Credit Risk Accounting (ACRA) method, which quantifies counterparty risk in the aforementioned three classes. This is a proactive marking-to-model solution permitting management to build up appropriate reserves before risk events happen, rather than doing so in the wake of their occurrence.

The Market Risk Amendment by the Basle Committee also promotes marking-to-model (see also Chapter 15). Marking-to-model is necessary when the instruments which have to be valued at market price are not actively traded. The main source of market risk is volatility.

In terms of loans, volatility concerns interest rate changes which quite often happen in a different direction from the one the bank's economists have projected. The no. 2 source of price risk is market liquidity. Liquidity and volatility often have a covariance, but, as the art of studying covariance is still in its infancy, I personally prefer to use a three-dimensional frame of reference, such as the one in Figure 14.2. The figure suggests that the cash flow from the loans portfolio of our bank is a good way to examine its soundness. Cash flow has become a crucial variable as some central banks, like the Bundesbank, require cash flow reports from the financial institutions.

Accounting for volatility, liquidity and cash flow is not identical to directly marking-to-market the loans portfolio. However, the fact is that, while some loans, like mortgages, can be marked-to-market because they are securitized, others, like corporates, cannot. We have to work through approximations.

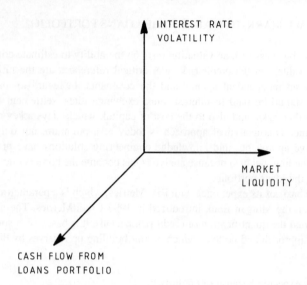

Figure 14.2   A three dimensional frame of reference into which to map market risk from loans

Approximations to marking the loans portfolio, as well as any other financial instrument, are inherent in the process of marking-to-model. They also come about because a certain method developed for one instrument is used in connection with another. An example is *duration*, using, for instance, MacCauley's algorithm[2] for corporates even though it was originally developed for mortgages.

As a matter of another approximation a corporate loan can be marked-to-market if we calculate the net present value. The key to this approach to accounting is to guess how much the bank will be getting at expiry of the loan.

- A valid way to proceed is to look at the loan as a *zero coupon* bond and discount at the appropriate interest rate.
- If there is probability of default, say at 5 percent, we should take the 95 percent of the loan in reference and discount.

A more sophisticated approach to loan valuation will consider the effects of convexity as well as credit risk, market risk and payoff profiles. There exists a correlation between:

- risk rating and loan portfolio optimization,
- bond ratings and expected default frequencies, and
- borrower risks and general transaction risks.

Attention should be paid not only to the evaluation of collateral, covenants and guarantees, but also to the auditing component of credit risk rating systems. Some banks are successfully using generic algorithms for credit risk rating,[3] over and above the rating which is provided by independent agencies, or in substitution for the latter.

But mathematical models alone will be powerless without database mining and the filtering of time series to provide the information elements necessary to the application of algorithms. Online *ad hoc* queries must be supported so that management can be provided with documented evidence on whether a loan, or a class of loans is:

- more profitable or less profitable than another loan or class of loans, and
- if the observance of predetermined levels of profitability leaves much to be desired, because of lending officers' practices.

As a matter of principle, profitability analysis does not have a payoff until the loan officer sits down to negotiate a new loan or a renewal with the customer. Therefore the profitability analysis system must be understandable and believable, not only to top management but also to the loan officer – and it must be easily accessible.

Able solutions require far more than simple calculations and a cost-of-funds rate that the loan officer feels is fair and realistic. Indeed, it is much more important for the system to be interactive, understandable and credible than that it be precise in its results.

Part of the degree of confidence an information system for loans can give to its users lies in its ability to provide qualitative and quantitative answers to the loan officers' concerns about risks and creditworthiness.

- Whether MacCauley's algorithm or the net present value method is used to value the contents of the loans portfolio is a matter open to the decision of the bank.
- What is not negotiable, in terms of maintaining a sound loans valuation practice, is the level of technological sophistication which makes it possible to do a clean job.

The solution which I am advising to the banks with which I work is extending the interactive computational finance system, designed for derivative financial instruments, into loans. Interactivity will make it possible to address market volatility and liquidity, in the way they have been treated in section 5, in real time.

A good way of judging interest rate volatility and market liquidity is through the simulation of a process of *loan liquefication*, or the creation of a secondary market for loans and similar financial paper. With loan liquefication a financial institution becomes the bank of the banks. This process involves three steps for which the bank gets a fee:

- origination,
- underwriting and
- distribution.

The originator does not keep the loan for years. It distributes it. But to be executed in an able manner this three-stage process imposes demands on the information system, such as fast and reliable data collection and dissemination; timely access to steadily updated databases; uninterrupted availability to stimulate and test different market hypotheses; and no time-zone barriers in terms of implementation.

It is not that easy to calculate the P&L pattern of the loans portfolio, but neither is the task impossible if we have well-established goals and knowhow to organize ourselves. The majority of banks, however, have not faced this issue in an able manner because they still rely on obsolete 'electronic data processing' rather than on interactive computational finance.

7   JUDGING A BORROWER'S ABILITY TO REPAY A LOAN

Many factors underpin a bank's ability to make loans and create credit. One of them is its financial resources, from capital to reserves, deposits and bought money. Another is the quality of its management and of its risk control system. Other factors depend on government policies, including the ratio of reserves that banks are required to keep on hand against their loans – as well as the central bank's monetary policy.

As regards management quality in terms of risk control, the first unpardonable offense of a loan officer is not making a bad loan, but that of forgetting about its consequences: for instance, not sounding the alarm when he starts recognizing that the loan is turning bad. The failure to think in terms of possible aftermaths and to take appropriate action means that banks have genuine difficulty performing what they are supposed to do best: judging a borrower's ability to repay a loan prior to making a commitment. This is a balancing act and it is not easy.

Not only are many decisions subjective rather than objective, but also there is a great deal of pressure around to make a loan. One of my professors at UCLA taught me 45 years ago that the boss of the credit division should be a man at the end of his career and with independence of means – in order to be able to say *No*!

- Between these two concepts lies the job description of loans officers.
- The only difference between then (1953) and now (1998) is that deregulation and globalization have changed some of the rules.

Banks do not operate in the economist's environment of perfect competition. Competition today is much more fierce than it was 45 years ago, but it is far from perfect. Because of deregulation, entry into the marketplace is no longer restricted, and there is plenty of money for lending in the hands of non-banks. While the argument of tougher competition is real, and many risks can be caught in the net of qualitative evaluations, there are also other factors which influence granting or refusing a loan: for example, qualitative evaluations which relate to the character of the person applying for a loan – whether such a person is single individual or the senior officer of an industrial firm.

Risk management is inseparable from the use of financial instruments, but also from the person to which loans are granted. Even if fully secured, every loan is a kind of speculation. The degree of risk varies according to

- the character and strength of the counterparty,
- the quality and spread of the collateral as well as the covenants, and
- the interest rate volatility and market liquidity of which we have spoken.

The *character* of the counterparty is the major component of credit risk which cannot be expressed in quantitative terms. The use of fuzzy engineering permits a better understanding of the qualification variables, but the best approach remans the direct human touch. As advice, this is no different from the answer J.P. Morgan gave during the 1912 investigation on the Money Trust by the US House Banking and Currency Committee. In his testimony, Morgan underlined that *the basis of credit is character.*

'Is not commercial credit based primarily upon money or property?' Samuel Untermyer asked. (Dr. Untermyer was special counsel to the US Banking Committee.)
'No sir. The first thing is character,' Morgan replied, 'because a man I do not trust could not get money from me on all the bonds of Christendom.'

J.P. Morgan was renowned for his ability to know each major client personally, thus judging both character and performance. This can be done with great difficulty if at all, in the present world of networks and electronic banking. Hence the wisdom of developing *quality databases* and mining them.

The mass market in which most banks operate today has reduced quite considerably the ability to judge a borrower – and whether or not he can repay – through the human touch. Yet a banker is not just another entrepreneur trading in risky goods. Without knowing the party he deals with, personally by means of relationship lending, or through rigorous computer-generated patterns, the banker is liable to make mistakes of judgment – and costly ones for that matter. Even if it is often subjective, personal judgment about the borrower's character is important. Despite the thrifts affair in the 1980s in America, the junk bonds collapse, and the huge problems the Japanese banks faced in 1995 and 1996, the lessons have not been sufficiently learned in order to put lending standards on a new and more solid base.

Where this leads in terms of excesses is best demonstrated by the troubles Scandinavian banks faced, which we study in section 8. As one example of foolish loans, during the easy-money 1980s, bankers rushed into plenty of dubious deals with Donald Trump, Robert Maxwell and many other high flyers who bet on their names. The results have been tales to write into every bank's training program in order to call for greater caution.

- Rarely have big-league loans officers been so willing to toss standards of prudence to the wind, as in the 1980s.
- Bankers failed to make sure that each new loan was adequately backed by collateral and, as we saw in section 2, covenants were watered down or discarded.

In Trump's case, banks lent him hundreds of millions secured only by his signature and junior claims on already heavily mortgaged assets. Some executives at financial institutions not involved in these deals suggest that that sort of exposure to the proprietor of such high-risk projects as casinos, airlines and real estate projects is highly unusual – yet it has happened.

Bankers who got burned with the Maxwell and other loans now say they could not have predicted the abrupt collapse of the real estate and junk bond markets. This is simply nonsense because prediction is the alter ego of good management. But when prudence goes missing, other sound loan practices also walk away.

Many bankers seem to have treated their huge exposure to high risk entrepreneurs almost as casually as a routine home improvement loan. According to officers of institutions involved in these dubious credits undertaken by the banking industry,

- few lenders subjected to anything more than cursory scrutiny the lofty asset valuations on the risk-taker's periodic net worth statements;
- also few took the trouble to analyze his rapidly rising debt levels; even if they know that wheelers-dealers are overburdened in exposure.

Donald Trump's Atlantic City ventures are an example of financing serious bankers should never do. Because the covenants were waived, few loans officers picked up the rapidly deteriorating operational cash flow. Yet Donald Trump barely broke even in 1988 and had a negative $60 million cash flow in 1989 – though by the mid-1990s he was again up and running.

Also few lenders sought to determine the full extent of unsecured debt. As one banker who several times declined to lend money to Trump puts it: 'These guys didn't do their homework' (*Business Week*, July 9, 1990). The problem is that this is becoming increasingly commonplace, not only with commercial banks but also with supranational bodies like the World Bank, which fall into the trap of complacency as a substitute for analytics.

8 LESSONS TO BE LEARNED FROM THE SCANDINAVIAN BANKING CRISIS

In 1990 and 1991, the Scandinavian countries underwent a severe banking crisis which was the worst of its kind since World War II. Half a dozen major banks in Norway, Sweden and Finland were in acute difficulty or were seized by regulators. These included the flagship Christiania Bank and Norway's no. 3, Fokus Bank; Finland's Skopbank; and Sweden's state-controlled no. 2 bank, Nordbanken, as well as Sweden's biggest savings bank, Foersta Sparbank.

Scandinavian banks ran into trouble for a variety of reasons. They suffered heavily from bad property loans, corporate bankruptcies and, in Finland's case, the collapse of trade with Russia. Many Norwegian, Swedish and Danish banks had to be bailed out by their governments as their foreign credit lines dried up.

- Even relatively healthy competitors were walking wounded because of their exposure to sick brethren.
- The bill to taxpayers has been staggering: The equivalent of about $15 billion, according to conservative estimates.

Scandinavian governments and central banks rushed in to rescue the mounting number of banks in critical condition, fearful that an outright failure might shatter international confidence in their financial systems. Meanwhile, the growing bailouts brought the Scandinavian region into recession.

Each country took a slightly different approach. The Finnish government guaranteed foreign borrowings for troubled banks and encouraged them to raise fresh capital from private investors. Norway's government forked out some NKr25 billion ($3.9 billion) of taxpayers' money to nationalize the biggest banks. It ended up owning 72 percent of Den Norske Bank and 69 percent of Christiania Bank, formerly the two biggest private banks.

Taking into account the size of the economy, the national budget and the central bank's reserves – therefore in relative terms – in Norway, where there have been three major commercial banks in serious trouble, the crisis was more serious than that of the S&Ls in the US. In the case of Norway, commercial banks were the hardest hit in terms of ailing financial institutions, while the savings banks prospered (which was not true in neighboring Sweden). Following the government's bail-out and takeover, some of the salvaged banks, such as Den Norske and Bergen Bank, were merged:

- at least a third of their staff were fired,
- headquarters buildings were closed down,

- loan portfolios were slashed, and
- collateral was sold at bargain basement prices.

Eventually, the salvaged banks started to come out of the shadow of government ownership. As with the savings and loans in the US, this has not been a showcase of recovery. The Norwegian banks continue to be assailed by former shareholders who bitterly resent the way they lost their equity and threaten to sue Den Norske Bank and Fokus Bank for the return of their money.

Also some critics claim the commercial banks went bankrupt only because the government and the auditors forced them to accept crippling provisions on bad loans too quickly. But to this there was no alternative, given

- the huge losses the Norwegian banks experienced in their loans book, and
- the Basle Accord of 1988 on capital adequacy requirements by which they had to abide.

The Swedish government tried a combination of both approaches. It issued general guarantees to support the foreign borrowing of several retail banks, while it bailed out Nordbanken. It also created a special holding company, SECURUM, that took the worst property and corporate loans off the troubled Nordbanken's balance sheet. SECURUM is now slowly selling many of the assets it acquired by foreclosing on the loans' collateral. The transaction which took place is shown in Figure 14.3. Problem loans with Nordbanken's client firms were passed to SECURUM, which was a holding company fully owned by the Swedish government.

- The value of the asset was calculated in common accord and Nordbanken compensated for it.
- From this point on, SECURUM did transactions at its discretion with Nordbanken or with other, competitor banks.

SECURUM'S organization is shown in Figure 14.4. The Finance division handles the bad loans. The Industry Holdings division addresses the other holdings SECURUM took over, apart from real estate. Four different departments manage the real estate assets by region: North, South, East and West. There is, as well, an International Business division endowed with those Nordbanken assets which were outside Sweden.

As a result of these transactions, Sweden's 71 percent state-controlled Nordbanken tapped the state coffers for SKr5.2 billion ($850 million). The Swedish government had no alternative as record loan loss provisions pushed Nordbanken below minimum capital adequacy standards. To SECURUM, which inherited Nordbanken's non-performing loans, real estate and other holdings, the government advanced SKr68 billion ($4.16 billion).

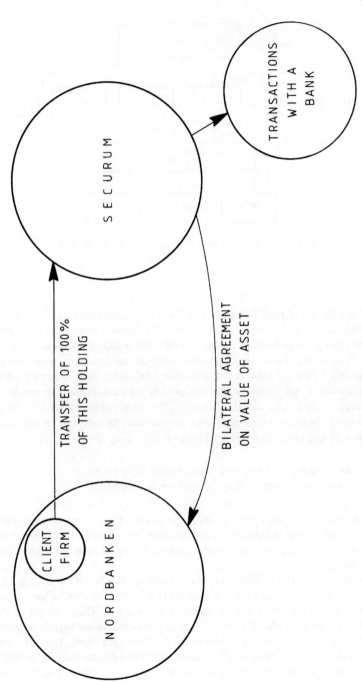

Figure 14.3 SECURUM's role in the liquidation of bad loans

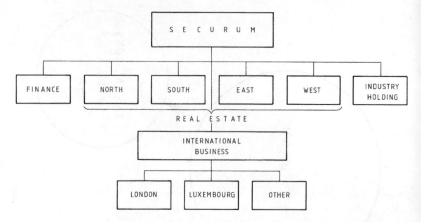

Figure 14.4   Organization and structure of the SECURUM holding and investment company

Finland's central bank invested 11 billion Finnish markkaa ($2.7 billion) in its bail-out of ailing Skopbank. Underscoring the industry-wide turmoil, virtually every major bank in Norway, Sweden and Finland installed a new chief executive over an 18 month period. The usual scene was that board members were brusquely forced out if they did not leave on their own. Obviously, the managements which were liquidated had underestimated the inherent risks in expanding so rapidly, and had underreacted to the signals of distress. The same pattern can be seen all over the financial industry: Japan and France provide other examples of up-and-coming banks with aggressive strategies grabbing for risk-taking clients.

- If the economy works as they planned, they make profits.
- If it works against them, they get very serious problems.

In Norway, for example, plunging oil prices in 1986 put the Norwegian economy on the skids. Five subsequent years of recession ate relentlessly into banks' reserves, decimating core capital and pushing the entire financial system to the breaking point.

From 1987 to 1990, Norwegian banks piled up NKr38 billion in loan losses and loss provisions, including a record NKr12.8 billion in 1990 alone. Analysts estimated the total losses and provisions at in excess of NKr20 billion in 1991, fueled by Christiania Bank's NKr7.2 billion pretax loss in the first three-quarters of that same year – the biggest loss ever by a Norwegian bank. The government agreed to take over Christiania as part of a NKr13.4 billion package to buttress the country's foundering banking institutions and avoid systemic risk. What does this experience teach us in regard to the mismanagement of loans and other assets?

9 ANALYTICAL APPROACHES TO THE CORRECTION OF FLAWS IN LOANS MANAGEMENT

Norway's banking crisis began in 1990, when the country's leading banks told the Ministry of Finance that almost half their loans were non-performing. Within a year, the government had injected a large amount of money to keep capital ratios within the Basle Committee rules, but fired most of the top managers and took over ownership of all the largest banks.

Correctly, in a move which found echos in the banking industry in other countries, for the next four years the new owner enforced a tough cost-cutting program. The exercise paid off and by 1995 the Norwegian government was taking back some of its money by means of:

- floating 31 percent of the stock of Christiania Bank to raise NKr2 billion, and
- selling 16 percent of Den Norske Bank for NKr1 billion.

But because the stockmarket could not afford more paper, the government was still left owning most of the rest of the two banks' equity. The silver lining has been that the paper value of these holdings has risen since the crisis. But the change did not come without pain.

First was the realization that in their lending policies, the failed Norwegian banks – like so many others – did not pay due attention to *contingent claims*: that is, assets where a new and volatile variable can occur, affecting the payment stream of a contractual agreement. This has an evident impact on liabilities and assets covered by such an agreement. Examples of contingent claims are:

- options contracts,
- floating rate loans,
- loans with caps and floors,
- different types of warrants, and so on.

Second, it was found that there was not in place a worthwhile system for scoring loans. Neither was there a system which significantly improves the loan officer's judgment, based on practices. Yet, in the case of companies, expert systems can be effectively used for *analyzing balance sheets* as well as *mining databases* to put together a *scoring of borrowers* applying for loans and reflecting on:

- profitability,
- cash flow,
- liquidity,

- the acid test (current assets over current liabilities),
- fixed long-term assets, and
- the capital ratio.

Other expert systems can be built to evaluate future perspectives of the company's business, including annual growth and productivity. The quality of management should also be part of the picture with the output presented in graphical form, like the radar chart in Figure 14.5. The grades are 1 to 3, with 3 being the highest grade.

Banks are not alone in misjudging the financial condition of themselves and their clients. Let me give, as another example of mismanagement, the Sears' misfortunes. In 1993/94 the Sears, Roebuck chain of department stores, made a net loss on merchandising of $179 million. It also landed its parent company with a pretax charge of $1.7 billion to pay for a massive restructuring of the chain.

Sears, Roebuck was once an ambitious retailing and financial empire which build its fortune in the post-World War II years by taking on Montgomery Ward. In the 1970s and 1980s, it expanded greatly, but during the early 1990s, it took the opposite road and substantially dismantled its operations:

- it sold Dean Witter, an investment bank, and
- floated off 20 percent of its Allstate insurance subsidiary.

This downsizing left the group hugely dependent on its retailing arm, but at the same time it became better focused on the merchandising job which was its

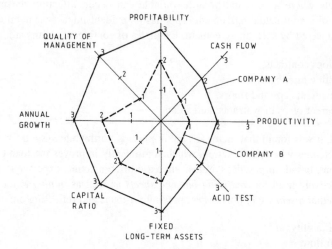

Figure 14.5 A radar chart permitting a snap judgment of a company

original source of income. I see a great parallel between Sears' case and that of retail banks which run off their tracks.

At times, not only poor management but also the law of the land conspires to bring and keep a financial company near the edge of chaos. One of the reasons for management's laxity is that the law sometimes not only condones but even supports bankruptcy cases and associated abuses – as, for instance, happens in several of the East Asian countries because of the 1997–8 financial crisis.

Bankruptcies in the United States surged in the early 1980s, not just because of the 1980–3 recessionary period but also, if not mainly, because of federal bankruptcy reform legislation. This made bankruptcy more attractive by allowing debtors to shield more assets from creditors.

- the use of credit began to be seen as a mark of success,
- debtors jumped on the debt bandwagon, as banks competed to have them as customers on increasingly favorable terms.

Reduced vigilance on loans in the banking sector led to huge loan losses and associated loss provisions. Therefore it is not unreasonable for investors to want to know whether their banks' portfolios contain risky loans that are likely to translate into future losses:

- How much did they set aside last quarter as a provision for loan losses?
- How much have they classified as non-performing loans?
- How much were they left with by way of reserves?

As both depositors and investors have painfully learned, historical information does not prevent surprise write-offs. Examples are the Bank of New England, with its unexpected $1.4 billion provision for loan losses in December 1989, and Valley National Bank's $384 million provision for loan losses during 1989.

The irony is that even bad news, correctly reported, would raise the bank's dependability. Hence the suggestion made some years ago that banks rank the loans they have outstanding along a standardized nine-point scale of riskiness. This will make it possible to compare the way the banks rank practically identical loans. It will also make it easier to see if what is considered 'minimal risk' by Bank A is taken as 'standard' by Bank B and 'high' by Bank C. Such a policy will also simplify the marking-to-market of loans on fairly comparable terms, as the Accounting Standards Board is now demanding.

In conclusion, loans must be prudently priced. They must also be marked-to-market or to model both in the short run and in the long run, based on estimates of their riskiness. The bank's loss experience should also be used as a factor in evaluating the rate of return on its loans. Nobody said that patient money does not run out of patience. This is as true of commercial banks as it is of supranational bodies.

Notes

1.   See D.N. Chorafas, *Managing Derivatives Risk* (Burr Ridge, IL: Irwin Professional Publishing, 1996).
2.   See D.N. Chorafas, *Financial Models and Simulation* (London: Macmillan, 1995).
3.   See D.N. Chorafas, *Rocket Scientists in Banking* (London and Dublin: Lafferty, 1995).

15 Credit Risk, Market Risk and the Basle Committee on Banking Supervision

1 INTRODUCTION

The Basle Committee on Banking Supervision was established in 1975 by the governors of central banks of the Group of Ten (G-10) countries and other authorities with responsibility in the supervision of banks. About five years after the Capital Accord of 1988 and in recognition of the fact this addressed only *credit risk*, in April 1993 the Basle Committee issued for comment by banks and financial market participants a package of supervisory proposals concerning *market risk*, with an improved second version released in April 1995.

Elaborated by representatives of banking supervisory authorities, this document suggested the application of algorithmic solutions and procedural approaches which could lead to capital charges because of market risks incurred by commercial banks. In January 1996, after responses to the second release were received, the document in question was redefined, refined and finalized.

Another major event of 1996 was the discussion paper by the Accounting Standards Board (ASB) of the UK, which suggested changes to the way accounts are kept by industrial enterprises and financial institutions. This concerns disclosure for on-balance sheet and off-balance sheet financial instruments and associated risk arising from movements in market prices.

For its part, also in 1996, the Bank of England announced changes in the way it regulates banks. These follow to a large extent recommendations made by Arthur Andersen, a consultancy. Since Barings collapsed in February 1995, there have been many outside assertions that a too laissez-faire regulation by the Bank of England was partly to blame for the Barings bankruptcy. Then, in 1997, the new British government took two steps: the first strengthened and the second weakened the position of the Bank of England. The Chancellor of the Exchequer loosened the ties between the Treasury and the central bank, granting the latter a degree of independence. But also it took away the reserve institution's bank supervision authority giving it to a new organization, in a pattern which is fairly similar to the policy followed in Switzerland and in Germany.

In America, the regulations on trading book and banking book reporting cast by the Financial Accounting Standards Board (FASB) are also in full evolution. In the 1990s, reporting on derivatives trades and portfolios became the theme of four Financial Accounting Statements: 105, 107, 119 and XXX. Statement XXX is the latest and it integrates the fine print regarding the control of derivatives risk.

2   THE BASLE COMMITTEE ON BANKING SUPERVISON REVAMPS AND RESTRUCTURES CAPITAL REQUIREMENTS

Practically everybody in the banking industry, particularly people in senior positions in central banks and other regulatory authorities, as well as commercial and investment banks, has been concerned about *market risk*. This includes interest rate risk, currency risk, commodity risk, equity risk, country risk, event risk and other exposures. Few people, however, have had a clear idea about:

* how to measure market risk in a dependable manner,
* how to account for its impact on the trading book and the banking book,
* what sort of reserves are needed to face market risk, and
* what may be the impact of its reporting on the financial health of a bank.

The first draft of a Market Risk Amendment (of April 1993) by the Basle Committee was received by the banking industry with mixed feelings. It was the right step towards establishing a concept and a process for measuring and counterbalancing market risk, and therefore a laudable effort. But it mainly rested on *netting*, which is not a rigorous manner for the control of exposure.

Some bankers were critical of this first draft, stating that it did not go far enough. For instance, top-tier American banks had already implemented sophisticated marking-to-model approaches (eigenmodels) and they would not go back to netting. Alternatively, other banks did not even have a clear netting culture. These and other responses were duly taken into account in the second release of the Market Risk Amendment draft, in April 1995. Most evidently they were reflected in its final form, made public in January 1996. The Market Risk Amendment took effect immediately and it became mandatory at the end of 1997. Capital standards for market risk are being implemented by all banks and supervised by the G-10 regulatory authorities.

* The effect of the Market Risk Amendment is most significant as a supplement to the Capital Accord of 1988 regarding capital requirements for loans.
* Even more sweeping is the cultural change regarding modeling expertise, which becomes necessary for its rigorous control of market risk.

The cornerstone to the Amendment is the concept of marking-to-market, also of *marking-to-model*, the trading book, though not yet the banking book. Also included is the concept of *backtesting* (see section 6), by means of post-mortem comparisons between results obtained through modeling and actual market performance in asset pricing.

* Marking-to-model has become necessary because the largest part of derivatives deals are over the counter (OTC).

Based on real-life statistics from a major money center bank, Table 15.1 presents the percentage of commitments made in notional principal amounts (see Chapter 9) in derivatives – contrasting OTC contracts with those exchange traded. As will be appreciated, more than three quarters are OTC. Table15.2 restructures these statistics, presenting a taxonomy of derivative instruments. Interest rate products have the largest share, followed by currencies.

- OTC positions typically have no active market and, therefore, they cannot be marked-to-market according to established banking practice.

To ensure that no abusive switching occurs between marking-to-model and netting, aimed to minimize capital charges, the Market Risk Amendment foresees that central banks will be vigilant to prevent such events, and also to ensure that

Table 15.1 Percentage of commitments made in notional principal in derivatives OTC versus exchange-traded

1.	OTC	77.1%
1.1	Currency products	41%
1.2	Interest rate products	30%
1.3	Equity derivatives	5.0%
1.4	Precious metals/commodities	1.1%
2.	Exchange-traded	22.9%
2.1	Currency products	1%
2.2	Interest rate products	21%
2.3	Equity derivatives	0.5%
2.4	Precious metals/commodities	0.4%

Table 15.2 Percentage of commodities in notional principal amounts by taxonomy of derivative instruments

1.	Currency products	42%
1.1	Over-the-counter (OTC)	41%
1.2	Exchange-traded	1%
2.	Interest rate products	51%
2.1	Over-the-counter (OTC)	30%
2.2	Exchange-traded	21%
3.	Equity derivatives	5.5%
3.1	Over-the-counter (OTC)	5.0%
3.2	Exchanged-traded	0.5%
4.	Precious metals and other commodities	1.5%
4.1	Over-the-counter (OTC)	1.1%
4.2	Exchange-traded	0.4%

gains trading in securities is being marked-to-market. Supervisory authorities will take precautions against cherry-picking between the *standardized* approach by BIS and the banks' proprietary models for risk management.

The Amendment stipulates that positions of less than wholly-owned subsidiaries will be subject to generally accepted accounting principles in the country where the parent bank is supervised. In a way similar to that regarding credit risk, capital requirements for market risk are to apply on a global consolidated basis.

The best way to recognize the sweeping impact of the 1996 Market Risk Amendment is the fact that the few advanced technology banks, with expertise in marking-to-model, saw the opportunity for cross fertilization in modeling from market risk to *credit risk*.

- J.P. Morgan developed and publicly announced CreditMetrics, a model-based approach which permits planning quantitatively for longer-term credit risk.
- On the basis of the CreditMetrics effort, Swiss Bank Corporation went further, developing and implementing the Actuarial Credit Risk Accounting (ACRA) model.

Both CreditMetrics and ACRA work on the principle that credit risk is the risk that the counterparty to a financial instrument will fail to discharge an obligation, causing the other party to incur a financial loss. But instead of lumping together in the same bucket all credit risks, they differentiate between those which are

- expected,
- unexpected, and
- quite exceptional supercatastrophes.

The model permits management to calculate the reserves necessary for each class well ahead of time. It also accounts for the fact that credit risk has many aspects, one of them being closely associated with liquidity risk which is defined as the risk that a bank will encounter difficulty in raising funds at short notice to meet commitments associated with contractual obligations it has taken. To control liquidity risk, we must know a great deal about the distribution of loans, the amounts involved and debt maturity. Everything is subject to analysis. In fact, such studies should cover in a detailed way all assets and liabilities.

By transferring basic modeling concepts from market risk to credit risk, some banks came to realize that both qualitative and quantitative information is necessary about counterparty risks, including current and potential future credit exposure and counterparty creditworthiness. Valuation reserves for actual credit losses should be in a form that permits a thorough evaluation of the bank's performance.

3 IMPLIED RISK AND THE PRECOMMITMENT APPROACH

There is another major benefit first-rank banks can obtain by integrating credit risk and market risk through modeling. During the last couple of years, the *precommitment* approach has been used in the United States for the supervision of financial conglomerates. This is done with the collaboration of the Federal Reserve System. Precommitment is aiming to assure that

- The total capital adequacy of a financial institution is able to face all contingencies; and
- A more rigorous process is in place for risk management than is otherwise possible.

Each bank using precommitment defines its expected variance in exposure. Based on this prognostication of *implied risk*, the Federal Reserve approves the corresponding capital requirements, which have been calculated by the financial institution and submitted to the supervisors.

The hinge is that the commercial bank must keep within its self-imposed limits, which become a guideline. Management must therefore have timely information and it must keep a tight lid on risks over the period the bank has been precommitted. This brings into perspective a new risk management culture

- Implied risks look into the future;
- The classical P&L focuses on the past.

To establish a precommitment statement, the bank's senior management must ask itself: 'Where does my next step bring me?' This obliges the Board of Directors and the executive committee to think ahead rather than *post mortem*. The computational procedure:

- Assesses market risk and credit risk by important client;
- Uses a sampling procedure for less important cases in relationship banking;
- Considers cumulative exposure by a counterparty or a group of clients;
- Establishes the level of total exposure as well as the variance.

In a significant measure, the implied risk underpinning this approach has more to do with what the market believes risk is, rather than the old ways where the calculation of risk was based on *post mortem* accounting procedures. Models are evidently instrumental in the prognostication of risk. Therefore, only high-technology banks can adopt this solution.

To be able to submit to the supervisory authorities risk variances by which it can stand, and to steadily update its own estimates, senior management has to consistently test the practical market results against those which have been calculated. It has also to keep in mind that even the most sophisticated solutions do not do away with real-life market risks and credit risks.

The bad news is that there will be a severe aftermath if the precommitted limits are broken. Penalties can reach $50 million, depending on the level of overshooting. The good news is that capital requirements for credit risk and market risk are significantly reduced. Equally important is the fact that the precommitment approach obliges the bank's senior management to become proactive.

4   GLOBAL SUPERVISION, THE BANK'S TOP MANAGEMENT AND THE TRADING BOOK

According to theory, a bank's *trading book* includes the institution's proprietary positions in financial instruments intentionally held for short term dealings or resale. Alternatively, such products may be taken on by the bank for benefits in the short term from expected differences in their buying and selling prices. At least, that is what I learned when, in the early 1950s, I studied banking at the Graduate School of Business, University of California, Los Angeles. But theory and practice are not quite the same things. Besides this, theory evolves to reflect a changing market perspective.

Over and above short-term commitments, today the trading book comprises all derivatives, and it is marked-to-market: on-balance sheet instruments are short-term; off-balance sheet instruments are long-term. Furthermore, in some countries, regulations oblige banks to value at market some instruments not falling into the trading book. At the same time, other regulators require that trading activities must be accounted for

- at book value, or
- at lower of cost and market value.

The emphasis, in all these exercises, is on market risk – or the risk that the value of a financial instrument will fluctuate as a result of changes in market prices. Every instrument is subject to market volatility, whether this is caused by factors specific to the individual security or its issuer, or by factors affecting the market at large.

The change which has taken place in the contents of the trading book is not the only one. Perhaps less appreciated, but just as crucial, is the fact that both the 1988 Capital Accord and the 1996 Market Risk Amendment constitute key elements of the new global supervision. While national markets get deregulated, internationally the Basle Committee establishes rules which lead to new (and necessary) prudent standards.

But there are no uniform reporting practices yet, even within the G-10. Given differences in regulatory practices and characteristics, the trading book is not exactly the same from one institution to another, or from one country to the other. But it does differ significantly from the *banking book*, in which are registered medium to longer-term commitments, particularly

- all sorts of loans,
- different types of deposits, and
- the bank's portfolio of longer-held securities

Because of these differences, which when ingeniously used can create loopholes, the fact that the Basle Committee's Market Risk Amendment does not address positions in the banking book creates some problems. One of them is organizational: not all financial institutions clearly differentiate between the items which enter the banking book and trading book. Another one is technical: the 1996 Market Risk Amendment is not addressing issues of an internal organizational nature, like internal controls. Neither does it imply uniform accounting standards, though a subcommittee of the Basle Committee is now working on this issue.

By contrast, the Amendment is quite comprehensive in regard to the type of transactions which should be targeted, and the way in which they should be handled. The main frame of reference consists of four sectors where market risk definitely applies:

1. *interest rate risk*, the risk that the value of a financial instrument will fluctuate owing to changes in interest rates defined by the market;
2. *currency risk*, the risk that the value of a financial instrument will be volatile owing to intraday changes in foreign exchange rates.

Closely related to currency risk is *country risk*: the risk that a country's loans obligations will go bust, or severely worsen its financial condition.

3. *Equity risk* may be specific to one security or to all securities traded in the market.
4. *Commodities risk*: practically everything, including currencies, is a commodity, but this specific reference is connected with metals, oil, agricultural products and so on.

There is as well a separate section which sets out methods for measuring price risk in connection with:

5. *Options*

From the day on which commitments are undertaken, all transactions, including forward sales and purchases, shall be included in the calculation of capital requirements to compensate for market risk. Supervisory authorities will ensure there is no window-dressing on specific dates in such reporting.

Banks incur an increasing amount of interest rate risk which, other things being equal, is greater the longer the maturity of the contracts into which they enter. The Basle Committee Amendment offers two alternative methods for measurement, one based on *maturity* and the other on *duration*.

- Under the maturity approach, long or short positions in debt securities and other sources of interest rate exposure are slotted into a maturity ladder composed of 12 to 15 time bands.
- With the duration method, banks can measure more accurately their general market risk by separately computing the price sensitivity of each position through MacCauley's duration algorithm.[1]

Developed in the mid-1930s, MacCauley's duration algorithm was one of the earlier models used in finance. However, it was preceded by other quantitative efforts, including

- the national economic model developed in the 1890s by Leon Walras, which set the pattern for input/output analysis, and
- the quantitative principle advanced by Vilfredo Pareto, also in the late 1890s, which became known as Pareto's law.

The Amendment stipulates that capital charges for currency exchange risk and commodities risk will apply to the bank's total currency and commodity positions, subject to some discretion. Two processes are necessary to calculate capital requirements for forex risk.

- the measurement of exposure in a single currency position, and
- the measurement of risks inherent in a bank's mix of long and short positions in different currencies.

Gold is to be dealt with as a foreign exchange position rather than a commodity, because its volatility is more in line with currency exchange. When gold is part of a forward contract, any currency interest rate exposure from the other leg must be reported.

An important aftermath of the 1996 Market Risk Amendment by the Basle Committee is that banks are now formally using quantitative information about market risk through value-at-risk models (see section 4) or other analytics. This changes the way in which institutions manage risk. An integral part of this approach is quantitative information about market activity and market liquidity. The Amendment distinguishes a specific market risk in the case where an individual debt, equity or other security moves in a way different from the general market in terms of day-to-day trading. This, too, has to be measured and reported.

Another clause of the Market Risk Amendment addresses *repo* deals. For supervisory purposes, a security which is the subject of a lending or repurchase agreement will be treated as if it were still owned by its lender. Swaps must be handled as two notional positions in securities with relevant maturities. Banks with large swaps books may use alternative formulae for the swaps into which they enter to compute positions in the maturity or duration ladder. The fact that the Market Risk Amendment addresses swaps is important, since swaps are being used to offset the risk of an uncovered position, seeing to it that there is a future cash flow which would move in the opposite direction to the hedged position. Also swaps are today instruments greatly favored by the banking industry.

A hedge of sorts is what many banks started using in order to weed mismatch risk out of their loans book. They make an *internal interest rate swap*, replacing fixed interest rates in the banking book with variable interest rate, bringing the fixed interest rate risk the bank has assumed into the trading book. There it will be marked-to-market or to model. Hedge accounting links the two transactions, and then maps them together at a future date. But in reality there are no perfect hedges, because one leg of the transaction may change much more than the other – which says volumes about netting. Hence the importance of being able to compute value-at-risk.

5   VALUE-AT-RISK, AND THE CONCEPT OF CONFIDENCE INTERVALS

The crucial question targeted through value-at-risk (VAR) models is: 'What can I lose under certain assumptions of market behavior, given the current exposure in my trading book?' The answer varies with the bank's outstanding forward interest rate contracts, currency and other swaps, options purchased and written, equity/ index derivatives and other over-the-counter deals, as well as futures and options traded in the exchanges.

There are many types of VAR algorithms, which largely fall into two classes, as we will see in the following paragraphs. Typically VAR models developed by banks for internal risk management try to measure the losses in a portfolio over a specified period of time, often a holding period of the next 24 hours which is extended to 10 days as required by BIS through a simple (and inaccurate) algorithm.[2]

This is the sense of marking-to-model the exposure taken by the institution. Banks utilize value-at-risk techniques to measure the possible losses in their trading book arising from the effect of market movements, but they should appreciate that the VAR calculation is an approximation.

- The simpler class of the VAR algorithms is a *parametric* model. It is based on the assumption that risks and returns are normally distributed.

Given its parametric nature, I identify this approach as VAR/P. But VAR/P is not monolithic. What characterizes its different versions is that they gravitate around this normal distribution hypothesis, which constitutes an approximation. By contrast,

- the more complex (and accurate) value-at-risk solution is based on non-parametric statistics and mathematical *simulation*, including Monte Carlo.[3]

Let us call it VAR/S. With VAR/S, no assumptions are made about the nature of the distribution. Therefore, other things equal, we take less of a risk of being wrong in our hypothesis. The counterpart of this is that simulation is a more sophisticated approach than the parametric solutions, and few banks have the knowhow necessary to handle it in an able manner.

The 1996 Market Risk Amendment accepts both the parametric and the simulation alternatives. It also promotes *stress analysis*. This, too, is a simulation procedure which makes it possible to look at the effects of extreme market movements (but not necessarily panics) on the contents of the portfolio under scrutiny. I will explain my tool for stress analysis in section 8.

Let us now take a closer look at the parametric and non-parametric models for the computation of value-at-risk. The parametric model is also known as *whole book* approach, or *variance/covariance analysis*. It

- uses statistics, calculated from historical data on price volatility, and
- employs correlations within and between markets, to estimate likely potential losses.

The hypothesis being made in regard to the normal distribution concerns price changes. The assumption of a normal distribution enables the bank to calculate a *confidence level* for the value at risk over the 'next' timeframe.

- The confidence level is calculated by reference to the standard deviation of past price changes multiplied by a scaling factor.
- This confidence level α is usually taken equal to 0.1, 0.05 to 0.01.

These levels of confidence, or significance, indicate how many times (in the long run) the estimate we make of a worst-case scenario in regard to trading book losses will be exceeded. An $\alpha = 0.1$ corresponds to 90 percent of assurance; $\alpha = 0.05$, to 95 percent; and $\alpha = 0.01$ to 99 percent.

In other terms, with $\alpha = 0.01$, in 99 cases out of 100 the estimate of trading book losses will not be exceeded. This is what the Basle Committee's Market Risk Amendment stipulates for the one-tailed statistical distribution.

- The smaller is the α, which in a statistical operating characteristics curve (OCC) is known as Type I error or producer's risk, the greater is the confidence that the calculated value-at-risk is the worst case which can happen.

Figure 15.1 gives an idea of how much the market risk seems to change as a function of level of confidence. In a way, this graph is an optical illusion because we should remember that at the 90 percent level the 10 percent of cases will fall outside that limit established by the nearly parabolic curve, while only 1 percent of future risks will fall outside the 99 percent level of confidence.

Let us also always recall that algorithms alone do not solve the problem of correct risk estimates. Critical to the application of this and of any other modeling approach is *database mining*.[4] A rich database is very important because, under the variance/covariance approach,

- we use statistics on the magnitude of past price movements, and
- we compute correlations between price movements.

The statistics are mined from the database, while the correlations are computed after we obtain the necessary information elements. Let me add that, though most banks today work with interday statistics, tier-1 financial institutions collect, database and use their *intraday* financial information. We have already spoken of this fact.

- Modeling can become so much more accurate if we have tick-by-tick data streams.
- This is true all over finance, from equities trading and currency exchange to derivatives instruments.

With the VAR/S approach also known as *historical simulation*, the trading book can be studied by means of analogical thinking. When two analogous systems are found to exist, projections and evaluations done on one of them can be used to

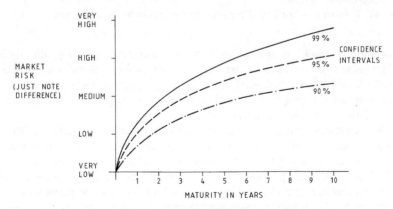

Figure 15.1 Market risk factor at three levels of confidence intervals

make inferences about the other. One way of looking at VAR/S is as a very sophisticated 'What if' scenario. By mining the database we play back past events and ask ourselves *what* would happen with current trading book exposure *if* such events were repeated. We can also test different hypotheses pertinent to the study at hand.

The more thoroughly a bank has classified and analyzed past data, the better it is positioned to use VAR/S. This statement is valid with risk and return, but also with national economic time series. Brandon Davies, the Treasurer of Barclays Global Corporate Banking, set his people to analyzing nearly 200 years of the British economy and its spikes, and they came up with some very interesting results. Analytically minded people also appreciate that, no matter how carefully they were built, models, too, can fail. Therefore, as a safeguard, the Basle Committee is stipulating that banks applying the proprietary model approach must use a rigorous and comprehensive backtesting procedure.

6   BACKTESTING AND THE GREEN, YELLOW AND RED ZONES

In each country, the central bank has the responsibility to supervise the results of VAR computing. It is therefore wise to conduct *a priori* tests covering a range of possibilities, particularly focusing on cases which could create extraordinary losses or gains. Examples of historical events of an extraordinary nature, during the last dozen years, are:

- the October 1987 equity market crash,
- the suspension of sterling's and Italian lira's membership of the ERM in September 1992, and
- the February to April 1994 meltdown of prices in the bond market.

As another check on the adequacy of the modeling approach, the Basle Committee requires that banks convey to their supervisory authorities information on the largest losses experienced during the reporting period. The resulting capital requirements can then be compared with the capital requirement for the same dates produced by the proprietary models.

Mathematically speaking, *backtesting* calls for a statistically valid number of observations. As with all experiments, a statistically valid sample is required in order to make a factual and documented judgement about the model's accuracy. The Basle Committee projects that there might be a need for increases in capital requirements if, over a 250 working day period (or one year), proprietary models underpredict the number of losses and the error rate exceeds the 1 percent cut-off point. This evidently corresponds to the *99 percent level of confidence.* Calling such losses *exceptions*, the Market Risk Amendment stipulates that:

- if the proprietary model has generated 0 to 4 exceptions, it falls into the *Green Zone*, which means that it is acceptable;
- if there are 5 to 9 exceptions, it finds itself in the *Yellow (Amber) Zone* and needs to be *closely monitored*; and
- if there are more than 10 exceptions, the proprietary model is in the *Red Zone* of low performance.

This procedure permits continuous testing of the model's accuracy. Regulators will not necessarily test the algorithms and heuristics of the bank's proprietary models themselves, which may become a forbidding job, but they will test the results. This is the sense of the Green, Yellow and Red Zones.

Let us look a little closer at the statistics. The reference to the 99 percent percentile, of the one-tailed distribution is the statistical level of confidence. It puts limits on the uncertainty connected with a likely but not sure outcome. The concept starts with the assumption of a normal distribution, which itself is an approximation.

- The mean of this distribution is the *expected value*, but it only provides a 50 percent level of confidence.
- The mean plus 1.65 standard deviations, for a two-tailed distribution, gives a 90 percent level of confidence.
- The mean plus 2.60 standard deviations is a 99 percent level of confidence – always for a two-tailed distribution.

The 99 percent level of confidence is what the 1996 Market Risk Amendment specifies, but for a one-tailed distribution. This would correspond to the mean plus 2.33 standard deviations. But I do suggest sticking to the mean plus 2.60 standard deviations, which in reality represents a 99.5 percent level of confidence for one-tailed distribution, increasing by so much the likelihood that there will be no errors, and therefore the model's results will fall in the Green Zone.

The reason for advising a higher level of confidence is justified by the fact that capital requirements for banks whose models are in the Red Zone *will* be increased by regulators. If they are in the Yellow Zone, the capital requirements *may* be increased, at the regulators' discretion.

If 'exceptions' are viewed as failures in the proprietary models' prediction, which they really are, the quality control implied by the Basle Committee is fairly tough – as it should be. In terms of percentage defective,

- a 0 to 4 failure rate means 0 percent to 1.6 percent in terms of acceptable quality,

- a 5 to 9 failure rate corresponds to up to 3.6 percent, and
- 10 or more failures represents to a quality level beyond 3.6 percent.

This emphasis on the quality level of the model's results means that the Basle Committee's backtesting provisions will affect banks rather significantly. If a bank's proprietary model underpredicts the number of larger losses, the capital requirement will be adjusted upwards. If the failure rate is high, capital requirements will need to be adjusted fairly frequently. Therefore banks must be very careful with the models they develop and use.

The Market Risk Amendment does not elaborate on the methodology to be followed for reporting to the bank's management off-balance sheet (OBS) risks, particularly concerning the results of a combined on-balance sheet and off-balance sheet exposure. Figure 15.2 shows a chart which can fulfill this mission, provided that:

- it is implemented in real time,
- it is supported by database mining to answer *ad hoc* queries, and
- its reporting structure can be interactively personalized by management, as the situation demands.

In conclusion, while national rules and regulations concerning supervision continue to apply, the Amendment guarantees a common frame of reference which in turn ensures a reasonable level of homogeneity in risk control and regulatory reporting. The Basle Committee has left a considerable amount of flexibility to the central bank of each of the G-10 countries in terms of the actual management of market risk.

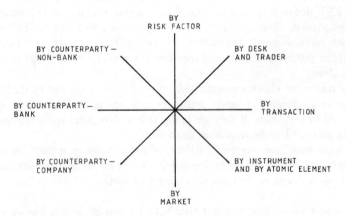

Figure 15.2   Framework for derivatives risk management

7 WHY MARKING-TO-MODEL IS A MAJOR CULTURAL CHANGE FOR MANY FINANCIAL INSTITUTIONS

One of the most important references in connection with the Market Risk Amendment is that marking-to-model has been legitimized as the solution to the valuation of the trading book while for valuation purposes banks can choose the so-called 'standard method' of the Bank for International Settlements (BIS); as an alternative to proprietary models, the more sophisticated institutions develop *eigenmodels*.

- A bank's own models are usually derived from database information concerning its internal risk management systems, procedures and results.
- Such models are subject to the observance of *adequacy criteria* and are controlled through *backtesting*, as described in section 5.

However, many questions of policy and organization remain to be answered. For instance, will the supervisory authorities in each country promote the development of models for risk management among the banks they regulate? If so, how big a group of rocket scientists[5] should each commercial bank have? What type of studies should it undertake? Further questions include the following. Will market risk studies consider volatility, liquidity and cash flow – or other criteria for market risk management? Will this be done strictly in the central bank's own national economy, the European Union, the North Atlantic Free Trade Area, internationally? Money center banks operate all over the globe.

Proprietary model solutions must evidently account for the fact that, whether a bank marks-to-model or not, the capital requirements for counterparty credit risk will continue to apply under the terms of the 1988 Capital Accord, as modified by subsequent amendments. With respect to derivative products, the new element is that:

- capital requirements for market risk must now apply on a worldwide consolidated basis;
- this will require additional capital, over and above the 1988 capital requirements for credit risk.

The proprietary model approach follows a practice which has already taken hold in America, at least among advanced technology banks. The Amendment respects a bank's internal risk measurement system and its way of applying capital charges. Not everything has been standardized. Those banks which are able to develop an eigenmodel culture for market risk are now cross-fertilizing the credit risk domain. J.P. Morgan first introduced, in 1995/6, RiskMetrics, which is a VAR/P type of model. A year later, in 1997, it brought to the market CreditMetrics for credit risk. We have already spoken of this.

- Banks with experience in credit risk modeling have found that, provided their loans portfolio is diversified, they will need for credit risk only half the capital stipulated by the 1998 BIS accord.
- Similarly, banks with experience in market risk modeling can demonstrate that, in the longer run, they need half the capital required by netting.
- Furthermore, by using models for credit risk and market risk, technologically advanced financial institutions have been able to integrate the client's profile in terms of exposure taken by the bank.

This makes sense both from a relationship banking viewpoint and in terms of risk management. Notice, however, that risk exposure is compounded not only because of market risk and credit risk reasons, but also owing to the fact that the networks, databases, computers and software of most banks leave much to be desired. That is why the 'haves' and the 'have nots' in the coming decade will be separated by the advanced or retrograde status of their information technology.

Few senior managements really have the necessary knowhow in networks, databases, computers and software to appreciate that the global bank's information elements are sitting all over the world, and in 9.9 cases out of 10 they cannot be readily integrated – if this is feasible at all.

- Major banks typically have different sites with heterogeneous computer systems, ill-coordinated among themselves.
- Not only are their software and their databases incompatible, but also each operating unit uses different ways to handle its risks.

Integration is a massive technology problem made more complex by the fact that most institutions still have legacy systems that use various types of basic software which do not talk to one another.[6] Quite often, even at the same site, a bank's trading and position-keeping systems are based on different technologies. This is highly counterproductive.

As cannot be repeated too often, a well-managed bank needs an integrative approach. The 1996 Market Risk Amendment does not say so, but knowledgeable bankers appreciate that this is what should be done. In its fundamentals, risk management boils down to an interactive three-dimensional frame of reference as shown in Figure 15.3 which should be steadily updated in real time.

Ideally, pricing, tracking and risk control should be accomplished at both the macro level and the micro level of market reference. Derivatives are instruments of the macromarkets, which are global, sophisticated and of vast size, able to satisfy the most demanding investors. Testing the macro level means stress analysis. (See section 7.) The sense of the micro level is detail.

In every financial institution, as well as in any other company, a sign of good management is both the establishment of sound policies and the use of high technology in the control of risk. Assisted by advanced technology, the right policies

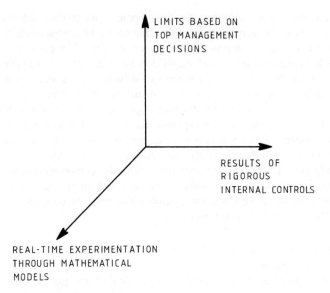

Figure 15.3 An interactive three-dimensional frame of reference for effective risk management

should see to it that senior management is able, without the assistance of intermediaries, to look at:

- the trader
- the instrument
- the counterparty, and
- the trading unit.

Not only should this presentation be *ad hoc* in real time, but it must also be fully integrated firm wide, in order to evaluate and control risk. Senior managers must be steadily linked to one another through interactive computational finance.

In other words, financial institutions must not only be able to provide regulators with risk measurement metrics, but also be in a position to assess the risk they have taken, and continue to take, on many different levels of operations for internal accounting reasons. This should be done intraday, immediately following deviations with the appropriate corrective action.

In order to ensure a degree of prudence, the Basle Committee has proposed quantitative and qualitative criteria for those banks which wish to use proprietary models. These might become the basis for generalized transparency and consistency regarding added capital requirements in a way valid across banks. As has been brought to the reader's attention, the Basle Committee's quantitative criteria, as well as those that will govern the use of proprietary models with the goal of determining capital charges, require that *value-at-risk* be computed daily, using a 99th percentile and a one-tailed confidence interval. The problem with this approach, beyond the use of realistic models for value-at-risk, is that VAR only answers about 60 percent to 65 percent of a bank's risk management require-ments. Different models are required for the balance of the transactions.

Stress analysis is an alternative, more sophisticated solution than VAR. The goal is to compute the extent of exposure under extreme assumptions. The stress test might be based on a yield curve, or on the notional principal amount. This is a different approach than the likely loss estimated through VAR.

Finally, one of the important issues in an objective computation of market risk exposure concerns the *timeframes* to be observed in the testing procedure. According to the Basle Committee, value-at-risk must be computed on a daily basis. The Market Risk Amendment

- specifies the employment of a minimum price shock equivalent to a holding period of 10 trading days, and
- instructs that the model incorporate a historical observation period of at least one year.

My regret is that daily statistics rather than *intraday* time series have been adopted. Given the rapid evolution in the financial markets, their globalization, the fact that there is 24-hour banking and a forex transaction happens every five to eight seconds, intraday financial time series are a 'must'.[7]

8   STRESS ANALYSIS, NOTIONAL PRINCIPAL AMOUNT AND ITS DEMODULATOR

As we have already seen in Chapter 9, the term *notional principal amount* is widely used with derivatives. Etymologically, it has been borrowed from swaps, where it signifies the quantity of money never actually to be paid or received. By contrast, the actual flows resulting from the trade will be paid or received at appropriate calendar periods. Today this notional principal concept is used in con-nection with forward rate agreements, caps, floors, forward contracts on Treasury bonds, guilds and bunds, as well as exotic derivative instruments like binary options. While not every trade in derivatives is expressed in notional principal, this concept is very important.

- Some central banks, like the Federal Reserve, consider the notional principal valuable metrics.
- Other central banks, like the Bank of England, relegate it to irrelevancy.

I belong to the class defined by the first point and believe that notional principal amount-to-loans risk equivalence is a process of calculation and adjustment that observes and exploits the characteristics of prevailing exposure. The challenge is to find conversion ratios which provide a common denominator and frame of reference. This can be done in either of two ways:

- establishing a common denominator for all derivatives contracts, which is accurate but not precise, or
- computing a demodulator of notional principal instrument-by-instrument.

Either approach sets the stage for *stress testing*. Once we have computed a demodulator of the notional amount (as explained in the following paragraphs), we can develop 'What if' scenarios and experiment interactively in real time. What if the volatility in the market increases? For this stress test, we decrease the demodulator of the notional principal (I will explain how to do it). The result is a corresponding increase in capital at risk.

Let us start with the second of the two alternative methods briefly described in the above two bullet points. Say that, for an interest rate swap, the notional principal of a contract is $100 million. We mine our interest rate swaps (IRS) database and find that, in the distribution of *absolute values* of gains and losses in connection with fixed/floating rates,

- the mean is 2.17 (the absolute values of gains and losses in IRS have been normalized to $100 million notional principal);
- the standard deviation is 1.

Then, at the 99 percent level confidence (one-tailed distribution), the risk being taken is:

$$\bar{x} + 2.33s = 2.4 + 2.33 \times 1 = 174.5 \text{ or } \$4.5 \text{ million}$$

where s is the standard deviation of the distribution, and $\bar{x}$ is the mean. The resulting demodulator is:

$$100/4.5 = 22.2$$

Based on past statistics, the $4.5 million represents the possible loss at the 99 percent level of confidence. It will be most likely exceeded only 1 percent of the time. But the demodulation also constitutes a *stress test*.

How should this demultiplier be chosen, and subsequent modeling done in the general case of the whole trading book? From my experience I suggest that a 1/30 demodulation for cumulative derivatives exposure might be right under quiet market conditions which typically involve reduced control. However, in tougher times it is wise to switch to 1/25 and 1/20, by stages – the1/20 accounting for a situation which might lead to systemic risk.

This transition from *reduced* inspection to *normal* inspection and *tightened* inspection has a mathematical basis developed in the World War II years at Columbia University, for the atomic bomb project. The necessary methodology and tables can be found in MIL-STD-105 (United States Printing Office, Washington, DC). As a matter of principle, derivatives transactions can be handled fairly well under this methodology:

- some are high-risk because the off-balance sheet instruments are not so well known;
- others are high-risk because the loss exposure the bank takes can be unlimited;
- still others are high-risk because of the long maturity horizon which they cover.

The use of already established military standards in quality control and in reliability engineering is very helpful because these risks are not so easy to hedge, in contrast to what is so often said in public by the executives of some financial institutions or treasury departments. Military standards for quality control can help those banks that look favorably on a rigorous control of risk.

With this, it becomes feasible to *integrate balance sheet and off-balance sheet exposure.* Such an approach also makes it possible to pay attention to other crucial factors that enter the risk equation. It permits proceeding with client-by-client consolidation for balance sheet and off-balance sheet deals, and a similar reference is valid for the calculation of instrument-by-instrument exposure done by each trader – as well as trader-by-trader comparisons.

So much for my notional principal amount method. Every financial institution will be well advised to re-evaluate its portfolio in a detailed manner in terms of specific

- rating of the counterparties,
- type and amount of derivative instruments,
- total exposure and specific mix, and
- maturity of trades and the time dimension.

Other crucial factors to be taken into account are initial conditions of the trade; in-the-money, at-the-money and out-of-the-money market valuation; possible all-or-nothing components in complex derivatives; prevailing market liquidity and volatility, and frequency of payments. A more sophisticated model will also consider initial and marked-to-model value, as well as other factors the bank believes to be critical.

9   NONLINEAR THINKING, LOANS EQUIVALENCE AND CAPITAL AT RISK

'Anything linear is probably wrong,' says Joel Moses, Dean of the School of Architecture and Planning, MIT. 'In complex systems you usually have feedback loops. In R&D, we've long had this notion of a linear chain from basic research to product development, and we know that that's wrong. Unfortunately, not enough people operate as if they know it's wrong' (*The MIT Report*, June/July 1996).

Financial markets are nonlinear adaptive systems whose behavior can become unpredictable. Both trading prices and transaction velocity tend to change in real time, with the result that complexity increases, as does the system's tendency to get out of control. The opinion is voiced among cognizant bankers and technologists that real-time networks may create unforeseen kinds of systemic risk, apart from the more obvious result that they will redefine competition among the main players in the financial industry. A basic but little appreciated fact is that technology increases both the efficiency and the complexity of the financial system.

- Sophisticated technology helps to manage risk and it amplifies risk at the same time.
- It also blurs the boundaries between retail and wholesale banking, as well as commercial and investment banking.

A similar statement can be made about new financial products which were originally thought to be hedging mechanisms, but whose nonlinear behavior bankers have not yet understood too well. Yet the need to do so is pressing.

The more sophisticated the models which we develop, the more nonlinear they are bound to be. The presence of rocket science in banking is irreversible, and financial institutions which do not get ready to face this fact are in for many surprises. Not only our algorithms and heuristics, but also our concepts about modeling are getting more complex.

Let me paraphrase the example which Brandon Davies, of Barclays Bank, presented in his lecture at the First International Conference on Risk Management (London, 17–19 March 1997). Davies demonstrated a very thorough analysis which covered interest rate volatility. If the treasury or the economics department of the bank works hard on financial studies, then there is plenty of scope for fine-tuning the model we use – like, for instance, the demodulator of the notional principal amount.

- Over an extended timeframe, we can take outliers as belonging to nervous markets: financial crises, war periods and their aftermath.
- By contrast, values from relatively calm markets will tend towards a normal distribution, which may well be handled parametrically.

This bifurcation in terms of complexity in our concepts and in our models can be effectively used in connection with interest rates, currencies, equities and other commodities, helping to tune the demodulator of the notional principal amount towards realistic values – and therefore to offer a valid estimate of outstanding exposure.

As with loans, risk-equivalent exposure calculation concerns the issuer and user of the instrument, as much as the prevailing market conditions. Starting with the premise that in the majority of derivatives trades the notional principal amount *per se* is not involved in any other sense than as a frame of reference, risk equivalence aims to produce a quantitative result so that actual and potential risks are appropriately estimated.

A sound solution will sustain real-time response and reporting, rather than provide figures to be given long after the facts. But no model solves all of the risk-related problems single-handed, as I have so often explained.

- While technology is a necessary and valuable companion, well above modeling are corporate policies and procedures aimed at controlling risk.
- These are the responsibility of the bank's board of directors and of the board of management.

To understand how a more sophisticated system works and be able to apply the method, let us take as an example a hypothetical Bank of Commerce with its financial instruments, markets and counterparties. Through this case study we would see how to:

- choose and use a demultiplier by derivative financial instrument,
- calculate a risk premium for the monetization of risk, and
- estimate a general decompiler for the contents of ABC's portfolio.

For reasons of simplicity, say that the Bank of Commerce has in its portfolio only binary options (a highly risky instrument), oil futures, gold futures, interest rate futures and currency futures. The bank's management has rated the counterparties from AAA to BB, largely guided by an independent credit evaluation agency with some internal evaluation added to it by the bank's own analysts. While nobody disputes the value of AAA, from AA downwards many banks superimpose their own criteria. Much depends on the institution and the analyst.

The Union Bank of Switzerland, for example, considers investment grades down to and including BBB. However, other banks and brokers also accept BB. In certain cases, even BBB may not satisfy investment grade standards. There are really no universal and absolute measures of counterparty risk.

The computation of capital at risk for six trades involving five instruments is shown in Table 15.3. To simplify this example, the same time to maturity has been chosen for all trades, equal to one year. Alternatively, the longer the time to

395

Table 15.3 Computation of capital at risk rates for six trade

Customer	Rating	Transaction	Time to maturity	Notional amount ($)	Demodulator	Loans equivalent ($)
1	AAA	Binary option	1 year	30 mn	1	30.0 mn
2	AA	Oil futures	1 year	250 mn	25	10.0 mn
3	AA	Interest rate swap	1 year	500 mn	40	12.5 mn
4	BB	Interest rate swap	1 year	100 mn	40	2.5 mn
5	BB	Currency futures	1 year	350 mn	30	11.6 mn
6	B	Gold futures	1 year	60 mn	35	1.7 mn
			Sum	1,290 mn		68.3 mn

maturity, the greater the risk the bank takes. The fate of a deal in binary options is decided by all-or-nothing. Therefore the whole notional principal is at risk and the demodulator to loans equivalence is 1.

Oil futures fluctuate but in the judgment of the ABC expert on oil prices the maximum exposure is 4 percent; hence the demodulator is 25. Another financial analyst working for ABC judged the maximum interest rate exposure at 2.5 percent. This gives a demodulator of 40. Currency futures were considered to be more risky than IRS within the same one-year timeframe. The chosen demodulator is 30. The risk associated with gold futures was considered to fall between currency futures and interest rate swaps; hence the divisor is 35.

The careful reader will appreciate that a better way to do these estimates is through mining the database of normalized gains and losses by class of instruments. This method has already been explained. Cognizant analysts will also associate a premium with time to maturity. If we have a yield curve, risk connected with an IRS demodulator should be differentiated by time bracket – in a way not dissimilar to the one BIS advises for netting.

Let us return to the simplified version of the compound example. If we sum the amounts shown in the two columns of Table15.3, notional amounts and loans equivalent, and divide the former by the latter, the general demultiplier results at about 19. This is loaded, however, because of the binary option.

- If the binary option is left out, the general demodulator becomes 33.
- This is near to the 30 level which I have suggested as a general case.

It is not necessary that the general demodulator and the demodulators by instrument correspond with precision. The two are based on different concepts and levels of detail. There are as well other factors which must be considered, such as the maturity of the commitment and the rating of the counterparty which, purposely, have been left out of the equation in this example.

10   THE COLLABORATION OF SUPERVISORY AUTHORITIES IN IMPLEMENTING THE MARKET RISK AMENDMENT

The type of collaboration which should take place among supervisory authorities regarding market risk is not explicitly specified by the Basle Committee. This was settled by the 20 May 1996 agreement among the G-10 central banks, which also involved the Bank for International Settlements (BIS) and the International Monetary Fund (IMF).

On 20 May 1996, at the annual meeting which took place in Frankfurt, Germany, two main bodies representing commercial banking and investment banking regulators from the G-10 countries issued a joint statement of principles for improved collaboration. Largely, this was in response to a request by the heads of government at the Halifax G-7 summit of June 1995.

While everybody talks of transnational collaboration, nobody likes to give up its prerogatives. As it currently stands, while establishing a cooperation, this accord does not commit supervisory authorities in any one country to specific ways of working with each other.

- The overall initiative has been promoted by the Basle Committee on Banking Supervision and its counterpart, the International Organization of Securities Commissions (IOSC).
- The most likely result of the May 1996 accord is that it will reinforce a move towards groups that combine banking and securities operations, bringing institutions under joint scrutiny of regulators from the two industries.

A further principle of the accord concerns adequate reporting and disclosure to ensure the transparency and integrity of markets. Still another is that markets must be able to survive the failure of individual firms – which goes beyond current systems and procedures implying that the supervisory process has to be constantly improved.

But the May 1996 meeting also saw some reservations expressed about a fully transnational supervisory and global risk control system. An example is the statement made that arrangements to improve coordination and cooperation 'will not in any way reduce the powers and responsibilities' of individual national supervisors (*Financial Times*, 21 May 1996). Still, even if limited, the decision on cross-country collaboration in commercial banking and investment banking is important because to date regulators have failed to share information among countries and between financial industries. Examples are BCCI, the Barings bankruptcy and the $1.8 billion derivatives losses by Sumitomo Corporation. Furthermore, there has been tension between regulators in the banking and securities sectors.

On-and-off tensions among supervisory authorities because of overlapping duties came to a head in 1992 with the breakdown of talks intended to provide a common standard for capital to cover trading risks. They surfaced again in the 1993 to 1995 timeframe with the delays experienced in regard to the approval of the Market Risk Amendment. On the other hand, the need for better cooperation has been spurred by:

- the consolidation of financial industries in recent years, and
- the increasing number of take overs of securities firms by commercial banks.

This takeover activity has been particularly intense in Europe. Examples are the takeover of Phillips & Drew by UBS, CSFB by Crédit Suisse, Warburg by Swiss

Banking Corporation, Morgan Grenfell by Deutsche Bank, Kleinwort Benson by Dresdner Bank and Barings by ING Bank.

A close cooperation between regulators of the commercial banking and investment banking institutions not only makes sense in itself, but also creates the infrastructure of a supervisory activity which should definitely be extended towards *non-banks* – both in regard to capital adequacy for credit risk and in connection with the new norms for market risk.

It is indeed curious that, in spite of their size and their risks, in non-banks: hedge funds, mutual funds, pension funds, postal banks and the treasuries of many corporations are regulated by nobody and there is no authority supervising them. Hence even the collaboration between central banks and securities commissions only covers part of the financial market. At present, this cooperation rests on the following basic principles.

- All banks and securities firms should be subject to effective supervision, and the supervision of capital should be adequate.
- Special supervisory arrangements will be provided for geographically and functionally diversified financial groups.
- In the longer run, supervision will be more homogeneous and as free as possible from different national impediments.

It escapes nobody's attention that regulatory arrangements should account for *globalization*. Somewhat less clear is the level of high technology which should be used by the financial industry. In my view, only the most advanced technology counts. Its aims are outlined in Figure15.4.

In May 1996, the supervisory authorities of banks and security companies stipulated, quite correctly, that new regulation can only become effective if all financial institutions have a proper risk management system at least at the state-of-the-art level suggested by the Market Risk Amendment. However, it is somewhat optimistic to expect this standard to be reached any time soon. In the first place, not only among the Group of Ten but all over the globe, the central banks themselves have to change their culture. The auditing and supervisory departments of central banks have so far relied mainly on procedural approaches, old data processing technology and simple, linear quantitative analyses. They often use spreadsheets to extract information from the commercial bank's database and manipulate numbers:

- measuring a bank's capital,
- looking into the biggest loan exposures,
- estimating the liquidity in its treasury, and
- evaluating the volatility of its portfolio.

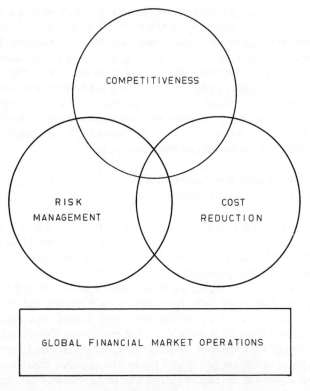

Figure 15.4 Aims of high technology implementation

All this may be necessary but it is not enough. Regulators must go well beyond the deterministic models they are currently using for quantitative analysis into heuristics – including genetic algorithms and fuzzy engineering. They should also move from linear to nonlinear solutions, as we saw in section 9.

Central banks should also acquire the skills necessary for testing the output of all models developed and used by commercial and investment banks, beyond those stipulated by the Market Risk Amendment. The same comment is valid for backtesting procedures which, as we have seen, should be in place throughout the life cycle of the model.

The ability of regulators to evaluate and control the quality of management of the banks they supervise is also highly relevant. Only recently has it begun to be appreciated that spotting *weak management* and *poor controls* is a very important supervisory task indeed. This qualitative analysis is not yet part of the central banks' culture.

Judging the quality of a bank's internal controls, its limit-setting policies and its risk management will require much more than supervisors visiting their charges more often. And there should as well be, throughout the G-10 and beyond, homogeneous regulatory procedures explaining how the central banks might better supervise the commercial banks' international operations. Such new policies and practices should be set by working more closely with securities regulators, like Britain's Securities and Futures Authority (SFA) and America's Securities and Exchange Commission (SEC). It is not possible to be successful in bank supervision if each regulatory authority continues in its own parochial way.

This last reference brings attention to compliance requirements for investment banks and brokers. In America, for example, a registered broker/dealer must comply with Securities and Exchange Commission rules:

- 15C3-1, Net Capital Computation, and
- 15C3-3, Customer Reserve Requirement.

These rules oblige the investment bank to calculate and set aside the amount of funds needed to protect its clients' assets. In addition, SEC Rule 17A-13 requires that the broker physically count and confirm all client securities at least once a quarter, including all fully paid for and excess margin securities.

Compliance with these regulations is quite strictly monitored by the Securities and Exchange Commission, the New York Stock Exchange and the National Association of Securities Dealers. The firm's own internal audit department is also expected to regularly monitor the stated procedures. I would expect these rules, or compromises which are similar to them, to be generalized throughout the G-10 countries in the not too distant future. But universal banks will be well advised to implement the best in current regulation without delay through dry runs, well before the rules in question become the law of the land. We should always be keen to learn, adapt and use important tools for risk management reasons.

Notes

1.   See D.N. Chorafas, *Financial Models and Simulation* (London: Macmillan, 1995).
2.   See D.N. Chorafas, *The 1996 Market Risk Amendment. Understanding Value-at-Risk* (Burr Ridge, IL.: McGraw-Hill/Irwin Professional, 1998).
3.   See D.N. Chorafas, *Chaos Theory in the Financial Markets* (Chicago: Probus/Irwin, 1994).
4.   D.N. Chorafas and H. Steinmann, *Database Mining* (London and Dublin: Lafferty, 1994).
5.   See D.N. Chorafas, *Rocket Scientists in Banking* (London and Dublin: Lafferty, 1995).
6.   See D.N. Chorafas and H. Steinmann, *Do IT or Die* (London and Dublin: Lafferty, 1992).
7.   D.N. Chorafas, *How to Understand and Use Mathematics for Derivatives, volume 1: Understanding the Behaviour of Markets* (London: Euromoney, 1995).

16 Technical Approaches to Security: From Smart Money to Dumb Money and Risks Galore

1 INTRODUCTION

The previous 15 chapters in this book have provided solid evidence that there is a revolution taking place in banking, most particularly in personal services supported by information technology. Underpinning this ongoing evolution is global networking, computer-based models and database mining used as competitive weapons by today's businesses as well as in payment systems.

Networks rather than standalone devices are in increasing demand, aimed at the efficient collection, dissemination and processing of information. The thrust towards networking is due to various economic and market forces which capitalize on available technology to solve any-to-any communications and computer-intensive financial problems.

But what about *security* in the new environment characterizing the banking business? Are we sure that the new systems which we develop and use are secure and as observant of personal privacy as they should be? Nobody can give a factual and documented confirmation, yet this is an issue of vital importance.

Tibor Vamos, of the Hungarian Academy of Sciences, says that it is really a basic interest of democracy to have not only strong financial control but also a secure transaction system. End-to-end transaction security, Vamos suggests, is in no way less important than military security, because it influences in an important manner the life of the whole population.

Nobody really says that there will never be a case for a new payments technology. The sense of my reference is that, to be successful, new payments solutions must turn technology upside-down. Their success rests on imaginative contributions like software agents, mobile computing, real-time database mining and 'Things That Think'.

To demonstrate how insecure are some of the products and systems *en vogue* today, I have chosen as a case study plastic money – most particularly smart cards and cybermoney. The plastic money's acceptance does not mean that there exist no security problems; indeed, there are many, and they start with magnetic strip credit cards.

- However, with some exceptions, recovery with magnetic strip plastic money functions relatively well.

401

Therefore credit cards are used in connection with a wide range of payments and many people consider them to be quite trustworthy.

- Lack of security is the rule with cybermoney and smart cards – with no rigorous solution yet in sight.

Knowledgeable executives in the financial industry, as well as in commerce, believe it will be some time before consumers and retailers welcome electronic cash in a way similar to their acceptance of magnetic strip cards. 'Notes and coins are fast and efficient for low-value transactions,' says Peter Hirsch, managing director of Retail Banking Research. This speaks volumes for the prospects of smart cards in the small payments market.

To sell themselves to the public, new payment methods require a deep concern about security, to be followed by effective solutions. This means much better forms of security and personal protection than so far invented or applied. Cryptography and firewalls may be necessary – but they are not enough.

Furthermore, a rigorous study of the new payments media cannot be dissociated from their effect (current and potential) on the monetary base and the velocity of circulation of money – and hence on the money supply, bringing to the fore another type of security, because in extremis insecure money adds to systemic risk.[2]

2   SECURITY ISSUES CURRENTLY POSED BY CREDIT CARDS

It is inevitable that, if we trade electronically in buying and selling different wares, we must also have a way to transact business at the financial end. The big question with electronic money is which security solution will prove to be acceptable and viable. It is still too early to make a bet, but we can learn some lessons by examining what happens with credit cards.

The restaurant where one gives one's credit card is also a security risk. The same is true of the hotel because, to make a reservation, the consumer has to give over the phone his credit card number. Consumers accept this risk because there is in place an infrastructure to catch waiters or reservations clerks who misuse the card information. But this is not true of hackers working on networks from their home.

Some people think that the perception of insecurity on the Internet has mainly to do with pornography. This is only partly true. Because most Web users are computer-literate, comparing credit card risks with those with cybermoney, many consumers start to realize that software modules are not people.

- One can look at the waiter and decide to trust him or not to trust him.
- But the consumer does not have the same feedback over the network – any network.

In terms of cybermoney, some hybrid solutions may be possible by learning from what is perceived as security advances in other domains. For instance, to reduce ATM-related crime, Huntington Bankshares (in the US) installed red buttons on its automatic teller machines. The client pushes this button and talks directly to the police department.

The acceptance of cybermoney has also to do with established social habits. Social habits can change. We are still in the early phase of the Web: publishing. (See section 8 on the legal aftermath of publishing.) From here a bifurcation develops. *Either* multimedia electronic commerce is not the order of the day and 3-D simulation permits visiting virtual malls, *or* consumers have still to go out and look at, say, home appliances, choosing what they want.

- Subsequently, they can use the Web to find the best deal and negotiate the price with the retailer.

But if *trusted* electronic commerce is not the order of the day, then there will be a payments bottleneck.

- *Either* the consumer trusts that cybermoney does not lead to fraud, or he continues using checks for payment.

A bifurcation will keep personal checks and credit cards as main players in the payment system. But there may also come half-way solutions, such as online payment accepted by the merchants and the consumer public only for minor settlements. Much will depend on the nature of security software which will be available.

Security risks on the Internet and credit card risks correlate. The $50 million lost by an AT operator when hackers got hold of 20,000 credit card numbers in an online database is just one example. The point is that insecure cybermoney can make such incidents look like minor events.

In many cases, what should have been a legitimate business turns out to be a deception. On a number of occasions in major hotels, from Les Vegas to McLean, VA, after I signed the bill somebody added an unidentified (and illegal) charge of a few dollars. Usually, this amount has been too small to be worth contesting, but in December 1996, when I received my Visa credit card account from the Barclays Bank, London, it showed that one of the hotels made a debit of $214.59, corresponding to £131.70. It took three registered letters to get back the money.

The lesson is that, once an unscrupulous merchant has the customer's credit card number, he can do whatever he pleases with it. This is, of course, no unique example of credit cards being misused. In 1995, in America, credit card companies lost about $1.3 billion as a result of fraud, according to estimates by MasterCard International. This did not happen for want of finding secure solutions, but in spite of them.

One of the reasons for the failure of many current security approaches is that they have not been tested to be fullproof and fool-proof. Thiefs are smart too. In one incident in Germany, pickpockets defrauded consumers' debit cards along with other personal information. Then they called the owners and said, 'This is your bank speaking. You are lucky that your card has been found. We will cancel it, but need your PIN. In a week you get a new one.' The victims were fooled by this fake call, and did not bother to double check with their bank. Rather, it was their bank which later informed them that their accounts were overdrawn.

For his own security, the debit card and credit card user has to do much more than to remember his personal identification number – rather than writing it down. He must be very vigilant, and he must also be aware that, as a security key, the simple PIN has outlived its usefulness.

The pros would say that track-2 magnetic strip cards used with swipe or insertion readers offer a low-cost security solution for an average of $0.35 per card. A track-2 card holds up to 40 characters of numerical data, such as name of holder, other personal numbers, expiration date and a list of directories that can be accessed. At the same time, however, a lost track-2 magnetic strip card rewards the person who stole it with all this information concerning its legitimate owner. The same is true of smart cards. Nor am I comfortable with the fact that so much attention is focused on directories. This is done in the belief that whoever controls the directory wins the security round, which is an oversimplification and therefore is false.

3   BEWARE OF COUNTERFEITING WITH PLASTIC MONEY

The last 10 years have seen a major new development: the counterfeiting of plastic money to run alongside the traditional counterfeiting of currency. Although counterfeiting typically accounts for just 26 percent of total fraud losses, in the 1990s it continued to grow at an alarming rate – just as the use of credit cards and debit cards exploded. In some instances, it increased by 74 percent in a year.

Overall, credit card fraud can be divided into *pre-status* and *post-status*. With pre-status, fraud occurs before the cardholder realizes something is wrong and informs the credit card company. With post-status, the credit card issuer has already been informed. Counterfeiting falls into the pre-status class, hitting both consumers and the credit card issuer.

Generally, it is easier to prevent and reduce post-status fraud but pre-status fraud occurs at the time when cards are most vulnerable to abuse. Statistics help to dramatize this reference. As the 1980s came to a close (to be precise, in 1988–91, as contrasted to the 1985–7 timeframe),

- cumulative growth in credit card crime stood at a staggering 240 percent, compared with only a 69 percent growth in card transactions over the same period;

- losses peaked at \$165.6 million in 1991. Though they have declined since then, many banks are worried about a new explosion.

Why did the credit card crime rate decline? In my judgment the no. 1 reason is that the industry realized that it had to get its act together and attack this financial bloodletting with all the resources at its command.

Part of the problem of the growing insecurity with credit cards has been that the classical instructions to consumers on how to handle their credit cards and debit cards have not changed for years: for instance, the traditional advice never to write down the personal identification number and never to leave the credit card unattended. Very few people follow the instruction not to write down their PIN, because they cannot remember their number. As for the second piece of advice, it simply does not make sense when one gives one's card to the waiter in the restaurant to pay the bill or, even worse, gives it over the phone to a hotel which proves to have few scruples. 'Do not let your card out of sight, even when paying in the best hotel or restaurant', is good advice. But it is impractical.

More rigorous approaches are necessary, and these are not forthcoming. True, some new instructions have been added to make consumers better aware of credit card risks. But these are elementary. For example:

- always check your billing statement, especially after a trip;
- always check sales vouchers when you sign them and keep the copy (which few people do).

New types of theft and counterfeiting make a mockery of these instructions. Since the value of plastic money is based on confidence, much tougher laws are needed to boost confidence by catching and speedily punishing the thieves.

Because the major credit card companies are global, the Internet could play a significant role in improving transaction security. Much will depend, not only on algorithms and online procedures, but also on bandwidth, leading to intellectual intimacy with good will practices associations and law enforcement agencies, with a site on the Web. This is the sense of what is starting to be called the *Bandwidth Law*. Easy connectivity over the Internet and high bandwidth can lead to many social changes, including better law enforcement procedures connected with electronic money. Police departments have not yet exploited this channel.

The Internet presents a new dimension in the security effort, but it is a double-edged sword. While about half the cards are still stolen in burglaries, car break-ins, muggings or pickpocketing, a closer collaboration between local police, Interpol and other law-enforcement agencies has led to the unearthing of new online schemes.

It takes imagination to counteract effectively different types of swindles. Some of the more advanced techniques of organized crime capitalize on the fact that credit card use worldwide is so great and is still growing. The Visa network alone processes globally more than six billion transactions a year. Hence

- even a 1 percent fraud rate is enough in itself to cause alarm because it represents 60 million cases of theft;
- while 99 percent of transactions are genuine, the balance causes serious financial loss to banks and other institutions funding the credit card companies.

In its fundamentals, globality makes the sheer size of the problem staggering. In Great Britain alone, 30 million people hold some 83 million plastic cards of which two million are lost or stolen every year and 210,000 subsequently used illegally. No wonder that, in a histogram of losses, those connected with credit cards exceed all others, as shown in Figure 16.1.

Business travelers and holiday-makers abroad are most at risk. In many countries, thieves like to use foreign cards because they feel that gives them a little bit of extra time to manipulate accounts.

- It is also easier to circulate counterfeit foreign cards than counterfeits of cards issued by local financial institutions.
- For law enforcement, merchants and banks, the trick is to spot the difference between a counterfeit card and the real thing.

Often the counterfeit card does not carry the name of a genuine issuing bank. Neither does it carry a Bank Identification Number (BIN) printed above the first four embossed figures of the card number.

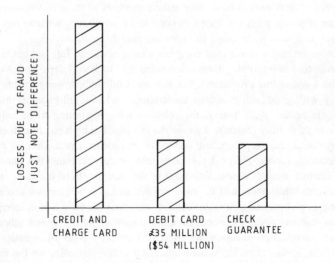

Figure 16.1 Annual plastic card fraud losses in the United Kingdom (order of magnitude)

Quite frequently, depending on the thief's sophistication, the dove hologram on the counterfeit card is a different design from the genuine one. But while at least some of the counterfeits use high technology, so do the genuine card issuers. A high-tech *electronic detective* is the latest device in Visa's battle against the card fraudster in Europe, the Middle East and Africa.

After year-long trials in the United States where it cut fraud by over $25.3 million, the Cardholder Risk Identification Service (CRIS) has been introduced to Europe, with the first pilot made in Spain (January 1995), then rolled out across the region. CRIS is aimed at business and holiday travelers from Britain, France and Germany to Southern Europe, North Africa and the Middle East, whose Visa cards roughly represent more than 50 percent of all Visa card fraud. Through Visa's global computer network and expert systems, user profiles are developed and an early warning system is put in place.[3]

4   CAN WE IMPROVE THE SECURITY OF CONSUMER PAYMENT SYSTEMS?

Using plastic cards to draw cash while traveling rather than relying on traveler's checks, has some attractions, although many people still prefer the use of old fashioned traveler's checks because they trust them more than plastic money – and the cost is lower. Among the advantages of cards are:

- their small size, making for easier portability, and
- the fact that the user does not need to pay in advance for the cash.

But, as we saw in sections 2 and 3, the risk of theft is also greater. While on a trip, the user of traveler's checks will typically leave them in the hotel safe – but he will carry along his credit card. What if, instead of the magnetic strip, the card had a chip?

- Being a cross between low-value traveler's checks and credit cards, smart cards can combine the disadvantages of both.
- But, as we will see in sections 5 to 7, their risks are still ill-studied, making their possession that much more profitable to the thieves.

Fraud exists in connection with all financial instruments, but the newer they are, the less secure they happen to be, hence the greater the risk of fraud. A 220-year old example comes from coinage. In 1779 the drain on the gold reserves of the Bank of England made it necessary to stop paying out gold in exchange for the Bank's notes, beginning a Restriction Period that was to last until 1821. To meet the shortage of coin, the government authorized the Bank, as an emergency measure, to circulate Spanish silver dollars from its reserves. These were counter-marked with the head of George III.

In addition, the Bank of England issued, for the first time, low denomination notes for 1 and 2. The poor quality of the new notes led to an epidemic of forgeries. With forgery carrying the death penalty, over 300 people were executed, while others were transported merely for possession of a forged note.

- Such rules are tough, but they can make the difference between security and insecurity.
- When tough rules are waived or forgotten, forgeries start all over again.

Forgeries of paper money in pounds were repeated during World War II with German-made counterfeits. This led the Bank of England to reissue notes on more secure paper, enriched with a metallic strip for better protection (based on a suggestion made by one of the helping hands in the Bank's printing shop).

What can we learn from this example to apply to the credit/debit card domain? A possible parallel to the paper money's metallic strip is *Card Watch*, a British awareness campaign that has taken the message of card care and alertness to the general public. This effort has reinforced the work done in earlier years under the check card scheme with retailer staff.

At the same time, with the collaboration of Abbey National Bank, the Department of Trade and Industry sponsored a project on the use of massively parallel computers for fraud detection. Conducted through mathematical models developed by university researchers, this project on safer credit cards

- focuses on the whole concept underpinning credit cards and their handling, simulated on parallel processors;
- its models permit detection of fraud patterns, leading to new distribution arrangements.

The goal of patterning and of the resulting channeling arrangements is to ensure that replacements or new cards are securely delivered to the rightful cardholder, together with a parallel enhancement of card issuers' own internal procedures.

Part of the work was oriented toward the development of a card authentication method (CAM) to combat counterfeiting. Research also took place on measures to verify automatically whether the presenter of the card is the genuine cardholder. This is important inasmuch as there is general agreement on the need for a cardholder verification technique better than the existing signature method and PIN.

In the opinion of many experts, there is need for many projects of that kind involving end-to-end simulation of payment systems, focusing on account statements and examining the use the consumer is making of plastic money. The current account or credit card statement shows the client that money has been withdrawn from his account with the card from a cashpoint machine. But the cardholder knows that he did not take it out:

- he has not written down his PIN, nor has he told anyone what it is;
- therefore, how could someone else have got into his account?

An interesting case that might (I said *might*) give the smart card a break is bridging for the Euro. Some people think smart cards should become part of stage three of the European Monetary Union (EMU).

Electronic money in stored-value cards denominated in Euros might be freely used within the Euro area even before the coins and notes are exchanged in retail trade. But, as Ben-Gurion once said, 'Two things which are wrong, don't make one which is right'. The answer is not so complex. The card could have been intercepted or stolen, then copied and replaced. The PIN number could have been intercepted in the post when it was on its way to the client under separate cover from the card, or obtained from the cardholder without his realizing it.

An estimated 100,000 people in Britain have had money taken out of their account through a phantom withdrawal. Banks have traditionally been reluctant to admit that their systems can fail – or that their machines can make mistakes. Though they have an audit trail and they can track back and find out what has happened,

- they are slow in responding to customer complaints;
- rather often, customer letters go unanswered.

Both in the United States and in England, some banks are using hidden cameras at some branches to make it easier to identify the person making the disputed withdrawal. Since 1992, the onus has been on the bank to prove the customer had been negligent, by telling someone else his PIN number or not taking enough care of his card.

There are, however, many sorts of fraud. In 1989, in America, federal agents found that a gang pulled the personal ATM code numbers of Bank of America customers from GTE phone lines. The lines transmit transactions from accounts at Bank of America and thousands of other banks linked to the Plus System, a national network of shared ATMs. The fraud confronting users of ATM money is becoming more serious as some banks are spicing up their ATM menus. ATMs can now issue rail passes in Portland, gift certificates in Tacoma, postage stamps in Pittsburgh and grocery coupons in the Midwest.

The banks hope that such programs will attract new customers and extract fees from those who keep their accounts elswhere. But if the corresponding studies on security are not rigorous, and no reliable solutions are developed, these marketing efforts may turn out to be counterproductive.

5   THE PERPETUAL MOTION MONEY MACHINE WITH SMART CARDS

Many people have criticized smart cards as a technology endlessly in search of meaningful applications. At the same time, the divergent experiences of different countries show that the issues behind prepaid plastic money are more complex than the smart card pros have been suggesting.

Theoretically, chip-in-cards have an edge over magnetic strip credit cards because they can carry much more information. For instance, they could be used to integrate a driver's license, insurance policies, health information or other records. But there is no rigorous proof they can do so more securely – and so far I am talking only of identification (ID) records.

- Today's classical ID cards often have a picture and signature so it can be visually tested that the bearer matches the card.
- Smart cards can store similar information and a PIN for security, but this is part both of their assets and of their liabilities.

The pros answer this by saying that smart cards can have a digital identity – the so-called 'certificate'. The thinking is that such certificates should be embedded in smart cards, with algorithms to protect them from outside attack. This argument forgets that, if a code cracker can run timing tests on the smart card, directly or by timing a network into which the card is plugged, its secret code will quite likely be broken.

Industry standards are being developed for smart cards to be used in applications as diverse as digital cellular phones, satellite and cable television and smart money. But are these standards safe, and is this really what the consumers want?

It never hurts to try, if the cost is not too high. Recently, Visa, MasterCard and Europay agreed on a common specification for smart cards that defines the basic protocols for communication between cards and readers. This is analogous to the RS-232 standards that govern communication between personal computers and modems. However,

- high-security standards which are just as important, or even more, have not yet been addressed in any valid way;
- no rigorous trusted solution has been developed which truly limits risks taken through the use of smart cards in financial transactions.

Some events which took place in Japan in 1996 serve as a reminder that, even if information technology provides tools for the fight against some criminal activity, it also opens other loopholes. Used in Pachinko machines, forged prepaid magnetic strip cards, which are the nearest kin to smart cards, have been at the center of one of the world's largest electronic crimes affecting some of Japan's blue-chip companies.

Pachinko is a combination pinball game and slot machine. In Japan, this business generates an annual estimated revenue of ¥32 billion ($27 million). This is roughly equal to the combined sales of the country's top 10 auto makers. As a public game, Pachinko is played in parlors where customers sit shoulder-to-shoulder on small stools in a haze of cigarette smoke. Some people consider this game a corrupting social force, as parlor owners evade taxes and they seem to funnel cash to organized crime.

In the late 1980s, with help from some blue-chip companies, the National Police Agency attempted to tame the game by issuing prepaid magnetic strip cards in place of cash. Today, 70 percent of parlors use only these cards, but

- reliance on a relatively simple encryption code, and
- the lack of a central database with which to reconcile card validity

left the cards vulnerable to a wave of counterfeiting. Once the code was cracked, the magmetic strips could be written over repeatedly, providing their users with a more or less endless supply of money.

As a result of the fraud, Mitsubishi's Nippon Leisure Card System, the major card manufacturer, posted huge losses. Next in line, Sumitomo-owned Nippon Game Card had losses of ¥8 billion ($6.5 million). The only way to reduce the losses was to take their higher-value Pachinko cards out of circulation.

- There is no proof that NatWest, MasterCard and their partners have learned from the Pachinko experience.
- The same is true as regards what other sponsors do with smart money card – and when they do not learn from failure they are condemned to repeat it.

Theoretically, to enhance their security, smart cards can carry valuable information such as biometric identifiers: voiceprints, fingerprints, retina scans, iris scans or dynamic signature patterns. But like any other card, smart cards can be stolen or lost and this information can be copied by high-tech thieves.

If the question of downloading money is left aside, smart cards could find novel applications. Or could they? Customs authorities in Holland have tested a system to speed passport checking at airports for frequent flyers:

- the user puts a finger on a glass plate, and a video camera captures the fingerprint,
- then a computer compares the video image with a reference print stored on the smart card.

With the template on a smart card, the Dutch authorities say, there is no need to connect to a centralized database to confirm a person's identity. Except that this is erasable memory and this can lead to serious risks of forgery. The day Holland is flooded by illegal immigrants rings, we talk again.

Furthermore, such matching techniques are as yet imperfect. The algorithms for deriving and comparing biometric patterns are still elementary – and solutions made in haste or based on wrong hypotheses lead to nasty results.

In other novel applications, in Japan, kidney patients can carry cards that hold their dialysis records and treatment prescriptions. This, however, is an application for the news media, because such cases do not require smart cards even if dialysis patients often need their blood cleansed two or three times a week.

More credible as a potential implementation is that of cellular telephones which could use smart cards to animate them. In current experimentation, the card holds the subscriber's phone number and other account information. It can also perform digital signal processing to encrypt the conversation. If all goes well,

- algorithms can foil the eavesdroppers who bedevil users of conventional cellular phones;
- but when a cellular phone is lost or stolen, the security embedded in the smart card can turn against its owner.

Here precisely is where the security risk comes in. Now consider a commercial/financial application (which is also being tested) with smart card readers which periodically transfer information to banks for credit to the merchant's account, either directly or through a clearing house. Who would like to have such a device falling into the hands of organized crime?

6   WHY SMART MONEY CARDS CAN BECOME DUMB MONEY

The pros argue that stored-value cards with a chip may be reloaded, while simple ones of EPROM type (erasable, programmable read-only memory like, the telephone cards) are discarded when their cash is used up. Reloading is an argument which is both part of the solution and part of the problem. Anybody can develop the technology to reload the smart cards. Like the example with the Japanese Pachinko, this will be a forger's paradise.

- Tests under way, such as Mondex, allow electronic currency to pass from hand to hand indefinitely, without being redefined.
- The lack of clearance operations is enough to strike out any traditional controls by commercial banks and central banks.
- Anybody can create fake electronic currency and bring it into the system, with illegal 'printing of money' perpetuated until the thief is caught.

That is why a rigorous study of smart money made by the Bank of France[4] concluded that, if smart cards are used, then *all* payments should transit by an accredited bank. And even that has not convinced the French regulatory authorities that smart cards should be authorized.

The argument I often hear, that pilot projects for cards containing only essential information for medical treatment are 'a good proof of their security' is for the birds. Notice that social security ID cards, too, can be forged. Yet they are supposed to give access to medical benefits.

The fact that the legitimate ownership can be verified by stored fingerprint is not an assurance because fingerprints can be reloaded – hence altered. There is as well the fact that, in terms of commerce, the shopping public will not go for smart cards. At the 1996 Olympic Games, in Atlanta, Visa's VisaCash stored-value card performed in a mediocre way.

- More than one million smart cards were made, and they were usable at Olympic sites, the transit system and several thousand stores.
- But what has become known by way of results falls awfully short of what the pros had thought would be the case.

This is still in the future. Today all there is in smart cards is gadgetry to catch the consumer's fancy. Fischer International Systems, for instance, markets a device that allows the cards to be plugged into a PC. Called Smarty, it resembles an ordinary 3.5" floppy, but with a slot for a smart card.

The sales pitch is the same with other push and pull efforts: 'There is no need to visit your local branch to add more cash to the card. Just download some money from your checking account.' The cost of the product is trivial compared to the potential for losses. The device costs $55 and it is advertised as making the home computer become a 'home ATM'.

- Forgotten in the sales pitch is the hidden price of insecurity.
- Organized crime would ensure that the venturesome with 'home ATMs' might be faced with a fraud disaster.

Of course, there are some advantages with smart cards. The pros say they are a nice way of processing penny-ante transactions. In 1994, some $1.8 trillion was spent worldwide on purchases of under $10, some $560 billion of that in the US. But, even if consumers are willing to move away from silver, they would go for *secure* devices.

If such devices existed, both merchants and consumers would stand to benefit – even if, because of costs, no one has been willing to ante up for the expensive equipment needed to process smart cards, let alone the cost of insecurity. But neither most cards nor the Internet are secure. Today, anyone with a modem and a PC is able to launch an attack on security. Even if developers are careful in the design of a product, things happen that were not anticipated.

One of the hypes going the rounds is that merchants would gain a lot of money with smart cards, given that today merchants have to pay some 5 percent to 7 percent of total cash receipts in connection with the costs of handling money. But this cost will not go away:

- part of it is credit card charges, which will remain;
- part of it is accounting charges, which will also stay put.

Another argument is that smart cards could speed customers through check-out lines and speed of service is critical to the merchant's business. Quite apart from the fact that a cash transaction takes only a couple of seconds, while credit cards tie up the line, because of security risks the smart money cards will

- be limited to $50 – a trivial amount, and
- require some authentication check-up, which takes time.

Few people seem to appreciate that, if the limit of money loaded onto a smart card is $50, the average value in a card will be $25 or less. This may be enough to buy a couple of beers or a pack of cigarettes – but not to shop in a supermarket or department store. (A limit of $50 is what the Federal Reserve is studying. Mondex has put the limit at $10. You can always buy peanuts.)

There is also another social effect, which should not be forgotten. Studies have shown that people paying with plastic money tend to spend more per purchase than cash customers. Some consumers think that plastic money grows on trees, until the day of reckoning when they have to pay the bills and find out that credit card bills eat up a quarter of their income.

Another of the heralded potential benefits is also half-baked. It is said that smart card issuers can keep the float, investing customer money while it sits idle on the chip in the card. This essentially emulates traveler's checks – but nobody today can prove that smart cards will be as safe as the good old traveler's checks in the case where they are lost or forged, and the merchant may be sued by consumers for fraud.

- When lost, the traveler's check is reported and the proof that its legitimate user did not employ it is the lack of his signature.
- With classical magnetic strip credit cards, the signature has been replaced by the PIN number (which we have said is not that safe).
- Smart cards cannot do away with the signature and the PIN at the same time. If they do so, they will be the most unsafe banking product ever invented.

Banks are also betting on the so-called *slippage*, money left on cards that never gets used. In the traveler's check industry, that amounts to a huge 7 percent, which makes some institutions salivate. Mondex, however, says that it would allow people to pass digital cash from one card to another. Good-bye slippage and good-morning fraud.

This does not mean that some niche markets for smart cards would not exist. AT&T is working with Delta Air Lines and selected customers of the East Coast, on shuttle loading tickets and frequent-flyer miles registered on chip-in-card. Hilton is doing something similar for hotel reservations. McDonald's and Blockbuster Videos are discussing a joint smart card capable of carrying electronic coupons and frequent shopper bonus points in addition to cash. And so on and so forth.

The pros say that, from fast-food joints to souvenir stands and gas stations, cash can be vacuumed instantly off the chip into the merchant's register. But does it work for niche markets and an occasional usage to develop bottom-up a vast and expensive network infrastructure? And even when we talk of niche markets, can we afford to forget about ironclad security?

There must also be a *legal system* supportive of security enforcement. The old legal framework should change to account for cyberspace, and the new rules must become global. Bell Labs recounts the story of a Dutch hacker who broke into its computers system. Although he attempted to destroy it, the hacker could not be prosecuted because hacking was not illegal under Dutch law (*ACM Member Net*, March 1998, Vol. 41, No. 3)

7 THE COMPETITION BETWEEN SMART CARDS AND SUPER-SMART CARDS: AN UNDERWORLD'S EDEN

In spite of the risks involved and the lack of a factual and documented business opportunity, worldwide there is a great number of competitors in a market which so far does not seem to exist. Offers come from Visa and MasterCard, Banksys (Proton), NatWest's Mondex, KZA (the German money card) and many others. Even governments rush into what they think might be a gold mine. In Spain, the National Mint has been given by the government an initial five-year contract to manufacture a smart card designed with a view to giving it a much wider scope in the future. Its basic characteristics include:

- microchip and magnetic strip,
- multi-application operating system,
- a 6805 microprocessor,
- 128-byte RAM memory,
- 6 Kbytes ROM memory, and
- a 3 Kbytes EPROM for storing data.

According to a Spanish government spokesman, this is a multi-issuer and multi-use card, therefore it has to be adaptable to many different functions. For the social security department, microchip technology was the obvious choice but, as the card is also to be used by the Spanish health services (which had already chosen magnetic strip technology), it was decided to include both options.

For the uninitiated, this is the Spanish version of Mardi Gras. For the moment, the card will allow holders to consult their personal social welfare files, obtain general information from the different bodies involved in the project, register changes in their situation, consult job offers, renew their status as job seekers and to sign on for unemployment benefit.

- This is the best example I could find of a modernized state-supermarket which tries to be all things to all people – and fails on all counts.
- It is also a prime case of a fraud paradise: smart thiefs can use dumb money, cheat on social security, extract unemployment benefits, and/or change their record and status at will – all on one card.

Beyond the vast opportunities for forgery, this sort of complex and unfocused device is the antithesis to systems thinking, the Eden for the underworld within anyone's reach, but for the Spanish government the super-smart card is also expected to go a long way towards performing, other unspecified miracles as well.

Another super-smart card initiative is Cost 219, a cooperation between 19 European countries concerned with future telecommunication and tele-informatic facilities for the disabled and elderly people. Participating countries are: Austria, Belgium, Croatia, Denmark, Finland, France, Germany, Greece, Hungary, Ireland, Italy, Malta, the Netherlands, Norway, Portugal, Spain, Sweden, Switzerland and the UK.

Cost 219 was established in 1986, with a mandate to continue until 1996. It did not produce results, but it did not die either. It still vaguely aims to identify areas of new research that need to be undertaken and to stimulate the setting up of new projects.

- Such cards research, one might say, is not unlike cancer research.
- A key reason why no effective medicine can be found for cancer, advises a French saying, is that more people are living from the existence of this disease than dying from it.

One of the stated intial goals of Cost 219 was to make a smart card tool able to tell cash dispensers what are the specific abilities of the users (!). The terminal will then automatically adapt itself and behave in a way that the user wants it to behave. Anyone who believes such garbage will believe anything.

Few people today seem to remember that, in the late 1980s, there was another device competing in the 'super' class: the optical card featuring two megabytes' storage. It had no chip and instead encoded information that could be read by a laser beam. But optical cards proved to be non starters and they got no market subscriptions, apart from initial tests by Blue Cross/Blue Shield, Sumitomo, Olivetti and some others.

At about the same time, the late 1980s, in Chicago, Andersen Consulting created a prototype supermarket of the future that used chip-based smart cards to personalize the store. At check-out, the smart card not only paid for the purchase but also recorded the customer's favorite foods, brands, even details like birthdays and anniversaries. The demonstration was interesting, but there were no takers.

In the early 1990s, the US Department of Agriculture launched a pilot program with taxpayers' money to issue food stamps on smart cards. Each recipient was supposed to receive a card programmed with a month's worth of benefits, along with a personal identification number.

- The shopper would plug the card into a store's computer terminal, which would verify his identity and subtract the cost of the purchase from the card's memory chip.
- The smart card was supposed to stamp out black-market and counterfeit food stamps, as well as eliminate cumbersome paperwork – it did neither.

This idea and its trial did not pass the test of time and it is indeed curious that serious people today contemplate a revolution with smart cards, years after the sparks have been spent. It is always good business to be aware of the messages given by the market.

The failures I have mentioned are not the only ones in ill-defined, if not outright useless, projects with super-smart cards. In 1990, Visa International and several Japanese companies, including Toshiba, NTT, Japan Airlines (JAL), JR Tokai (one of the privatized regional railway companies) and the Hankyu railways-to-department stores group, conducted a research project with super-smart cards. When used with a video screen attached, these supercards were supposed to allow their owners to buy goods or make airline reservations from an armchair and then to transfer the funds to pay for what was being bought. The results have not been conclusive. This and other super-smart cards projects were supposed to go beyond what the smart card does with a chip – the Bull and Casio variety.

It puzzles me that the highly paid market researchers who are supposed to know what they are doing do not take care to study the mistakes and failures of the past. Often, they do not even ask what the banks and the merchants think before reaching conclusions.

- Few banks are willing to shoulder the cost of replacing their ATM hardware, as would be required with smart cards and the supers.
- Also consumers are not biting and ATM makers are not eager to change their designs.

Furthermore, with regard to security, several bankers figure that hackers will eventually break any code they confront on the smart card or the network. As it cannot be repeated too often, with smart cards and with cyber money the top issue is lack of security.

The second sticky point is who pays for the readers – and generally for the system. Once it was retailers who paid, just as they paid banks for handling cheques and credit cards. But this has changed, and in the last analysis both insecurity and the costs fall on the consumer.

Every smart card in the market can be duplicated because of the electromagnetic signals it emits. Then, it can be reproduced in thousand of clones.

8   INTERNET, ELECTRONIC MAIL AND LEGAL RESPONSIBILITIES

If one asks why all these failures, I would not hestitate to answer because of rush and the unwillingness to learn a lesson taught by the facts of life. But other people who are more critical may add because of lust and greed that is integral part of any battle for market share. Quite often,

- Little attention is paid to the hard issue of value differentiation as most 'solutions' are quite similar from a technical viewpoint.
- Is this also true with electronic commerce and electronic banking on the Internet? What about electronic mail?

Until quite recently, nobody seriously contested electronic mail in terms of legal responsibilities, other than the fact that messages could be intercepted on the network, as happens everywhere with electronic lines. But this, too, has changed. The week beginning 14 July 1997 saw a pace-setting libel judgment in the UK against insurer Norwich Union (NU). This is the first case in which a British company has received damages for an E-mail libel, and it has been ordered by the High Court to pay £450,000 ($742,500) in damages and costs to Western Provident Association.

The reason for the court decision is found in electronic mail messages written by NU staff spreading unfounded rumours about a business rival. These messages were posted on Norwich Union's internal system, but they reached brokers and clients (*Lloyds List*, 25 July 1997). The ruling spread the message that, in the eyes of the law, anyone communicating or disseminating information on the Internet is deemed to be *publishing*.

- As electronic publishers, both companies and individuals using the Internet are becoming exposed to libel and defamation risks.
- Previously, wherever they existed, such cases faced only the traditional civil responsibilities of the media industry.

With this High Court ruling, a new frame of reference has been established which suggests that the risks to businesses and consumers presented by the very wide circulation of E-Mail messages have widened. This is the direct result of the almost effortless copying and dissemination facilities at people's fingertips.

- The underworld's Eden of which we spoke in section 7 rests on this simple fact.
- If the less sophisticated E-mail can become a legal liability, think how fast smart money can turn into dumb money.

At the root of the problem is the fact that people tend to be rather more casual in their use of E-Mail than in other forms of publication. They also think E-mail messages have disappeared once they have been sent. But, to the contrary, internal messages between friends and colleagues can be spread across many organizations in just a few hours or a few days.

As far as E-mail is concerned, because the legal risk is real, employers should adopt adequate procedures to protect themselves against it. They should educate their staff and set strict rules for the use of E-mail. They should also handle sensitive information with great care. It goes without saying that even stiffer rules must apply with electronic money.

It is surprising that only a very few people appreciate the risks associated with electronic banking, electronic commerce or even simply electronic information. Substandard privacy and security on the Internet does not seem to bother the majority of people, but the US Social Security has taken another at the Web and decided otherwise.

In 1997, in America, the Social Security Administration shut a Website that supplied information about people's personal income and retirement, out of concern that the site could violate privacy rights.

- To keep up with the times, the US agency began offering detailed estimates of future benefits on the Internet.
- But experts on computers and privacy law expressed concern that safeguards were not enough to keep people from obtaining confidential electronic data.

Under the Federal Privacy Act of 1974, individuals are guaranteed access to information the government holds about them. But with Social Security numbers and mothers' maiden names available in public databases, the government had no way to confirm that the people requesting information on the Internet were the ones authorized to use the information.

This action by the Social Security Administration in the US joins the decision by the UK High Court in more than one way. Even if some of the best-known companies – from Microsoft to IBM – are now working on creating a universal method for keeping track of resources, with

- endusers,
- passwords,
- E-mail addresses,

- attached devices and
- software modules,

secure solutions do not seem to be around the corner. Yet a high level of security is important, whether we talk of a private corporate network or the public Internet.

As if to make matters worse, code breaking in networks has shaken confidence in the security of some very popular encryption schemes. Both cryptographers and computer experts are stunned at how easy it can be to unravel securely coded messages. Indeed, code breakers have recently found a back door through massive computer power:

- a wily snooper can figure out what the secret key is by keeping track of the length of time a computer takes to decipher messages;
- this approach can also be used with the so-called *certificate*, which essentially tells what the holder is – his digital identity. (See section 5.)

The cryptographic code may have leaks, with evident consequences for electronic money and Internet commerce. This is amplified by the fact that online users see the Web primarily as a channel for information gathering rather than for electronic banking.

- According to a survey of Internet users done by Georgia Tech and the University of Michigan, people are not inclined to trust Internet with important business deals, and even less with their financial payments and settlements. A major obstacle to online purchases is indeed security.

Let me add a note of scientific interest. The method currently used by hackers to break supposedly secure encryption codes is not too different from that employed by Alan Turing and his code breakers during World War II in connection with the German Enigma. Turing had constructed a machine which scanned each intercepted message for 'eins':

- 'eins' show up frequently in the German language;
- intercepting their location in military messages created a message content pattern.

Code breakers are smart and they live within the same user community as the bankers and the merchants. Hence they know which of the popular software makers uses which technique to prevent attacks on encrypted transmissions.

9   CYBERMONEY, FINANCIAL REGULATION AND MONEY SUPPLY

An even bigger challenge than security, in the classical sense of the word, is the study of the consequences of electronic money. These can hit the dollar, the pound, the DM, the yen – and also create new kinds of composite currencies beyond ECU and SDR.

Let me start with a brief definition. Today's popular term *electronic money* came to be used in connection with stored-value cards, which this chapter has covered in detail. By contrast, tomorrow's meaning of the same term shifts toward *network money*:

- payment units in computer networks define electronic credit balances in movable or fixed computer storage;
- movable storage may be in smart cards or the hard disk of a personal computer. Fixed storage is at the bank's computer center.

What underpins electronic money is that it can readily serve as a means for payment, to fulfill various payment obligations. This can be done by transferring the credit balance from one storage device to another, over some medium.

What will be the effect of electronic money on money supply? What if tomorrow smart card payments go well in excess of \$50, rivaling or even exceeding the average transaction with credit cards? How great will be the effect of counterfeiting on money supply? Will it hit some currencies more than others?

Financial regulators in the United States have set up a task force to examine how emerging electronic transactions, and most particularly transactions on the Internet, will affect current rules for payment systems. As Robert Rubin, the US Treasury secretary, stated:

- electronic money poses difficult issues in consumer protection,
- while central banks and governments want to avoid inappropriate regulation (*Financial Times*, 20 September 1996).

Two US agencies, The Federal Deposit Insurance Corporation (FDIC) and the Treasury, are looking at the necessary regulatory measures jointly regarding the development of electronic money, Rubin suggested. But there is still a great deal of work to be done.

Because digital cash is not necessarily part of a government-guaranteed insurance scheme, a non-bank type of digital cash is inherently riskier for the consumer or the merchant than bank-issued digital cash. It is actually more like coupons than cash. But the money supply magnification effect which it possesses is the best prescription possible for a global system risk.

The problem is very complex, and the ongoing study may lead to a change in the current position, where the prevailing legal advice from the government is that money held on most smart cards offered by banks does not technically qualify as a deposit. Therefore

- it does not count in the money supply;
- also it does not have state insurance.

In the US, the Smart Card Forum, a grouping of the largest card offerers, is broadly supportive of the government's stance to rethink deposits qualifications. But it also cautions that it would be premature to introduce detailed regulations now as they might be rendered technologically obsolete within a year or so.

This problem of rapid obsolescence of regulatory ruling because of technology is not going to disappear with time. If anything, it will become more accute. During the working meeting I had at the Bank of England on 25 September, 1996, central bankers expressed concern about the Internet and cybermoney, because there are still too many problems with unknowns, from network access and security, to the effects of cybermoney on money supply. In the background was the issue that, in both cases, one can get a great deal of exposure. Therefore, the whole question of electronic money is now elaborated in the UK by the Bank of England and internationally by the Bank for International Settlements (BIS). Many subjects are being debated among central banks:

- Who should be allowed to issue cybermoney, and who should not?
- Is electronic money like deposit-taking or is it not?
- How should cybermoney be regulated? On which statistics?
- Which will be the most likely effect of cybermoney and smart cards on the money supply?

The Swiss National Bank comes closer than other central banks to accounting for digital cash, having instituted the *transactions account* as part of M1, but, to complicate matters, digital cash is not always cash. Figure 16.2 explains what enters into M1 metrics of money supply. Notice that this definition provides a common ground. It is accurate but not precise, because no two central banks count M1 the same way, nor are the statistics exactly the same in the different countries.

About a third of M1 is M0. M0 is a British definition which counts coins and notes in circulation. Smart cards target the role today played by coins and small notes. Hence they should be part of M0. There is no ruling yet to that effect.

About two thirds of M1 is banking book money. There is no limit to the amount the banking system can expand the money supply, advised Marriner Eccles, a former chairman of the Federal Reserve. Cybermoney used for payments and settlements of commercial transaction should, in principle, fall into this class.

- Here again there is no decision yet on this matter by central banks.
- Indeed, there can be no decision as long as cybermoney is considered to be off the banking book (non-deposits).

If cybermoney was in the banking book and a financial institution were to issue digital cash, its creation would be considered a withdrawal from its deposits, or,

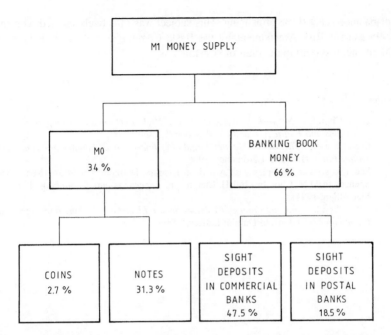

Figure 16.2 Notes, coins and banking book money as percentages of M1 money supply

alternatively, the printing of new money. In a way, the bank would be obliged to credit user accounts for deposits of digital cash.

Most foggy is the issue of whether or not electronic money would need real funds to back it up, other than a legal reserve limit for the original deposits. As the practice of using cybermoney spreads, and statistics point to substantial amounts, it could be considered cash in circulation – thereby significantly increasing the money supply.

If the issue of cybermoney is taken to be a money withdrawal, then withdrawing digital cash reduces the amount of deposits the bank has available for extending loans. It also reduces the expansion of the money supply. But is this a sound policy? No documented answer has yet been given to this query.

If a non-bank bank were to issue digital cash, taking on central bank functions, this would open Pandora's box in terms of aftermaths. Leaving aside the fact that such an operation could be backed up only by the willingness of merchants to accept electronic cash as a unit of payment, how is the reserve bank going to supervise such an operation when it has no control over non-banks?

The more I look into these issues, the more I am under the impression that we are moving towards a repetition of the mistakes made in the 1980s with off-balance sheet (OBS) financing. This subject was effectively tackled with the 1996 Market Risk Amendment by the Basle Committee, only after it brought the financial system to the limit of systemic risk.

Notes

1.   D.N. Chorafas, *Network Computers versus High Performance Computers: New Directions and Future Applications* (London: Cassell, 1997).

2.   D.N. Chorafas, *The Money Magnet. Regulating International Finance and Analyzing Money Flows* (London: Euromoney, 1996).

3.   See also similar examples with American Express, Diamond Credit and Marks and Spencer in D.N. Chorafas and H. Steinmann, *Expert Systems in Banking* (London: Macmillan, 1991).

4.   D.N. Chorafas, *Internet Financial Devices Secure Electronic Banking and Electronic Commerce*? (London and Dublin: Lafferty, 1998).

Appendix: What is the Sense of Branding?

Because *branding* has become a key word in retail banking, and more generally in commercial banking, I felt it necessary to explain to the reader some basic issues concerning its concept and its process. This short essay is not a critique of branding in the banking industry as such, but of the fact that some bankers think that they can survive and prosper through gimmicks.

Let us start with the fundamentals. Visa, MasterCard and Eurocard are *brands*, but no single financial institution has a lock on them. The American Express credit card is a brand of AmEx, which is not a bank. Only Citibank can say that it owns a credit card brand: Diner's Club.

Branding usually implies the registration of a *brand name*, and patent protection as well. Coca Cola, Procter and Gamble, Unilever and the Imperial Chemical Industries (ICI) can do so. There are, however, two industries where patents and copyrights do not truly hold. These are banking and software.

- There is no copyright in the banking industry.
- Any competitor can do the same – and do it better or cheaper.

Yet, with innovation, deregulation and globalization being the moving gears of the financial industry today, there is plenty of scope for a solution on which is able effectively to

- protect intellectual property, and
- permit differentiation of one bank from another.

By 1999, in the United States, banks and savings and loans will have the same charters, eliminating the legal difference between the two entities (*Business Week*, March 24, 1997). In the United Kingdom, too, several building societies are converting into banking institutions. In a way, the distinction which formally existed between savings banks and commercial banks, and commercial banks and investment banks is disappearing. To compensate, banks try to find some other way to differentiate. Technological leadership, for instance, offers such an opportunity, but also poses stiff requirements in terms of investments and skills. Is *branding* a softer approach?

Many retail bankers think that today, and well into the 21st century, the cornerstone of retail marketing is the development of a brand concept. Therefore they drive for *own-brand products* and look at them as the means to

- produce improved margins, and
- increase pressure on competitors.

The banking industry has taken this concept from merchandizing, where brand management is seen as the way to create strong identities for cosmetics, soaps, pharmaceuticals, cars, trucks, cornflakes and toothpaste.

Another critical issue associated with branding is that of public recognition because of being a known leader in the industry. In high technology, for instance, Intel, Microsoft and Cisco share the distinction of being ranked in the top five among *Fortune 500* companies both by:

- Return on sales, and
- Return on assets.

Microsoft has a market value of $200 billion. But even though Cisco has a market value of $58 billion (nearly 30 percent more than General Motors), this company is still unknown even to many dedicated computer users.

Financial analysts say that Cisco is now obsessed with getting brand recognition – and it plans an 'Intel inside'-type ad. The company can capitalize on its market share as it already has close to a 70 percent of the market in its core router business:

- Cisco is either first or second in every other market in which it operates.
- It also has the policy of buying any company that has a technology it fancies.

As in the banking industry, many high technology firms now feel that serious brand-building is important because big IT contracts are increasingly being awarded at Board level, rather than through a decision by IT managers.

There is a growing number of companies who believe that their future will greatly be influenced by choices made at the Board of Directors' level of firms that operate far beyond the confines of their core business. In the technology industry, for example, brand recognition can help to win over non-technical executives, raising the barriers to smaller, less known rivals – as IBM did.

Among the myriad of players in the global market, few companies, however, understand that, whether we talk of banking products, semiconductors, software or minivans, the key to *brand management* is to stop chasing your competition and start chasing your customer – with something he or she cannot afford to miss. This must be done in a coordinated manner, and there must be clear incentives:

- with the brand manager's pay linked to the brand's success, and
- with advertising, pricing and planning handled by a competent person for each brand.

This type of approach can be very costly in banking, particularly so for the smaller banks. Branding is a business of segmenting the mass market, keeping for ourselves the better segment. But even the big banks do not have as wide a market follow-up as, say, Procter and Gamble, where branding makes sense.

In some countries, such as the United States, few of the larger banks operate coast-to-coast – and even when they do so, it is through acquisitions, hence under a different name. In a country where about 15 percent of households move house every year, closing bank accounts and opening new ones at a different bank in their new town, mobility turns branding on its head. There is, however, a counter-argument to what I have just said. The contrarian view is that, operating the traditional way, banks lose the business of many of their customers who are moving. Therefore some banks have started using networks with two main goals:

- to keep within the fold most customers who were moving, and
- to win a large share of the business of technology-oriented people moving into the bank's own region.

This strategy blends branding with technology, but it is subject to the constraints identified in the early part of this Appendix. Besides this, branding as a dream or as a cure for eveything would not do. The key ingredients must be *focus* and *ingenious* tactics. Master performers provide examples. At Microsoft, the strategy guiding difficult tactical decisions regarding the direction of product development is referred to as *embrace and extend*. For instance, rather than invent a whole new service to compete on the Internet, Microsoft would

- embrace current net standards,
- then extend them through added value.

If Netscape lets Web browsers look at pages from around the world, Microsoft would let users look at Web pages from within familiar applications. If the Navigator could play sound, Explorer would play quality sound. In other terms, Microsoft wins by *outfeaturing* its competitors.

In essence, that is what Coca-Cola, Unilever and other ingenious mass marketers do with their brands, while relying on relentless advertising through television and other media to imprint the brand message on the public's mind. Asked about the secret behind his company's success, Coca-Cola's chairman answered: 'Early to bed, early to rise and advertise, advertise, advertise.' Retail banks are not well positioned to do this. They do not have the concept, they do not have the margins and they do not have the market.

There are cultural and structural constraints as well. Brand-oriented organizations should be keen to avert the risk of competing brand managers ending up brawling among themselves as they vie for marketing money and management attention. In fact, such rough corners led Procter and Gamble itself to *abandon brand management* in 1988. It is, therefore, a little difficult to see why, 10 years down the line, some commercial banks become so excited and eager to jump on the branding bandwagon.

Deciding that its system was pitting brands like Camay and Ivory soaps against one another, Procter and Gamble switched to *category management,* in which managers oversaw whole product categories. This solution is indeed much closer to what the bank industry needs. At Citibank, for instance, the categories are called *channels,* and they are the main product lines on which senior management is focusing attention – through which it reaches the market and makes good profits.

Acknowledgments

The following organizations, their senior executives and system specialists, participated in the research projects which led to the contents of the present book and its documentation.

UNITED STATES

Federal Reserve Bank of Boston

* William N. McDONOUGH, Executive Vice President – Legal
* Richard KOPCKE, Vice President and Economist
* Peter FORTUNE, Senior Economist
* George ALEXAKOS, Examiner
* Katerina SIMONS, Economist
* Joanna STAVINS, Economist
* Jane KATZ, Editor, Regional Review

600 Atlantic Avenue, Boston, MA 02106-2976

Seattle Branch, Federal Reserve Bank of San Francisco

* Jimmy F. KAMADA, Assistant Vice President
* Gale P. ANSELL, Assistant Vice President, Business Development

1015, 2nd Avenue, Seattle, WA 98122-3567

Federal Reserve Bank of San Francisco

* Matthew FOSS, Manager, Capital Markets
* Nigel OGILVIE, Banking Supervision and Regulation

101 Market Street, San Francisco, CA 94120

State Street Bank and Trust

* James J. DARR, Executive Vice President, US Financial Assets Services

225 Franklin Street, Boston, MA 02105-1992

Bankers Trust

* Dr. Carmine VONA, Executive Vice President for Worldwide Technology
* Shalom BRINSY, Senior Vice President Distributed Networks
* Dan W. MUECKE, Vice President, Technology Strategic Planning
* Bob GRAHAM, Vice President, Database Manager

One Bankers Trust Plaza, New York, NY 10006

Citibank

* Colin CROOK, Chairman Corporate Technology Committee
* Dr. Daniel SCHUTZER, Senior Vice President, Information Technology
* Jim CALDARELLA, Manager, Business Architecture for Global Finance
* Nicholas P. RICHARDS, Database Administrator
* William BRINDLEY, Technology Officer
* Michael R. VEALE, Network Connectivity
* Harriet SCHABES, Corporate Standards
* Leigh REEVE, Technology for Global Finance

399 Park Avenue, New York, NY 10043

Morgan Stanley

* Gary T. GOEHRKE, Managing Director, Information Services
* Guy CHIARELLO, Vice President, Databases
* Robert F. DE YOUNG, Principal, Information Technology

1933 Broadway, New York, NY 10019

* Eileen S. WALLACE, Vice President, Treasury Department
* Jacqueline T. BRODY, Treasury Department

1251 Avenue of the Americas, New York, NY 10020

Goldman Sachs

* Peter T. HOVERSTEN, Vice President, Information Technology
* Leo J. ESPOSITO, Vice President, Information Systems
* David FLAXMAN, Advanced Technology Group
* Malcolm DRAPER, Architect, Communications Systems
* Fred M. KATZ, Applications Architect, Equity Sales and Trading
* Vincent L. AMATULLI, Information Technology, Treasury Department

85 Broad Street, New York, NY 10004

J.J. Kenny Services Inc.

* Thomas E. ZIELINSKI, Chief Information Officer
* Ira KIRSCHNER, Database Administrator, Director of System Programming and of the Data Center

65, Broadway, New York, NY1006

Merrill Lynch

* Kevin SAWYER, Director of Distributed Computing Services and Executive in Charge of the Mainframe to Client-Server Conversion Process
* Raymond M. DISCO, Treasury/Bank Relations Manager

World Financial Center, South Tower, New York, NY 10080-6107

Teachers, Insurance and Annuity Association/College Retirement Equities Fund (TIAA/CREF)

* Charles S. DVORKIN, Vice President and Chief Technology Officer
* Harry D. PERRIN, Assistant Vice President, Information Technology

730 Third Avenue, New York, NY 10017-3206

Financial Accounting Standards Board

* Halsey G. BULLEN, Project Manager
* Jeannot BLANCHET, Project Manager
* Teri L. LIST, Practice Fellow

401 Merritt 7, Norwalk, CN 06856

Teknekron Software Systems, Inc.

* Vivek RANADIVE, President and CEO
* Robert RECTOR, Senior Vice President, Client Technical Services
* Martin LUTHI, Senior Director, Client Technical Services
* Gerard D. BUGGY, Vice President, Global Financial Sales and Marketing
* Norman CHEUNG, Director, Quantum Leap Group
* Bradley C. RHODE, Vice President, Core Technology Engineering
* Tugrul FIRATLI, Director, Network Consulting Services
* John E. McDOWALL
* Tom JASEK, Director, Market Sheet

* Glenn A. McCOMB, Senior Member of Technical Staff, New Technologies
* Murat K. SONMEZ, Member of Technical Staff
* Murray D. RODE, Member of Technical Staff

530 Lytton Avenue, Suite 301, Palo Alto, CA 94301

Evans and Sutherland

* Les HORWOOD, Director New Business Development
* Mike WALTERMAN, Systems Engineer, Virtual Reality Applications
* Lisa B. HUBER, Software Engineer, 3-Dimensional Programming

600 Komas Drive, P.O.Box 58700, Salt Lake City, Utah 84158

nCUBE

* Michael MEIRER, President and Chief Executive Officer
* Craig D. RAMSEY, Senior Vice President, Worldwide Sales
* Ronald J. BUCK, Vice President, Marketing
* Matthew HALL, Director of Software Development

919 East Hillside Blvd, Foster City, CA 94404

Visual Numerics

* Don KAINER, Vice President and General Manager
* Joe WEAVER, Vice President OEM/VAR Sales
* Jim PHILLIPS, Director Product Development
* Dr. Shawn JAVID, Senior Product Manager
* Dan CLARK, Manager, WAVE Family Products
* Thomas L. WELCH, Marketing Product Manager
* Margaret JOURNEY, Director Administration
* John BEE, Technical Sales Engineer
* Adam ASNES, VDA Sales Executive
* William POTTS, Sales Manager

6230 Lookout Road, Boulder, Colorado 80301

Massachusetts Institute of Technology

* Prof. Dr. Stuart E. MADNICK, Information Technology and Management Science
* Prof. Dr. Michael SIEGEL, Information Technology, Sloan School of Management

* Patricia M. McGINNIS, Executive Director, International Financial Services
* Prof. Peter J. KEMPTHORNE, Project on Non-Traditional Methods in Financial Analysis
* Dr. Alexander M. SAMAROV, Project on Non-Traditional Methods in Financial Analysis
* Robert R. HALPERIN, Executive Director, Center for Coordination Science
* Professor Amar GUPTA, Sloan School of Management
* Professor Jean-Luc VILA, Finance Dept., Sloan School of Management
* Professor Bin ZHOU, Management Science, Sloan School of Management

292 Main Street, Cambridge, MA 02139

* Eric B. SUNDIN, Industrial Liaison Officer
* David L. VERRILL, Senior Liaison Officer, Industrial Liaison Program

Sloan School of Management
50 Memorial Drive, Cambridge, MA 02139

* Henry H. HOUH, Desk Area Network and ViewStation Project, Electrical Engineering and Computer Science
* Dr. Henry A. LIEBERMAN, Media Laboratory
* Valerie A. EAMES, Media Laboratory
* Prof. Dr. Kenneth B. HAASE, Media Arts and Sciences
* Dr. David ZELTZER, Virtual Reality Project

Ames St., Cambridge, MA 02139

University of Michigan

* Professor John H. HOLLAND, Electrical Engineering and Computer Science
* Dr. Rick L. RIOLO, Systems Researcher, Department of Psychology

Ann Arbor, MI 48109-2103

Santa Fe Institute

* Dr. Edward A. KNAPP, President
* Dr. L. Mike SIMMONS, Jr., Vice President
* Dr. Bruce ABELL, Vice President Finance
* Prof. Dr. Murray GELL-MANN, Theory of Complexity
* Prof. Dr. Stuart KAUFFMAN, Models in Biology
* Dr. Chris LANGTON, Artificial Life

* Dr. John MILLER, Adaptive Computation in Economics
* Dr. Blake LE BARON, Non-Traditional Methods in Economics
* Bruce SAWHILL, Virtual Reality

1660 Old Pecos Trail, Santa Fe, NM 87501

**School of Engineering and Applied Science,
University of California, Los Angeles**

* Dean A.R. Frank WAZZAN, School of Engineering and Applied Science
* Prof. Richard MUNTZ, Chair, Computer Science Department
* Prof.Dr. Leonard KLEINROCK, Telecommunications and Networks
* Professor Nicolaos G. ALEXOPOULOS, Electrical Engineering
* Prof.Dr. Judea PEARL, Cognitive Systems Laboratory
* Prof.Dr. Walter KARPLUS, Computer Science Department
* Prof.Dr. Michael G. DYER, Artificial Intelligence Laboratory
* Ms. Susan CRUSE, Director of Development and Alumni Affairs
* Joel SHORT, Ph.D. Candidate
* David Chickering, Ph.D. Candidate

Westwood Village, Los Angeles, CA 90024

School of Business Administration, University of Southern California

* Dr. Bert M. STEECE, Dean of Faculty, School of Business Administration
* Dr. Alan ROWE, Professor of Management

Los Angeles, CA 90089-1421

Prediction Company

* Dr. J. Doyne FARMER, Director of Development
* Dr. Norman H. PACKARD, Director of Research
* Jim McGILL, Managing Director

234 Griffin Street, Santa Fe, NM 87501

Nynex Science and Technology, Inc.

* Thomas M. SUPER, Vice President, Research and Development
* Steven CROSS, NYNEX Shuttle Project
* Valerie R. TINGLE, System Analyst
* Melinda CREWS, Public Liaison, NYNEX Labs.

500 Westchester Avenue, White Plains, NY 10604

* John C. FALCO, Sales Manager, NYNEX Systems Marketing
* David J. ANNINO, Account Executive, NYNEX Systems Marketing

100 Church Street, New York, NY 10007

Microsoft

* Mike McGEEHAN, Database Specialist
* Andrew ELLIOTT, Marketing Manager

825, 8th Avenue, New York, NY

Reuters America

* Robert RUSSEL, Senior Vice President
* William A.S. KENNEDY, Vice President
* Buford SMITH, President, Reuters Information Technology
* Richard A. WILLIS, Manager International Systems Design
* M.A. SAYERS, Technical Manager, Central Systems Development
* Alexander FAUST, Manager Financial Products USA (Instantlink and Blend)

40 E. 52nd Street, New York, NY 10022

Oracle Corporation

* Scott MATTHEWS, National Account Manager
* Robert T. FUNK, Senior Systems Specialist
* Joseph M. DI BARTOLOMEO, Systems Specialist
* Dick DAWSON, Systems Specialist

885 Third Avenue, New York, NY 10022

Digital Equipment Corporation

* Mike FISHBEIN, Product Manager, Massively Parallel Systems (MAS-PAR Supercomputer)
* Marco EMRICH, Technology Manager, NAS
* Robert PASSMORE, Technical Manager, Storage Systems
* Mark S. DRESDNER, DEC Marketing Operations

146 Main Street, Maynard, MA 01754
(Meeting held at UBS New York)

Unisys Corporation

* Harvey J. CHIAT, Director Impact Programs
* Manuel LAVIN, Director, Databases
* David A. GOIFFON, Software Engineer

P.O.Box 64942, MS 4463, Saint Paul, MN, 55164-0942

Hewlett-Packard

* Brad WILSON, Product Manager, Commercial Systems
* Vish KRISHNAN, Manager R+D Laboratory
* Samir MATHUR, Open ODB Manager
* Michael GUPTA, Transarc, Tuxedo, Encina Transaction Processing
* Dave WILLIAMS, Industry Account Manager

1911, Pruneridge Avenue, Cupertino, CA 95014

IBM Corporation

* Terry LIFFICK, Software Strategies, Client-Server Architecture
* Paula CAPPELLO, Information Warehouse Framework
* Ed COBBS, Transaction Processing Systems
* Dr. Paul WILMS, Connectivity and Interoperability
* Helen ARZU, IBM Santa Teresa Representative
* Dana L. STETSON, Advisory Marketing IBM New York

Santa Teresa Laboratory, 555 Bailey Avenue, San José, CA 95141

UBS Securities

* A. Ramy GOLDSTEIN, Managing Director, Equity Derivative Products

299 Park Avenue, New York, NY 10171-0026

Union Bank of Switzerland

* Dr. H. BAUMANN, Director of Logistics, North American Operations
* Dr. Ch. GABATHULER, Director, Information Technology
* Hossur SRIKANTAN, Vice President Information Technology Department
* Roy M. DARHIN, Assistant Vice President

299 Park Avenue, New York, NY 10171-0026

UNITED KINGDOM

Bank of England

* W.D.R. SWANNEY, C.A., Head of Division, Supervision and Surveillance
* Patricia JACKSON, Special Advisor, Regulatory and Supervisory Policy
* Mark LAYCOCK, Banking Supervision

Threadneedle Street, London EC2R 8AH

British Bankers, Association

* Paul CHISNALL, Assistant Director

Pinners Hall, 105-108 Old Broad Street, London EC2N 1EX

Accounting Standards Board

* A.V.C. COOK, Technical Director
* Sandra THOMPSON, Project Director

Holborn Hall, 100 Gray's Inn Road, London WC1X 8AL

Barclays Bank

* Alan BROWN, Director Group Credit Policy
* Brandon DAVIES, Treasurer UK Group

54 Lombard Street, London EC3P 3AH

* Peter GOLDEN, Chief Information Officer, Barclays Capital Markets, Treasury, BZW
* David J. PARSONS, Director Advanced Technology
* Christine E. IRWIN, Group Information Systems Technology

Murray House, 1 Royal Mint Court, London EC3N 4HH

Abbey National Bank

* Mac MILLINGTON, Director of Information Technology

Chalkdell Drive, Shenley Wood, Milton Keynes MK6 6LA

* Anthony W. ELLIOTT, Director of Risk and Credit

Abbey House, Baker Street, London NW1 6XL

Natwest Securities

* Sam B. GIBB, Director of Information Technology
* Don F. SIMPSON, Director, Global Technology
* Richard E. GIBBS, Director, Equity Derivatives Derivatives

135 Bishopsgate, London EC2M 3XT

Credit Swiss Financial Products

* Ross SALINGER, Managing Director

One Cabot Square, London E14 4QJ

Credit Swiss First Boston

* Geoff J.R. DOUBLEDAY, Executive Director

One Cabot Square, London E14 4QJ

Bankgesellschaft Berlin

* Stephen F. MYERS, Head of Market Risk

1 Crown Court, Cheapside, London

British Telecom

* Dr. Alan RUDGE, Deputy Managing Director

BT Centre, 81 Newgate Street, London EC1A 7AJ

Association for Payment Clearing Services (APACS)

* J. Michael WILLIAMSON, Deputy Chief Executive

14 Finsbury Square, London EC2A 1BR

Oracle Corporation

* Mr. Geoffrey W. SQUIRE, Executive Vice President, and Chief Executive
* Mr. Richard BARKER, Senior Vice President and Director British Research Laboratories

* Mr. Giles GODART-BROWN, Senior Support Manager
* Mr. Paul A. GOULD, Account Executive

Oracle Park, Bittams Lane, Guildford Rd, Chertsey,
Surrey KT16 9RG

E.D. & F. Man International

* Brian FUDGE, Funds Division

Sugar Quay, Lower Thames Street, London EC3R 6DU

Prudential-Bache Securities

* Stephen MASSEY, Regional Director – Europe

9 Devonshire Square, London EC2M 4HP

SCANDINAVIA

Sveriges Riksbank

* Gran ZETTERGREN, Economics Department

Brunkebergstorg 11, S-103 37 Stockholm

Vaerdipapircentralen (VP)

* Mr. Jens BACHE, General Manager
* Mrs. Aase BLUME, Assistant to the General Manager

61 Helgeshoj Allé, Postbox 20, 2630 Taastrup, Denmark

Swedish Bankers' Association

* Mr. Bo GUNNARSSON, Manager, Bank Automation Department
* Mr. Gösta FISCHER, Manager, Bank-Owned Financial Companies Department
* Mr. Göran AHLBERG, Manager, Credit Market Affairs Department

P.O. Box 7603, 10394 Stockholm, Sweden

---

440 Acknowledgments

Skandinaviska Enskilda Banken

* Mr. Lars ISACSSON, Treasurer
* Mr. Urban JANELD, Executive Vice President Finance and IT
* Mr. Mats ANDERSSON, Director of Computers and Communications
* Mr. Gösta OLAVI, Manager SEB Data/Koncern Data

2 Sergels Torg, 10640 Stockholm, Sweden

Securum AB

* Mr. Anders NYREN, Director of Finance and Accounting
* Mr. John LUNDGREN, Manager of IT

38 Regeringsg, 5 tr., 10398 Stockholm, Sweden

Sveatornet AB of the Swedish Savings Banks

* Mr. Gunar M. CARLSSON, General Manager

(Meeting at Swedish Bankers' Association)

Mandamus AB of the Swedish Agricultural Banks

* Mrs. Marie MARTINSSON, Credit Department

(Meeting at Swedish Bankers' Association)

Handelsbanken

* Mr. Janeric SUNDIN, Manager, Securities Department
* Mr. Jan ARONSON, Assistant Manager, Securities Department

(Meeting at Swedish Bankers' Association)

Gota Banken

* Mr. JOHANNSSON, Credit Department

(Meeting at Swedish Bankers' Association)

Irdem AB

* Gian MEDRI, Former Director of Research at Nordbanken

19 Flintlasvagen, 19154 Sollentuna, Sweden

AUSTRIA

Bank Austria

* Dr. Peter FISCHER, Senior General Manager, Treasury Division
* Peter GABRIEL, Deputy General Manager, Trading
* Konrad SCHCATE, Manager, Financial Engineering

2, Am Hof, 1010 Vienna

Creditanstalt Bankverein

* Dr. Wolfgang G. LICHTL, Director of Foreign Exchange and Money Markets
* Dr. Johann STROBL, Manager, Financial Analysis for Treasury Operations

3, Julius Tandler-Platz, 1090 Vienna

Association of Austrian Banks and Bankers

* Dr. Fritz DIWOK, Secretary General

11, Boersengasse, 1013 Vienna

Wiener Betriebs- und Baugesellschaft mbH

* Dr. Josef FRITZ, General Manager

1 Anschützstrasse, 1153 Vienna

Management Data of Creditanstalt

* Ing. Guenther REINDL, Vice President, International Banking Software
* Ing. Franz NECAS, Project Manager, RICOS
* Mag. Nikolas GOETZ, Product Manager, RICOS

21-25 Althanstrasse, 1090 Vienna

GERMANY

Deutsche Bundesbank

* Eckhard OECHLER, Director of Bank Supervision and Legal Matters

14, Wilhelm Epstein Strasse, D-6000 Frankfurt 50

Deutsche Bank

* Peter GERARD, Executive Vice President, Organization and Information Technology
* Hermann SEILER, Senior Vice President, Investment Banking and Foreign Exchange Systems
* Dr. KUHN, Investment Banking and Foreign Exchange Systems
* Dr. Stefan KOLB, Organization and Technological Development

12, Koelner Strasse, D-6236 Eschborn

Dresdner Bank

* Dr. Karsten WOHLENBERG, Project Leader Risk Management, Simulation and Analytics Task Force Financial Division
* Hans-Peter LEISTEN, Mathematician
* Susanne LOESKEN, Organization and IT Department

43, Mainzer Landstrasse, D-6000 Frankfurt

Commerzbank

* Helmut HOPPE, Director Organization and Information Technology
* Hermann LENZ, Director Controllership, Internal Accounting and Management Accounting
* Harald LUX, Manager Organization and Information Technology
* Waldemar NICKEL, Manager Systems Planning

155, Mainzer Landstrasse, D-60261 Frankfurt

Deutscher Sparkassen und Giroverband

* Manfred KRUEGER, Division Manager,
  Card Strategy

4 Simrockstrasse, D-5300 Bonn 1

Media Systems

* Bertram ANDERER, Director

6, Goethestrasse, D-7500 Karlsruhe

Fraunhofer Institute for Computer Graphics

* Dr. Ing. Martin GOEBEL
* Wolfgang FELBER

7, Wilhelminerstrasse, D-6100 Darmstadt

GMD First – Research Institute for Computer Architecture, Software Technology and Graphics

* Prof. Dr. Ing. Wolfgang K. GILOI, General Manager
* Dr. BEHR, Administrative Director
* Dr. Ulrich BRUENING, Chief Designer
* Dr. Joerg NOLTE, Designer of Parallel Operating Systems Software
* Dr. Matthias KESSLER, Parallel Languages and Parallel Compilers
* Dr. Friedrich W. SCHROER, New Programming Paradigms
* Dr. Thomas LUX, Fluid Dynamics, Weather Prediction and Pollution Control Project

5, Rudower Chaussee, D-1199 Berlin

Siemens Nixdorf

* Wolfgang WEISS, Director of Banking Industry Office
* Bert KIRSCHBAUM, Manager, Dresdner Bank Project
* Mark MILLER, Manager Neural Networks Project for UBS and German banks
* Andrea VONERDEN, Business Management Department

27, Lyoner Strasse, D-6000 Frankfurt 71

UBS Germany

* H.-H. v. SCHELIHA, Director, Organization and Information Technology
* Georg SUDHAUS, Manager IT for Trading Systems
* Marco BRACCO, Trader
* Jaap VAN HARTEN, Trader

52, Bleichstrasse, D-6000 Frankfurt 1

FRANCE

Banque de France

* Pierre JAILLET, Director, Monetary Studies and Statistics

*   Yvan ODONNAL, Manager, Monetary Analyses and Statistics
*   G. TOURNEMIRE, Analyst, Monetary Studies

39, rue Croix des Petits Champs, 75001 Paris

**Secretariat General de la Commission Bancaire –
Banque de France**

*   Didier PENY, Head of Supervisory Policy and Research Division
*   Michel MARTINO, International Affairs
*   Benjamin SAHEL, Market Risk Control

115, rue de Reaumur, 75002 Paris

**Ministry of Finance and the Economy, Conseil National de la
Compatibilité**

*   Alain LE BARS, Director International Relations and Cooperation

6, rue Louise WEISS, 75703 Paris Cedex 13

ITALY

Banca d'Italia

*   Eugenio GAIOTTI, Research Department, Monetary and Financial Division

Banca d'Italia, Rome

Istituto Bancario San Paolo di Torino

*   Dr. Paolo CHIUMENTI, Director of Budgeting
*   Roberto COSTA, Director of Private Banking
*   Pino RAVELLI, Director Bergamo Region

via G. Camozzi 27, 24121 Bergamo

LUXEMBOURG

Banque Generale du Luxembourg

*   Prof. Dr. Yves WAGNER, Director of Asset and Risk Management
*   Hans-Jörg PARIS, International Risk Manager

* Dirk VAN REETH, Manager Department of Companies and Legal Structures
* Dr. Luc RODESCH, Investment Advisor

27, avenue Monterey, L-2951 Luxembourg

Cedel

* André LUSSI, Chief Executive Officer
* Ray SOUDAH, Chief Financial and Investment Officer

67 Bd Grande-Duchesse Charlotte, L-1010 Luxembourg

SWITZERLAND

Swiss National Bank

* Robert FLURI, Assistant Director Statistics Section
* Dr. Werner HERMANN, Risk Management
* Dr. Christian WALTER, Representative to the Basle Committee

15, Brsenstrasse, 8022 Zürich

Bank for International Settlements

* Claude SIVY, Director, Controllership and Operational Security
* Frederik C. MUSCH, Secretary General, Basel Committee on Banking Supervision

2 Centralbankplatz, Basel

Swiss Bank Corporation

* Dr. Marcel ROHNER, Director, IFD Controlling

Swiss Bank Center, 8010 Zürich, Switzerland

BZ Bank Zurich

* Martin EBNER, President
* Peter SJOSTRAND, Finance
* Olivier WILLI, Analyst
* Roger JENNY, Analyst

50 Sihlstrasse, 8021 Zürich, Switzerland

BZ Trust Aktiengesellschaft

* Dr. Stefan HOLZER, Financial Analyst

24 Eglirain, 8832 Wilen, Switzerland

Ciba – Geigy AG

* Stefan JANOVJAK, Divisional Information Manager
* Natalie PAPEZIK, Information Architect

Ciba-Geigy, R-1045, 5.19, 4002 Basle Switzerland

Ecole Polytechnique Federal de Lausanne

* Prof. Dr. Jean-Daniel NICOUD, Director, Microinformatics Laboratory
* Prof. Dr. Boi FALTINGS, Artificial Intelligence
* Prof. Dr. Martin J. HASLER, Circuits and Systems
* Dr. Ing. Roman BOULIC, Computer Graphics

1015 Lausanne, Switzerland

Eurodis

* Albert MUELLER, Director
* Beat ERZER, Marketing Manager
* B. PEDRAZZINI, Systems Engineer
* Reto ALBERTINI, Sales Engineer

Bahnhofstrasse 58/60, CH-8105 Regensdorf, Switzerland

Olsen and Associates

* Dr. Richard OLSEN, Chief Executive Officer

232 Seefeldstrasse, 8008 Zurich, Switzerland

JAPAN

Bank of Japan

* Harry TOYAMA, Counsel and Chief Manager, Credit and Market Management Department
* Akira IEDA, Credit and Market Management Department

2-1-1, Kongoku-Cho, Nihonbashi, Chuo-ku, Tokyo 103

Dai-Ichi Kangyo Bank

* Shunsuke NAKASUJI, General Manager and Director, Information Technology Division
* Seiichi HASEGAWA, Manager International Systems Group
* Takahiro SEKIZAWA, International Systems Group
* Yukio HISATOMI, Manager Systems Planning Group
* Shigeaki TOGAWA, Systems Planning Group

13-3, Shibuya, 2-Chome, Shibuya-ku, Tokyo 150

Fuji Bank

* Hideo TANAKA, General Manager Systems Planning Division
* Toshihiko UZAKI, Manager Systems Planning Division
* Takakazu IMAI, Systems Planning Division

Otemachi Financial Center, 1-5-4 Otemachi, Chiyoda-ku, Tokyo

Mitsubishi Bank

* Akira WATANABE, General Manager, Derivative Products
* Akira TOWATARI, Manager, Strategic Planning and Administration, Derivative Products
* Takehito NEMOTO, Chief Manager, Systems Development Division
* Nobuyuki YAMADA, Systems Development Division
* Haruhiko SUZUKI, Systems Development Division

7-1, Marunouchi, 2-Chome, Chiyoda-ku, Tokyo 100

Nomura Research Institute

* Tomio ARAI, Director, Systems Science Department
* Tomoyuki OHTA, Director, Financial Engineering Group
* Tomohiko HIRUTA, Manager, I-STAR Systems Services

9-1, Nihonbashi, 1-Chome, Chuo-ku, Tokyo 103

Mitsubishi Trust and Banking

* Nobuyuki TANAKA, General Manager, Systems Planning Division
* Terufumi KAGE, Consultant Systems Planning Division

9-8 Kohnan, 2-Chome, Minato-ku, Tokyo 108

Sakura Bank

* Nobuo IHARA, Senior Vice President and General Manager, Systems Development Office VIII
* Hisao KATAYAMA, Senior Vice President and General Manager, System Development Office VII
* Toshihiko EDA, Senior Systems Engineer, Systems Development Division

4-2, Kami-Osahi, 4-Chome, Shinagawa-ku, Tokyo 141

Sanyo Securities

* Yuji OZAWA, Director, Systems Planning Department
* K. TOYAMA, Systems Planning Department

1-8-1, Nihonbashi, Kayabacho, Chuo-ku, Tokyo 103

Center for Financial Industry Information System Systems (FISC)

* Shighehisa HATTORI, Executive Director
* Kiyoshi KUMATA, Manager, Research Division II

16th Floor, Ark Mori Building, 12-32, 1-Chome Akasaka, Minato-ku, Tokyo 107

Laboratory for International Fuzzy Engineering Research (LIFE)

* Prof. Dr. Toshiro TERANO, Executive Director
* Dr. Anca L. RALESCU, Assistant Director
* Shunichi TANI, Fuzzy Control Project Leader

Siber Hegner Building, 89-1 Yamashita-Cho, Naka-ku, Yokohama-shi 231

Real World Computing Partnership (RWC)

* Dr. Junichi SHUMADA, General Manager of RWC
* Hajime IRISAWA, Executive Director

Tsukuba Mitsui Building, 1-6-1 Takezono, Tsukuba-shi, Ibarahi 305

Tokyo University

* Prof. Dr. Michitaka HIROSE, Dept. of Mechano-Informatics, Faculty of Engineering

* Dr. Kensuke YOKOYAMA, Virtual Reality Project

3-1, 7-Chome, Hongo Bunkyo-ku, Tokyo 113

Tokyo International University

* Prof. Dr. Yoshiro KURATANI

9-1-7-528, Akasaka, Minato-ku, Tokyo 107

Japan Electronic Directory Research Institute

* Dr. Toshio YOKOI, General Manager

Mita-Kokusai Building – Annex, 4-28 Mita, 1-Chome, Minato-ku, Tokyo 108

Mitsubishi Research Institute (MRI)

* Masayuki FUJITA, Manager, Strategic Information Systems Dept.
* Hideyuki MORITA, Senior Research Associate, Information Science Dept.
* Akio SATO, Research Associate, Information Science Dept.

ARCO Tower, 8-1 Shimomeguro, 1-Chome, Meguro-ku, Tokyo 153

NTT Software

* Dr. Fukuya ISHINO, Senior Vice President

223-1 Yamashita-Cho, Naka-ku, Yokohama 231

Ryoshin Systems (Systems Developer Fully Owned by Mitsubishi Trust)

* Takewo YUWI, Vice President, Technical Research and Development

9-8 Kohman, 2-Chome, Minato-ku, Tokyo 108

Sanyo Software Services

* Fumio SATO, General Manager, Sales Department 2

Kanayama Building, 1-2-12 Shinkawa, Chuo-ku, Tokyo 104

Fujitsu Research Institute

* Dr. Masuteru SEKIGUCHI, Member of the Board and Director of R&D
* Takao SAITO, Director of the Parallel Computing Research Center
* Dr. Hiroyasu ITOH, R&D Department
* Katsuto KONDO, R&D Department
* Satoshi HAMAYA, Information Systems and Economics

9-3 Nakase, 1-Chome, Mihama-ku, Chiba-City 261

NEC

* Kotaro NAMBA, Senior Researcher, NEC Planning Research
* Dr. Toshiyuki NAKATA, Manager, Computer System Research Laboratory
* Asao KANEKO, Computer System Research Laboratory

3-13-12 Mita, Minato-ku, Tokyo 108

Toshiba

* Dr. Makoto IHARA, Manager Workstation Product Planning and Technical Support Dept.
* Emi NAKAMURA, Analyst Financial Applications Dept.
* Joshikiyo NAKAMURA, Financial Sales Manager
* Minami ARAI, Deputy Manager, Workstation Systems Division

1-1, Shibaura, 1-Chome, Minato-ku, Tokyo 105

Microsoft

* James LALONDE, Multinational Account Manager, Large Accounts Sales Dept.

Sasazuka NA Bldg, 50-1 Sasazuka, 1-Chome, Shibuya-ku, Tokyo 151

Apple Technology

* Dr. Tsutomu KOBAYASHI, President

25 Mori Bldg, 1-4-30 Roppongi, Minato-ku, Tokyo 106

Digital Equipment JAPAN

* Roshio ISHII, Account Manager, Financial Sales Unit 1

2-1 Kamiogi, 1-Chome, Suginamiku, Tokyo 167

UBS Japan

* Dr. Peter BRUTSCHE, Executive Vice President and Chief Manager
* Gary P. EIDAM, First Vice President, Regional Head of Technology
* Charles UNDERWOOD, Vice President, Head of Technical Architecture and Strategy
* Masaki UTSUNOMIYA, Manager, IT Production Facilities

Yurakucho Building 2F, 1-10-1 Yurakucho, Chiyoda-ku, Tokyo 100

Index